P.t.

Ang.

MEETING THE NEEDS OF OUR CLIENTS CREATIVELY:

The Impact of Art and Culture on Caregiving

Editor:

John D. Morgan, Ph.D.

*King's College of
the University of Western Ontario
London, Canada*

Death, Value and Meaning Series
Series Editor: John D. Morgan

Baywood Publishing Company, Inc.
AMITYVILLE, NEW YORK

Library of Congress Catalog Number: 99-12799
ISBN: 0-89503-193-0 (Cloth)

Library of Congress Cataloging-in-Publication Data

Meeting the needs of our clients creatively :   the impact of art and
  culture on caregiving / editor, John D. Morgan.
     p.   cm. - - (Death, value, and meaning series)
  Includes bibliographical references and index.
  ISBN 0-89503-193-0 (hardcover)
    1. Grief.   2. Death- -Psychological aspects.   3. Counseling.
  4. Arts- -Therapeutic use.   I. Morgan, John D., 1933- .
  II. Series.
  BF575.G7M443 1999
  158' .3- -DC21   99-12799
                                                    CIP

Table of Contents

PART II: CREATIVE CAREGIVING: PRACTICAL APPLICATIONS

Introduction

THE NATURE OF GRIEF

When we were very, very little, our parents, grandparents, aunts and uncles, perhaps even older brothers and sisters picked us up, made funny faces at us, made strange sounds, held us; we felt warm, we felt safe. This is what is known as bonding or attachment. This bonding relationship is the root of our ability to love, and it is at the same time the root of our ability to grieve. As has been said so often, grief is the price we pay for love. It is the price we pay for security, it is the price we pay for a sense of warmth, and for a sense that our lives have meaning.

When our parents or caregivers did not respond immediately to our needs, we cried. We cried not only because our needs were not immediately satisfied, but we cried also because we were afraid that the bond was being broken. We felt safe as long as this person was there to respond to us, we felt threatened when that person did not come immediately. What every parent knows is that when the child was left with a babysitter, the child protested and screamed. Sometimes the protest worked. Sometimes the parents decided that they would not go out and that they would stay home with the child. Grief is the little kid inside of us protesting. Grief is that little kid inside of us thinking that if I yell loudly enough, if I scream loudly enough maybe my loved one will come back.

Bereavement comes from the French word *ravir* which means to steal. And every grieving person knows the truth of this etymology. We believe that something important, someone important has been stolen from us. The Buddhists tell us that the foremost reality of human life is loss; life is pain. The Buddhists suggest that the way to remove pain is to live without attachment. That is one alternative, but that means to live without love, because attachment is love. There is another alternative, and that is to face up to grief. That is what the focus of this book is. This book is a way of helping ourselves, and the people with whom we work, face up to the reality of grief.

1

Grief Theory

While grief has probably been discussed since time immemorial, especially in literature, grief theory, that is, a reasoned analysis of the emotional and physical responses to death, dates back to Freud's 1917 publication of *Mourning And Melancholia* [1]. Freud told us of the naturalness and normality of grief. His insights have been lost in the death denying reality of Western culture. We seem to believe that if we didn't think about it, if we didn't talk about it, it will not happen. Since, as Herman Feifel taught us, our intellectual energy focused on the empirical sciences, those elements of life not susceptible to experiemental tests were lost [2]. Dr. Robert Kastenbaum has indicated that if one can look at the Social Science publications of the last fifty years, one would assume that nobody ever died or no one ever grieved [3]. There was very little research done in these areas.

We date Contemporary grief theory to the 1943 publication of Eric Lindemann's article *The Symptomatology and Management of Acute Grief* [4]. Dr. Lindemann had been a psychiatric resident in Boston at the time of the Coconut Grove fire in which many young people had died. He visited grieving families asking about their reactions to the loss. At the time Dr. Lindemann decided that the normal grief process would be over with in about two weeks. When Colin Murray Parkes published his first addition of *Bereavement: Studies of Grief in Adult Life* [5], he said that grief would normally last about a year. What we now know of course is that grief never ends. Grief has been likened to scar tissue. We are not always conscious of the pain, but on certain "rainy" days we are very conscious of it. Whatever analogy is most appropriate, we know that grief is the most truly human situation in which we will find ourselves. "We manage to avoid thinking about a highly emotionally charged event that has a 100 percent chance of happening" [6, p. 7].

Not only do family members grieve, but the dying person him or herself also grieves. This reality is called anticipatory grief. Although there is still much debate about it's nature, we can say with some degree of assurance that dying persons go through a process of grief. In a death, the family member grieves because he/she has lost one person at the same time the dying person is losing everyone and everything that he or she has ever loved, "to prepare for the impending loss of all the love objects" [7, p. 77].

The Uniqueness of Grief

Two identical twins growing from the same genetic base, having been raised in the same household, grieve very differently when one or the other of their parents dies. Grief is not automatic. The impact of the death is, as it were, a chemical reaction caused by mixtures of variables both inside the grieving person and variables outside of the grieving person.

The internal variables of the grieving person are their age, gender, personality, health, feelings toward the deceased, and their own dependency behavior [8, p. 39]. Age is a factor because adults of sixty have, as a rule, more grief experience than an adult of forty or twenty. An adult of twenty has more grief experience than a young child or teenager. Adults know that, as painful it is, they have grieved before and survived, so too they will grieve again and survive. Gender is a factor in grief for two reasons. Men are not socialized to share the burdens of life as readily as women. Women tend to confide and seek solace not only in their spouse, but also in relatives and close friends. Men tend to confide only in their spouse. Consequently, the death of the spouse leaves the man in a more fragile position than does the death of a spouse leave the woman. Secondly, it has been argued that men are genetically less capable of handling frustration than are women. The testosterone that gives men their sex drive interferes with their ability to handle frustration. Consequently when grief occurs, again the man is less able to handle it [9]. Mr. Tom Golden argues that men are less able to produce tears and are less conscious of their own emotional state because of the structure of the corpus callosum [10, pp. 73-74]. Gender is a factor. Personality is a factor. If someone has had personality difficulties, trouble coping with life as it has been presented to them before the death of a significant other, they're going to continue to have coping difficulties. Health is a factor. Grief is hard work. If one doesn't have the health to cope with grief, that person is going to find it more difficult to handle than persons whose health is better. Finally, ambivalence is an internal factor in grief. If one cannot look back at the relationship with a great deal of satisfaction, the unfinished arguments and unhealed wounds will resonate throughout the grief process. All relationships are ambivalent, but those persons who can look back at a long relationship in which the normal tensions of life were resolved find grief easier.

In addition to these internal mediators there are external factors in the grieving situation [8]. The most important mediator is the perceived availability of social support and the willingness to use it. Social support is more than knowing many people. The fact that one knows many people does not mean that one has a great deal of support. That there are many people who find themselves in the sandwich generation where they are caring for elderly persons, perhaps those affected by Alzheimer's, at the same time caring for young children. If their spouse should die, they might have a large social network, no doubt co-workers, fellow parents from the schools and so on, but that does not necessarily mean that they have a large network of support. Social support has best been described by Sister Francis Dominica Ritchie of Helen House Hospice in Oxford England. Sister Francis says that social support is asking someone how they are and *staying long enough to get the answer*. If it takes half an hour to get the answer, that's fine and if it takes two hours to get the answer, that's fine too [11]. Dr. Pittu Laungani, whose two chapters are included in this volume, indicates that in his village in India when a wife dies, the men of the village will come together to the grieving spouse and will not leave until the widower has acknowledged the death and is weeping. It is the same with women. When a man dies the women of the village come together and will not leave until the widow has acknowledged the death and is weeping [12]. This form of social support gives someone permission to grieve, tells them that grief is normal, and it starts them on the process of grief. Social support, as Vachon, Freeman, Lyall, Rogers, and Freman indicated some many years ago, is still the number one predictor of grief resolution [13]. A second variable in the reaction of grief is whether or not someone had the opportunity to prepare for the death. We human beings are capable of handling almost anything as long as we know it's going to happen. Sudden death denies us this anticipatory period to get our emotional house in order. A third variable is who has died. There is a truism that when a child dies we lose our future: when a parent dies we lose our past; when a spouse dies we lose our present. We can no longer look forward to the child's entering school, graduating from university, getting married, having their own family, the way that we would have, had our child lived. When a parent dies, we are no longer able to call someone and get information about what we were like when we were young. When our spouse dies we lose our future. We become a fifth wheel socially. We are no longer invited to parties because people feel awkward. We lose identity, economic status, and friends. An important aspect in the impact of grief is religiosity. Religiosity has to be distinguished from church attendance; because there are many people who attend church or synagogue who are not necessarily religious, and there are many people who do not attend church or synagogue who might very well be religious. Religiosity is a sense of being in good hands, the sense of finding meaning in the face of adversity. There is no question that religiosity is an important aspect in the grieving situation. People move from one sphere of grief to another to the extent that they have found meaning in their own life and meaning in the life of the person who has died [8]. There is another aspect of religion that is advantageous. For many religious people there is a built-in social support system.

Grief impacts us on various levels. It affects us emotionally, biologically, sexually, economically, socially, and spiritually [14]. There is no aspect of our lives that is not affected by grief. When someone is facing grief they go through various phases. In general, these phases are shock, in which the reality of the situation can be denied or at least will not be felt; becoming aware of all that has been lost in their life; withdrawal and recuperation of energy; then healing and reinvestment in life [8]. There is a continual vacillation between the "pangs of grief" and putting grief aside [15, p. 244]. Guilt and self-reproach are common, as is searching and sensory apperations [15, p. 245].

Helping the Bereaved

How do we help ourselves and others get from the shock of the death to the reinvesting in life? As indicated above, social support, a sense of meaning, and allowing grief to proceed are important. Funerals and other rituals are important because they provide social support and meaning [16]. Once the funeral is over, the long process toward resolution begins. The bereaved need education and (additional) support [15, p. 251]. This book provides these steps. The purpose of this book is to give the griever and caregiver tools to understand the process of grief and tools to facilitate the movement from shock to resolution.

REFERENCES

1. S. Freud, Morning and Melancholia, in *A General Selection from the Works of Sigmund Freud,* Doubleday, New York, 1917.
2. H. Feifel, Psychology and Death: Meaningful Rediscovery, *American Psychologist, 45*:4, pp. 537-543, 1990.
3. R. Kastenbaum, The Reconstructing Death in Postmodern Society, *Omega, 27*:1, pp. 75-89, 1993.
4. E. Lindemann, Symptomatology and Management of Acute Grief, *American Journal of Psychiatry, 101,* pp. 141-148, 1943.
5. C. M. Parkes, *Bereavement: Studies of Grief in Adult Life,* International, New York, 1972.
6. L. Goodman, *Death and The Creative Life,* Springer, New York, 1981.
7. E. Kübler-Ross, *On Death and Dying,* Macmillan, New York, 1969.
8. C. Sanders, *Grief: The Mourning After,* Wiley, New York, 1989.
9. J. Stillian, *Death and The Sexes,* Hemisphere, Washington, 1985.
10. T. Golden, *Swallowed by a Snake: The Gift of the Masculine Side of Healing,* Golden Healing, Kensington, Maryland, 1996.
11. F. Ritchie, *Asking the Experts,* video, King's College, London, Ontario, 1995.
12. Laungani, P. Personal communication.
13. M. L. S. Vachon, K. Freedman, W. A. L. Lyall, J. Rogers, and S. T. F. Freman, Stress Reaction to Bereavement, *Essence, 1*:1, pp. 23-33, 1976.
14. P. Anderson, Working with Widows in Groups, in *Readings in Thanatology,* J. D. Morgan (ed.), Baywood, Amityville, pp. 327-337, 1997.
15. C. M. Parkes, Bereavement: What Most People Should Know, in *Readings in Thanatology,* J. D. Morgan (ed.), Baywood, Amityville, pp. 241-253, 1997.
16. G. Howarth, *Last Rites: The Work of The Modern Funeral Director,* Baywood, Amityville, 1996.

PART I

Creative Caregiving:
Theoretical Considerations

In this first part of the book, we examine certain theoretical aspects of the grief process and how we might approach a dying or grieving person. We examine what it is to be human and how we can bring the best of humanity to the grieving person.

As strange as it may seem, grief and creativity are natural partners. Both are uniquely human characteristics. While all animals die, the human person is the only one that is aware of death as a universal fate, and thus the only animal that "lives a whole lifetime with the fate of death haunting one's dreams and even the most sun-filled days" [1, p. 27]. Creativity, too, is uniquely human in that it arises from the rational nature of the person, the ability to transcend the limits of immediate sensibility [2, p. 1040a]. Joining the two ideas together, we draw the conclusion that the awareness of our own death, or the deaths of those who are dear to us, acts as an impetus to make something that will last, to act creatively. Creativity is the ability of the human mind to move from what it perceives to be a lack, to create something that was not there before.

The fact that all creativity is rooted in the awareness of death is the main focus of John Morgan's chapter. Our own insufficiency in the face of death creates tension or anxiety. But this tension can be a good thing. Instability causes energy [3]. This energy can be used either creatively or will fester and cause fundamental dissatisfaction with life. The Spanish existentialist philosopher Miguel de Unamuno said that the ultimate moral maxim ought to be that we live so that if extinction is the final end for us, it will be seen as an injustice. "Act so that in your own judgement and in the judgement of others you many merit eternity; act so that you may become irreplaceable" [4, p. 263]. This theoretical position is reflected in the article by Samuel Silverman. Dr. Silverman examines the works of five composers: Brahms, Mussorgsky, Mahler, Strauss, and Shostakovitch. Each of these authors had a death awareness that influenced their life work. As Unamuno said, they created something that lasted, the world was richer because of their existence and poorer because of their deaths.

It is not simply enough to be with the dying or grieving person. We must bring to them the best that we have to offer. We bring them ourselves, our knowledge, and our skill so that the process of dying or grieving might be a fulfilling part of life. In order to do this we have to know where the client is in his or her life journey. Since each of us moves on in dying and grieving only when we have found meaning in the process [5, p. 69], it is important to understand the basic meaning context of the persons with whom we work. People make decisions not simply on the basis of facts presented to them, but how those facts fit into their system of values. Pittu Laungani reminds us that we are dealing with a concrete individual sitting with us, not some abstracted human nature. What Dr. Laungani teaches us is that if we are going to be true to the uniqueness of the client, which is the great contribution of the death awareness movement of the last fifty years, we must meet the client in the midst of their culture not simply as a problem to be solved. A therapeutic relationship works best when there is a common set of assumptions or, at the minimum, a mutual awareness of assumptions. These assumptions deal with language, interpretation, or non-verbal signals, but most importantly they must take into account the ethical and spiritual commitments of the client.

Culture is the sum total of the ideas by which we live [5]. If we are going to treat a client in a meaningful way, we must be attentive to their cultural traditions, but cultural knowledge presents us with hypotheses for working with people, not a cookbook. Being attentive to cultural traditions does not take away from us the obligation to listen to the individual person. It is important to have knowledge of the culture, as it is important to theoretical knowledge about the process of dying and grieving, but when working with individuals we must treat them as concrete individuals and not as embodiments of some tradition. Dr. Victor Baez and Dr. Kevin Ann Oltjenbruns caution us that we cannot treat all Catholics alike, all Jews alike, all North Americans alike, all Black persons alike; each person is a unique individual. Culture is only a starting point. Diversity leads to the realization that there is diversity within diversity, that the differences within a group may be as large as differences among groups, and that there are not only intercultural assumptions but cross cultural ones as well. It is only being actively aware of all of these elements that we can be true to the needs of our clients.

Dr. Eleanor Pask shows how this cultural awareness and sensitivity can work in the concrete setting of a hospital, especially in working with children and their families. She explains concrete principles of working with a client in a hospital setting. These principles are 1) that the patient has a right to have his/her socio-cultural background understood and respected; 2) that health care professionals have an obligation to meet cultural needs in a meaningful way; 3) that treating all patients alike is not only ineffective, but unscientific, and unethical; 4) that health care professionals have an obligation to be prepared to meet the socio-cultural needs of their clients; and 5) that the assessment of the cultural needs must take place before the treatment of the client begins. Dr. Pask tells the tragic story of a man who was reported to the police because his child was brought into the hospital with lacerated skin. The man cut his child because his traditions demanded that the "evil spirits" in the child must be allowed to leave the body so that the child's health can be restored. The man was so misunderstood that he suicided. The tragedy is not that the man was reported to the police, there are very good reasons for doing so. The tragedy is that the matter was handled in such a way that the man saw no alternative to suicide.

Glennys Howarth takes us a step toward understanding of individualization. Dr. Howarth has us realize that examining the social structures in which people live, the material of Sociology ever since August Compt, is not enough. We must examine the person as he or she is in the immediate. Analyses of bodily behavior and meanings produce insights into how people perceive their bodies and the effect of bodily transformation on their sense of well being. We seem to have a quasi love-hate relationship with our bodies. The body is the source of pleasure, but also of pain; of health and well-being, but also of sickness and infections. Only by examining how the client perceives his body can we truly be of service to the client.

In this first part of the book, we examine some theoretical issues in dealing with clients, with emphasis on taking seriously the cultural views and expectations of the clients, as well as our own. The maxim of the Delphic Oracle [7] "Know thyself," is as appropriate today as it was in the fifth century before the common era. Before we can be of service to others, we must be aware of their orientation to life and values. However, we cannot do that until we are aware of our own values and culture. This reminds us of the demands that health-care workers, clergy, funeral directors, and other counselors, need first of all, to be well-rounded men and women. We must resist the "shopping mall" orientation to education which allows students to pick and choose what they choose to learn and demand an integrated education based on the time honored liberal arts.

REFERENCES

1. E. Becker, *The Denial of Death,* Free Press, New York, 1973.
2. Aristotle, Nicomachean Ethics, in *The Basic Works of Aristotle,* R. McKeon (ed.), Random House, New York, pp. 935-1145, 1941.
3. L. Goodman, *Death and the Creative Life,* Springer, New York, 1981.
4. Unamuno y Yugo, M., *The Tragic Sense of Life in Men and Peoples,* J. E. Crawford Fitch (trans.), Dover, New York, 1954.
5. C. M. Sanders, *How to Survive the Loss of a Child,* Prima, Rocklin, Calfironia, 1992.
6. J. Ortega y Gasset, In Search of Goethe from Within, in *The Dehumanization of Art and Other Writings on Art and Culture,* Doubleday, Garden City, pp. 123-160, 1956.
7. Plato, Apology, in *The Dialogues of Plato,* B. Jowett (trans. and ed.),Volume 1, Oxford, Oxford, 1964.

CHAPTER 1

The Knowledge of Death is a Stimulus to Creativity[1]

John D. Morgan

Although we glibly use such phrases as "life and death" decisions, fundamentally we know that there are none. Death always wins, always has the last word. The choices with which we are faced deal with death sooner or death later, but never life versus death. The realization of this fundamental fact reminds us of the limited control we have over life, and is the root of some answers to the problem of euthanasia.

There are many possible responses to the knowledge that death will end our lives and all our relationships. These responses can, in general, be divided into those which see death as a totally negative, meaningless intrusion into life; or to see it as an opportunity to create meaning in our lives. If one can look at death, and continue to say that life is good, then life has won.

In this chapter I explore the relationship between creativity and the knowledge that our lives and our relationships will end in death. I believe that many people, perhaps in one way or another most people, find meaning in their lives in spite of death. A few persons even take the opportunity to create something beautiful with their grief [1, p. 62].

[1] This chapter was originally published in "The Knowledge of Death as Stimulus to Creativity" by John D. Morgan, pp. 345-360 in DEATH AND THE QUEST FOR MEANING, Stephen Strack, Ed. Copyright © 1997 Jason Aronson, Inc. Northvale, New Jersey. Reprinted with permission of the publisher.

THE HUMAN CONDITION

Since at least the fifth century before the common era, philosophers have sought to understand what it is to be a human person, and having arrived at some tentative answers to that question, have asked what it is to be a good human person.

The terms "individual" and "person" are often interchanged in ordinary discourse, but if we are to gain some understanding of what it is to be a human person, it is essential to make an accurate distinction. "Individual" is a term from logic, the science of efficient reasoning. An individual refers to "one out of the many," that is, the individual is thought of as having no other important characteristics than those common to the whole [2, p. 250]. The distinguishing specifics the individual *qua* individual might have are not considered. The computer on which I am working, an IBM Thinkpad type 2620-8yf, is fundamentally no different from any other Thinkpad of that type. The individual characteristics which it might have, the amount of wear on the keys, the smudges on the cover, or, more importantly, the data contained in RAM and ROM do not change the fundamental makeup of the computer.

If we were content to define human persons as individuals, as philosophers did until fairly recently, we would conclude that the human person is properly understood as a living, sensate, reasoning, valuing creature. A second conclusion would be that life history and other personalizing characteristics, such as values and goals, disappointments and joys, beliefs and doubts, are incidental and do not change fundamentally the nature of what it is to be this human being, this person. We would think that the characteristics of persons are limited to the characteristics of the class rather than resulting from personal life experiences.

The computer mentioned above is judged a "good" computer to the extent that it does what one expects of all computers, it stores and processes information effectively. The characteristics uniquely specific to it do not enter into the evaluation. In analogy to the computer, if a human person is fundamentally only "one of the many," then as long as one is living, sensing, reasoning, and evaluating then one has adequately achieved the goals which life has to offer. The unique specifics are irrelevant.

It is precisely because we doubt that the human being is merely an individual that the term "person" is so important. A person, according to Boethius, a fourth-century philosopher, is a unique substance of a rational nature [3, p. 57], that is, a *unique* source of knowing and valuing. Each person is a once-in-the-lifetime-of-the-universe-event. It is precisely the specific knowledge one has gained, and the specific values asserted, life history, that constitute each of us as a person. In a word, we are our biographies, the sum total of the decisions we have made [4, p. 32]. This view of the person is reflected in such clinically successful treatment modalities as music or art therapy, and telling the story of one's life. One may be healed by putting together the pieces of one's life into a consistent whole.

Persons differ from other creatures in that they determine for themselves what evidence they take seriously, the goals toward which they strive, and the values to which they commit. We are told in the Hebrew Bible that God made persons in Its image. In a sense this is a truism. Since whatever exists manifests some aspect that the Divine deemed to exist, everything is made in the image and likeness of God. When we say that persons are made in the image of God, however, we hold that persons not only share in God's act of existence, not only share in Its living and sensing characteristics, but also share in Its ability to understand and to set goals. Persons self-create values, decide for themselves what the goals of life shall be [5, p. 787]. They decide for themselves what kind of person they want to be and evaluate themselves in terms of the goals they set.

This self-creation of goals reflects human spirituality, that is, it comes from the ability to transcend the limits of a particular space and time. Spirituality is shown in many ways, but primarily in rational thinking, second in ethical activity, third in religious consciousness, and fourth in creativity. In rational thinking, the intellect moves from the concrete to the abstract. In ethical thinking, the person moves from the needs of the particular moment to more universal needs. In religion the person considers the "ground of all being" and considers the possibility of trying to establish a relationship with that Ground.

In creativity, perhaps the highest form of spirituality, the person transcends what is, to establish an imagined might be—to expand the universe. All of the above characteristics point to a quest for meaning, "the journey of the soul—not to religion itself but to the drive in humankind that gives rise to religion in the first place" [6, p. 8]. We are meaning creating beings.

Each moment of our lives demands a conscious awareness of who we are and who we want to be. We cannot not choose. Sartre reminds us that, "We are condemned to be free" [4, p. 23]. Being a self-creating person is not easy for at least two reasons which interest us in this chapter. The first difficulty persons face is insecurity of choice, the second is the knowledge of death.

Choice

The first great challenge of life is the confrontation with freedom. "Once you pose the problem of what it means to be a person, even dumbly, weakly, or with a veneer of pride about your imagined difference from others, you may be in trouble" [7, p. 24]. The fact that persons are self-creating is a double edged sword: the agony and ecstasy of being human. On the one hand, persons are not directed only by an in-built nature or genetic code, they have free will. This is the ecstasy. On the other hand, persons must take full responsibility for their own decisions and thus their own lives. They have no one to blame but themselves for their lives. This is the agony.

As Becker stated with his usual eloquence, "The fall into self-consciousness, the emergence from comfortable ignorance in nature, had one great penalty for man; it gave him *dread*, or anxiety" [7, p. 69]. It is precisely because self-creation demands so much attention and is a risk, that much of the human race chooses a form of slavery—to political or religious ideologies or to consumerism [7, p. 80]. While the approach of "slavery" is safe, what it misses is the daring to make a contribution with one's ephemerality, either through those great deeds recorded in history, or simply through a commitment to one's family, community, or profession [7, p. 299].

If persons are fundamentally self-creative, we must ask why it is so difficult to achieve what Maslow spoke of as actualizing one's full humanity. If there is a natural urge to do so, why is it so difficult? Maslow believes that "We fear our highest possibility (as well as our lowest ones). We are generally afraid to become that which we can glimpse in our most perfect moments . . ." [7, p. 48]. Becker takes this a step further and holds that we fear our highest possibilities because of our terror of death.

Death

In spite of the achievements since the 1950s, ours are still death denying cultures accentuated by four centuries of scientific thought and the materialism of the twentieth century. Wandering through the Vatican Museum, the Hermitage, the Louvre, or the Metropolitan Museum of Art, one is struck by how few paintings depict the central fact of life, that all life ends in death—"the collapse of personal time and space" [8, p. 200]—and all human relationships are limited. Deaths are often depicted in the visual arts, in opera, or in popular music, but they are usually the deaths of political or religious personages. Rarely, outside of Pieta-type expositions, is grief depicted at all. Philosophy and theology have traditionally examined questions of death, but rarely grief, and the impact that philosophy and theology have on the culture at large is minimal. The social sciences are no more helpful. In a recent article, Robert Kastenbaum stated that, "Basically, one could have subtracted dying, death, and grief from human experience and it would have made little difference to the studies, texts, and courses promulgated by the social and behavioral sciences until the last few years" [9, p. 79]. He indicates that the dominant attitude of our culture is that "Death is for losers" [9, p. 78]. We continue to find ourselves in a situation in which "we manage to avoid thinking about a highly emotionally charged event that has a 100 percent chance of occurring" [10, p. 7].

Death teaches us the absolute limits of life as we know it. Sickness is an "uncovering of the limitations and fragility of our earthly condition" [11, p. 91]. Personal disasters, such as the death of a child or a spouse, end the feelings of security with which we may have grown. Fundamental assumptions in life are overthrown. Beliefs about the justice and orderliness of the universe are challenged and what remains is the feeling of helplessness. A Trappist monk in Utah, while showing me the monastery cemetery as part of the tour of the monastery, said, "one does not have their feet on the ground, until they have put someone into it." This confrontation with death forces us to accept the basic limits of life and love.

What is perhaps most important, however, is that from death we learn to distrust that physical forces constitute the essential part of what it is to be a human being. "The biological forces indeed make a fine animal, but there is something else in man, something that cannot be mistaken for natural forces" [11, p. 95]. We are spiritual, meaning-creating beings. Joseph Campbell believes that the realization of personal death is *the* differentiating characteristics of humans.

[I]f one should ask why or how any such unsubstantial impulsion ever should have become dominant in the ordering of physical life, the answer is that in this wonderful human brain of ours there has dawned a realization unknown to the other primates. It is that of the individual, conscious of himself, and aware that he, and all that he cares for, will one day die [12, p. 22].

Personal death has had several major depictions over the centuries. For some of our ancestors, it was the dropping-in of an expected neighbor; for others, the last act of a personal drama; for others yet, the end of a relationship. For those who live in an achievement oriented culture, as we presently do, it is consummate failure [13, p. 602]. Whatever else it may be, for us all it is absolute loneliness. "All the masks must fall, all roles too must come to an end; all the parts that man plays before the world and before himself" [14, p. 165].

Coping with the Human Condition

Ernest Becker believes that there are three fundamental responses to the finality of death [7]. The first, the most typical of our culture, is to deny the reality of death—to act as though it won't happen or that it is not important. The great medieval Italian poet Dante might refer to those who live this way, because they never threw themselves into life, as ones who were never alive [15, p. 527]. The second response is that of mental illness, to become so engaged with death that one refuses to "play the games of society." According to Berdyaev, Dostoevsky teaches us that, "For the deeps of human nature are sounded not in sanity but in insanity, not in law-abidingness but in criminality, in obscure unconscious tendencies and not in daily life and in the parts of the soul that have been enlightened by the daylight of consciousness" [16, pp. 21-22].

The third response is heroism—to realize that since no one can do more than nature already has done—cut life short—then there is nothing to lose by being a hero, by living as fully as possible [7, p. 260]. We learn from Don Quixote that death is, "the great reality, the triumphant enemy of all illusion" [17, p. 49]. No longer having illusions about the temporal nature of life, the hero realizes the possibilities of creating a greater level of human achievement, who leaves behind "something that heightens life and testifies to the worthwhileness of existence" [18, p. 299]. The hero is the one who realizes that an awareness of death enhances life.

Creativity

[Art] must confront and reflect not only reality at its most painful, but at its most beautiful and meaningful as well. It must, in other words, present evidence of a transcendence over chaos and despair [19, p. 59].

Creativity: What Is It?

The human mind functions in two radically different ways. The "speculative intellect" knows simply for the sake of knowing. "All men by nature desire to know" [20, p. 689]. In addition to this speculative function, the human mind knows for the sake of production. This productive function is known as "practical intellect" [21, p. 45]. Practical intellect concerns itself with two basic areas, the production of human actions to be done (moral activity or the virtue of prudence), and the production of works to be made (art) [21, p. 45]. Prudence deals with the development of a good person, art deals with the development of a good product.

There are different types of art, the "right way of doing something" [22, p. 1026]. The arts have been traditionally divided into the servile arts, the liberal arts, and the fine arts. In the servile arts, the only purpose is the production of something useful (boiled water, a clean floor, a clean desk). In the liberal arts, the purpose is the production of a disciplined mind, one liberated from prejudice. The fine arts differ from servile arts or even the liberal arts, in that they create products, but not "mere products"; the products which the arts produce embody a vision.

Creativity is a power of engendering, of producing; but not simply reproducing what was already there, but in bringing into existence what has yet to be. Creativity can be defined as a "unique mental process leading to the expansion of experienced reality beyond the already established categorization and classification of it" [23, p. 156]. It is a uniquely human gift; not part of the material world, but "a privilege of spiritual organisms" [21, p. 56]. Essentially, creativity is an urge to expand in every dimension of being meaningfully alive. Every person desires to be creative, to fulfill the need to form, shape, and express deep feeling [19, p. 53]. As is seen in the clinical setting of a hospice, the mastering of new skills or the re-adaptation of old ones has a positive effect: "It is tangible proof that one is still alive and learning" [24, p. 41].

Creativity expands reality by taking the imagined awareness of the human mind and producing it externally. Reality is expanded by the external expression of the internal vision [23, p. 156]. This vision is what Maritain refers to as "poetic intuition, a musical stir, an unformulated song, with no words, no sounds, absolutely inaudible to the ear, audible only to the heart" [21, p. 301]. This is the "truth" that the creative person wishes to produce. "The fine arts are constituted by the intellect's need to produce externally what is grasped within itself in creative intuition, and to manifest it in beauty, is simply the essential thing in the fine arts" [21, p. 56]. By this process the human person is liberated from the strictures of reality and has the ability to transform reality and control it [21, p. 73].

Creativity: Why Is It?

Most of the time, we use length of years as the criterion of the appropriateness of a death, thinking that one should die in advanced age. Correspondingly, we determine that a death is "natural" when it occurs because physical functions fail, regardless of the individual's state of fulfillment at the time [10, p. 13]. For Jung, however, the ultimate aim of life is development and integration of each system and function of personality. An "appropriate death" would occur when one has reached wholeness, completeness, and self-realization; when all potentialities are actualized and integrated [10, p. 14]. A premature death would not be determined by length of years but by the incomplete actualization of a person's life [10, p. 36]. This is confirmed by the life-review studies of old or terminally ill patients which show that if a person looks on the past in despair, feeling that life has been wasted, s/he finds it difficult to come to terms with death [10, p. 22].

If physical survival were to be the same as actualization of potential, our orientation toward life and attitudes toward death would be fundamentally different. An ideal outcome of life should be the coincidence of the meaning of the words—"His work is done"—for the dying patient and the community. The patient should be "ready to go," when at the same time the community, the physician, has done his best to facilitate a dignified and meaningful death [25, p. 39]. If Jung is correct, the deaths of most men and women today are *"almost always* premature" [10, p. 14]. As Sam Keen said, "Contentment is probably the rarest of all human virtues. No matter how much we have, few of us are satisfied. We always want more" [26, p. 122].

Creative persons seem to be satisfied with their lives and their demands. The pianist Beveridge Webster states "It never felt like making sacrifices" [10, p. 48]; the actress Eva Le Gallienne adds, "My profession has been the passion of my life" [10, p. 58]. Keen tells us that, "The enlightened person, according to Zen Buddhism, has learned the true miracle of human consciousness—to be satisfied with what is given. The master of everyday life eats when he eats and sleeps when he sleeps and is content [26, p. 124]. The Irish playwright George Bernard Shaw says:

> This is the true joy in life, the being used for a purpose recognized by yourself as a mighty one; the being thoroughly worn out before you are thrown on the scrap heap; the being a force of Nature instead of a feverish selfish little clod of ailments and grievances complaining that the world will not devote itself to making you happy [27, p. 2].

Is it death of which we are afraid or the incompleteness of life? "Once one has succeeded in reaching self-fulfillment by giving form to all the latent possibilities within, death no longer presents a threat: one has won the race with death" [10, p. xi]. In a series of interviews conducted with twenty-three highly creative persons, eleven from the arts and twelve from the sciences, Goodman heard more concern about dying prematurely than about dying. Dying prematurely was defined as dying before one's psychological needs were satisfied [10, p. 15]. Rather, the creative person is future oriented, rather than present oriented or past oriented [10, pp. 22-23]. "One lives on one's hopes! I am always contemplating, always planning long in advance" [10, pp. 88-89]. What seems to be important for creativity is a different orientation to one's time span. Creativity demands more than a mere long life [10, p. 16].

A creative person's orientation to time differs from that of less creative persons. George Bernard Shaw tells us that, "Life is no brief candle to me. It is a sort of splendid torch which I have got hold of for the moment, and I want to make it burn as brightly as possible before handing it on to future generations" [27, p. 2]. The creative person seems to have little concern with the past and seems to be almost exclusively present or future oriented. The violinist Nathan Milstein says, "Present and future [are important]. Living is important" [10, p. 39]; writer Alan Arkin adds, "Since I have done 'my thing' I am no longer afraid of death" [10, p. 56]. The violinist Isaac Stern says basically the same thing, "Happily, in the interpretive search there is never an end" [10, p. 45]. Sam Keen, who combines philosophical analysis with his own creative writing, says that "the creative personality as one who is totally here—now, one who lives without future or past" [28, p. 25]. This future concern of creative people does not seem to extend to some far distant future, fifty or one hundred years. The artists and scientists that Goodman interviewed were concerned about accomplishing what they needed to accomplish but were not interested in seeing the effects of it in some remote future [10, p. 70].

Some creative persons are explicit about the effect of the awareness of death on their lives. The tenor Luciano Pavarotti believes that witnessing the execution of members of the Resistance in the Second World War had a great effect on his life [29, p. 13] The effect was so great that it is mentioned in the first few pages of his autobiography.

> This was the most important effect the war had on me. Twice during my life I have come very close to death myself. These two experiences—one,

an illness when I was twelve, the other, a plane accident just a few years ago—reinforced my reverence for life, my feeling of how precious it is [29, p. 13].

Rainer-Maria Rilke warns us not to believe that an author leads an untroubled life, rather, "His life has much difficulty and sorrow and remains far beyond yours. Were it not otherwise, he would never have been able to find those words" [27, p. 138].

We rely on commentaries for the death awareness of other creative persons. Trilling believes that the following lines from Chekhov's "Three Sisters" reflect the writer's own concern with death, "Where has it all gone? Where is it? . . . life's slipping by, and it will never, never return . . ." [30, p. 254]. "And when Chekhov wrote that 'it will be winter soon, and everything will be covered with snow,' he may well have wished to suggest that in the cycle of seasons the spring will follow and that, sad as we may be over what befalls ourselves and others, life itself is to be celebrated" [30, p. 255]. Trilling also believes that Tolstoi's "Death of Ivan Illych" was written for Tolstoi's religious purposes, "for religion often tries to put us in mind of the actuality of death, not in its terrors, to be sure, but in its inevitability, seeking thus to press upon us the understanding that the life of this world is not the sum of existence and not even its most valuable part" [15, p. 525]. The musicologist, George Martin, believes that Verdi's operas were almost all responses to death. "Life, [Verdi] suggests, is hard, happiness fleeting, and death the only certainty. He never pretends in his call for generous, noble action that these do not often end in suffering, but offers them as the best response to death" [31, p. 41].

The symbolic nature of art allows the person to do several things that are more difficult to do from the standpoint of ordinary thinking and acting. First of all, the languages we speak are already structured before we learn them. We inherit other persons' categories [10, p. 69]. The arts, but perhaps especially music, allow us to by-pass the limits of language [32, p. 49; 33, p. 291]. Logical thought processes are by their very nature objective, that is they separate out the personal issues of the thinker from the data being considered. The arts demand no such separation and allow people to "live their questions" [34, p. 85]. The arts also allow the person to express insights that would be too conflicted or too emotionally demanding to be expressed logically [35, p. x]. We read in *Dr. Zhivago* that, "Your health is bound to be affected if, day after day, you say the opposite of what you feel, if you grovel before what you dislike and rejoice at what brings you nothing but misfortune" [36, pp. 65-66]. "A culture that reveres life maintains its myths and symbols; without them, we dehumanize the life we live" [37, p. 21].

Art is therapy in that it facilitates healing by putting us in touch with the basic issues of life. This is obviously true in such treatment modalities as art and music therapy. "The arts help us to keep our imaginations alive and our connection to the earth and created order of the universe" [38, p. 17]. Wald tells us that "Engaging in an arts experience can serve to create a sense of integration and community that bridges cultural, religious and racial divisions" [38, p. 18]. Porchet-Munro believes that the effectiveness of art therapy results from the fundamental healing nature of music [39, p. 41]. Salmon adds that the music that a dying or grieving person chooses reflects the particular concerns of the person at the time. In other words, the music is chosen precisely for the purpose of healing [32, p. 50].

Music as therapy might be considered a placebo, but placebos work, as Norman Cousins tells us, because of the fundamental will to live [36, p. 56]. Cousins quotes Albert Schweitzer that, "The witch doctor succeeds for the same reason all the rest of us succeed. Each patient carries his own doctor inside him. They come to us not knowing that truth. We are at our best when we give the doctor who resides within each patient a chance to go to work" [36, p. 69]. On the basis of his living for a time with the Cellist Pablo Casals and the physician-organist-author-missionary Albert Schweitzer, Norman Cousins says, "What I learned from these two men had a profound effect on my life—especially during the period of my illness. I learned that a highly developed purpose and the will to live are among the prime raw materials of human existence" [36, pp. 71-72].

More fundamentally the arts heal because they give a reason for living [39, p. 40]. Creation frees the person from the arbitrary limits culture imposes [23, p. 158; 7, p. 46; 12, p. 4].

> On those rare occasions when I allow myself to think about death, The Terror rises from the pit of my stomach to my throat. How can the universe be designed so that I am to be eradicated? The thought fills me with anger, rage, defiance. And then I get back to work polishing a project that will create a sea wall against the tide of death [26, p. 102].

Do we back into death afraid to face it, or do we face it and live in spite of it? We tend to value what we cannot have or whatever is in short supply. If there would always be a tomorrow—if we didn't take seriously that every goodbye could be forever—our only goal would be the satisfaction of immediate needs, as we witness on the animal level. Death, understood to be loss, or fear of loss, naturally causes distress. We create to counteract that distress. On the most basic level the person works actively against its own fragility by seeking to expand and perpetuate itself; instead of shrinking, the person moves toward more life [7, p. 21]. Culture is what human beings of all times do to challenge death [23, p. 155]. Perhaps the noblest human characteristic is our desire to challenge destiny, and fight against extinction. The very source of all our endeavors has always been to conquer death, "though it is a goal that probably cannot and should not ever be reached" [10, p. 6].

Energy Can Be Produced Only When Systems are in Imbalance

Artistic creations are examples of sublimated energy. The creative process is a blend of two elements; the overwhelming awareness of death, and the confrontation of our own possibilities, what Havelka calls "the Holy" [23, p. 160]. Facing death creatively releases energy. A set of keys resting on a table, a battery in complete balance, produce no energy. In the words of the Spanish philosopher Ortega y Gasset, each of us is a "radical solitude" [40, p. 153]. At the root of each of us is an incommunicability—a solitude—that no one else can penetrate. This solitude causes us anxieties about who we are and what we should be doing with our lives. It is precisely our anxieties, our confusions, our weakness that are the causes of creativity. The lack of balance of our lives gives us the energy to do something creative with our lives. The violinist Nathan Milstein says, "Satisfied with what I have done so far, yes. But 'fulfilled' is not the correct word." "I don't feel I have reached the peak" [10, p. 39]. Pianist Vladimir Askenazy adds, "I am satisfied with the kind of life I am leading, that is, with my whole life-style—I am doing what I want to do professionally—and with my personal life, my children, my wife. But feeling fulfilled? No—that would be the end; I would be finished" [10, p. 52].

A creative life is a quest for "salvation." Meaningfulness is created *intentionally*, "Such intentionality, as Rollo May correctly notices, is life's organized patterning which gives meaning to our experience. We intend *to be* to such an extent that the fear of non-being weakens" [23, p. 155]. Keen states that, "There are so many lives I want to live, so many styles I want to inhabit" [28, p. 119]. The philosopher Nicholas Berdyaev believes that all Russian writers, but especially Dostoevsky, write for "salvation" [16, p. 30]. Campbell says that the need to transcend human mortality is the first great impetus to mythology [12, p. 22]. Trilling reminds us, however, that even the great writers treat death in a manner that limits its fearsomeness [15, p. 525]. The scientist Albert Einstein states his view of human fate:

> How extraordinary is the situation of us mortals! Each of us is here for a brief sojourn; for what purpose he knows not, though he sometimes thinks he senses it. But without going deeper than our daily life, it is plain that we exist for our fellow men—in the first place for those upon whose smiles and welfare all our happiness depends, and next for all those unknown to us personally but to whose destinies we are bound by the tie of sympathy [27, p. 228].

Creative people do fear death, but deal with it in a different manner [10, p. 10]. As meaning seeking, self-creative beings, each human life is a compromise between what is and what might have been, "an intermediate state between the fullness of ideal life and death" [11, p. 91]. Becker reinterprets Freud's Oedipus complex to "the Oedipal *project*, a project that sums up the basic problems of the child's life: whether he will be a passive object of fate, an appendage of others, a plaything of the world or whether he will be an active center within himself— whether he will control his own destiny with his own powers or not" [7, pp. 35-36]. The question that each person must ask is the same. Are we playthings of the gods, or do we take our fate in our hands. The response of creativity is to create so as to perpetuate oneself.

What seems to be necessary for a meaningful life is neither refusal to accept death nor acceptance pure and simple, but a "synthesis of revolt and acceptance" [11, p. 97]. The more positively one evaluates life, the more positively one tends to evaluate death; the less positively one views life, the more negatively one views death [10, p. 34]. An acknowledgment of our finiteness intensifies our awareness of life and acts as a force, propelling us toward the realization of talents or desires. We become free to open ourselves widely and boldly to experience and are exempted from oppressive anxieties about death [23, p. 158]. By transforming death into a product of our own creation, we gain some control over it. It is a way of doing actively what otherwise we would suffer passively. We intend *to be* to such an extent that the fear of non-being weakens [23, p. 155]. Freedom to act as one desires is possible only with control over one's resources and the ability to channel one's energy in the direction one chooses. The experience of creation can help to restore meaning to the lives of persons who, through illness, have felt a lack of self-worth [38, p. 78]. The fear of death can be conquered by reaching self-fulfillment and, as a consequence, experiencing life completely. Those who are the least apprehensive of death seem to be free to explore vaster, unfamiliar time regions and can therefore project their needs, wishes, thoughts, and when applicable, their own person into the far distant future as well as extend themselves backward in the distant past [10, p. 32].

CONCLUSION

Aristotle reminds us that we ought not seek for more precision than is possible in a given investigation [22, p. 936]. When dealing with fundamental realities, we must do the best we can while continually striving for exactitude.

The most important reality human beings must deal with is mortality and death. Whether this topic is approached from the perspective of medicine, psychology, religion, philosophy, music, or poetry, death is often described in terms of figurative images or phrases. Unlike language, the arts have the potential to express diverse themes simultaneously. Through the arts, one can confront life and death on many levels at once. By engaging in an experience in the arts, people can be assisted as they mourn, grieve, celebrate life; they can overcome fragmentation, and find a sense of meaning in their lives. Because the arts are regenerators of the body, mind, emotions, and spirit, persons can be enabled to live more fully while they are dying and grieving.

Becker believes that culture is a hope that the things which individuals create will outlive death, "that the person and his products count" [7, p. 5]. In the same vein, the ethician Daniel Callahan says that death becomes acceptable when it comes at the point when there is a good fit between the biological inevitability of death in general and the particular timing and circumstances of that death in the life of the individual [41]. The achievement of such a peaceful death should be the goal of life, and therefore of medicine. "The process of dying is deformed when it is extended unduly by medical interventions or when there is an extended period of loss of consciousness well before one is actually dead" [41, p. 189]. We are, in the words of the philosopher, writer Sam Keen, part of an evolving cosmic adventure. "Nature-God-Life intends something through you" [28, p. 45]. The universe has not come ready-made from the hands of God. Each person completes his/her destiny by creating, by embodying the vision that they have produced. This is both the cause and the effect of creativity.

REFERENCES

1. D. Edwards, Grieving: The Pain and the Promise, in *Personal Care in an Impersonal World*, J. D. Morgan (ed.), Baywood, Amityville, New York, pp. 39-72, 1993.
2. W. L. Reese, *Dictionary of Philosophy and Religion*, Humanities, Atlantic Highlands, New Jersey, 1980.
3. M. De Wulf, *Philosophy and Civilization in the Middle Ages*, Dover, New York, 1953.
4. J. P. Sartre, Existentialism, in *Existentialism and Human Emotions*, J. P. Sartre (ed.), B. Frechtman (trans.), Philosophical Library, New York, 1957.
5. T. Aquinas, *Summa Theologica*, Part I, Question LXXXIII, Article 1, in *Basic Writings of Saint Thomas Aquinas*, A. Pegis (ed.), Random House, New York, pp. 786-729, 1944.
6. J. Fortunato, *AIDS: The Spiritual Dilemma*, Harper and Row, San Francisco, 1987.
7. E. Becker, *The Denial of Death*, Free Press, New York, 1973.
8. T. Flynn, Dying as Doing: Philosophical Thoughts on Death and Authenticity, in *Thanatology: A Liberal Arts Approach*, M. A. Morgan and J. D. Morgan (eds.), King's (Ont.), London, Ontario, pp. 199-206, 1987.
9. R. Kastenbaum, Reconstructing Death in Postmodern Society, *Omega*, 27:1, pp. 75-89, 1993.
10. L. Goodman, *Death and the Creative Life*, Springer, New York, 1981.
11. F. H. Lepargneur, Sickness in Christian Anthropology, in *The Mystery of Suffering and Death*, M. J. Taylor (ed.), Doubleday, Garden City, pp. 91-100, 1974.
12. J. Campbell, *Myths to Live By*, Viking, New York, 1972.
13. P. Ariès, *The Hour of Our Death*, Knopf, New York, 1981.
14. L. Boros, Death: A Theological Reflection, in *The Mystery of Suffering and Death*, M. J. Taylor (ed.), Doubleday, Garden City, pp. 161-178, 1973.

15. L. Trilling, Commentary on Tolstoi's "Death of Ivan Illych," in *The Experience of Literature*, L. Trilling (ed.), Doubleday, Garden City, pp. 525-527, 1967.
16. N. Berdyaev, *Dostoevsky*, Meridian, Cleveland, 1964.
17. J. B. Priestly, *Literature and Western Man*, Harper and Brothers, New York, 1960.
18. S. Keen, The Heroics of Everyday Life: A Theorist Confronts His Own End, *Psychology Today*, April 1974.
19. H. Mitchell, Visual Arts, in *Creativity and the Close of Life*, S. Bailey et al. (eds.), The Connecticut Hospice, Brantford, pp. 53-59, 1990.
20. Aristotle, Metaphysics, in *The Basic Works of Aristotle*, R. J. McKeon (ed.), Random House, New York, pp. 689-926, 1941.
21. J. Maritain, *Creative Intuition in Art and Poetry*, Pantheon, New York, 1953.
22. Aristotle, Nicomachean Ethics, in *The Basic Works of Aristotle*, R. J. McKeon (ed.), Random House, New York, pp. 935-1112, 1941.
23. J. Havelka, Creativity and Death, in *Thanatology: A Liberal Arts Approach*, M. A. Morgan and J. D. Morgan (eds.), King's (Ont.), London, Ontario, pp. 155-162, 1986.
24. B. S. Melendez, Fabric Arts, in *Creativity and the Close of Life*, S. Bailey et al. (eds.), The Connecticut Hospice, Brantford, pp. 35-50, 1990.
25. T. Parsons, R. C. Fox, and V. M. Lidz, The "Gift" of Life, in *Death in American Experience*, A. Mack (ed.), Schocken, New York, pp. 1-49, 1973.
26. S. Keen, *Faces of the Enemy*, HarperCollins, New York, 1991.
27. D. Larson, *The Helper's Journey: Working with People Facing Grief, Loss, and Life-Threatening Illness*, Research, Champaign, 1993.
28. S. Keen, *To a Dancing God*, HarperCollins, New York, 1990.
29. L. Pavarotti, Growing up in Modena, in *Pavarotti: My Own Story*, L. Pavarotti and W. Wright (eds.), Doubleday, Garden City, pp. 3-17, 1981.
30. L. Trilling, Commentary on Chekhov's "Three Sisters," in *The Experience of Literature*, L. Trilling (ed.), Doubleday, Garden City, pp. 250-255, 1967.
31. G. Martin, Verdi and *Risorgimento*, in *The Verdi Companion*, W. Weaver and M. Chusid (eds.), W. W. Norton, New York, pp. 13-41, 1979.
32. D. Salmon, Music and Emotion in Palliative Care, *Journal of Palliative Care*, 9:4, pp. 48-52, 1993.
33. L. M. Ross and H. R. Pollio, Metaphors of Death: A Thematic Analysis of Personal Meanings, *Omega: Journal of Death and Dying*, 23:4, pp. 291-307, 1991.
34. S. S. Bailey, Music, in *Creativity and the Close of Life*, S. S. Bailey, M. M. Bridgeman, D. Falkner, C. M. Kitahata, E. Marks, B. B. Melendez, and H. Mitchell, Connecticut Hospice, Brantford, pp. 17-30, 1990.
35. F. Wald, Foreword, in *Creativity and the Close of Life*, S. Bailey et al. (eds.), Connecticut Hospice, New Haven, 1990.
36. N. Cousins, *Anatomy of an Illness*, W. W. Norton, New York, 1979.
37. C. A. Hammerschlag, *The Theft of the Spirit*, Simon and Schuster, New York, 1993.
38. S. S. Bailey, Introduction, in *Creativity and the Close of Life*, S. S. Bailey, M. M. Bridgeman, D. Falkner, C. M. Kitahata, E. Marks, B. B. Melendez, and H. Mitchell, Connecticut Hospice, Brantford, pp. 1-3, 1990.
39. S. Porchet-Munro, Music Therapy Perspectives in Palliative Care Education, *Journal of Palliative Care*, 9:4, pp. 39-42, 1993.

40. J. Ortega y Gasset, In Search of Goethe from Within, in *The Dehumanization of Art and Other Writings on Art and Culture*, J. Ortega y Gasset (ed.), Doubleday, Garden City, pp. 123-160, 1956.
41. D. Callahan, *The Troubled Dream of Life*, Simon & Schuster, New York, 1993.

CHAPTER 2

Expressing Death And Loss Through Music

Sam Silverman

"The tongue is the pen of the heart, but melody is the pen of the soul." So said Rabbi Schneur Zalman of Ladi, the first Lubavitcher Rabbi. Commenting on this thought, the sixth Lubavitcher Rebbe, Rabbi Joseph Itschok remarked, "Speech reveals the thought of the mind, but melody reveals the emotions of longing and delight. These stem from the inner self, from the very soul, and are much higher than reason and intellect." No one knows why music excites emotions, or in what way it operates, but clearly music is a primary vehicle for expressing our deepest feelings. This has been true from biblical times, with the Psalms meant to be sung.

The experience of loss, the presentiment of death, are among the most basic human emotions, and composers have used this vehicle to express their own feelings about death, to memorialize lost friends, and even for the loss of communities. A composer sometimes confronts his own mortality, sometimes faces the loss of others. How do people adjust or accommodate to the loss of others who have been important to them? People generally use one of two mechanisms: either denial of the loss, or negation of its finality. Denial may be part of the initial reaction. Denial is a way of acting as if nothing has happened. It does not call for a creative solution for the composer, only silence. Negation, on the other hand, involves a more active resolution of the dilemma. Negation, as a mechanism [1, 2] is the negation of the significance of death by the introduction and presence of new life and continuing life. Negation is an adaptive mechanism which facilitates learning to deal with a new reality. Negation gives significance to the death by providing for a new or continuing life. The composer, through his music, provides for a continuing bond with one who has been important to him (for a discussion of the importance of these continuing bonds, see Silverman and Klass [3]; see also Bertman [4]).

In this chapter I shall consider, as case studies, five composers, and outline losses in their lives which have been reflected in their music. Composition becomes for them a way of dealing with the consciousness of their own mortality, and accommodating to the losses of people, or even of entire communities, important to them. Composing then becomes a creative strategy for healing, and its use exemplifies the process of negation.

JOHANNES BRAHMS

Brahms (1833-1897), in a number of his compositions, showed an awareness of death. This was particularly evident in his *German Requiem*, composed after the deaths of his friend Robert Schumann and his mother. Toward the end of his life his song cycle *Four Serious Songs,* Op. 121, also reflected this concern. The first three texts are from Ecclesiastes and Ecclesiastics. The first is about the vanity of human existence. The next two are about the blessing of death.

His settings of German folk songs in 1894, three years before his death, include at least two which deal with death. In one, *Es ging ein Maidlein zarte*, a young girl in the garden meets a terrifying man, no flesh, no blood, no hair, only flesh and sinews. He is death. She offers him all her father's estate. It is no good. She lies full of bitter fear and sorrow. In the other, *Es reit' ein Herr and auch sein Knecht*, a master and his squire go riding. For desire of the master's wife the squire kills him, returns to her, informs her, and asks for her. She goes off to the heath where the master lies, confirms his death. She will go to a nunnery and pray for him to go to heaven. In another late work, *Ach, Arme Welt, Op. 110, No. 2*, by an anonymous poet, the singer talks of how valueless are the things of this world:

Ah, wretched world, thou deceivest me.
Yes, I know that from my own experience;
And yet I cannot flee from thee. Thou false world, thou art untrue.
Thy glitter vanishes, that I know full well.
With grief and with great suffering. Thy glory, thy wealth, thou wretched world,
In death, in times of real trouble, fail thee;
Thy treasure is vain, spurious coin.
Therefore, help me, Lord, to peace.

In one of his earliest works, *Four Songs for Women's Voices*, Op. 17, composed in 1860, he includes *Come Away, Death*, after Shakespeare, and *The Death of Trenar*, from Ossian's poem *Fingal. Come Away Death* was also used by

Gerald Finzi (1901-1956) in a tribute to Vaughan Williams on his seventieth birthday, October 12, 1942. Another early work of Brahms, Romances from Johann Tieck's *Magellone*, Op. 33, includes: *Sind es Schmerzen, Sind es Freuden* [Are they sorrow, are they pleasure], about a young man despairing over the possibility that his lover may have left him. Tearful, he swears that he will end his life if they part; in *Verzweiflung* [Desperation] the desperate man no longer cares whether the rough sea takes him to his grave or not; and in *Muss es ein Trennung geben* [Must we then once more be parted] the song talks of the bitterness, grief and pain of parting from a loved one. In 1880 *Nanie*, Op. 82, for Chorus and Orchestra, was triggered by the death of his friend, Anselm Feuerbach.

For Brahms the deaths of his friends seems to have triggered in him primarily the awareness of his own mortality, and it is this he attempts to resolve in his music.

MODEST MUSSORGSKY

In 1874 Modest Musorgsky (1839-1881) composed what is perhaps his best known composition, *Pictures at an Exhibition*, as well as a desolate, subjective song cycle *Without the Sun* [5]. A good friend, Victor Hartman, a painter, had died the previous summer and his close friend Nadezhda Opochinina was to die in June 1874. His drinking problem, which eventually killed him, was also firmly established in this year. Hartman's death greatly upset Musorgsky, who also blamed himself for not recognizing and doing something about the aneurism which killed Hartman. An exhibit of Hartman's paintings was held in February and March of 1874, and Musorgsky decided to memorialize his friend by putting some of his paintings to music. One of these is of Hartman, a friend, and a guide examining the Parisian catacombs, and reflects Musorgsky's somber side. Death recurs in his other work, as in the death of Tsar Boris, in his opera *Boris Godunov*. The deaths of his mother, Hartman, and Opochinina deeply affected him. For Musorgsky, death was simply a waste [5, p. 46]. A year after the completion of *Pictures,* Musorgsky composed *Songs and Dances of Death*, again dealing with this theme. Shostakovich felt particularly close to Musorgsky, especially since his death from drink was so similar to that of Shostakovich's close friend Sollertinsky [6, p. 239]. For many years his favorite work was Musorgsky's *Songs and Dances of Death*, which he orchestrated, and which was connected to his Fourteenth symphony; a later favorite was *Without the Sun* [6, p. 240, 182].

For Musorgsky the deaths of those close to him not only triggered his reflections on death, but led him to memorialize his friend, at least in the case of Hartman.

Gustav Mahler

Gustav Mahler (1860-1911), like Shostakovich, was aware throughout his life of death. Unlike Shostakovich, Mahler's awareness was intensely personal, with no echo of the political situation of his time and place. This consciousness showed very clearly in two works composed between 1901 and 1904, the *Kindertotenlieder* [Songs on the Deaths of Children], and his Sixth Symphony. Both works were completed during a period when Mahler's life and work were thriving. He had met Alma Schindler in November 1901, and they were married in March 1902. Two children were born, in November 1902 and June 1904. He was the established director of the prestigious Vienna Court Opera since 1897, and his musical career was progressing well.

The *Kindertotenlieder* consists of settings of five poems by Friedrich Rückert (1788-1866), written following the deaths of two of his children. Rückert is said to have written over 400 poems expressing his grief at their loss. Mahler set three poems to music in 1901 and the remaining two in 1904. Each poem presents an aspect of the pain of bereavement. The first poem contrasts the effect of sunrise on one who has lost a child the previous night, with the joy it brings to the rest of the world. The second deals with memories of the child's eyes and the anticipation of the coming loss. In the third, he cannot see his wife entering the door without remembering the missing child, who used to accompany her. In the fourth he thinks that perhaps they are only out walking, and they will meet again in bright sunshine in the hills. The last poem deals with the funeral in a raging storm— he thinks that he would never have let the children out in such bad weather, but now nothing can affect them anymore. Mahler's wife Alma found these pieces deeply disturbing:

> I can understand setting such frightful words to music if one had no children, or had lost those one had. . . . What I cannot understand is bewailing the deaths of children, who were in the best of health and spirits, hardly an hour after having kissed and fondled them.

The Sixth Symphony was considered by Mahler to be his "Tragic" symphony. Bruno Walter, who had been assistant conductor to Mahler, noted the pessimism of the work:

> . . . it reeks of the bitter cup of human life. . . . above all in its last movement, where something resembling the inexorable strife of "all against all" is translated into music. "Existence is a burden; death is desirable and life hateful" might be its motto. . . . the work ends in hopelessness and the dark night of the soul.

The symphony ends with three "hammer blows of fate" which fell the hero. Alma wrote: "Not one of his works came so directly from his inmost heart as this. We both wept that day. The music and what it foretold touched us deeply."

Three years later, in 1907, Mahler himself suffered from the three hammer blows of fate. His eldest daughter, four years old, died; he was diagnosed with the heart condition which eventually killed him in 1911; and social pressures in Vienna led to his resignation as director of the Opera. Mahler himself believed that in the symphony he had predicted these blows of fate, and that in the *Kindertotenlieder* he had foretold the loss of his child. It is not necessary, however, to see the two pieces as clairvoyant presentiments of later developments in Mahler's life. Reik has suggested that Mahler's interest in Rückert's poems was fueled by the fact that the name of Rückert's child, Ernst, was the same as that of the brother, a year younger than him, who died when Gustav was thirteen [7]. Mahler's father and mother had both died in 1889, and his brother Otto committed suicide in 1895, and it is possible to speculate that the memories of the entire series of deaths were triggered by the name of Rückert's dead son, and that this led over the next three years to both works.

Mahler's awareness of death continued in perhaps a heightened manner after the events of 1907. Two years later he refused to designate his latest symphony as the Ninth Symphony, remembering those as the last symphonies of Beethoven and Bruckner, and called it instead *Das Lied von der Erde* [The Song of the Earth], a setting of German translations of six Chinese poems. Having now disguised the actual Ninth, he designated the next symphony as number 9. He was working on the Tenth Symphony when he died. Both Das Lied and the Ninth Symphony were first performed after Mahler's death, conducted by Bruno Walter. Several performing versions of the partially completed Tenth Symphony are available. Deryck Cooke, creator of perhaps the best known of these performing versions, writes of these three last works:

> These three works represent a three-stage pilgrimage in the process of "learning to walk and stand"—learning to find a meaning in life on the threshold of death without the assurance of any religious faith in immortality. In *The Song of the Earth*, the first stage, the sudden bitter awareness of imminent extinction is confronted and fused with a hedonistic delight in the beauty of nature and ecstasy of living, both now possessed so briefly and precariously. Then, in the second stage, the Ninth Symphony, this evidently goalless hedonism becomes a mere starting-point which vanishes as bitterness and horror come uppermost with terrible violence and lead to ultimate heartbreak. Finally, in the third stage, the Tenth Symphony, a deeper self-exploration eventually exorcises bitterness, horror and heartbreak, and culminates in a hymn to human love and a serene, unlamenting acceptance of the inevitable human lot [8].

For Mahler it was the deaths in his immediate family: parents, siblings, children, which were reflected in his music.

RICHARD STRAUSS

Unlike both Mahler and Shostakovich, Richard Strauss (1864-1949) does not show an awareness of death throughout his career in music. But early in his career, at the age of twenty-five, he composed the tone poem, *Death and Transfiguration*, and near the end of his life, his last compositions, the *Four Last Songs*, deal with approaching death. A few years after its composition Strauss described his conception in *Death and Transfiguration* [9, Vol. I, pp. 77-78]. The music deals with the last hours of a dying artist, reviewing his life, his aspiration and his attempt to reach artistic perfection, and his inability to do so. In the end, his soul leaves his body "in order to find gloriously achieved in everlasting space those things which could not be fulfilled here below." It is perhaps surprising to find in such a young man the sense that he could never achieve perfection. Strauss' lack of self-esteem was lifelong. He himself considered that he was not of the first rank. Strauss was constantly denigrated by his wife, but justified this as being treatment which was "just what he needed" [9, Vol. II, p. 239]. Perhaps death seemed to him like a release from his own imperfections.

Near the end of his life, between May and September of 1948 [9, Vol. III, p. 460], Strauss composed four songs, one of them connected with *Death and Transfiguration* through the quotation of a motif from the earlier work. These songs were his last compositions, finished about a year before his death, and performed for the first time eight months after his death. A portion of the music, sung by Kiri Te Kanawa, was used as a recurring theme, played by the sensitive Indonesian man, in the movie *The Year of Living Dangerously*. The first poem *Im Abendrot* [In the Twilight], by Eichendorff, describes an old couple, having gone together through the vicissitudes of life, watching the sunset and asking, as they prepare for the end, "Is this then death?" The other three, composed after the first, are by poems of Hesse. The first of these extols the beauties of spring. The second tells of the soul's fatigue and its desire for sleep. The third, entitled "September," deals with the end of summer, when summer "slowly closes his weary eyes." Strauss died before the first performance, and never indicated the order in which the songs should be sung. The editor of the published version gave the following order, which has been used since: Spring, September, On going to sleep, and In the Twilight.

Strauss' identification with his early work, *Death and Transfiguration*, came out clearly as he was dying. One of the last remarks he made to his daughter-in-law was: "Dying is just as I composed it in *Tod und Verklärung*" [10, p. 209].

With Strauss, his own physical death and the death of his creativity were the concerns of his music, and the problems he tried to resolve.

DMITRI SHOSTAKOVITCH

Dmitri Shostakovitch (1906-1975), in a conversation with Volkov (1979)[1] stated: "Fear of death may be the most intense emotion of all. I sometimes think that there is no deeper feeling. The irony lies in the fact that under the influence of that fear people create poetry, prose, and music; that is they try to strengthen their ties with the living and increase their influence on them." To write about death was a way of thinking through things related to death, thus losing the fear of death [6, p. 181]. Shostakovich's life spanned the period from the czars, through the early hopefulness of the Communist era, the Stalinist autocracy, to the more moderate autocracy of Brezhnev. During the thirties, friends were executed and he was himself in danger of losing his life. In the war years he saw death during the early part of the siege of Leningrad (now St. Petersburg) and the consequences of war with the massive destruction of people.

Shostakovitch epitomized his study of death in his fourteenth symphony, which consists of eleven poems, all concerned with death, and which he considered his most important statement on the subject. The symphony premiered in 1969, not too long after a near-fatal heart attack in 1966 [12, p. 143ff]. The orchestration of the symphony is very sparse, thus emphasizing the messages of the poems. Shostakovitch, speaking at a public rehearsal of the symphony said:

> I think that in my Symphony I'm following in the footsteps of the great Mussorgsky. His cycle Songs and Dances of Death—perhaps not all of it, but certainly The Field Marshall—is a great protest against death, a reminder that one must live one's life honestly, nobly, honorably, never committing evil acts [13].

Shostakovitch was also concerned with anti-semitism, and the mass murders resulting from this. During the Second World War, in September 1941, the Germans had carried out the mass murder of an estimated 70,000 Jews in a deep ravine, Babi Yar, in the outskirts of Kiev. The Germans, and subsequently the Ukrainians, tried to destroy the memory of this massacre of Jews. In 1961, Yevgeny Yevtushenko published his famous poem on the subject, in which he identified with every one killed at Babi Yar. Shostakovitch used this poem in the first movement of his thirteenth symphony, completed in 1962. As in the fourteenth symphony, the orchestration is restrained, serving as a backdrop for the poem. Both the poem and the symphony were upsetting to the Soviet authorities, who tried to give the impression that anti-semitism did not exist in the Soviet

---

[1] The credibility of Volkov's book has been questioned. It appears now to be generally accepted that whether or not the reported conversations were verbatim reports, they nevertheless reflect Shostakovitch's thinking and attitudes. A review and evaluation of this question is given by MacDonald [11] in the opening section of his book.

Union, and some passages were first required to be changed, and then performance of even the revised version was banned after 1965. Shostakovitch's reaction to anti-semitism was also reflected in his Violin Concerto, the Jewish Cycle and the Fourth Quartet [6, p. 157].

Shostakovitch responded also to the loss of individuals. When the person who he felt closest to, and whom he had first met in 1921, Ivan Sollertinsky, died in 1944, Shostakovitch dedicated his Second Piano Trio in memory of him. The Trio reflected both his grief at the loss of a close friend and a revulsion to the horrors of the Nazi death camps, liberated by the advancing Red Army. In a letter to Sollertinsky's widow, Shostakovich noted that he and Sollertinsky had talked about death:

> We talked about that inevitable thing waiting for us at the end of our lives—
> about death. Both of us feared and dreaded it. We loved life, but knew that
> sooner or later we would have to leave it [13, p. 116].

Shostakovitch lived in turbulent times, times of revolution and war, Stalinist purges in which many innocent people lost their lives. His music reacted to and reflected awareness and concern with his own death, with the deaths of his family and friends, and with the deaths of whole communities and peoples during the Nazi barbarities. Unlike the other composers discussed above, Shostakovitch's work covered a very wide spectrum of death.

DISCUSSION

Denial leads to creative stagnation and an absence of healing, since if the perception is that nothing has happened there is no need for any action. The underlying problem, however, remains unresolved and can lead to further difficulties, and an ongoing expenditure of energy in suppressing reality. Negation, as exemplified by the above composers, allows, hopefully, for at least an emotional resolution, and for ongoing creativity.

Noy [14, see also Rose, 15] argues for a two-level system of human communication. Language exemplifies a secondary level, based on social conventions based on agreed-upon symbols, signals, and signs. A primary level conveys the most significant part of the information, expressing experiences and emotions by means of tone, pitch, intensity, rhythm, resonance, timbre, duration, and inflection of the speaking voice. Music uses this primary mode of communication of meaning. This non-verbal means derives from and is the same as the pre-verbal means which an infant uses, prior to the acquisition of language, in communicating with the mother. This framework suggests to me that the composer, who has suffered grievous loss, acts to re-establish connection by symbolically returning to the prototypical union with the mother through the non-verbal, pre-verbal means present in music (see Silverman [16] for an analogous treatment of suicide as a return to prototypical union).

In many examples above the composer has set a text to music. By doing this he uses both verbal and non-verbal cues. Both cognitive and emotive processes are involved. In the language of the sixth Lubavitcher Rebbe cited at the beginning of this chapter, both mind and inner self come into play. Involving the conscious as well as the deeper levels of the mind should help the healing process.

Preserving the memory of the dead provides a continuing bond with those we have lost. In Greece during the period of Homer this was also seen as essential to the spirit of the deceased [17, p. 235]. The person was seen as consisting of body and soul. When the body was gone the spirit could live after death only if he was remembered. Even today one often hears the comment that people live on as long as they are remembered. Thus a composer, in memorializing a lost one, not only resolves his own grief, but provides a boon to the one he has lost, who continues to live as long as the music is performed.

This chapter has concentrated on the composer, and the role of his compositions in helping to resolve his awareness of his own mortality and in coping with the loss of a loved one and even whole communities. But music is also listened to by others. To the extent that it speaks for them, and to them, a musical composition, either directly through language or indirectly through non-verbal cues, or both, should help also in resolving their pain and dilemmas. The Beatles song, *Eleanor Rigby*, speaks to lonely people everywhere. The impact on listeners, however, is outside the scope of this chapter.

Additional notes: I have used several books for the discussion of Mahler: Cooke [8], Del Mar [7], Filler [18], Floros [19], and Keegan [20]. Much of the information in these books is the same, so I have not given specific references in the text.

Much information on composers is also available in the liner notes of the recordings of their music, and I have used these as well, generally without attribution, except where translations of material is involved.

Very useful collections of articles, which include discussions of the connections of music with death and mourning, from a psychoanalytic perspective, can be found in Feder, Karmel, and Pollock [21]. See especially the work of George Pollock in these and other sources.

REFERENCES

1. S. M. Silverman, [untitled], *Omega Newsletter, 3*:3, p. 29, 1968.
2. S. M. Silverman and P. R. Silverman, Parent-Child Communication in Widowed Families, *American Journal of Psychotherapy, 33*, pp. 428-441, 1979.
3. P. R. Silverman and D. Klass, Examining the Dominant Model, in *Continuing Bonds: New Understandings of Grief,* D. Klass, P. R. Silverman, and S. Nickman (eds.), Taylor & Francis, Washington, 1996.

4. S. L. Bertman, Communicating with the Dead: An Ongoing Experience as Expressed in Art, Literature and Song, in *Between Life and Death*, R. Kastenbaum (ed.), Springer, New York, pp. 124-155, 1979.

5. M. Russ, *Musorgsky: Pictures at an Exhibition*, Cambridge University Press, Cambridge, 1992.

6. S. Volkov (ed.), *Testimony: The Memoirs of Dmitri Shostakovich*, Harper & Row, New York, 1979.

7. N. Del Mar, *Mahler's Sixth Symphony—A Study*, Eulenburg Books, London, 1980.

8. D. Cooke, *Gustav Mahler: An Introduction to His Music*, Cambridge University Press, Cambridge, 1980.

9. N. Del Mar, *Richard Strauss*, three volumes, Cornell University Press, Ithaca, New York, 1986.

10. M. Kennedy and R. Bailey, Richard Strauss, in *The New Grove: Turn of the Century Masters*, W. W. Norton & Company, New York and London, 1985.

11. I. MacDonald, *The New Shostakovich*, Northeastern University Press, Boston, 1990.

12. R. Blokker with R. Dearling, *The Music of Dmitri Shostakovich: The Symphonies*, Tantivy Press, London, 1979.

13. D. Sollertinsky and L. Sollertinsky, *Pages from the Life of Dmitri Shostakovich*, Harcourt Brace Jovanovich, New York and London, 1980.

14. P. Noy, How Music Conveys Emotion, in *Psychoanalytic Explorations in Music, Second Series*, S. Feder et al. (eds.), International Universities Press, Madison, Connecticut, pp. 125-149, 1993.

15. G. J. Rose, On Form and Feeling in Music, in *Psychoanalytic Explorations in Music, Second Series*, S. Feder et al. (eds.), International Universities Press, Madison, Connecticut, pp. 63-81, 1993.

16. S. M. Silverman, Loneliness, Relationships, and the Dynamics of Suicide: An Essay-Review of Kokoro by Soseki Natsume, in *Suicide and Bereavement*, B. L. Danto and A. H. Kutscher (eds.), MSS Information Corporation, New York, pp. 176-193, 1977.

17. K. Meyer-Baer, *Music of the Spheres and the Dance of Death: Studies in Musical Iconology*, Princeton University Press, Princeton, 1970.

18. S. M. Filler, *Gustav Mahler and Alma Mahler: A Guide to Research*, Garland Publishing, Inc., New York, 1989.

19. C. Floros, *Gustav Mahler: The Symphonies*, Amadeus Press, Portland, Oregon, 1993 (English translation of German original edition, 1985).

20. S. Keegan, *The Bride of the Wind: The Life and Times of Alma Mahler-Werfel*, Secker & Warburg, London, 1991.

21. S. Feder, R. L. Karmel, and G. H. Pollock, *Psychoanalytic Explorations in Music, First Series*, International Universities Press, Madison, Connecticut, 1990; Second Series, 1993.

CHAPTER 3

The Advantages of Culture-Centered Counseling Over Client-Centered Counseling

Pittu Laungani

Client-centered counseling, which is also referred to as person-centered counseling, involves a subtle, close, and complex encounter of two minds: the mind of the client and the mind of the counselor. For the encounter to be meaningful, in other words, for both the client and the counselor to be able to pursue a meaningful and productive dialogue over time, it is necessary that both of them are aware or become aware of the rules which guide and foster their dialogues. Insofar as the two actors in the encounter are fully cognizant of the rules, communication is likely to proceed smoothly. But for either party to misunderstand the rules, or to flaunt the rules, or to arbitrarily change the rules during the course of the encounters, is likely to lead to an impasse—which of course has serious repercussions on the outcomes of these encounters. The rules that guide these encounters are generally unwritten. They are seldom articulated, nor are they ever specified. They exist within the social, existential, and cultural milieu of the client and the counselor. They are part of the cultural legacy inherited by the two dramatis personae.

This needs some elaboration. For effective communication between the counselor and the client it is essential that the following three conditions are met:

1. That the persons concerned share a common set of assumptions.
2. That the persons concerned share, to a large extent, a common cultural ideology.
3. That the counselor and the client share, to a large extent, the theoretical assumptions underlying the process of client-centered counseling.

Let us examine the three conditions briefly.

1. SHARING COMMON SETS OF ASSUMPTIONS

Each culture, or a sub-group within a given culture, comes to acquire over time a set of shared assumptions. It is not easy to define what shared assumptions are, nor is it particularly easy to articulate them with any degree of precision. However, it is reasonable to suggest that most of us have an intuitive understanding of what the concept subsumes.

Assumptions refers to commonly held beliefs, attitudes, and values shared by people in a given culture. Each culture, over time, comes to acquire its own notions concerning right and wrong, good and bad, proper and improper, healthy and unhealthy, normal and abnormal. When pressed why we hold such beliefs dearly and not others, why this is important and that less so, we may be unable to offer plausible explanations. Nonetheless our beliefs and values whose origins are often lost in antiquity pervade our cultural atmosphere. Like air, we imbibe them, often without a conscious awareness of their origins. What is not always fully appreciated is the extent to which one is a prisoner of one's culture, handcuffed to it, as it were, by past history.

The mechanics by which such beliefs are culturally transmitted and internalize are of course open to conjecture. However, it is the sharing or not sharing of such beliefs which, in a sense, brings cultures close to one another, or moves them apart. Clearly, some cultures are "closer" to one another, and others "apart." Although geographical location may play a vital role in the closeness or otherwise of cultures, it need not always be the case, as is evidenced by the similarities between Britain and Australia. And although cultures may be enjoined by a common course of history, they may yet remain apart, as is evidenced by the differences between Britain and India. If the underlying assumptions commonly shared by members of one culture are *not* shared by members of another culture, nor is any serious attempt made to understand them, effective communication is likely to be imperiled, and may, under some circumstances, breakdown altogether.

An example or two may clarify our meaning further. A woman living in India may accept a firmly established system of folk "theories" as to what constitutes illness and its causes. The belief system which she takes for granted is the one which is culturally accepted in her country. To her, the dysentery in her child might seem to be the definite influence of the "evil eye," and although it may be diagnosed as due to bacteria by an Indian doctor trained in Western medicine, her view would be unlikely to be subjected to ridicule. The two views—the natural and the supernatural—would reside side by side; pills, potions, and amulets, mixing freely with antibiotics. Over time, the woman in question may come around to believing that her child's illness was caused by armies of unknown, unseen "germs." Thus, the bacteriological view might ultimately come to prevail.

But whether she does or does not come around to accepting the bacteriological view, her own views concerning the causes of her child's illness are the ones which find ready acceptance among her own people and within her own community.

In England, however, the same Asian woman would find herself out of step, and out of sympathy—with the added danger of finding her own sanity being questioned were she to persist in supernatural explanations of her child's illness.

Thus, the assumptions shared by two persons or a group of people may be *linguistic* (e.g., sharing a common language), *semantic* (e.g., an ability to interpret and understand the subtle nuances of the shared language), *non-linguistic* (e.g., an understanding of the non-verbal means of communication, which would include the expression of feelings, emotions, and empathy conveyed through gestures, eye-contact, facial expressions, bodily postures, etc.), *ethical* (e.g., an appreciation of the normative moral rules which prescribe one's private and social behaviors), *political* (e.g., an internalization of the values underlying an elected constitutional government, notions of "natural justice," etc.).

Without shared assumptions, effective communication between two or more persons is likely to be seriously impeded. Such impediments can and do occur even between indigenous groups of people sharing a common language and, to a large extent, the fundamental values of their own culture. This can be evidenced in England where members of different social classes often experience serious difficulties in communicating with one another—and more poignantly, between medical doctors and their patients [1].

2. SHARING A COMMON CULTURAL IDEOLOGY

It is not being suggested that meaningful intercultural communications are never possible unless the persons concerned share a common cultural ideology. Such an argument would involve the acceptance of an extreme relativistic position. Relativistic doctrines, despite their seeming attractions and their recent upsurge within certain academic circles, have very little merit in them [2]. The value of relativism as a valid explanatory concept has come to be seriously questioned by several writers [2-7]. The acceptance of an extreme relativistic position is to present an argument which ends all arguments—for there is nothing left to say. It leads to what Popper refers to as an epistemological cul-de-sac [8]. Such a position does not permit any meaningful comparisons within and between groups of people on factors of significant importance. From a practical point of view, the acceptance of a relativistic position is likely to lead to arbitrary, pejorative, and even dangerous divisions within any society.

It is asserted that meaningful intercultural communications are possible. However, such processes are not without their own unique hazards. The potential hazards of intercultural communication—in our case inter-cultural counseling and therapy—and the means by which they may be overcome will be examined later.

What distinguishes one culture from another is the fact that cultures vary with respect to their value systems, which have a significant bearing on the religious beliefs, kinship patterns, social arrangements, communication networks, including regulatory norms of personal, familial, and social conduct [9, 10]. Values are best defined as the currently held normative expectations that underlie individual and social conduct [9]. Salient beliefs concerning right and wrong, good and bad, normal and abnormal, appropriate and inappropriate, proper and improper, and the like, are, to a large extent, influenced by the values operative in the culture. Because certain values are culture-specific, it follows that many assumptions and expectations underlying the appropriateness or otherwise of certain behaviors are also culture-specific. This factor evidently has extremely serious implications for counseling persons from different cultures. It is argued that Western cultures in general and English culture in particular can be distinguished from non-Western cultures in general and Indian culture in particular along four major factors, which are:

Individualism . . . . Communalism (Collectivism)
Cognitivism . . . . Emotionalism
Free Will . . . . Determinism
Materialism . . . . Spiritualism

It should be pointed out that the two concepts underlying each factor are not dichotomous; they need to be understood as extending along a continuum, starting at, say, Individualism at one end and extending into Communalism (or Collectivism) at the other. The salient values and behaviors of groups of people may be described as more individualism-oriented and less communalism-oriented and vice versa. In fact, the values can be described at any measurable point along the continuum, and over time may even move along the dimension from one end to the other. The concepts to the left of each factor are applicable more to Western cultures (including Britain) and those to the right to non-Western cultures (including India). The theoretical basis of the above dimensions and the kinds of private and social behaviors subsumed under each of the dimensions has been extensively described elsewhere [1, 2, 11-14]. Several hypotheses deduced from the above formulation have been subjected to rigorous empirical tests in India and in England [15, 16], thus providing empirical validity to the above formulations. Although no attempt will be made to discuss the above formulations in detail, references will be made to those features which have a direct bearing on the problems related to the nature, the process, and the product of client-centered and culture-centered counseling/therapy.

3. THEORETICAL ASSUMPTIONS IN CLIENT-CENTERED COUNSELING

All therapies—and client-centered therapy is no exception—have their own theoretical assumptions. In some instances, the assumptions are clearly stipulated (e.g., in Freudian psychotherapy and in behavior therapy) and in others they may not be clearly articulated and may need to be inferred from the nature of the relationship between the therapist and the client, the process of counseling, and the types of interpretations offered by the counselor or therapist. No form of counseling in that sense is atheoretical. It should also be recognized that theories are not constructed in a social vacuum. All theories are social constructions [8, 17]. They are rooted in social reality. As has been argued elsewhere:

> . . . a theory also needs to take into account its historical antecedent, its prevalent social, religious, economic (and other) conditions, including the objective and subjective states of knowledge which exist in a given society at a specific point in time. All these factors collectively influence the manner in which theories are conceptualized, formulated, and tested. Failure to take account of these factors may impose severe constraints on rationalist theories and may even render them meaningless [2, p. 2].

The theoretical assumptions underlying Rogerian counseling are too well known to merit a detailed discussion. However, the major features which have a pertinent bearing on our subsequent discussions of culture-centered counseling are shown in Table 1.

The theoretical assumptions which underlie client-centered counseling are seldom or never presented to the client as one might a menu, a price list, or a catalogue. Although the counselor may offer some initial insights into the nature of the counseling process, it is, however, the client who, over a series of encounters, is expected to infer the theoretical basis of the counseling process.

Table 1. Major Features Underlying Client-Centered Counseling

1. Secular.
2. Holistic.
3. Rooted in the neo-Kantian humanist tradition.
4. Importance of non-hierarchal relationship between client and counselor.
5. (Total?) Acceptance of client's beliefs, attitudes, and values.
6. Cognitive factors important in the counseling process.
7. Non-directive.
8. Counselor as facilitator.
9. Relationship between client and counselor "contractual."
10. Individuality of client (and counselor) recognized and respected.

Right from the beginning, the client is (unwittingly) involved in a guessing game and this naturally places the client at a disadvantage and the counselor at a distinct advantage because the counselor knows and the client doesn't. Such a practice compromises the fundamental assumption of non-hierarchal relationships. Like most relationships in psychotherapies of one kind or another, this one too turns into an asymmetrical relationship in which the counselor is in a position which is superior to that of the client. All the other factors, too, "conspire" to perpetuate the non-hierarchal nature of the relationship. It is the client who is expected to keep his/her appointments with the counselor. It is the client who is kept waiting should the counselor, for one reason or the other, be busy. On the other hand, it is not the client but the counselor who initiates the session, and who, after the agreed hour or fifty minutes, terminates the session. It is the counselor who is construed as the "expert" who has within his or her means the power to unravel the complexities and conundrums of the client's existential dilemmas, and "guide" him or her along a path which will lead to a successful resolution of the client's psychological conflicts. Whether such constructions of expertise of the counselor are justified or not is not the point. Whether the counselor is imbued with the powers to understand the client's conflicts is also not the point. It is sufficient that such constructions form part of the world view of the client and that the counselor is seen as the expert. Without such a construction it is hard to envisage how the very process of counseling can be initiated.

It would seem therefore that at an overt level there is a semblance of a non-hierarchal relationship, but at a covert level the relationship between the counselor and the client is one based on a hierarchial structure, in which the counselor unintentionally (or intentionally) occupies a superior position to the client. However hard the counselor tries, however genuine the counselor's intentions, it is quite difficult to discard the asymmetrical nature of client-counselor relationships.

To a large extent the theoretical assumptions which underlie the nature of client-centered counseling must be seen against the backdrop of the shared cultural ideology between the client and the counselor/therapist. Let us now discuss the problems of transplanting client-centered counseling/therapy.

1. Non-Hierarchal Relationships

The idea that the relationship between the client and the counselor must be based on a premise of equality stems from the fundamental notion of Individualism, which is one of the distinguishing features of Western society. Individualism, among other things, implies the acceptance of an individual's uniqueness, a recognition of and a respect for the other person's individuality. Individualism also recognizes the individual's ability to pursue their own clearly defined goals, take responsibility for their actions, cope with their problems, take credit for their successes, and accept blame for any failures encountered on the way.

When one turns to Indian culture, one finds that the concept of individualism has little meaning among people of that culture. Indian society has always been and continues to be a community based society. People live in extended family networks, where relationships are maintained on a hierarchical basis. A community in India has several unique features. People within a group are united by a common caste rank. Caste itself operates on a ranking or a hierarchial system. Elders and persons in positions of authority, e.g., teachers, gurus, etc., are accorded special status and are generally deferred to. On important issues, members of the family and one's *jati* (sub-community) may meet and confer with one another, and any decisions taken are often binding on the rest of the members within the community. Given the early socialization of Indians into a hierarchal social and familial structure, it would be difficult, if not impossible, for an Indian client to accept a counseling relationship based on the premise of equality. It is a situation in which the Indian client would feel extremely uncomfortable.

2. The Counselor/Therapist as the Expert

The Indian client is likely to search for a therapist he/she can respect, look up to, and defer to. To an Indian client, the counselor or therapist is seen as a special person, as the expert, a *guru*, a person who is imbued with special powers, even in some instances with *psycho-magical powers* which can be used to alleviate the client's personal and familial problems [18]. For an Indian client to operate on terms of equality with his/her therapist/counselors is totally alien to his/her way of thinking. Once the Indian client recognizes and accepts the "special" powers of the therapist or counselor, the client then is eager to abide by the counselor's wishes. It is through obedience, reverence, and respect of the counselor's psycho-magical powers, that the client hopes to make a rapid recovery.

3. Acceptance of Personal Responsibility

Again, while the philosophy of individualism permits an individual to take credit for his/her successes and accept blame for his/her failures, this attitude is also alien to an Indian way of thinking. A strong belief in a deterministic philosophy allows, for instance, a Muslim client to explain away failures and successes in terms of The Will of Allah, and for the Hindu, to the inexorable consequences of his/her Karma. The acceptance of personal responsibility for the consequences of one's actions is not as straightforward a concept as would appear at first sight. It is in need of a careful analysis.

4. Non-Directive/Directive Counseling

While some Western clients would be willing to attempt to arrive at an understanding of their inner conflicts and dilemmas with only a minimal assistance from their therapists/counselors, Indian clients would find it virtually impossible to follow such a lead. Because of their imbuing their therapist/counselor with superior powers bordering, in some cases, on the magical and mystical, they would expect to be guided and directed by them at every stage in their attempts at seeking a "cure" to their psychological problems. This attitude seriously compromises the fundamental assumption related to non-directed counseling/therapy.

5. Cognitivism . . . Emotionalism

It should also be recognized that Indian society, in contradistinction to Western society, operates on an emotional mode, whereas Western society operates on a cognitive mode. These different constructions of their private and social worlds stem from their inheritance of their different philosophical legacies. As a result, Westerners are able to engage in work-related contractual arrangements with their therapist/counselors. A therapist is a person with whom one *works* in order to resolve a personal problem. Note the emphasis on the word "work." The relationship is contractual. Both the parties in the contract have specific obligations toward one another. The fact that the nature of the transaction between the therapists and the client is of an emotional nature does not alter the contractual arrangements.

Indians, on the other hand, operate on an emotional mode. Indian society, therefore, tends to be relation-centered rather than work-and-activity centered. Work is often seen as a by-product of relationships. Consequently, Indians find it extremely difficult to enter into impersonal contractual arrangements. They look for a greater emotional connectedness with their therapists, which would allow them to express their dependency needs. As Roland points out:

> In contrast to Western hierarchal relationships—which tend to be based on a fixed status and power relationship, governed by contractual agreements and an ideology of essential equality—Indian hierarchal relationships are oriented toward firmly internalized expectations in both superior and subordinate for reciprocity for mutual obligations in a more closely emotionally connected relationship [18, p. 32].

The few examples which have been offered demonstrate quite clearly that any attempt to impose the client-centered therapeutic model on people from non-Western cultures, particularly those from the Indian sub-continent, is doomed to failure. Counselors need to realize that knowledge of Indian culture and history and/or the ability to speak one of the scores of Indian languages is not the same thing as understanding how Indians function psychologically. Sadly, there are no instant recipes for understanding how people of other cultures construe their own private and social worlds, how they relate to themselves, to their kith and kin, and to the members of the host community. To rely on superficial accounts related to the dietary practices of people of non-Western cultures (e.g., Muslims eat beef, but not pork; Hindus may eat pork, but do not eat beef; Jains eat neither) their religious beliefs (e.g., Hinduism is a pantheistic religion; they worship several Gods), the languages which they speak (e.g., Gujarati, Bengali, Urdu, Hindi, Punjabi, etc.), the clothes which they wear (e.g., the saris and shalwar kurtas worn by the women, the five k's worn by Sikhs), the customs which they follow (e.g., the Diwali festival of Hindus, the Ramadan practices of Muslims), the traditions which they abide by, the rites and rituals which they observe at christenings, engagements, weddings, and funerals, etc., may form the basis of a good beginning. These, however, are superficial observations. They do not help us to go beyond such superficialities. Such knowledge is certainly not enough for a Western counselor to impose a client-centered therapeutic model on those people.

An unintentional error which counselors—and indeed the majority of Westerners all over the Western world—make is to be misled by the perceived Westernization of their Indian clients. Should they meet with an Indian who speaks English fluently and colloquially, one who dresses in a Western manner, is involved in a professional occupation, and for all appearances gives the impression of being a Westerner, is also assumed to be a Westerner. *The Indian is then imbued with a Western mind!* He/she is then divested of most, if not all his/her cultural inheritance.

Why this is done is in itself an interesting issue. Several speculative observations can be made. There is a widespread Eurocentric belief that all developing countries over time will be influenced by Western science, technology, and know-how, to such an extent that they too, in the process, will become Westernized and indistinguishable from other Western countries. The West sets, so to speak, the gold standard, which developing nations attempt to achieve. If developing nations and/or members of ethnic minorities living in Western nations are all driven to getting Westernized, there is hardly any point in trying to understand an Indian from his/her own unique cultural perspective. What Westerners find difficult to understand and consequently come to terms with is the fact that the psyche of the members of ethnic minorities (as indeed of every person) is made up of several layers of which the Western persona is the most easily observable one. Such a persona no doubt is desirable. It dilutes, if not conceals, differences which would otherwise be difficult to accommodate in one's psychological schema. It facilitates intercultural relationships at a functional level. But beneath the easily acquired cosmetic Westernized persona is to be found a psyche whose roots can be traced back to one's own ancestral cultural upbringing which exercise a profound influence on the individuals in terms of their evaluations of themselves, their identities, and their own unique world views.

CONCLUSION

It is evident that client-centered therapy/counseling runs into serious problems not only among the indigenous members of Western society, but more importantly among members of ethnic minorities, particularly those from the Indian sub-continent. We have seen that it does not live up to its fundamental assumptions. There are within it serious inconsistencies which only further research ought be able to clarify.

The main problem with client-centered therapy/counseling—as indeed with all therapies—is the one of commensurability. Does it work? If so, how does it work? How do we know that it works? Vital though the issue is, most practitioners tend to shy away from it. This is a question which pleads for an answer. Just because a therapy is seen as being attractive, or is seen as being politically correct, or that it is in keeping with current social trends, does not in itself merit its usage unless one can establish its validity as clearly, as comprehensively, and as unequivocally, as possible. To turn away from the notion of validity and even look upon it as obscene as some therapists do, is to adopt an ostrich-like attitude, which in the long run will harm the very clients we are meant to help.

Let me end the chapter with a quote from a personal experience. When I was single and lived in a flat in central London, I had appointed a sort of major-domo whose job it was to look after my flat, clean it, paint it, do my shopping, iron my shirts, answer my telephones in my absence, and so on. One day, out of the blue, Bernie paid me, what he thought was a supreme compliment:

> "You know, Dr. Laungani, you are almost a true Brit! Almost one of us."
> I was aware that he was paying me a genuine compliment. However, in his compliment lay several implicit cultural assumptions:
> 1. Britain provided the gold standard for cultural development all over the world;
> 2. A desire to being British was the standard to which all non-Britishers automatically aspired;
> 3. That however hard one tried, one would never become a true Brit— whatever the term "true Britisher" might mean;
> 4. That other cultural developments were not even worth consideration.

It did not occur to him that I might have felt perfectly secure with my own cultural identity, and had never entertained a desire to acquire a "British" identity although I have lived and worked in Britain for several years. I did not wish to enter into a discussion with him over these issues. Since it would have been too complicated to explain to him all the implications, positive and negative, of his compliment, I merely smiled and replied: "Vive la difference."

REFERENCES

1. P. Laungani, *It Shouldn't Happen to a Patient: A Survivor's Guide to Fighting Life-Threatening Illness,* Whiting & Birch, London, 1992.
2. P. Laungani, Mental Illness in India and Britain: Theory and Practice, *Medicine and Law, 16,* pp. 509-540, 1997.
3. A. Bloom, *The Closing of the American Mind,* Penguin, London, 1987.
4. L. Doyal and R. Harris, *Empiricism, Explanation and Rationality: An Introduction to the Philosophy of the Social Sciences,* Routledge, London, 1989.
5. E. Gellner, *Relativism and the Social Sciences,* Cambridge University Press, Cambridge, 1985.
6. F. Musgrove, *Education and Anthropology: Other Cultures and the Teacher,* John Wiley & Sons, Chichester, 1982.
7. B. Williams, *Ethics and the Limits of Philosophy,* Fontana, London, 1985.
8. K. Popper, *Objective Knowledge: An Evolutionary Approach,* Clarendon Press, Oxford, 1972.
9. P. Laungani, Death and Bereavement in India and England: A Comparative Analysis, *Mortality, 1:2,* pp. 191-211, 1996.
10. C. M. Parkes, P. Laungani, and B. Young, *Death and Bereavement Across Cultures,* Routledge, London, 1996.
11. P. Laungani, Cultural Differences in Stress and Its Management, *Stress Medicine, 9:1,* pp. 37-43, 1993.
12. P. Laungani, Cultural Differences in Stress: India and England, *Counselling Psychology Review, 9:4,* pp. 25-37, 1994.
13. P. Laungani, Stress in Eastern and Western Cultures, in *Stress and Emotion, Vol. 15,* J. Brebner, E. Greenglass, P. Laungani, and A. O'Roark (eds.), C. D. Spielberger and I. G. Sarason (Series eds.), Taylor and Francis, Washington, D.C., pp. 265-280, 1995.
14. P. Laungani, Death in a Hindu Family, in *Death and Bereavement Across Cultures,* C. M. Parkes, P. Laungani, and W. Young (eds.), Routledge, London, 1997.
15. D. Sachdev, *Effects of Psychocultural Factors on the Socialisation of British Born Indian Children and Indigenous British Children Living in England,* unpublished doctoral dissertation, South Bank University, London, 1992.
16. D. Sookhoo, *A Comparative Study of the Health Beliefs and Health Practices of British Whites and Asian Adults with and without Myocardial Infarction,* paper read at the 53rd Annual Convention of the International Council of Psychologists, Taipei, Taiwan, August 1995.
17. J. Ziman, *Reliable Knowledge: An Exploration of the Grounds for Belief in Science,* Cambridge University Press, Cambridge, 1978.
18. A. Roland, *In Search of Self in India and in Japan: Toward a Cross-Cultural Psychology,* Princeton University Press, Princeton, 1989.

CHAPTER 4

Diversity within Diversity: Strategies for Developing Insight among Professionals

Victor Baez and Kevin Ann Oltjenbruns

BACKGROUND

Most modern societies face a number of challenges related to accommodating human differences. Coping with the issues related to multiculturalism is a characteristic of numerous societies. This pursuit of multiculturalism is evident in various ways; it affects the development of public policy, the delivery of social services, as well as many aspects of personal life. Until recently, we did not understand the importance of paying attention to different group cultures or gender differences in providing support. Many of us lacked the insight that the delivery of services in a professional and caring manner may be affected by the ethnicity/race or gender of the client. Fortunately most professionals now understand that these differences must be taken into account if appropriate services are to be provided.

Before we begin our discussion as to how to be more sensitive to persons of various backgrounds, it can be helpful to develop insight about the world's changing demographics. There are many factors contributing to our growing pursuit of multiculturalism. Since Word War II, there has been, on a global basis, major resettlement of peoples from all over the world. For example, the United States, long recognized as a society of immigrants, has seen the number of immigrants steadily increase from the 1950s to the 1990s. Further, the countries of origin of these new immigrants shifted significantly in favor of Latin America and Asia. Not only were there larger numbers of persons entering the United States, these individuals tended to come from areas of the world whose languages and cultures were different from what many regard as Anglo-Saxon American norm. In addition to an increased rate of immigration, the high birth rate of various ethnic minority groups (African Americans, Hispanics, and Native Americans) has tended to substantially alter the proportion of Americans of non-European descent.

It is increasingly evident that, in all aspects of life including professional practice, the chances of encountering persons from cultural backgrounds different from our own have increased dramatically. According to Brislin and Yoshida one must add a third certainty in life to Benjamin Franklin's death and taxes: "People must interact with others from very different cultural backgrounds, whether they are well-prepared to do so or not" [1, p. 1].

Although important demographic changes help to explain the increasing diversity of most modern nations, they cannot entirely account for the pursuit of multiculturalism. For example, as noted, the United States is considered a nation of immigrants. Relatively little attention was paid to cultural or other differences until fairly recent times. Everyone was expected to adapt to the predominant cultural norms and values. The ferment of the civil rights movement provides a more appropriate starting point for understanding the changes in ideology that furnish key dimensions to the current pursuit of multiculturalism. During this period, many minority groups came to believe that the educational and other institutions of society failed to provide adequate services to members of their groups precisely because these institutions had failed to recognize their unique identity, and in doing so failed to treat them with dignity. This striving for recognition of the uniqueness of members of certain groups and the pursuit of dignity is àt the heart of a widespread move toward "multiculturalism" which calls for acknowledgment and respect for human differences. Many strive for recognition and attention to gender differences, religious differences, ethnic/racial differences, among others, in various aspects of social interaction. Social service providers have come to realize that language, culture, traditions, gender, and skin color cannot be ignored, indeed they must be consciously recognized and appreciated if appropriate services are to be delivered.

In recent years, increased attention has been given by professionals who serve the dying and the grieving in developing new skills, insights, and information in relation to meeting the needs of various groups as defined along certain dimensions (e.g., ethnicity, religious background, gender). Numerous professional conferences have recently focused on issues of diversity and many helpful resources have recently been published including such edited volumes as: *Ethnic Variations in Dying, Death and Grief: Diversity in Universality* [2], *A Cross-Cultural Look at Death, Dying, and Religion* [3], *Personal Care in an Impersonal World: A Multidimensional Look at Bereavement* [4], and *Coping with the Final Tragedy: Cultural Variations in Dying and Grieving* [5].

CONTENT/MODEL

This chapter presents a *practical and interactive* model useful in examining human differences, the impact of these differences on social and professional relationships, and the experiences of individuals with these differences at times of death and bereavement. The model is founded on seven basic elements related to human diversity which the authors deem essential for beginning to develop the knowledge and skills necessary for cultural competence in offering services at times of death and bereavement. From these seven basic elements flow specific activities to help practitioners learn and apply practice principles. Specifically, the model is built around a series of interactive exercises that help to explicate the major points.

Essential for this approach to diversity is the caution that we be careful of over-generalizations that may lead to stereotyping. Properly understood, diversity leads to the realization that:

- there is diversity within diversity;
- differences within a group are often as large as differences between groups;
- members of any group may share important characteristics with members of their own group, but also with members of other groups (e.g., a Mexican American[1] person with a serious illness has that experience of a serious illness in common with non-Mexican Americans who are also experiencing a serious illness).

The seven basic elements of the model are derived from an interactive view of human identity and can be summarized as follows:

1. Cultural competence begins with self-awareness. Knowing oneself, one's personal biases and interests, and having some sense of how one's religion, ethnic/racial group, family, gender have contributed to making each of us who we are can contribute greatly to making us more open and better able to understand others. Knowing one's own thoughts, feelings, and reactions to death and bereavement as well as how one's background in terms of family, culture, religion, gender, and other unique features has influenced these thoughts, feelings, and reactions will enhance our capacity to try to be helpful to others who are experiencing death and bereavement.

2. We must understand that a person's identity has many facets which includes race/ethnicity, but also includes such dimensions as religious background, gender, sexual orientation. In addition, identity is influenced

---

[1] Examples used throughout this chapter refer to Mexican Americans. The authors felt it would be clearer to refer only to one group. However, it should be apparent that similar examples could be drawn with reference to any other cultural group.

by other individual "conceptual" experiences. These include where we live (geographic location), whether we are rich, poor, or middle class (SES), our generation status, etc. (Although El Día de los Muertos or The Day of the Dead is an important cultural practice acknowledging the place of death in life, a Mexican-American teenager living in Los Angeles, and a middle aged Mexican immigrant living in a small town in Colorado are likely to have very different experiences and viewpoints about this cultural practice.)

3. In order to provide culturally appropriate and sensitive care for dying and grieving, it is not enough to simply learn descriptive information about broadly defined population groups. This descriptive information is crucial, but not enough. (Knowing that, among Mexican Americans, open grieving is expected at a wake service (velorio) is crucial but not enough, for this is not always the case.)

4. General knowledge of someone's ethnicity, someone's religion, someone's gender, etc. provides us with a source for hypotheses to be tested about how best to provide care to an individual or family. (Knowing that, in Mexican-American culture, death is very much a family event, allows us to create a hypothesis about how certain individuals and families might react. It does not allow us, however, to conclude that this pattern really exists in every situation. Not all Mexican Americans have close family ties. Each individual's experience of closeness to family is influenced by many factors in their own individual lives.)

5. Many of the definitions and concepts and much of the information in the area of human diversity appear, at times, to be inconsistent and even contradictory. Because of the complexity of human life and behavior, we often use paradoxical language to communicate about human differences. It is not unusual for someone who is culturally different to express to a helping professional that they are just like everyone else, but still insist on being recognized as a member of a specific group.

6. One's race and also one's sense of ethnic belonging may not be reflected in one's everyday behavior. My race or my ethnic identity do not necessarily explain how I carry out my life from day to day. It is usually not possible to predict behavior from prior knowledge of race or culture. (For example, although Mexican-American culture has often been described as fatalistic, Mexican Americans facing a life-threatening illness will not necessarily easily accept their condition.) There will be wide variation in terms of coping behaviors in these situations. Many other factors will influence individual decisions.

7. Understanding the experiences of others requires that we pay special attention to what those who are "insiders" (to an experience) tell those of us who may be outsiders (to that experience). As practitioners, we have to come to develop knowledge and skill that will help us answer the

questions: Can we really understand someone else's experiences? Can any of us ever really understand the life (or death) experience of those who are significantly different from ourselves? We may not understand completely, but we need to try, and our best source of knowledge is communication with those who are most directly involved in a given experience. (For example, a Mexican-American parent who has lost a child is the best source of information about how they are experiencing that loss and how their cultural milieu may be influencing their grief process.)

From these seven elements, the authors have developed a number of activities and insights which can inform culturally sensitive practice. These activities (exercises and examples) are presented in the next section, and can be used by practitioners to help themselves and others develop personal insights in the development of "cultural competence." For each activity, a statement of rationale provides a backdrop that explicates the principles being explored, a description of the activity follows, and finally a summary/discussion is included.

ACTIVITY: SELF-AWARENESS: AN UNDERSTANDING OF ONE'S MULTIPLE IDENTITIES

Rationale

One of the best ways to appreciate the complexity of another human being is to deepen an understanding of ourselves first. We will ask you to do this as you reflect on many different personal dimensions. Rather than examining identity as a uni-dimensional descriptor of one's self, you can think of it as if you had many "identities." Consider the many contributors to your own definition of self. Think for a moment of your family roots. What is your ethnic heritage? Think, too, of the impact that such things as your religious upbringing, your gender socialization, your family's socioeconomic status, and significant historical events have had in your lifetime. All of these helped shape who you are.

Description of Activity

Use Chart 1 to think through the many facets of your identity. These variables impact the beliefs you have, the behaviors you engage in, the type of support/intervention you desire; the customs/rituals you participate in as they relate to various aspects of illness, death, grief, and so on. Evaluate these various beliefs, behaviors, etc.—how were they tied to your ethnic heritage? to your religious upbringing? to your gender socialization? and so on. How do these variables—singly or in combination—affect outcomes as related to illness, healthcare, dying/death, bereavement?

Beliefs About • Behaviors in Regard to • Type of Support/Intervention Desired • Customs Related to	Variables Defining Who You Are	Broader Context	Factors You Feel Influence Your beliefs, behaviors, support/intervention desired, customs you participate in, other
My "Identities"	• ethnic heritage • religion • gender • sexual orientation • other	• socioeconomic status • geographic locale • cohort group • your past history (experiences) • your family history (experiences)	
Death Illness Dying Process			
What Constitutes Appropriate			
• Assessment			
• Care			
• Who is involved?			
• Techniques/tools used?			
Funeral Rituals			
Burial Practices			
Life After Death			
Grief • what is felt? • how is it expressed? • what is regarded as "normal"? • from whom do you seek support?			

Source: Oltjenbruns/Baez, May 1997, King's College; 15th International Conference on Death and Bereavement: "Delivering Care in a Multicultural Setting," Session—"Diversity Within Diversity."

Summary/Discussion

Doing an exercise such as the one described here will help refine the insight you have about the many factors which intersect to make *you* a unique individual—you have unique characteristics, unique needs, unique strengths, and so on. You can now generalize this insight to gain better insight regarding those persons with whom you work (e.g., clients, patients, parishioners, family members). They are also unique and must be treated as such.

This is not to say that knowing something of a person's general characteristics is useless information. The point we are stressing is that, while knowledge of general characteristics does provide important insight, it does *not* provide us with an answer as to precisely what an individual needs in terms of support. It does not provide us with a recipe as to how to interact with a particular person simply based on knowledge of a single dimension (e.g., race or religious beliefs). To the contrary, there is risk involved that a caregiver may come to a very inappropriate conclusion based on a single descriptor. A name on a patient's chart may cause some to assume that the patient they are about to meet is, for example, a male of a particular heritage. Many might jump to the conclusion, for example, that the Kevin Oltjenbruns (one of this chapter's authors) whose name appears on a patient chart is a male of German heritage and begin to plan interventions accordingly. A significant problem (or at least embarrassed laughter) might arise upon discovery that this individual is, in fact, a woman of Irish heritage. Recall that information along a particular dimension (e.g., a name), while it provides a hypothesis, does not necessarily lead to an accurate conclusion.

As a continuation of the exercise, discuss with a partner any experiences you may have had when either you or a colleague jumped to a conclusion about a patient/client—based on a simple descriptor of that person.

ACTIVITY:
SIMILARITIES AND DIFFERENCES

Rationale

On occasion, we look at one another and may conclude that we have little in common because we are of different races, ethnic backgrounds, religious backgrounds, etc. Figure 1 is a tool for helping persons to discover their similarities as well as their differences.

Description of Activity

Divide into groups of two or three individuals. Draw as many circles as there are people in the group. Decide which of you is "A," which is "B," and so on. If you discuss a characteristic and find that you are similar in regard to that

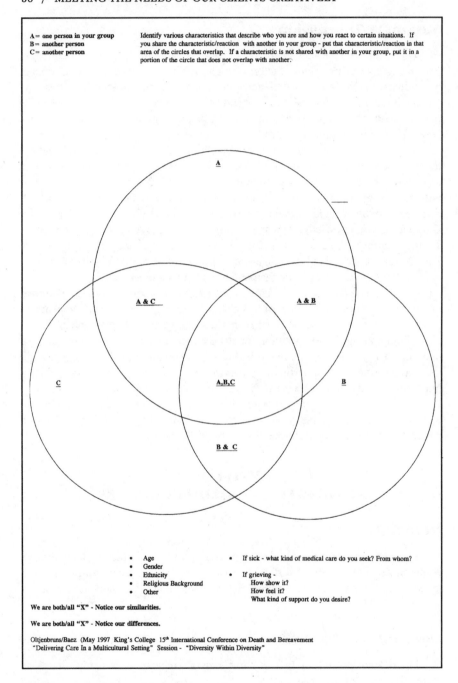

A= one person in your group
B= another person
C= another person

Identify various characteristics that describe who you are and how you react to certain situations. If you share the characteristic/reaction with another in your group - put that characteristic/reaction in that area of the circles that overlap. If a characteristic is not shared with another in your group, put it in a portion of the circle that does not overlap with another.

A

A & C   A & B

C   A,B,C   B

B & C

- Age
- Gender
- Ethnicity
- Religious Background
- Other

- If sick - what kind of medical care do you seek? From whom?
- If grieving -
  How show it?
  How feel it?
  What kind of support do you desire?

We are both/all "X" - Notice our similarities.

We are both/all "X" - Notice our differences.

Oltjenbruns/Baez (May 1997 King's College 15ᵗʰ International Conference on Death and Bereavement "Delivering Care In a Multicultural Setting" Session - "Diversity Within Diversity"

Figure 1.

characteristic—write it in the area that is created by the intersection of circle A with circle B. If you are different in terms of that characteristic, write those descriptors in the separate circles. For example, if your group has one woman and one man, write down "male" in the A-circle and "female" in the B-circle. If on the other hand, both team members are female—write "female" in the intersecting area. Using one color of ink, plot similarities/differences along such fundamental characteristics as: gender, ethnicity, religious heritage, socioeconomic status, etc. Now, change color of ink and write in descriptors for such things as the following:

If you are sick, what kind of medical help do you seek?
From whom?

If you are grieving—
How are you likely to show your grief?
What feelings/thoughts are likely to be most intense?
What kind of support from others would you likely desire?

If someone in your family has died, would they most likely be cremated?
Buried?

Note that these are only examples of the types of questions you might ask. You are free to define questions that are personally relevant to you.

Summary Discussion

The goal of this activity, "Similarities and Differences," is to illustrate that people may typically share significant characteristics, beliefs, values, etc., even though they may be different on key dimensions of identity. Alternatively, persons who share a given characteristic (e.g., sex or gender), may still be quite different from one another on other dimensions. For example, not all women desire the same type of support when they are ill nor do they show their emotions in the same way when they are grieving.

Again, there is a need to build a hypothesis about a given individual prior to coming to a conclusion about the type of care that might be most appropriate for a given individual or family.

CASE STUDY:
THE NEED TO TEST HYPOTHESES

Rationale

Obtaining and using information about diverse groups is essential for work with individuals and families from various backgrounds. (For example, it is important to learn the specific ways in which Mexican Americans express grief and common gender differences that may characterize these expressions.) However, this general insight about common reactions needs to be informed by strong cautions concerning the potential harm of over-generalizing. Again, remember that cultural descriptions need to be considered as *hypotheses to be tested* in individual situations. Although general information about a given cultural group is useful, it should not serve as the basis for action without first trying to see if it actually applies in a particular situation. For example, a person may exhibit few, if any, strongly visible cultural traits yet still be very much Mexican American. For whatever reason, one Mexican American may not align with certain stereotypes (e.g., eating tacos or expressing grief openly) but that person may still identify strongly as a Mexican American. It is crucial to focus not simply on the cultural traits a client may exhibit, but also on that person's perceptions and understandings of her/his ethnic/racial identity.

Description of Activity

Read the following vignette, and in small groups discuss the questions that follow.

Carmen Maria Solano is a thirty-five-year-old immigrant from Central America. She is a very sociable person and soon made a number of rather close friends in her neighborhood and at work. About a year after her arrival in the United States, the mother of one of these friends died. Carmen had interacted with the deceased and was truly saddened by this loss. Being a person who cries very easily, and having heard that Americans don't cry at funerals (or at least that they don't do so in public), Carmen went to her doctor to obtain a prescription for tranquilizers. She didn't want to make a fool of herself by being the only one at the funeral to cry. When Carmen arrived at the funeral she was surprised to see that many people were crying, some even loudly. After the funeral, she shared with her husband her disappointment about being tranquilized and thus unable to express her grief openly by crying, something natural to her way of showing her grief and her caring.

1. Was Carmen Maria's perception that there is an American cultural norm about not expressing grief in public (e.g., by crying loudly) correct?
2. How might Carmen Maria have tested the cultural information she obtained about Americans not crying at funerals?
3. Think about some cultural information you have about how various cultural groups express grief. Have you found this information to be true in some instances? All instances? How might you go about testing appropriate hypotheses?

4. Evaluate how you could interact with clients who are culturally different from yourself in order to confirm/deny knowledge you have about their cultural group. Tie to a discussion of death and bereavement.

5. Assume there is a cultural norm in the United States to not express grief openly in public (e.g., by loud crying), how would you explain to Carmen why some persons at the funeral felt comfortable crying?

Summary Discussion

The primary goal of this case study is to illustrate the importance of treating all generalized cultural information with caution. This generalized knowledge is a beginning point for cultural competence, but may lead to unfortunate consequences if not tested. Recall that there is a wide range of variation within any cultural group. Most importantly, one's race and/or sense of ethnic belonging may not be reflected in everyday behavior. (My race or my ethnic identity do not necessarily explain how I carry out my life from day to day. What defines a person as Mexican American? Is it a list of traits? Brown skin? Eating tortillas, tacos, chiles? Speaking Spanish? Listening to Mariachi music? Celebrating *El Día de los Muertos*? Using *curanderas/curanderos* (folk healers) as part of a spiritual support system?)

Some practitioners tend to focus on specific ways in which people within certain cultural groups behave, what and how they eat, how they express grief, their views of death and the afterlife. However, it is as important, if not more so, to focus on a person's perceptions of their ethnicity, gender, or racial identity. Think about this in terms of your own work. Even if a person does not exhibit typically ethnic, typically "Mexican American" behaviors in their daily lives, how important might it be to acknowledge, support, and encourage people to express their sense of identification with a particular ethnic group at times of death and bereavement?

ACTIVITY:
UNDERSTANDING THE USE OF PARADOX

Rationale

As we learn to become more competent in understanding other cultures, it is also essential to understand that human differences, cultural knowledge, the lives of human beings, and human emotion are so complex that we frequently have a difficult time talking about them using ordinary language. Much descriptive information about a culture is inherently paradoxical. This does not mean it is not true, or not useful, or not relevant. It means that we often need to resort to language that is out of the ordinary to deal with many aspects of diversity.

Activity

Read the following definition of paradox and the short excerpt from a poem by Pat Parker. In small groups, discuss the questions that follow.

paradox: A person, condition, or action with seemingly contradictory qualities. Paradoxical statements are often used to indicate situations which are very complex and hard to explain in ordinary language.

Poem Title: *To the white person who wants to be my friend*

The first thing you do, is forget that I'm Black.
Second, you never forget that I'm black.

1. What is the main idea behind the excerpt from Pat Parker's poem?
2. Why do you think she chose to use paradoxical language to make her point?
3. Can you think of ways in which paradoxical statements might be useful to practitioners and clients dealing with death or bereavement?

Summary Discussion

The two lines from Pat Parker's poem are an excellent example of a paradoxical statement. It sounds like a contradiction: "forget that I'm Black; never forget that I'm black." But if we think about it, these two short lines also contain a very profound statement. Using ordinary language, it would take many more words to fully express what Pat Parker has been able to express in very few words. In addition, the use of ordinary language would not have the impact of the paradoxical statement. You see this in your own work with families and individuals who are struggling with deeply felt emotions. Ordinary language often fails us.

ACTIVITY:
COMMUNICATION BETWEEN INSIDERS
AND OUTSIDERS

Rationale

Can one really understand someone else's experiences? Can any of us ever really understand those who are different from ourselves in some significant way? As practitioners, we must ask ourselves this question and come to some understanding of what is involved. We assume in the helping professions that understanding someone else's perspectives/experiences is important to building a helping relationship. Empathy is at the core of the helping process, and empathy requires a degree of understanding. (Can I, a Hispanic male, really understand the grief process of a female non-Hispanic client? Can a non-Hispanic therapist really understand the grief experience of a Mexican-American client?)

The notion of insider/outsider is useful to gain insights that are helpful in communicating across differences. For example, when we experience the loss of a loved one, we are said to be "insiders" to that experience. We own it. We are ultimately the ones who know what that is really like. Others may also be experiencing that loss, but not in the same way. Experts may have some general knowledge about what it is like to lose a loved one, but, ultimately, I experience that loss in my own way. I am an insider to that experience. Everyone else is an outsider.

We also know that in these situations, it is often difficult to communicate with those who are outside of my experience. I try to explain how I feel, what I am experiencing, but words fail me. Insights from these experiences are important in practice. One must come to understand these two different positions and develop strategies for communicating across the difference.

Activity

Take a few minutes by yourself to think about the following. It is helpful if you jot down some notes while doing this exercise.

What was the last time you experienced the loss of a loved one (or a similar grief experience)? Take particular note of how you felt and how you behaved under these circumstances. How did you feel? What did you do? You are an "insider" to this experience. It is uniquely your own.

Then think about having to explain your situation, including feelings and behaviors, to an "outsider" in an attempt to help them understand what you are experiencing. Take particular note about how you would want that "outsider" to behave toward you under these circumstances. Also, pay attention to your use of language. What kinds of phrases would you use to explain your feeling? Your behaviors?

Next, choose a partner and try to talk through what you experienced doing this exercise.

Summary Discussion

In beginning to think about understanding another's experience, it is useful to understand that we have all experienced being insiders in some situations and have also been outsiders in other situations. We know from these experiences that it is difficult, sometimes very difficult, to explain to an "outsider" what one is feeling or experiencing. Yet, there are certain important insights to be derived from being an outsider which are useful to keep in mind in trying to think about and resolve the question of whether one can really understand someone else's experiences, the experiences of someone who is different from us. Think about a client who is of a different background than you are; that person is grieving the loss of a spouse. Think of that client as being the "insider" to that particular experience. You are the "outsider." Then consider the following principles for communicating across differences:

1. Outsiders must approach "insiders" with humility and caution. Insiders have more immediate, subtle, and critical knowledge of their own experiences than anyone else. They are the experts about their own experiences. You, the outsider, are the learner.
2. Be careful about overt denials or minimization of the insider's understandings or responses. (Although you yourself may not experience it the same way, the grief of someone experiencing an early miscarriage may be as real as that of someone who loses a two-year-old child.)
3. Don't cut someone off by saying you understand. Allow the other to explain.
4. Don't judge what insiders "ought to do" or how they "ought to feel."
5. One of the best ways to communicate across the boundary of insider and outsider is to use analogies. Help your client/patient explain his/her feelings to you. "Explain to me how you felt when your father died? (It felt like my heart exploded into a thousand pieces.)"

ACTIVITY: CASE VIGNETTE

This last activity helps to summarize principles presented earlier in this chapter through the use of a case vignette. The situation presented, although fictional, describes a scenario that is true to the many forms of diversity and the very complex ethnic reality experienced by most families in the modern world. It points to the fact that, in addition to cultural differences, one must pay attention to other types of differences including those tied to one's generation, gender, level of education, individual experiences, etc.

Read the case vignette found in the next section, concerning death and bereavement in a Mexican-American family, or substitute a similar experience from an ethnic/racial group more familiar to you. After reading the vignette (based on your knowledge of the cultural group) create hypotheses in regard to each member of the family. Bring to mind your expectations about such things as their perceptions and attitudes toward the use of medical technology, their spiritual beliefs, and how each person might deal with the death and ensuing grief.

Case Vignette

Maria Guadalupe Sánchez is a seventy-one-year-old woman dying of cancer. She has been married for over fifty years to José Antonio Villa who is seventy-three years old. They had three children, one of whom died in childhood. They remain close to their two surviving children.

1. The younger, Mónica Maria Pérez, is twenty-nine and a medical student. She is married to Juan Hugo Pérez. They have two young children, Samuel (8) and Samantha (10).
2. The older son, Joe, is aged thirty-three. He is divorced and has not seen his ex-wife or three children for a number of years. They live in another part of the country.

Family Members
Maria Guadalupe Sánchez (71)
José Antonio Villa (73)
Daughter: Mónica Maria Pérez, (29) married to Juan Hugo Pérez
      Two children: Samuel (8) and Samantha (10)
Son: Joe Villa (33) divorced. Has not seen ex-wife or three children in years.

Based on your knowledge of Mexican-American culture, how might you go about planning to provide services for this family? What expectations might you have? What hypotheses might you want to test (see Figure 2)?

Summary/Discussion

The use of this case vignette is a good way to try to understand the complexities inherent in diversity. After discussing the scenario as it was originally defined, change the scenario in the following (or similar ways). Try to think through how these changes might affect your expectations.

What if Maria Guadalupe has some deep seated and unresolved fears of death because of the early loss of one of her children?

What if Mónica Maria studied medicine in Mexico where she married Juan Hugo who comes from a very traditional Mexican family?

What if the older son Joe was deeply affected by his divorce and sought professional help in trying to deal with the grief related to the separation from his children?

What if José Antonio has recently converted to a fundamentalist religious group that emphasizes the need for physical suffering to atone for sin?

Name	Hypothesis/Information (that you as caregiver would like to test)
Maria Guadalupe Sánchez	
José Antonio Villa	
Mónica Maria Pérez	
Juan Hugo Pérez	
Samuel and Samantha	
Joe Villa	
Source: Oltjenbruns/Baez, May 1997, King's College; 15th International Conference on Death and Bereavement: "Delivering Care in a Multicultural Setting," Session—"Diversity Within Diversity."	

Figure 2.

SUMMARY

The purpose of this chapter has been to provide caregivers of various backgrounds a number of tools by which they might develop insight regarding those they serve. Often, we can better appreciate "diversity" if we come to understand better our own heritage. When we understand that our own background, socialization, interactions with others, etc., can help shape who we are but does not absolutely define us, we can better understand those dynamics as they relate to those we serve. Just as we do not want anyone to *assume* that they know all about us by knowing general descriptors (e.g., gender, religious background, ethnicity), we should not *assume* that we know how best to intervene by knowing those same descriptors relevant to our clients and patients. Instead, we must test hypotheses about given individuals to truly appreciate that although there are many commonalties among persons of the same group, there are also many differences—that is, there is "diversity within diversity."

ENDNOTE

Information in this chapter, as well as the specific activities included herein, were developed for a conference presentation: Kevin Ann Oltjenbruns/Victor Baez (May 1997) King's College; 15th International Conference on Death and Bereavement: "Delivering Care in a Multicultural Session"—"Diversity Within Diversity." The authors would also like to credit earlier work done for Colorado State University's multicultural infusion project.

REFERENCES

1. R. Brislin and T. Yoshida, The Content of Cross-Cultural Training: An Introduction, in *Improving Intercultural Interactions,* R. Brislin and T. Yoshida (eds.), Sage, Thousand Oaks, California, pp. 1-4, 1994.
2. D. P. Drish, K. F. Lundquist, and V. J. Nelsen, *Ethnic Variations in Dying, Death and Grief: Diversity in Universality,* Taylor and Francis, Washington, D.C., 1993.
3. J. K. Parry and A. S. Ryan, *A Cross-Cultural Look at Death, Dying and Religion,* Nelson-Hall Publishers, Chicago, 1995.
4. J. Morgan, *Personal Care in an Impersonal World: A Multidimensional Look at Bereavement,* Baywood, Amityville, New York, 1993.
5. D. R. Counts and D. A. Counts, *Coping with the Final Tragedy: Cultural Variations in Dying and Grieving,* Baywood, Amityville, New York, 1991.

BIBLIOGRAPHY

Banks, J. and Banks, C., *Multicultural Education,* Allyn and Bacon, Boston, pp. 5-6, 1993.

Iglehart, A. and Bercerra, R., *Social Services and the Ethnic Community,* Allyn and Bacon, New York, 1995.

Locke, D., *Increasing Multicultural Understanding,* Sage, Newbury Park, California, 1992.

Narayan, U., Working Together Across Differences, in *Social Work Processes,* C. Compton and B. Galaway (eds.), Brooks/Cole, Pacific Grove, pp. 177-188, 1994.

Portes, A. and Rumbaut, R., *Immigrant America,* University of California Press, Berkeley, 1990.

CHAPTER 5

Culture: Caring and Curing in the Changing Health Scene

Eleanor G. Pask

As health care professionals we know only too well how the impact of the culture of the child and family affect the care we provide and the perception of that care. The multicultural nature of the families for whom we care is shaping the future of health care. It wasn't too many years ago that one rarely encountered a family who was not of Anglo-Saxon origin in the hospital. Now it is the norm. In urban hospitals professionals work with about a 50 percent ethnic population with a very large number of cultures represented. The pediatric population for whom we care will never be the same again and a carefully planned approach to adapting health care and nursing practices now will go a long way to preventing problems in the future.

The issues and concerns of a multicultural nature which health care professionals are facing are universal across industrialized countries. No one, it seems, was adequately prepared for the rapidity of movement of large numbers of people from one country to another. Many countries have felt the impact of immigration. A few years ago it was thought that immigration would pose no problem. At that time it was felt that the goal should be to "assimilate" the newcomers into the mainstream culture as quickly as possible. That did not happen, nor should it have happened. We have learned that people's cultural heritage cannot and should not be left behind when they emigrate. Culture is an integral part of everyone's life. Health care professionals were caught unaware and for the first time began to experience the effects of other health care practices and beliefs on their prescriptions for health. Words like noncompliance filtered in and were heard more frequently with reference to the lack of adherence to our prescribed care, especially by patients of cultures other than the mainstream.

Every health care professional can think of situations which have arisen in interactions with patients of another culture.

Roberto D. was a six-month-old baby with a rare metabolic disease. It was known since birth that he would not survive. The parents visited him daily in the hospital and sat quietly by his crib. When he died, nearly forty family members came to the hospital and wept and wailed loudly around his bed. Initially, R. nurse was distressed at the "disruptive" behavior and wondered why the family could not support the parents. She was reassured by the head nurse that the family was indeed supporting the parents and without this overt show of grief the parents would have been unduly distressed.

Madeleine Leininger was one of the first nurse-anthropologists to examine carefully the role that the patient's culture exerted on the care being provided [1]. When Leininger worked in a children's residential care facility, she was distressed by the psychiatric labeling of the children. As she watched, children of different cultures were diagnosed in terms of psychiatric pathology. She was struck, however, by the fact that their parents were shocked and didn't recognize any problem with their children. She began to question: what was the effect of culture on the children?; what was the effect of culture on their personality?; and whether culture alone had provided the basis for the mislabeling. Leininger believed these questions were relevant, and that the culture of the children was paramount in determining their behaviors. Leininger then examined the implications of these questions for health care providers.

Leininger defines culture as:

• Patterns of learned behaviours and values passed from generation to generation.
• A blue print for thought and action.
• Dynamic and changing.
• Accumulated ways by which a group of people solve problems.
• Material and nonmaterial.
• Dominant force in determining health, illness and caring patterns [1, pp. 119-120, passim].

This last statement is essential for health care providers to understand because culture dictates how to be healthy, how to behave when ill, how to care, and how to cure.

Based on extensive research Leininger developed principles of transcultural caring [1, pp. 85-108, passim].

These principles she first applied to nursing, but it is evident that they bear relevance to all health professions. The principles provide the framework for planning, implementing, and assessing the effectiveness of care.

- Patients have a right to have their socio-cultural background understood in the same way they expect to have their physical and psychological needs identified and understood.
- Health care professionals must respond to social and cultural needs and use this new knowledge in a helping way.
- Treating all patients alike is unsafe, unscientific, and a questionable way to meet health care.
- Health care professional-patient cultural differences and ways to facilitate a better intercultural process should be anticipated rather than entering into a relationship blindly.
- A health care professional should not begin to care for a patient before making a cultural assessment.

It is important for health care professionals to recognize that the majority of health care globally is provided outside the Western model. For example, 70 to 90 percent of health care is provided by family, friends, and the community [2, p. 251]. Folk, or non-professional, healers include the following: diagnosticians, diviners, herbalists, singers, specific practitioners such as bone setters, naturopaths, and homeopaths. Many of these more traditional types of practices have recently found their way into urban areas and can be readily accessed.

Work in this field is not new, but it took some time before the immensity of the issue was sufficiently apparent to demand responses from the health care sector and subsequently to influence care. Becker's Health Care Model, as early as 1978, identified the variable of culture as one of the key determinants by which an individual perceived not only his or her susceptibility to illness, but also the seriousness of that illness [3]. These perceptions in turn influenced the likelihood of the individual's adherence to recommended treatment.

THE PATIENT'S EXPLANATORY MODEL

Every health care professional has undoubtedly worked with patients and their families who did not seem to understand, or agree with them, about their illness or treatment. There may be several reasons for this, but in many instances it is because the questions the physician asks, which in fact are similar to the ones the patient asks, elicit completely opposing answers.

What makes us healthy and what makes us ill are two fascinating factors which we rarely consider until we are ill. Our culture has taught us how to behave when we are sick and we begin to learn "illness behavior" as children. An astute and sensitive professional will learn and understand from the patient just how she or he explains the illness.

When a mother brings her child to a health care professional she already has an idea of why the child is ill based on the "Patient's Explanatory Model" [2, p. 256]. The mother may not express her understanding in our terms, but her comprehension of the events certainly affects how she feels and how she describes her child's illness. An adult patient has his or her own explanation of the illness and presents the symptoms in the context of how he or she understands them.

A ten-month-old Portuguese baby was brought by his distraught mother to the Emergency Department of a large children's hospital. The baby was quickly diagnosed with meningococcaemia. The mother was convinced that the baby was ill because he was possessed by evil spirits and could never be cured until he was freed from them. She was intent on having the spirits exorcised. The medical team agreed, but insisted on beginning therapy immediately while she arranged though her family to seek an exorcist. The baby was treated medically and also was exorcised. The baby survived. The mother believed that the baby's recovery occurred because the evil spirits had left the child.

The physician will diagnose a disease and will prescribe treatment within the scientific parameters as he or she has studied and learned them. Often we label patients and families as apathetic, noncompliant, uncooperative, or difficult when really the main problem lies in the disparity between how the patient and the physician understand and explain the same illness and the treatment.

It is interesting to note that both patients and doctors ask basically the same questions, but they use very different language. The physician using the paradigm of the medical model will frame specific questions about etiology, onset of symptoms, pathophysiology, course of illness, and treatment. No patient will articulate his or her questions about, or understanding of, the illness or symptoms in those terms. The patient, however, addresses precisely the same questions in a manner meaningful to him and in terms he or she readily understands. In the patient's mind the five questions of the medical model must be rephrased into five questions which make sense.

The intent remains the same, but the terminology changes as the medical model phraseology is transformed into questions the patient understands and can answer.

- *Etiology*
  1. What do you think caused your illness?
- *Onset of Symptoms*
  2. Why do you think it started when it did?
- *Pathophysiology*
  3. What do you think your illness does to you (how does it work)?
- *Course of Illness*
  4. How severe is your illness; will it have a long or short course?
- *Treatment*
  5. What kind of treatment do you think you should have?

In most instances a sensitive health care professional can elicit a great deal of valuable information from a patient by asking these five questions and using the terminology the patient uses. In some cases it may be necessary to ask additional questions, such as:

* What are the most important results you hope to achieve from your treatment?
* What are the chief problems for you because of your illness?
* What do you fear most?

It is important to examine each of these questions in a bit more depth as the patient might. The first question "What caused your illness?" might elicit answers such as a medical reason, for example, a virus, or religious reasons, or the Evil Eye (Malojo), bad winds, Yin and Yang, hot or cold, or ecological reasons.

As we all know, patients who come already having explained their illness by a medical reason are not often greeted with open arms. They tend to dictate the type of treatment they wish and they usually bring a list of questions for which they have already established the answers.

The ecological model is gaining credibility rapidly in the "consumer" population. It has three major foci: the biological, which is the relationship of man to his environment; the social, which is the interdependence between people and the institution; and the cultural. This model gives broad and plausible reasons for illness. Recently over 12,000 health care consumers attended a week-long conference based on an extensive roster of diseases such as cancer, arthritis, and diabetes. The conference focused on the ecological model as an integrated approach to understanding and living with a chronic illness.

Patients who have explained their illness in religious terms may be experiencing a natural or an unnatural illness. These are often difficult to distinguish. A natural illness is one that has been sent by God as punishment for sin. The wrath of God may be the final explanation for the illness and in these instances the doctor may not be able to help until God has interceded.

Maria was a ten-year-old Italian girl with a chronic renal disease. Her health was maintained by medication, but eventually she would require a transplant. Her mother was certain that Maria was ill because of the mother's sin. The mother received very little help from her husband and son. When Maria was hospitalized the mother worked at her full-time job, visited Maria every evening and maintained her home, providing meals for her family. The mother was near to exhaustion, but the health professionals were unable to arrange help for her, because she firmly believed Maria's illness was her "cross to bear." Eventually, a priest was contacted and he was able to encourage Maria's mother to accept limited help.

An unnatural illness occurs when people are unprotected, fall prey to evil spirits, or become possessed by the devil. The gift of healing is a powerful gift and those in a community who possess it are very respected.

Bad medicine such as spells, the Evil Eye, or harmful magic is believed to be a very real source of illness by many cultures. These can only be counteracted by good medicine such as taboos or magic. Taboos are injunctions to do or not to do something. The Evil Eye is a prevalent belief in many countries and through this belief some people have the ability to harm others by looking at them, especially children. Admiring children may subject them to the Eye and a child who is under this spell may suffer from fever, vomiting, diarrhea, loss of weight, and irritability. The child will have to be relieved from the spell of the Evil Eye before any other treatment can be effectively introduced. There are several methods for determining whether a child remains under the spell and one of the most common is the olive oil test. Drops of olive oil are dropped into a vial or a glass of water. If the oil seals the water the child is still possessed. If the oil remains in small droplets or goes to the bottom the child has been freed.

Bad Air or Bad Winds is a belief common to the Vietnamese and other Asian cultures. It is the presence of these bad winds in the body which can cause disease, sometimes as serious as paralysis. The bad winds must be allowed to escape from the body before healing can occur.

Shortly after the major influx of refugees, a Vietnamese father brought his son to a children's emergency because of the child's high fever and apparent illness. On examination the doctor noted multiple petechiae over the child's vertebral column and ribs. The father could not understand English, or explain what these marks meant. The doctor called the SCAN team. Unfortunately the father was arrested and later hanged himself. This tragedy could have been avoided had only an interpreter been called. Someone who not only understood the father's language, but also understood that the practice which resulted in the bruising was a traditional practice designed to let the bad winds which had caused the illness escape from the body.

Yin and Yang is basically an oriental theory. Yin is a female force, negative, cold, and empty. Yang is the male force, positive and moving toward light, warmth, and fullness. All things within the universe consist of a balance of Yin and Yang and in order to achieve health the two forces must be in equilibrium. Excess Yang causes fever, dehydration, and irritability. Excess Yin causes gastric disorders and the propensity for catching colds. Yin stores the vital strength of life. It is a very complex belief with some parts of the body such as the skin having the nature of Yang whereas the inside of the body is more Yin. Some organs are Yang and some are Yin.

The hot and cold theory is also very prevalent in certain cultures such as the Hispanic. Some diseases are hot and must be treated with cold foods or remedies and others are cold and must be treated with hot. Cancer is a cold disease.

Recently a Chinese girl, N. W., was diagnosed with leukemia and was admitted to a children's hospital. Her mother was certain she had cancer because she had eaten too many cold foods. It made no sense what-so-ever to the mother for the staff to begin chemotherapy when the child's illness was caused by a situation which required a completely different intervention, namely the restoration of the balance between hot and cold.

A Chinese child, H. N., was admitted with severe bilateral otitis media. This is considered a hot disease and the Chinese mother refused to allow her child to eat her breakfast of scrambled eggs, because this was a hot food. The staff felt that the mother was not acting in the child's best interests by preventing her from eating a nutritious breakfast. The mother could not understand why the staff reacted in the manner in which they did. Again, this a situation which could have been avoided had time been taken to ask the mother why she removed the child's breakfast but more importantly why she thought the child had leukemia.

The assignation of hot or cold has nothing to do with the temperature of the food, rather it refers to some of its qualities. Certain herbs are cold, others are hot. Some foods are cold, others are hot. It is a complex belief, difficult for the uninitiated to understand.

There are many other reasons which patients use to explain their illness and by asking the first question of the model "What do you think caused your illness?" with sensitivity and respect, the health care professional will glean the information essential to implementing appropriate care.

The second question which asks "Why do you think it started when it did?" often elicits responses such as "God's punishing me," for something the patient will then go on to describe, or "I went out without a hat on," or "I got my feet wet." These events generally do not precipitate illness.

The answers to the third question "How does your illness work?" really depend on how the patient has responded to the first two questions. It may be an imbalance of Yin and Yang, or hot and cold, or the presence of demons or spirits. Often patients express stress related disease processes as "It's eating away at me."

It is common knowledge that the lay person's understanding of physiology and basic anatomy is generally lacking. Often in an attempt to explain how the illness works the patient develops quite unique interpretations which preclude a proper perception of both the illness and the treatment. It is important to gain some understanding of the perspective the patient has on how the disease is affecting his or her body. Only then can effective teaching begin.

The fourth question "How severe is your illness?" brings an interesting analogy with the expression of symptoms, for example, the expression of pain varies greatly. There is a case reported citing the expression of pain by two women with the same eye disorder. An Irish lady simply complained that she could no longer thread the needle when she wanted to sew. An Italian lady complained bitterly and overtly about her painful running eyes, headaches, and generalized symptoms. Chinese and Jewish people describe pain very differently. Canadians differ in their expression of symptoms across the country. In some countries certain diseases are expected. In some lower socioeconomic groups, lower back pain is an expected part of life and treatment for it would not be sought. North America has clinics dedicated to treating back pain because people will not tolerate it. Trachoma is endemic in some areas of Greece. Nausea in pregnancy is very culture specific.

"What kind of treatment do you expect?" is an extremely important question and produces some very interesting answers. Mothers who bring their fevered babies all bundled up to the hospital most likely do not expect the treatment they receive when all the blankets are removed. Patients who come expecting antibiotics for their cold are often very disappointed and accuse the doctors of treating them unwisely. In societies where folk medicine is practiced, many people are involved in the treatment of the patient. Friends, relatives, and immediate family members all play certain roles in effecting the cure. Different types of practitioners may well be involved. The Taiwanese often go to three different health care practitioners—a diagnostician, an herbalist, and an Eastern doctor—before entering the Western health care system.

A six-week-old Chinese baby girl, Amy, with a cardiac condition was admitted to the cardiac unit of a children's hospital. Her parents, both professionals, had resided in Canada for several years and were fluent in English. They quickly learned how to check Amy's apex, measure, and administer her digoxin. Amy was discharged. Two weeks later she was rushed to the Emergency Unit. At that time her apex was 20. The information quickly unfolded and Amy's grandmother who resided with the family had been preparing a mild preparation containing fox-glove. In her traditional role she would provide this care for the baby. Unfortunately, the staff at the hospital before Amy was first discharged had not asked who would be treating Amy when she went home. Amy recovered and the grandmother refrained from any future administration of fox-glove tea. Another situation which could have been avoided had the right question been asked.

Food plays an extremely important role in treatment. Some foods are accepted and others are not. We feel it is important to eat a lot of protein to improve healing—all cultures do not adhere to this thought.

A seven-year-old Italian boy had been operated on for a ruptured appendix. He returned to the unit and had a naso-gastric tube with suction. For two days despite aggressive intravenous antibiotic therapy he failed to respond as expected. On the third day the nurse observed the mother feeding the boy pasta by mouth. Using her discretion the nurse suggested to the mother that she might bring in some clear home made soup for her son rather than the pasta. The mother agreed and the boy began to recover quickly. The nurse understood the importance of the role of the mother to feed her son and respected that, but negotiated a more acceptable type of food based on the child's surgical status.

If patients believe in a religious cause for their illness, they need faith to get them better. In many cases a physician is unable to intervene. Faith healers are more effective than doctors in some instances. All religious models have elaborate rules for caring and curing such as blessings, prayers, rites, and incantations. All are very important and all cultures depend on them in some way to restore health.

Folk medicine is gaining in popularity. It provides a very interesting approach to healing. Folk medicine is actually comprised of components of classical early medicine, selected beliefs, and early tenets of Christianity. This makes as much sense to someone who believes in it as do the scientific principles of medicine to a medical school graduate. Folk medicine has achieved extraordinary results and in many places in the world it is the only medicine practiced. In combination, folk medicine and modern medicine can achieve cures which independently they cannot. Modern medicine's pharmacopoeia is extensive and, if it were combined with the humanitarian, family approach and the additional knowledge of cures of folk medicine, all the world would benefit. Slowly the medical model is expanding from the paternalistic doctor-patient diad or the nurse-doctor-patient triad to a much more extensive involvement of the family. As this occurs the blending of health care beliefs will also occur.

In the field of geriatric care, patients rarely expect what they receive from their treatment. Many cultures see aging and death as a natural phenomenon of life and resist the option of institutional care for the elderly. North Americans are often viewed as less than compassionate and respectful of their elderly. Our society often preserves life until no vestige of the humanity remains. The impact of these opposing views can destroy a family.

If health care professionals ask the remaining three questions, they will be able to elicit additional information, but it is more than likely the patient will have touched on them already. The answer to the sixth question about the most important result of treatment may suggest whether the patient feels the treatment will work. In our culture the most significant problems caused by illness might be the fear of intractable pain, loss of work, or the inability to support a family. Answers such as these alert the health care professional to enlist the help of additional supports and family members. The answer to the final question regarding how long the patient feels he will suffer from the illness often discloses how realistic the patient is and what gap exists between the doctor's and the patient's expectations. Sometimes this disparity leads to labeling such as denial or noncompliance. Instead of becoming impatient, we must learn to listen.

The information gleaned from the questions of the Explanatory Model provides a rich and important framework on which to base care which includes teaching and psychosocial support. Health care professionals will have a very good idea of the patient's perceptions and beliefs about the illness. The questions can be asked during a regular health care or nursing assessment and the facts that impinge upon the patient's care and treatment added to the plan of care. The Patient's Explanatory Model is an efficient and effective manner in which to approach patient care. It leaves room for negotiating and contracting, teaching and learning. These modest questions yield information on which the most exquisite care can be provided. The consequence is that for both the patient and the professional elements of frustration, stereotyping, disrespect, mis-communication, and misunderstanding are supplanted by elements of success, recognition of the importance of cultural diversity, respect, effective communication, and understanding. In the end, both the family and health care professionals have gained immensely.

There are many practical points we can take away, but I would like to stress just two. The first is the important point of learning how to ask questions, to conduct a cultural assessment, and incorporate the information into the patient's care. The second point is that we need to learn to listen and not translate the answers into textbook responses. Adherence to these two points will contribute immensely to the elimination of words such as non-compliance and will shape a meaningful future for the health care of our children.

REFERENCES

1. M. Leininger, *Transcultural Nursing: Concepts, Theories, and Practices*, Wiley, Toronto, 1978.
2. A. Kleinman, L. Eisenberg, and B. Good, Culture, Illness and Care: Clinical Lessons from Anthropologic and Cross-Cultural Research, *Annals of Internal Medicine, 88*, pp. 251-258, 1978.
3. M. H. Becker, The Health Belief Model and Sick Role Behaviour, *Nursing Digest*, pp. 35-40, Spring 1978.

CHAPTER 6

The Sociology of the Body

Glennys Howarth

Social anthropologists have long acknowledged the importance of the body and have recorded insights into cultural aspects of its nutrition, dress, decoration, and preparations for disposal after death. Sociologists, too, are now recognizing that their traditional emphasis on social structures has obscured the significance of the body "as one of the crucial instances of the complex interrelations of nature, culture and society" [1, p. viii]. This being so, the examination of the body is fast becoming a central theme in sociology. Turner, for example, contests in his claim for a sociology of the body, that

> . . . sociology is genuinely a sociology of action, and . . . the social actor is not a Cartesian subject divided into body and mind but an embodied actor whose practicality and knowledgeability involve precisely this embodiment [2, p. 169].

Turner's case is that by concentrating primarily on social structures sociology has neglected the significance of the body. The way in which the body is socially constructed and the meanings associated with particular aspects of bodily behavior, for example dieting [3], have been overlooked and are only now being recognized as rich sources of sociological knowledge. Beyond that, in modern Western cultures the demeanor of the body can be identified as a critical key to personhood. Exploring the link between body images and personhood, Hockey and James show that individuals with bodies failing to conform to images of the adult body in mainstream culture are not afforded the privileges reserved for those whose bodies do [4]. According to this argument, possessing the body of a child or that of an elderly or disabled person endows the owner with limited capacity to fulfil the cultural requirements which confer the entitlement to personhood.

For medical sociologists in particular, analyses of bodily behavior and meanings have produced insights into how people perceive their bodies and the effect of bodily transformation on their sense of well-being and self-identity. Research has focused on aspects of ill-health, for example on issues of anorexia and obesity [5], and on the impact of bodily pain [6]. Studies of the impact of bodily changes on self-image have included work on ageing [4, 7], exercise regimes [8, 9], and disability [4, 10]. More commonly, when we report illness to our doctors they examine the body and read it for signs of malaise and disease. Indeed, we examine our own bodies and the signs of health or illness which we find affect the way we feel and the confidence with which we face the world. So for Turner, building on the work of Brumberg [5], analysis of the body needs to be central to the whole sociological enterprise and he contends that research projects with a focus on the body,

> . . . define the major theoretical topics which embrace the complex relationships between cultural change, social structure, personal identity and body transformations [2, p. 168].

THE BODY IN MODERN SOCIETY

In modern society there has been an increasing emphasis on the body as a source of well-being. Many quarters of the media and much health promotion literature are replete with images of the beautiful, young, sexual, fit, muscular, slim bodies to which we are all invited to aspire. Inextricably linked with these images is the growth in mass consumerism and the expansion, since the mid-century, of consumer products to aid and encourage us in our attempts to achieve the "perfect" body. The clothing and cosmetic industries tempt us with products that sell on the understanding that they will enhance the youthful and beautiful appearance required by cultural mores. Advertisements for hair and for other beauty products similarly entreat us, with claims of efficacy, to purchase consumer goods—from anti-wrinkle cream to plastic surgery—which fan the fires of our quest for eternal youth and beauty. Furthermore, we are continually reminded of the value of exercise to keep our bodies healthy. Innovation in technology brings refinements in training equipment which, together with marketing ingenuity, produces a steady stream of new and more therapeutic exercises. The proliferation of gymnasia and fitness classes bring "healthy" exercise within everyone's reach.

This emphasis on the importance of diet and exercise reinforce the individual's personal and social responsibility to keep his/her body healthy and free from disease. On the level of bio-politics, government statements and policies are regularly released with the objective of stimulating the individual to care sufficiently about bodily self-maintenance. For example, the importance of diet and exercise are common features of the British government's campaign to prevent and reduce the instances of heart disease [11]. A nation which successfully monitors its own health can produce a substantial saving in the government's health budget.

But if the body is a source of pleasure, health, beauty, and youth, it is also potentially dangerous and threatening as a site of disease, infection, and contamination [12-14]. Bodies, as reflected in the preoccupations of consumer culture, are at risk from body odor, decaying teeth and gums, spots and blackheads, and may fall prey to numerous other unpleasant and unsociable fates. Moreover, body fluids are perceived as especially threatening of contamination [14]. The spread of HIV/AIDS is a recent and powerful reminder of the danger of the body. Here again, individuals have been encouraged by government campaigns and media attention to reform their sexual behavior and so to escape contamination by other bodies which may carry this deadly virus. Thus the body is also a public health issue and one which requires strict and disciplined maintenance to contain its dangerous potential.

THE DEAD BODY

If representations of the living body have been drawn so thoroughly into the public sphere, what of the dead body? Concentrating attention on the corpse can be equally important to an understanding of the significance of the body in modern culture. The social management of the dead body has implications for cultural attitudes to the living body as well as for perceptions of death. What can a sociological analysis of the corpse tell us about social attitudes to mortality and the significance of the body in modern society? To answer this question the corpse must first be located in relation to cultural representations of the living body. Having examined the cultural context which determines its management, this chapter will then turn to look in detail at the mortician's treatment of the corpse. It is here, in the deathworkers handling and care of the body that it is possible to identify some of the social taboos regarding proximity to the cadaver and to trace the process by which the corpse is transformed from a defiling or profane object into a sacred one.

There are three features of the modern understanding of the corpse which provide the keys to its treatment and insight to attitudes to mortality. First, the corpse is perceived as a site of disease and a *source of pollution* [12, 15]. As such, it has become the subject of medical knowledge [16] and is seen as requiring professional or expert handling to contain its threat to public health. Second, in increasingly secular societies, the dead body has become the *material reality of death;* the signifier of mortality. Third, in Western consumer cultures the corpse, like the living body, has become subject to *commodity* production. Let us consider each of these characteristics in turn.

The Corpse as a Source of Pollution

We have discussed aspects of the living body which can be understood to have dangerous potential. The dead body, however, has fulfilled this potential and, although bereaved people continue to be emotionally attached to the body of their loved one, there remains, nevertheless, a cultural perception of the corpse as a source of disease and contamination. This view of the dead body as polluting is common to many societies. For example, in Cantonese society survivors can be contaminated simply by proximity to the corpse or merely by inhaling the "killing airs" [17]. In Western societies, since the nineteenth century, there has developed a physical and symbolic separation between the living and the dead. It was during the last century that the link between disease and hygiene was first established and this, together with the physical separation of the living from the dying and the dead, has led to an increased perception of the corpse as polluting. Lindsay Prior contends that the root of the relationship between death and disease is to be found in the science of pathology and the increasing concern with health and sanitation.

> Death and disease were to be located in the human body, diseases caused death, and the causal sequence which linked the one to the other were made visible in human organs and tissues [15, p. 9].

If the cause of death is located within the body, then the corpse is not simply a by-product of death but is at once a source of disease and a symbol of mortality. In modern societies, therefore, the dead body is seen as highly polluting: both physically and symbolically. Physical pollution stems from the fear of contamination by disease and decay; symbolic pollution from the fear of mortality and bodily decay, of which the corpse is a signifier.

The Corpse as the Material Reality of Death

The cadaver has always been a symbol of mortality [18]. Writing of the middle ages, Huizinga noted that *ars moriendi* focused on the decaying body. For example, there remain many tombs dating from that period with effigies of decaying bodies lying prostrate. These semi-decomposed bodies, carved in stone, are depicted with worms and insects of the same material. Their purpose was to remind all of the process taking place below. In Christendom these images provided people with a constant reminder that they should not become too attached to this life and all their worldly possessions, including their own bodies, because they would eventually corrupt and decay. Thus, the corpse was simply a reminder of human finitude. Solace came from the priest who preached a Christian belief system which celebrated Christ's triumph over death and allowed good people to look beyond death and to anticipate the life hereafter.

In modern Western societies, however, the role of the priest, once central to death ritual, has declined and medics have taken control over the dying process [19]. The emphasis of medical science is on the treatment of the body and not on the well-being of the soul. In the contemporary Western world the declining role of institutionalized Christianity and the escalation of materialism and individuality have led us to a society where the body (rather than the soul) has come to be identified as the site of the self [20]. Where once the body was understood to be merely the vehicle for the soul it is now afforded central significance in the construction of the self. The loss of mainstream Christian faith has been matched by the force of individualism. If one cannot anticipate reunion with those gone before, one can at least control the interpretation of death by commemorating the life of the individual and by revering that which remains, that is, the body—the material reality of death.

The Corpse as a Commodity

It was noted earlier that Western cultural images of living bodies are predominantly those of vitality, health, and beauty. These representations embody the notion of individuality—the prime motive force in their construction. By contrast, the corpse (before it receives *post-mortem* treatment) represents the very opposite of these images. For the body, sacred in life, is profane in death. The dead body lacks health, vitality, and beauty;[1] the deceased, the erstwhile owner of the body having once and for all lost control over its presentation and individuality. Thus the corpse as a symbol of mortality signifies a lack of individuality, a lack of control, and irreversible decay. It forces recognition that the personal quest for dominion and body beautiful is lost. Indeed, it is the perception of the dead body as the antithesis of our aspirations for the living body that amplifies the conviction that the corpse is such a dangerous and polluting object.

To combat the horror of this tragedy, funeral rites, both preparatory and celebrationary, are constructed which strive to transform the dead body into an object resembling the living one. Mortuary rituals convert the corpse, the material reality of death, from an unmanageable spectre into a collection of goods and services. In so doing, the body becomes a commodity, reconstructed according to the culturally acceptable characteristics of the living body. To exalt the body of the individual, mourners purchase goods (burial clothes, casket, etc.) and services (embalming, cosmetology, etc.) which revitalize or "humanize" [12] the cadaver; acting as antidotes to the threatening images of mortality and bodily decay. After treatment by the morticians (the nature of which is discussed below) visitors who come to view the body are able to comment on its *well-being* [23]. It is via these

---

[1] Some would perceive the dead body as beautiful, but this is usually in romantic representations; in literature, art, and music (see Bronfen [21] and Foltyn [22] for discussions of beauty in death).

processes that the humanized and preserved body of late twentieth-century Western society symbolizes the continuity of individualism and the victory over death.

Let us now consider the way in which morticians interpret these three cultural characteristics of the body and the influence this has on the performance of their roles in the cultural management of death. In so doing, this chapter will draw from a study of the work of modern funeral directors. The research, which took the form of ethnography, was conducted primarily in London, England [12]. The similarities between the deathworkers in this study and other morticians in Western societies, however, can be discerned in that they share much in terms of codes of conduct, philosophy and practice.[2]

THE MORTICIAN'S ROLE IN THE SOCIAL MANAGEMENT OF THE CORPSE

The three characteristics of the dead body outlined above are central to the work of morticians. The way in which operatives interpret these features informs mortuary philosophy and is translated into practice. Their conception, and hence their transformation into practice, of cultural approaches to the dead body can be summarized as follows. First, perceiving the corpse as polluting, these death-workers aim to *protect* both their clients and the public from contamination. Second, if the body is the material reality of death then it must be *cared* for appropriately. Finally, as purveyors of goods and services morticians strive to *humanize* the cadaver and so to retrieve the individuality that is lost in death. In the negotiation between deathworkers and their clients there is an emphasis on the care of the body both from bereaved families and friends and also from the funeral professions. Furthermore, through the funeral it is possible to transform the corpse (the material reality of death) into a package of material goods and services which (a) publicly demonstrate the extent of care, and (b) make mortality less threatening.

If we trace the role of the mortician in his/her treatment of the body it is possible to observe the way in which these three objectives influence their work.

Giving Custody of the Polluting Corpse to the Expert

The concern with public health, first noticeable in the nineteenth century, meant that the dead came to be separated from the living and the body of the

---

[2] For a detailed discussion of methodology, see Howarth [24]; for a full ethnographic account of the study, see Howarth [12]; for studies of funeral workers in North America, see Pine [33], Bowman [25], Habenstein [26], Mitford [27].

deceased began to be removed to the mortuary. Perceiving the corpse as a source of pollution and a danger to public health led to a social requirement for the services of an expert, a professional skilled in negating the corpse's power to contaminate. Morticians soon came to utilize pseudo-scientific techniques (such as embalming) to render the corpse harmless to the living. Indeed, the handling of the dead body is usually subject to public health regulations and these rules guide deathworkers in decisions pertaining to the appropriate location and sanitization of the corpse. As a signifier of pollution and a symbol of death, bereaved families in contemporary Western societies normally concede custody to the funeral director who in turn, is

> prepared to carry out the duty which is the fundamental core of his respon-
> sibility, namely, to take into his care and charge the body of the deceased
> [28, p. 102].

In taking custody, the mortician is aware that for the family, the body of the deceased is not merely a shell but is vested with memories and they retain an emotional attachment to it. Deathworkers must, therefore, treat their charge with care; in public at least, they must acknowledge that the body is a valuable object which is entitled to respect. Indeed, the families are usually concerned to ensure that they have done their best for their loved one as, within the confines of their budget, they purchase the most luxurious goods and the most beneficial services which the funeral director is able to provide. For their part, deathworkers see their obligation to the family to be protecting them from pollution while enabling them to enjoy meaningful contact with the deceased. In order to achieve this, morticians work to transform the corpse from a defiling object into a life-like representation of its former self.

In pursuit of this aim the funeral worker resorts to "humanization" techniques. By this I refer to the procedures they adopt to present the corpse in the most "life-like" manner possible. This entails removing the most obvious signs of death which linger and can be read on the body. After death, the body loses the human qualities associated with vitality: it lacks vigor, the skin becomes discolored and slack, the hair limp, limbs are stiff and inactive, and further deterioration is inevitable as corruption rapidly erodes the organs and tissues. If the deceased is to regain any semblance of individuality the decay must be arrested, the body preserved, albeit temporarily, and its human features redeemed. The intention is to the make the corpse appear life-like. To succeed in this objective the cadaver must first be washed and laid out, but the most effective tools available to further the humanization process are embalming, reconstruction work, the application of cosmetics (cosmetology), dress, and presentation.

Embalming, Reconstruction and Cosmetology

In introducing the concept of embalming to the bereaved families, funeral directors often adopt the language of preservation and hygiene. The practice, with its promise of restoring a life-like appearance in the corpse, is said to afford both psychological and physical protection to undertakers and their clients as it temporarily preserves human tissue. A primary rationalization for its use issues from public health discourse with its concern for the dangers which the decaying body potentially holds for the public. Indeed, the funeral industry in Britain claims that,

> (s)ince the treatment destroys all pathogenic bacteria, there is little danger of infection or contagion from an embalmed body [28, p. 59].

A further justification for the practice of embalming is that while protecting mourners from death pollution, it enables them to view their loved one as though s/he were alive. In other words, the mortician is tasked with making the dead body resemble the living one. For them, embalming is the most powerful weapon in the battle against the corruption of the body.

> This is perhaps the most valuable aspect of the treatment. The change effected is truly remarkable—gone is the deathly pallor and the discoloration of the lower features. Instead the family sees a life-like presentation of their loved one appearing as though peacefully sleeping. This result is a source of great comfort and has a decided psychological value [28, p. 59].

The practice itself entails draining body fluids from the cadaver and replacing these with formalin—a preservative chemical. This chemical revitalizes some of the fundamental human characteristics of the corpse—features such as facial color and elasticity of the skin. In the performance of their work, however, embalmers come into direct contact with bodily discharge; blood, mucus, and excreta, perceived in many cultures as dangerous sources of pollution [12-14]. But rather than handling, and thus becoming contaminated by these dangerous fluids, the embalmer's role is to cleanse the corpse and to expel its impurities. Replacing body fluids with formalin neutralizes the harmful effects of the cadaver. The first step to humanization is complete as the corpse has been rendered physically harmless. The next imperative is to make the corpse appear life-like.

If the deceased met with a violent death, the mortician may have to undertake substantial reconstruction work on the body. In cases where the bereaved wish to view the body and there is considerable disfigurement, morticians will attempt to restore the corpse to its former dignity. Extensive physical damage, such as that which frequently results from a road fatality, may require lengthy and intricate work. Relatives are usually grateful, however, and morticians are proud of their reconstruction skills. During the course of my research one funeral director who practiced embalming described the lengths to which he had gone when undertaking the facial reconstruction of a woman who had been involved in a collision with a truck. Briefly surviving the crash, her condition had not initially been diagnosed by the medics as fatal and the hospital team had stitched a large gash which ran from her hairline to her nose. The surgery had left a hideous scar which the funeral director was determined to remove.

> After she was embalmed and the skin had dried a bit I stuck the skin together with superglue and then removed the stitches. I carefully shaved off the surplus glue and filled in the cracks. I spent a couple of hours blending in the colour and putting back the lines and the pores [12].

The woman's relatives had been delighted at the reconstruction which allowed them to view their loved one without fear of confronting a damaged and horrifying spectacle. In other words, although ignorant of the details of restoration work, clients are perceived by deathworkers as requiring it because it removes the physical damage imposed by death. As another embalmer suggested:

> What we do is for the living, so they have a positive picture of their loved ones . . . Once they see they're all right, so to speak, then the process of grieving can begin [29].

One may interpret this funeral director's notion of being "all right" as appearing whole and life-like again.

When embalming and reconstruction work are complete the mortician applies a number of additional props to enhance the life-like appearance of the body. For example, the feet of the corpse may be tied together to produce a more "natural" posture (a concept that will be commented upon later); cotton wool may be packed beneath the eyelids to avoid a sunken appearance; lips are often sewn together to prevent a sagging jaw. Once this stage is finished the next step in the process of humanization is cosmetology.

The application of make-up can transform the face of the deceased. In the majority of cases the mortician relies on cosmetics which simply add color and vivacity to the face of his/her subject. If restoration work is likely to necessitate substantial cosmetology, morticians may ask for a photograph of the person as s/he was in life to assist them to achieve accuracy and perfection. However, provided the mortician does not totally misrepresent the appearance of the deceased in life, in the final analysis, accuracy and replication of the living individual is only secondary to the dramatic effect. It is the presentation of the body of the deceased as undamaged, serene, and life-like which dictates mortuary practice.

Dressing and Presentation

The clothing worn by the deceased is normally chosen by the relatives and it is common for people to request that their loved one be dressed in a favorite garment. Although burial gowns and shrouds are manufactured for the purpose, another popular option is to chose nightwear that had belonged to the deceased. Dressing the body in everyday clothing has the effect of amplifying the individuality of the person as s/he was in life. Nightclothes also make the body appear "normal" but are more fitting to his/her reclining state when presented by the mortician as sleeping.

When placing the body in the casket or coffin, the final stage in the humanization process, morticians pay special attention to the way in which it is positioned.

The aim of the funeral director or his assistant should be to attain a natural restful posture (with) the head resting on pillows of just the right height, possibly inclined a little to one side.

The posing of the arms and hands is also worthy of careful attention for hands can be expressive . . . Whatever the position chosen ensure that it looks natural.

A coverlet is supplied so that the finished result is . . . that of the deceased lying on a divan or bed. The judicious use of wadding to pack the arms in position can help retain a natural restful posture [28, pp. 57 and 63].

In the above extracts from a funeral association's manual, it is worth noting the stress that is placed on the need to capture a *natural* positioning for the corpse. The concern that the dead body should look "natural," however, is really an attempt to have the deceased appear to the mourners as s/he would have done in life—a sleeping person, for example, would not lie rigid with nose pointing to the ceiling and arms folded across the chest.

CONCLUSION

When the funeral company accepts custody of the body of the deceased their charge is polluting in the sense that it is both a physical receptacle of disease and a symbol of mortality. The deathworkers must negate the contaminating properties of the cadaver and enhance its human and individual qualities. Once the mortician has completed his/her work on the cadaver, its polluting aspects have been erased and its human dignity has been restored through careful attention and the application of goods and services. Although the *post-mortem* procedures have only temporary impact, the illusory effect is sufficient because the practice of humanization is not a denial of death but an extension of life [12]; it is simply one more version of consumerism aimed at the body. Mourners do not primarily desire to see the body as it was in life but to see it as a representation of death transformed: the body of the loved one rescued from the depths of the profane to the realm of the sacred. The image lauds individuality and vitality and hints at immortality.

In terms of the sociology of the body, if this academic discipline has hitherto analyzed society through disembodied social structures and agents, these disembodied actors have also been *immortal*. Yet what could be more fundamental to an understanding of the embodied social agent than a sociological appreciation of the human condition, that is, mortality? By applying a sociological analysis of the *post-mortem* treatment of the body, this chapter has attempted to augment the search for bodily themes current in sociology. In this way it has examined the way in which the body in death is made to reflect modern society's preoccupation with the body in life.

It was once stated with confidence that in modern Western societies death was taboo. According to this interpretation such societies were defined as death denying [30-34]. It is now more commonly held, and it may well be the case, that death is no longer the taboo of modern societies [35-36]. The discussion of mortality and the relative ease with which we can now address issues pertaining to dying, living wills, euthanasia, hospice, and funeral rituals heralds a new found openness. But although it may now be possible to speak relatively candidly of such matters, discussion of the nature, treatment, and the social significance of the dying and dead body continues to be socially outlawed in this new, frank discourse on death. Indeed, it is argued here, that in modern Western societies, pre-occupied as they are with the living body and its properties of vitality, there continues to be tremendous difficulty and fear entailed in confronting a material entity, that is the dead body, which abrogates the powerful cultural drive for body beautiful, healthy, and youthful.

REFERENCES

1. M. Featherstone, M. Hepworth, and B. S. Turner, Preface, *The Body: Social Process and Cultural Theory*, M. Featherstone, M. Hepworth, and B. S. Turner (eds.), Sage, London, p. viii, 1991.
2. B. S. Turner, *Regulating Bodies: Essays in Medical Sociology*, Routledge, London, 1992.
3. S. Mennell, On the Civilizing of Appetite, in *The Body: Social Process and Cultural Theory*, M. Featherstone, M. Hepworth, and B. S. Turner (eds.), Sage, London, 1991.
4. J. Hockey and A. James, *Growing Up and Growing Old*, Sage, London, 1993.
5. J. J. Brumberg, *Fasting Girls, the Emergence of Anorexia Nervosa as a Modern Disease*, Harvard University Press, Cambridge, 1988.
6. R. Melzack and P. Wall, *The Challenge of Pain*, Penguin, Harmondsworth, 1982.
7. M. Featherstone and M. Hepworth, Changing Images of Middle Age, in *Transitions in Middle and Later Life*, M. Johnson (ed.), British Society of Gerontology, London, 1980.

8. M. Featherstone, The Body in Consumer Culture, in *The Body: Social Process and Cultural Theory*, M. Featherstone, M. Hepworth, and B. S. Turner (eds.), Sage, London, 1991.

9. S. B. Linder, *The Harried Leisure Class*, Columbia University Press, New York, 1970.

10. I. K. Zola, *Missing Pieces*, Temple University Press, Philadelphia, 1982.

11. *The Health of the Nation*, HMSO, London, 1990.

12. G. Howarth, *Last Rites: The Work of the Modern Funeral Director*, Baywood, Amityville, New York, 1996.

13. M. Douglas, *Purity and Danger: An Analysis of the Concepts of Pollution and Taboo*, Routledge and Kegan Paul, London, 1966.

14. S. Laws, *Issues of Blood: The Politics of Menstruation*, Macmillan, Basingstoke, 1990.

15. L. Prior, *The Social Organization of Death: Medical Discourse and Social Practices in Belfast*, Macmillan, Basingstoke, 1989.

16. D. Armstrong, Silence and Truth in Death and Dying, *Social Science and Medicine, 24*:8, pp. 651-657, 1987.

17. J. L. Watson, Of Flesh and Bones: The Management of Death Pollution in Cantonese Society, in *Death and the Regeneration of Life*, M. Bloch and J. Parry (eds.), Cambridge University Press, Cambridge, 1982.

18. J. Huizinga, *The Waning of the Middle Ages*, Doubleday, New York, 1954.

19. R. Porters, Death and Doctors in Georgian England, in *Death, Ritual and Bereavement*, R. Houlbrooke (ed.), Routledge, London, 1989.

20. A. Synott, Tomb, Temple, Machine and Self: The Social Construction of the Body, *British Journal of Sociology, 43*:1, pp. 79-110, March 1992.

21. E. Bronfen, *Over Her Dead Body*, Manchester University Press, Manchester, 1992.

22. J. L. Foltyn, Dead Beauty: The Preservation, Memorialization and Destruction of Beauty in Death, in *Contemporary Issues in the Sociology of Death, Dying and Disposal*, G. Howarth and P. C. Jupp (eds.), Macmillan, Basingstoke, 1996.

23. V. R. Pine, *Caretakers of the Dead: The American Funeral Director*, Irvington, New York, 1975.

24. G. Howarth, Investigating Deathwork, in *The Sociology of Death*, D. Clark (ed.), Blackwell, Oxford, 1993.

25. L. Bowman, *The American Funeral: A Study in Guilt, Extravagance and Sublimity*, Public Affairs Press, Washington D.C., 1959.

26. R. W. Habenstein, *The American Funeral Director and the Sociology of Work*, unpublished Ph.D. thesis, University of Chicago, 1954.

27. J. Mitford, *The American Way of Death*, Hutchinson, London, 1963.

28. National Association of Funeral Directors, *Manual of Funeral Directing*, NAFD, London, 1988.

29. A. Puxley (embalmer), quoted in *The Independent* (UK) newspaper, December 15, 1991.

30. P. Ariès, *The Hour of Our Death*, Penguin, Harmondsworth, 1981.

31. N. Elias, *The Loneliness of Dying*, Blackwell, Oxford, 1985.

32. G. Gorer, The Pornography of Death, 1955, reprinted in G. Gorer, *Death, Grief and Mourning in Contemporary Britain*, Cresset Press, London, 1965.

33. I. Illich, *Limits to Medicine*, Marion Boyars, London, 1976.
34. L. Pincus, *Death and the Family*, Faber and Faber, London, 1976.
35. A. Kellehear, Are We a "Death-Denying" Society? A Sociological Review, *Social Science and Medicine, 18*:9, pp. 713-723, 1984.
36. T. Walter, Modern Death—Taboo or Not Taboo? *Sociology, 25*:2, pp. 293-310, 1991.

PART II

Creative Caregiving: Practical Applications

In this part of the book, we will apply the theories found in the first part to the concrete situation of working with the dying, the grieving, their families, and their caregivers.

In creativity, the usual boundaries are not in effect [1, p. 156]. Creativity brings out the best in us because in creativity the individual is in touch with the transcendent. Whether that transcendent is called God, the inner self, Brahman, or the transcendental ego really doesn't make any difference. Creativity opens the door to true religiosity because it takes us outside the normal limits we impose upon ourselves and that we have been taught by our culture. Every religion is a combination of a cosmology, that is a theory of how things come together in the universe, and a morality, about what things are important to human beings and has the effect of teaching us how to cope [2]. We have two chapters dealing with the role of a religious caregiver in working with a client. While Rev. Richard Gilbert and Dr. Leslie Kawamura come to the client with different world-views, they have much in common in the concrete situation.

Rev. Richard Gilbert discusses the role of the hospital chaplain. Gilbert believes that the first, most important, function of the chaplain is simply to be there, journeying with the dying and grieving. This mutual journeying demands an openness to the other, as well as an openness to oneself. Gilbert believes that one of the major functions of the chaplain is to be a mirror, that is, to provide an opportunity for the client to reflect on his/her own spiritual journey. Rev. Gilbert examines the importance of preparation, observation, and evaluation as well as the most important role of presence.

Eastern philosophies and religions have a more immediate orientation than we find in Western thought. First of all, Eastern religions put emphasis on the immanence of God rather than transcendence. Secondly, Eastern philosophies place more emphasis on living in the moment, rather than the historical or future orientation found in Judaism, Christianity, and Islam. Dr. Leslie Kawamura explains the Buddhist beliefs about life and death and shows how the hospital chaplain can be present to a person in need, and journey with the client, while being true to the immediacy of the moment.

Rev. Bailey examines the specific use of the arts in a hospice setting. The arts enable a person to mourn, to grieve, and to celebrate life. An increasing number of hospice programs have instituted arts programs which range from music therapy to artists in residence. This work has proven effective with a variety of clients from those with HIV to holocaust survivors and their children. Perhaps the most important aspect of the arts is integration. The philosopher Jacques Mairitan said that the arts are expressions of the inexpressible [3, p. 301]. Expression is articularly important in crisis moments of life and the arts often are the best and perhaps sometimes the only way for the dying and grieving to find a means of expression.

While Rev. Bailey provides us with a general orientation to the arts in dealing with the dying and the grieving, Lora Heller, Paul Alexander, Mindy Gough, and Gerry Cox provide us with the specifics. Each draws on the concrete clinical or teaching situations in which they have been involved and give us specific methods that work with specific clients.

In the next three chapters we move to applications specific to children. Dr. Sandra Bertman shows how the arts can be used for death education because they identify sources of concern and consolation; offer materials for expressing emotion, and underscores the universality yet individuality of the child's experience. This chapter is particularly important for teachers of counselors who work with children. Dr. Bertman gives very specific material that can be used and shows how to use them effectively. On perhaps a more historical note, Mrs. Elizabeth Lamers shows how the fairy tales that we are accustomed to have developed over the years. Fairy tales reflect the death system, that is the socio-physical network of orientations to mortality [4, p. 193] as well as modify the death system because of the ways that they teach children to deal with death and loss. A fairy tale is more than a story to quiet a child before sleep, it personifies inner conflicts, makes demands, reassures, and offers hope for the future.

Professor David Adams teaches us the importance of using the tools mentioned in the prior chapters in dealing with traumatized children. Much has been written recently about the relationship between grief patterns and post traumatic stress reactions. Professor Adams shows how children are dis-enfranchised grievers because they do not have the sophisticated language abilities that adults use to communicate feelings and stress. Professor Adams gives very specific intervention techniques to the parents and teachers of traumatized children, one of which is the use of music, play, and other arts for consolation and expressions.

It is instructive that most of us do not think of a funeral as a creative expression. The funeral has several purposes: the sanitary disposal of the body, the beginning of the grief process by a confrontation with the body, the support in the grief process by those who come to offer consolation, the celebration of the life of the deceased, and the reaffirmation of one's values and belief systems. It is in the latter two functions particularly that creativity and the arts can be useful. Dr. Pittu Laungani indicates the psychological importance of a funeral, particularly a funeral which is attentive to and respectful of the cultural traditions of the dead person and his/her mourners. In India, the place of Dr. Laungani's birth, not to attend a funeral is considered an act of impiety by not respecting the person who died, the family, and the community at large. A death is a significant event in the life of a community which demands the restructuring of roles [5, p. 170]. This is not only true for the family but for the community as a whole. The human need to "do something" can be expressed at the funeral in a way that is most helpful for those involved. Dr. Lloyd Smith shows us that the need to celebrate a life, offer support, and reaffirm values is not limited to those who belong to one of the traditional faith systems. The "unchurched" also have these needs although they may express them in other terms. Dr. Smith gives some very specific suggestions such as examining the personal mythology of those involved.

Each of us brings to each new grieving situation the hangover of a lifetime of losses. Patricia Zalaznik examines the specific needs of those who have been abused as children. Hospice philosophy particularly, with its emphasis on meeting needs in a unique way, should be attentive to the background of the dying and grieving. Ms. Zalaznik believes that sexual and physical abuse that occurs in childhood meets the criteria for post traumatic stress disorder, and, although the pain may have been suppressed throughout a lifetime, as one "gets his house in order" at dying or death, the pain will resurface. Ms. Zalaznik tells us that the responses of the formerly abused will be different from those who had not been abused, so this must be taken into account in end of life issues.

While Patricia Zalaznik's chapter deals primarily with the care for the dying, Thomas O'Neill's focuses on the bereaved. He believes that the native people of North America have a powerful tool in the "dream catcher." Mr. O'Neill shows us one meaning behind the dream catcher and advises us how to use it in working with grieving adults and children.

We end with care for the caregiver. In order to work with persons in need we must ourselves have a meaning system, even if it is not described in traditional ways. Dr. Darcie Sims shows the need for personal exploration and examinations of expectations. This self-awareness provides the foundation for hope and for ministry to those with whom we work.

While the focus of these chapters vary, the attentive reader will find material to stimulate his/her thinking and tools in dealing with the dying and grieving.

REFERENCES

1. J. Havelka, Creativity and Death, in *Thanatology: A Liberal Arts Approach,* M. A. Morgan and J. D. Morgan (eds.), King's (Ont.), London, Ontario, pp. 155-162, 1986.
2. H. Smith, *The Religions of Man,* Harper and Row, New York, 1986.
3. J. Maritain, *Creative Intuition in Art and Poetry,* Pantheon, New York, 1953.
4. R. Kastenbaum and R. Aisenberg, *The Psychology of Death,* Springer, New York, 1953.
5. M. A. Bull, Structure and Stresses: When a Family Member is Dying, in *Readings in Thanatology,* J. D. Morgan (ed.), Baywood, Amityville, New York, 1997.

CHAPTER 7

Pastoral Caregiving: Caring As Presence

Rev. Fr. Richard B. Gilbert

"Code 99, room 434," and we're off and running. Half way down the hall a physician, also responding to the code, saw me, smiled, and said, "Gee, chaplain, give us a chance!" Of course, he was kidding. But he also was very serious. His style seemed to be, "When all else 'fails,' call the chaplain."

That physician and I came to be good friends, and he quickly learned that pastoral care was not just about caring for the dying and those who mourn. He found woven through all that encompasses chaplaincy the clear thread of commitment to the whole person, and to the whole story.

In this story is the reminder of the power and presence that accompany pastoral care when approaching the dying patient, and when providing bereavement care. Dying and death are ultimately spiritual matters, and, because of these spiritual dimensions, challenge patient, caregivers, and professional staff to listen to the spiritual story. Because death is final, it is also "ultimate." It brings us to the essence of what it means to live, to die, and to face eternity as we understand it. The dying patient and the support system surrounding that patient, however it is defined, are engaged in a "dialogue with life's ultimates," and thus provide a pathway for pastoral caregiving.

This chapter is committed to the important role of pastoral caregivers, however they see their prescribed roles, and it is about their own grief issues and journey.

It is important to stress at the outset that we are dealing with several levels of experience and protocol. First, we are talking about pastoral caregiving. The biblical image is that of a shepherd, that is, a guide or friend. Many call their spiritual leaders pastors, for they seek in those individuals their call to provide

95

guidance and direction. It is about providing direction in all of life's wilderness experiences, including death and the subsequent grieving,

Second, it is imperative that pastoral caregivers be informed about grief and grieving, as well as their own grief issues as caregivers. Too many theological schools and seminaries provide courses in eschatology, but you may feel more a Sherlock Holmes than a grief caregiver, trying to find any evidence of grief support in the ministry. Ministers are surrounded, and sometimes deafened by, the cries of the bereaved (though not limited to death experiences), and we cannot be complete in our work of equipping others until we equip ourselves with insights into the grief experience and the resources that provide both definition and comfort.

Third, pastoral caregiving is NOT pastoral counseling, and they must not be confused or interchanged. Sometimes it is a boundary issue. At other times it is a recognition of needs or skill limitations. Foremost is the realization that most bereaved need guidance, information, comfort, and counsel; they do NOT need therapy. Of course, this is not just a strategy issue or job formula we are describing. It is the mandate that is placed before all pastoral caregivers: be shepherds! To transcend the pastoral caregiving role is to put that crucial relationship at risk. To become the therapist is to lose out on the vital link of pastor (shepherd) and person. That very peculiar or unique level of intimacy must be nurtured, not threatened.

One final reminder: boundaries are crucial to the process. To become emotionally available, to be willing to share of yourself so that others may experience the care they so desperately need, is to put yourself equally at risk. A commitment to pastoral care with the bereaved is to be equally committed to yourselves. This means that you continue to assess and care for your own grief issues, especially tending to the feelings that emerge (rightfully so) because you have linked so intimately with the bereaved. The emergency room nurse cannot see trauma after trauma without being caught up in (or snared by) those tough "why" questions that chip away at the veneer of safety and protection that provides space between yourselves and those in your care. To become involved is to become vulnerable, and you cannot continue that vulnerability without sufficient personal refreshment.

To be a bereavement caregiver, especially with a pastoral identification, is to be a reflector. You are a mirror, and when standing before that mirror the bereaved need to see themselves, their hurts, their questions, their victories, and their spiritual connections. Look out! As they look into the mirror of their own "souls," you too will be looking, and the mirror is facing toward you. You will be seen, by others and by yourself. That can become a gift (a pathway to healing), but also a risk (a possible pathway to destruction for self and those in your care) if you choose to ignore it, and thus ignore yourself.

As the pastoral caregiver, it is imperative that the shepherding posture be understood and maintained. There are times when the shepherd is right in the midst of the flock, guiding, prodding, nurturing, coercing. At other times, the shepherd stands afar off, looking at the whole flock, claiming a different perspective. The pastoral caregiver has responsibility to (though not always "responsibility for") the entire flock, and this includes the advocacy role for those "sheep" that stray or that otherwise may feel cut off ("disenfranchised") from the group.

What follows is an outline for pastoral care with the bereaved. Because your task is not to direct but to lead, to walk with, and sometimes follow those on the journey, it is not a "how to" book. What appears to be a blueprint for one griever can be disastrous for another. Thus we speak of caregiving as the "be with" book. It is in being with people who hurt that one can receive the gift of affirmation that enables them to find the sources for healing that are within themselves. There are no quick pathways to the high standards worthy of pastoral care. The P.O.P.E. outline (Prepare, Observe, Presence, Evaluate) offers a useful guide for our discussion.

PREPARE

Preparation is essential for the work of ministry, and that includes the care of the bereaved. Balance is essential, and that means both the balance between *professional* and *personal*, as well as the balance of both *timeless* and *timely*.

I remember visiting a church where the minister displayed impeccable care of things related to worship and other liturgical matters. Twice I saw him flick dust off the altar (as if that was a grave sin), and, on several occasions, he would fuss with his eucharistic vestments to make sure every fold and crease was in its proper place. In the five times I visited that church, the minister never remembered meeting me, a colleague, and seemed distant from the hurting parishioners who tried to share prayerful concerns on the greeting line following worship. He had lost that crucial balance.

Much of the "trouble" that arises in grief work occurs because we tip the scales and destroy the balance. We are to be professional. This means an awareness of our vocational responsibilities, the boundaries that exist between people in various relationships, and the integrity that respects and fosters a keen professional responsibility that is balanced with the personal issues, feelings, and needs. You cannot move the scales too far in either direction without doing damage to the pastoral relationship. To be too professional is to hide in the safety of "head stuff," knowing all of the "right answers" (or at least the title of a few good books and where to find them), but without risking the emotional awareness that identifies with the bereaved in an empathetic way.

To be professional for example means to "understand" that grief often includes anger, fear, loneliness, and guilt, to name a few of the more common feelings. To be personal is to be aware of the aforementioned issues because he or she has *experienced* anger, fear, loneliness, or guilt, knows that caregiving risks the exposure of those feelings, and can stay personally integrated to allow the sharing of those feelings without either jeopardizing the relationship or one's own health.

BALANCE

Preparation is also a balance of the timeless with the timely. Ministry, both ordained and lay, involves the timeless preparation of the self, the constant learning of skills for the work of ministry, and also the spiritual development that recognizes one cannot be a spiritual nurturer of others until he or she is able to tend to his or her own spiritual needs and grief issues.

Timeless preparation recognizes the opportunities and challenges of ministry, of lifetime service AND learning, and is committed to that. Here is one of the many major downfalls for ministers in bereavement work.

First, it means the *recognition* that ministers are confronted with constant revisions in the pastoral agenda, and in the human experience. In other words, we are never entirely "ready" for anything that comes into the minister's study. Most of us have been woefully under-prepared for ministry generally, and specifically for grief work. A look at a seminary transcript may identify courses in eschatology (the study of "last things"), but that doesn't guarantee any clue of what loss and grief are all about.

It is further compromised by the refusal of all too many in the ministry to see their own need for continued study in grief. As one bereaved parent once shared at a workshop, "I can understand that they (ministers) do not 'understand' how I feel. What I cannot excuse is their unwillingness to learn." Professional recognition or ranking demands that bereavement ministry be of the highest priority both in *action* and in *preparation* for that action.

The temporal preparation for bereavement work is also a dyad. We prepare with the double focus of *self* and *client*. You cannot enter into the life of another person, to enable "connection," until you check on the connections in your own life. Preparation means, "How am I doing *today*? "What are my issues *right now*?" Am I ready *at this time* to be personally and professionally available to another person?"

Any caregiver must maintain the "discipline of preparation" for every person encountered. It doesn't mean you are ever really "ready" for that person, for the agenda for ministry rests with the client. This means that there can be plenty of surprises. It means that I pay attention to myself, and what may be ahead for me and for my client, so that I am very clear (to self and others) who I serve, what I can offer, and territory that must remain closed off for me (or for the client).

Preparation is also timely. What is the parishioner bringing to me now? What am I bringing to him or her? Am I overburdened or overtired? Are they presenting messages (verbal or otherwise) that do not seem to fit, and need further exploration? What do I have to remember *now* about this person, either from past visits or based on the type of loss or circumstances surrounding the loss? For example, most of us have some level of stress and/or distress as Christmas approaches. We "know" that Christmas is a stressful time. We should also "know," as professionals, that Christmas can be a particularly difficult time for the bereaved. To be aware of that, and to make that connection of "head with heart" available to the client as a *possibility* for ministry is to be prepared for ministry.

OBSERVE

Granger Westberg, author of the still popular grief book, *Good Grief,* has frequently reminded us that God gave us one mouth and two ears for a reason [1]. Don't dismiss that too quickly. Listening is at the heart of bereavement caregiving. So is observing. To take a person at face value, or his or her words at the base level of meaning, is to fail to integrate the whole story and a whole list of possible meanings, issues, and needs.

Observe. Check things out. Is what you are seeing match with what you are hearing, or what your professional and personal experiences suggest might be present in this given moment of ministry?

When visiting a hospital room shared by two patients, and you see the patient in bed one with several visitors, lots of cards, flowers, and other gifts, and the area of the second patient to be void of any sense of community support, aren't your eyes telling you something? Yet how often do we jump right into the fray and not check out all of the messages right in front of us?

The bereaved person in your support group, in their home, passing by in a "hallway ministry" may be sending out messages of hurt, conflict, despair, and fear. Are you seeing the signals? For them to enter into your presence and say, "Everything is OK," may say a lot about his or her sense of safety or trust with you. It may say even more about how they can or cannot touch their feelings. These folks are grieving, they are following a totally new route with few, if any, landmarks, and yet somehow they feel obligated to keep themselves "presentable" at all times.

Observe. Check things out. Listen to their story. Listen to your understanding of that story, as well as the larger story we call loss. What is missing? What is really being said? Are you truly available to that person on the journey?

PRESENCE

Harry was a corporate executive. He wielded more power through his telephone receiver than many of us will ever know or experience. He also was dying of cancer. Day after day we would visit. He felt very comfortable letting me know how the company was doing, how much he was needed, and how he was irreplaceable. All of this may well have been true, as true as the fact that he was dying of cancer.

We visited, we "talked around" his disease, and daily I was reminded by professionals and family that, "He just is kidding himself if he thinks he will beat this cancer, and really, Reverend, can't you *do* something about it?"

To "do" something about anyone or anything is to confuse ministry with rescuing. At times one must step in. There are occasions when a person may be at personal risk, or a risk to others. That seldom is the case for the bereaved. What is common is the risk of the minister to try to rescue, direct, or otherwise do things for the patient or client.

With Harry, the family members and professionals had a valid concern. Harry's perceived inability to touch his true issues or feelings compromised both his healing and theirs. Could it also be that Harry was doing exactly as he was doing before cancer entered his life, namely, providing the loving gift of his leadership and care for both company and family? He was where he thought he either needed to be or should be. He didn't know. He was never terminal before.

A "doer" either would have experienced profound resistance ("get out of my room"), or otherwise destroyed the essence of the grief journey, that it is "my" journey. Presence is to walk with the person, neither directing nor following, surrendering the right or need to control for one of simply listening. It is to be present out of love, willing to listen (and to wait) to the person wherever he or she may be.

By listening to Harry and staying *with* him, the minister was able to await the opportunity for Harry to risk looking at other issues and other feelings. Harry was terrified of his cancer and of his dying. He stayed within the safe boundaries of that which was familiar to him. He did what he did every day. He went "to" work. Presence enabled Harry to risk (when he was ready) his fears, his uncertainties about the eternal in his life, his worries over the future provisions for his family, and to come to terms with his own dying.

Some just "walk by" and ignore ministry altogether. Others do a long list of tasks or chores, presumably to comfort the bereaved and certain to address the emotional needs of the caregiver. Presence, like Jesus on the road to Emmaus, was so comfortable with himself and so emotionally available to those two men, that he was able to love, to observe, to be with, and wait "Until their eyes were opened and they recognized him" (Luke 24:13-32).

EVALUATE

All of us, both bereaved and those who care for them, need constant reminders that "Grief's best friend is *time*."

Day after day there are plenty of reminders that time is being stolen from them. Those hurtful remarks like, "You should be over this by now," offer little comfort, and often do tremendous damage. Such remarks not only display the discomfort and apathy of the commentator, but also rob the bereaved of the one thing they have left to get them through their journey, *time*.

To protect both the journey and the time that it requires, it is essential that the caregiver display a commitment to that timetable. No one knows that timetable, for healing is often a fleeting moment grabbed during the turbulence of sorrow. The minister does know that it is his or her responsibility to commit his or her style or bereavement ministry to one that is rooted in presence, and that is a respect of all time and no time. The bereaved's best "friend" is time.

One demonstration of this commitment is the evaluation that follows *every* engagement in ministry. That is the final stage in our little P.O.P.E. formula. In reality, it is not final, but a coupling or link from moment to moment, visit to visit, a spot on the "map" of the grief journey to the next stop along the way.

To sit down and to evaluate, both with the client and alone, is to suggest to the client (who may or may not be able to "hear" what is being offered) that there is still time, and that the minister remains present with them. It is also a reminder to the minister that grief is a journey, the journey demands and deserves time, and that each minister's own journey has just found a "spot" along the way, a spot that requires time for self and self care.

Evaluation, like the other pairings in this lesson on ministry, is twofold. It is to evaluate the client as well as to evaluate the caregiver.

For those who chart frequently in health care institutions, you may know the familiar "SOAP" method (situation, observation, assessment, plan). It makes charting much easier, and also enhances team work for those who share responsibility for a particular patient.

It is at the heart of evaluation. What has the client presented? What have I observed? In assessing ("listening to the story"), what has been shared, what has been identified but yet to be explored, what seemed to be missing? What is the plan of action for that client? Am I to see them again? Did they decline a future appointment, but still suggest a gentle invitation "down the grief road?" Did I make a specific commitment to them for a specific task, such as a referral to a provider, to send an article or some other resource, to provide information needed for the journey, and how and when am I to respond to this? How will I evaluate the effectiveness of that process? What needs to be remembered from this session? What do I need to keep in mind for the next session? Is there something I should check out or do before the next session?

A widow came to talk to me some time ago. She shared, often with great rage, her dissatisfaction with her husband's management of the financial affairs of the family, and how, with his death, she was left less than adequately provided for. She also was angry with herself for living out the expectations of the "helpless female." She also felt terribly guilty about these feelings. In evaluating the session it was clear that the woman felt very safe to express (ventilate) some very tough feelings, that the feelings seemed very appropriate to the situation (that is, both expressive of the facts in the story and simply just what she was feeling), and that she presented no symptoms that would warrant intervention or some other alarm on my part. She was on her journey and right where she needed to be.

Further evaluation after the session also brought the reminder that she raised some very legitimate and specific questions about the family accounts, the insurance policies, banking, and other matters that required both immediate and long-term attention. They also were issues that I was not qualified to address, and even those matters which I could address were deserving of the kind of attention that only an accountant, banker, or insurance agent could handle. If I were to travel too far into her financial woes, I could risk both giving the wrong information and also straying too far from the pastoral relationship, which could then become blurred or damaged.

When we talked about these concerns, she was able to conclude for herself that perhaps she did not have sufficient information either to judge the actions or inactions of her husband, and also the tasks (if any) she needed to perform in order to bring some order into the financial chaos of her life.

She needed a safe place to ventilate, reassurance in this "madness" we call grief, but also some very specific answers to the questions that were emerging through her journey. By staying present with her, she was able to express all of what she was feeling, and also to recognize for herself her need and her right to receive help. Then, and only then, could we explore the possibilities for resolving these matters. I had agreed to furnish the names of a banker who understood both estates and insurance matters, and also the name of a support group for young widows who would appear more appropriate for her needs. The evaluation process (taking the time to review both the generalities and the specifics of any and all moments in ministry) forced me to ask of myself:

1. What was I asked to do?
2. Was this a reasonable request?
3. What have I committed to do in response?
4. Do I have the necessary information?
5. What is the best way to retrieve and then share this information?
6. Have I accomplished the necessary task(s)?

Self-evaluation is equally important. You may have only a few minutes between visits or clients, but to fail to provide self-evaluation is to put both self and the clients (both the previous one and the next one) at risk. You cannot continue to make yourself available to the bereaved without making yourself available to your own issues and agendas.

To evaluate yourself to ask:

1. Did I learn something today about myself?
2. What from my story presented a possible gift to the client?
3. What from my story may have got in the way of the moment in ministry? Where was that coming from, and what was it all about?
4. Did I gain new insights into myself as person and as professional? What am I to do with these new insights?

The heart of presence is helping people find the connections that they need to cope, indeed, to survive. This is where spirituality becomes so important, and is often ignored. Spirituality is where we turn to face life's challenges and questions, and where, in that very process, are often so easily derailed. When Jesus cried out, "My God, my God, why have you forsaken me?" he was not asking a question. He was making a statement of feelings (abandonment), and was trying to get God's attention (and ours). People in grief are desperately searching for healing, and often journey through questions. If we are to be present, then we must be willing to explore these essential spiritual issues. Remember, there are very few answers. Ultimately, it is not found in answers, but in connections to our spiritual center and being.

Why presence? In presence . . .

   . . . guilt can find forgiveness;
   . . . despair can experience hope;
   . . . sorrow can welcome comfort;
   . . . doubt gives way to trust;
   . . . pain is embraced with presence;
   . . . loneliness is open to community;
   . . . "hunger" is offered "bread";
   . . . disconnection becomes connection.

In her handsomely packed collection of cards with helpful sayings about grief, *TouchStones*, Darcie Sims offers very wise counsel both for the bereaved and those who watch over them [2]. One strikes me as particularly helpful to the discussion of pastoral care and the bereaved. If people are to find their connections back to God or that which is eternal for them (which is the work of pastoral care) it comes as we walk more and talk less. This *TouchStones* card invites us into the pastoral care for all who are bereaved:

> We cannot protect ourselves from the rain, but we can go together in search of the parade [2, #T-21].

REFERENCES

1. G. Westberg, *Good Grief,* Augsberg Fortress, Minneapolis, 1971.
2. D. Sims, *TouchStones,* Big A and Company, Wenatchee, Washington, 1993.

BIBLIOGRAPHY

Anderson, H., Holst, L. E., and Sunderland, R. H., *Ministry to Outpatients: A New Challenge in Pastoral Care,* Augsburg Fortress, Minneapolis, 1991.
Booth, L., *The God Game, It's Your Move: Reclaim Your Spiritual Power,* Stillpoint, Walpose, New Hampshire, 1995.

Clark, D. (ed.), *Clergy Response to Suicidal Persons and Their Family Members,* Exploration, Chicago, 1993.

Del Zoppo, P., *Pastoral Bereavement Counselling,* Saint Paul Bereavement Centre (Video), Staten Island, 1992.

Droege, T., *The Faith Factor in Health,* Trinity Press, Philadelphia, 1991.

Cox, G. R. and Fundis, R. J., *Spiritual, Ethical and Pastoral Aspects of Death and Bereavement,* Baywood, Amityville, New York, 1992.

Doka, K. and Morgan, J. D., *Death and Spirituality,* Baywood, Amityville, 1992.

Fitchett, G., *Assessing Spiritual Needs,* Augsburg Fortress, Minneapolis, 1993.

Fraser, L., *Water From the Rock: Finding Grace in Time of Grief,* Paulist, Mahwah, 1994.

Gilbert, R., Protestant Perspectives on Grief and Children, in *Bereaved Children and Teens,* E. A. Grollman (ed.), Beacon, Boston, 1995.

Gilbert, R., *HeartPeace: Healing Help for Grieving Folks,* Abbey Press, St. Meinrad, 1997.

Gilbert, R., *Use and Abuse of Religion in Grief*—(Recorded workshop).

Grollman, E., *Bereaved Children and Teens: A Support Guide for Parents and Professionals,* Beacon, Boston, 1995.

Hickman, M., *Healing After Loss: Daily Meditations for Working Through Grief,* Avon, New York, 1994.

Holst, L., *Hospital Ministry: The Role of the Chaplain Today,* Crossroad, New York, 1985.

Hope for the Bereaved, *Hope for the Bereaved,* Syracuse, 1995.

Hover, M., *Caring for Yourself when Caring for Others,* Twenty-Third, Mystic, Connecticut, 1993.

Levang, E. and Ilse, S., *Remembering with Love: Messages for Hope for the First Year of Grieving Beyond,* Deaconess, Minneapolis, 1992.

Meyer, C., *Surviving Death: A Practical Guide to Caring For the Dying and Bereaved,* Twenty-Third, Mystic, Connecticut, 1993.

Miller, J., *What Will Help Me? 12 Things to Remember When You Have Suffered a Loss,* Willowgreen, Fort Wayne, 1994.

Pruyser, P., *The Minister as Diagnostician: Personal Problems in Pastoral Perspective,* Westminster, Philadelphia, 1996.

Richards, L. and Johnson, P., *Death and the Caring Community: Ministering to the Terminally Ill,* Multnomah, Portland, 1980.

Sims, D., *If I Could Just See Hope,* Big A and Company, Wenatchee, 1993.

Simsic, W., *Cries of the Heart: Praying Our Losses,* St. Mary's, Winona, 1994.

Williams, D., *Grief Ministry: Helping Others Mourn,* Resource, San Jose, 1991.

CHAPTER 8

Facing Life and Death: A Buddhist's Understanding of Palliative Care and Bereavement

Leslie Kawamura

The minister stopped beside the bed of the ailing woman, whose leg was giving her much pain. "Pray for me," she whispered to him. He shook his head. "In my religion we do not pray," he replied then added: "But we have sutra chanting—would that help?" She shrugged and he chanted a few lines of sutra, the narrative of Buddhist religious canon, perhaps from the dialogues of Buddha. "It seemed to help her—even if it wasn't a 'prayer'," marveled the Rev. Tesshi Aoyama, who is a minster of the Buddhist Church of America. As a matter of fact, he is a nineteenth-generation Buddhist minister, born in Japan.

"There is no chaplaincy in Buddhism—I am a pioneer," he laughed [1, p. 69]. The above words, quoted from Dan L. Thrapp's article "Buddhist Helps Solace Sick at L.A. Hospital" in the Sunday, February 23, 1973 edition of the *Los Angeles Times* newspaper, relates perhaps the first ever qualified Buddhist ministerial graduate from a clinical pastoral education program. The information that Rev. Tesshi Aoyama, a Buddhist minister of the Japanese True Pure Land tradition, became a qualified counselor is one thing, but the dilemma in which both the minister and patient were placed is more interesting for the contents of the present chapter. The minister faced the dilemma of having to respond to an ailing patient's request for prayer when his own tradition lacked such a practice and the patient faced the dilemma of having to be satisfied with the chanting of a sutra, a practice which was quite foreign to her. That the situation ended on a positive note was owing to Rev. Aoyama's ". . . sensitivity and awareness of the meaning of relationships and social structures. From his experiences he learn[ed] to help

105

persons resolve personal conflicts, grow in maturity, and search for meaning" [1, pp. 69-70].

In recent times, there is a tendency for people to think that if one can find a response to the question of death and dying, then one can live in accordance with that response a meaningful life. This way of managing one's life can be understood as "teleo-centric" which is based upon a "theo-centric" religious tradition. By "theo-centric" I mean those religious traditions that prescribe a way of life on the basis of a divine intervention of some kind that governs the manner one lives now in anticipation of a life hereafter. Thus, "theo-centric" religious traditions tend to be "teleo-centric" also. However, not all world religions are theo-centric" or "teleo-centric." Such traditions represented by some forms of Buddhism and by "existential-phenomenological" philosophies tend not to ask questions about life or death but tend to emphasize the importance of participating in the act of living. This participation in living can be understood as an "insta-centric" or "insta-matic," because it focuses upon the importance of the "here and now" and upon the "loneliness" of being in the world alone by oneself. In contrast to the "theo-centric" which places the responsibility of life and death in the hands of an "other," the "insta-centric" puts the responsibility of life and death upon the individual.[1] The distinction between the "teleo-centric" and the "insta-centric" is an important distinction to keep in mind throughout this chapter, because it will be the foundation upon which the following exchange of ideas rest. Further, without a clear discernment about this distinction, we will have a tendency to conclude that a particular way of dealing with death and dying is the only correct way. This rather myopic view prevents one from becoming aware that the view of the majority culture need not be the most appropriate way of responding to the process of death and dying. In the words of Donald Irish, we should realize that:

The United States and Canadian societies have traditionally been predominantly white in race and Christian in religion. Thus the professional personnel who have daily been involved in the treatment of the dying and the nurture of the bereaved will most commonly have been related to white Roman Catholics and mainline Protestant patients and clients. The specialists themselves—physicians, nurses, clergy, social workers, hospice and hospital chaplains, and funeral directors—as trained professionals have usually also been members of the dominant groups. For both reasons, these practitioners have tended to be better acquainted with the beliefs about life and death, related rituals, patterns of emotional response, and attitudes toward the body that prevailed within the majority cultures [2, p. 1].

---

[1] I have coined phrases such as "teleo-centric," "insta-centric," "theo-centric," and "existential-phenomenological" in order to distinguish ways of thinking that produces a different way of seeing reality, although I am uncertain whether one is justified in coining such phrases.

Inasmuch as these words reflect the situation in the past, perhaps through discussions of the kind that we are holding now, the professionals from the "majority cultures" will become more sympathetic observers and listeners of the "minority cultures" within our predominantly Roman Catholic and mainline Protestant society. But a word of caution is in order. Paul C. Rosenblatt has pointed out that we must be attentive to the fact that:

> It is easy, in looking at the emotions and experiences of people from other cultures, to adopt a superficially helpful but nonetheless ethnocentric stance that implies, "Of course, our understanding are the right ones, but we will communicate with you in your own terms while still remaining assured that our way of thinking is correct." We will never understand people whose language or culture is different from ours if we translate what they say into our own terms and assume the transcendent realty of those terms [3, p. 14].

Buddhism is a relatively recent guest to the palliative care scene within Canada, and this means that many religious activities and thoughts that are natural to a Buddhist's way of understanding will undoubtedly strike the "majority culture" as unusual, strange, and odd. Consequently, in discussing the topic "Facing Life and Death—A Buddhist's Understanding of Palliative Care and Bereavement," those religious practices and beliefs common to the "minority culture" must be clearly understood, not as bizarre, eccentric, and strange phenomena, but as meaningful activities within the context of that "minority culture."

With the above as a background, it should be made clear that the terms "a Buddhist's Understanding" in the title of this presentation are meant to reflect my own understanding of palliative care and bereavement, and therefore one should not conclude that what I am about to explain is an archetypical, normative, and unequivocal Buddhist stance on the subject. It is my opinion that such a standard Buddhist stance cannot be attained even among the Buddhist traditions. But, I must quickly add that this does not exclude the possibility of establishing a common thread among those traditions that call themselves Buddhist. The ideas developed in this chapter have been derived from the research and textual information of a few experts in the field of death and dying which I have consulted and from my own experiences as a retired clergy of the Jodo-shin-shu, that is, the Japanese True Pure Land Buddhist tradition. The remainder of this chapter will be developed through a discussion of the following topics.

1. Foundational teachings of the historical Buddha, Shakyamuni
2. The Expressions of Death
3. The way we die, place of death, and timeliness or untimeliness of death
4. Rituals, Mourning and Funeral Customs; Memorial Service
5. Conclusion.

1. FOUNDATIONAL TEACHINGS OF THE HISTORICAL BUDDHA, SHAKYAMUNI

The Buddhist religion began in India with the life of a prince of the Shakya clan, Siddhårtha (one who attains one's aim). As a child he was moved by various situations of dis-ease that seemed to strike all living beings.

> . . . He grew up enjoying all the comforts and luxuries, pleasure and amusements proper to His age and class. . . . Eventually he was married, probably to more than one wife, and had a son. Yet despite so deep an enjoyment of worldly happiness he was not satisfied. The problem of existence tormented him. In particular He was obsessed by the pitiableness of the human predicament. Was there no way out for beings subjected to the miseries of birth, old age, disease and death [4, p. 12]?

In a quest for a response to the question of release from the miseries of birth, old age, disease, and death, the prince renounced his status and family and departed on his journey to the various religious leaders of his time. None could give a response to how to be released from such miseries. Resolved not to move from his meditation spot beneath a pipal tree until he had understood and gained an answer, he practiced the four contemplative stages by which he was able to reflect on his former activities; was able to see how his actions had their retribution; was able to direct his mind toward the destruction of his biases regarding sensual desires, conditioned existence, and opinionated views; and finally was able to realize that there was no permanency to mundane existence. Having passed through the four contemplative stages, the prince awakened to the reality of life as a process of interdependent arising and decaying. In other words, the prince attained the state of enlightenment—buddhahood and thereby realized that there is no way out of the miseries of birth, old age, disease, and death. Whatever comes into existence is bound to age, to decay, and to die. According to *Sammāditthi Sutta (Right View)* found in *The Middle Length Discourse of the Buddha (Majjima Nikāya)*:

> . . . With the arising of birth there is the arising of ageing and death. With the cessation of birth there is the cessation of ageing and death [5, p. 136].

Because there is no state of existence spared from the reality of impermanence and change, change or impermanence is foundational to "existence." According to Bhikkhu Bodhi:

> The notion of impermanence (*aniccatā*) forms the bedrock for the Buddha's teaching, having been the initial insight that impelled the Bodhisattva to leave the palace in search of a path to enlightenment. Impermanence, in the Buddhist view, comprises the totality of conditioned existence, ranging in

scale from the cosmic to the microscopic. At the far end of the spectrum the Buddha's vision reveals a universe of immense dimensions evolving and disintegrating in repetitive cycles throughout beginningless time. . . . In the middle range the mark impermanence comes to manifestation in our inescapable mortality, our condition of being bound to ageing, sickness, and death (MN 26.5) of possessing a body that is subject to being worn and rubbed away, to dissolution and disintegration" (MN 74.9). And at the close end of the spectrum, the Buddha's teaching discloses the radical impermanence uncovered only by sustained attention to experience in its living immediacy: the fact that all the consitutents of our being, bodily and mental, are in constant process, arising and passing away in rapid succession from moment to moment without any persistent underlying substance. In the very act of observation they are undergoing "destruction, vanishing, fading away, and ceasing" (MN 74.11) [6, p. 26].

These words indicate that impermanence lies at the basis of existence and that to exist is possible only in the process of birth, decay, and death. Death is a natural outcome of birth and of the decaying process.

The picture which I have portrayed so far is not, however, exclusively Buddhist. It seems that anyone who has pondered seriously over the question of life and death must come to such a conclusion. For example, in the "Introduction" to her book, *Death. The Final Stage of Growth*, Elisabeth Kübler-Ross makes the following observation:

Death always has been and always will be with us. It is an integral part of human existence. And because it is, it has always been a subject of deep concern to all of us. Since the dawn of humankind, the human mind has pondered death, searching for the answer to its mysteries, for the key to the question of death unlocks the door of life [7, p. 1].

To question the mystery of death is to question the process of life, and to question the process of life is to ponder about death. Death should not come as a surprise to anyone born and, consequently, death should not be a mystery to any of us here today. However, for example, if I or any one of you should die while reading this chapter, everyone, excepting perhaps the person who died, would be surprised that a death took place. However, death itself should not surprise us, because death is a natural outcome of life, and we are not surprised that we are alive. However, in spite of the Buddhist teaching of impermanence, in an actual life and death situation, I would suspect that even a Buddhist will mourn when death occurs and feel a sense of loss and grief just like any other sentient being. It seems absurd, therefore, to conclude that by following the Buddhist teachings a Buddhist adherent will not be disturbed should a death occur to someone close or even to oneself.

2. THE EXPRESSIONS OF DEATH

In more recent times, with the advent of professionals—death counselors, psychiatrists, geriatricians, funeral directors, clergy, and others—whose job it is to conceal the natural process of dying, stigma attached to death has increased and as a result death has become a phenomenon that is encountered at arm's length. Elisabeth Kübler-Ross states:

> Death is a subject that is evaded, ignored, and denied by our youth-worshipping, progress-oriented society. It is almost as if we have taken on death as just another disease to be conquered. But the fact is that death is inevitable. We will all die, it is only a matter of time. Death is as much a part of human existence, of human growth and development, as being born. It is one of the few things in life we can count on, that we can be assured will occur. Death is not an enemy to be conquered or a prison to be escaped. It is an integral part of our lives that gives meaning to human existence. It sets a limit on our time in this life, urging us on to do something productive with time as long as it is ours to use [7, p. x].

What is it that prevents us from examining death as a reality within life? What is it that keeps us from expressing our feelings to ourselves and to others so that we would reveal truly who we are. What is it that brings our emotional life to an end? According to Clark Moustakas:

> In the extreme, the person stops feeling altogether and tries to live solely by rational means and cognitive directions. This is the terrible tragedy of modern life—the alienation of [one][2] from one's own feelings, the desensitization of one to one's own suffering and grief, the fear of one to experience one's own loneliness and pain and the loneliness and misery of others [8, p. 34].

When Moustaka states, ". . . the person . . . tries to live solely by rational means and cognitive directions," I understand that he is referring to the feeling of guilt that arises when one lives in accordance with one's feelings. This ". . . desensitization of one to one's own suffering and grief, the fear of one to experience one's own loneliness and pain" and consequently "the loneliness and misery of others" arises from the need of one to protect what one has rationalized and cognitively determined to be the image of the self.

In my previous discussion on the reality of impermanence as the existential reality of a person, what was implied, but not clearly defined, was the fact that whatever exists does not possess an inherent nature by which its existential status

---

[2] I have deliberately changed the words "man" to the neutral form "one" and "his" to "one's" throughout this quotation.

is established. Within the Buddhist tradition this has been known as *an ātman*, which unlike the expected understanding that Buddhist believe in no-self or non-self, means that existence lacks essence. Now, if I should apply this Buddhist view of non-self to the human situation, I would come to realize that what is taken to be the "self" is nothing more than a cognitive reality, that is, an idea. An idea, owing to its reality of being an idea, cannot reveal a substantive existence, because if an idea were able to reveal something substantive, one should be able to carry an idea around in one's pocket, hand it over to another person, and have that idea take up space and time. As absurd as that may seem, the idea of handing an idea over to another person is not as absurd as it seems, because although we know that ideas are not substantive, we would be mislead if we thought that ideas had no efficacy. Ideas do have efficacy; one needs only to look back at the human history of war to verify that. However, even though ideas have efficacy, we should not conclude therefrom that an idea is substantive. What we should see in reflecting upon human history is that history has taken place to a large extent upon the strength of efficacy of ideas that have resulted from a non-substantive reality. In terms of understanding who we are, this means that the self-image that we imagine to be the real self is nothing more than a projection of our cognitive faculty and consequently the "real self" thus conceived has as much substance as one could expect from a son of a barren woman or the hair-net seen by a person with cataract. The same applies to what we have mentally determined to be the reality of death.

Death is not something distinctly separate from life nor is life something distinctly separate from death.[3] Usually, death and life are seen as if they were unique and distinct from each other, because we are capable of thinking of them in that manner instead of thinking of them as one and the same, a reality, by the way, which can be equally imagined. In his article, "The Death that Ends Death in Hinduism and Buddhism," J. Bruce Long states:

> There are, at least, two images of death which seem to inform a large proportion of contemporary fiction, drama and cinema. On the one hand, death is pictured as an ancient enemy who, after centuries of fruitless struggle, is being brought under submission by man's scientific and technological ingenuity. Second, death is imagined as a chilling wind, blowing wherever it wills to snuff out the flame of life in anyone who gets in its way, leaving for those who remain behind only a sense that life is an inexhaustible draught of ennui or anxiety [9, pp. 52-53].

---

[3] For an interesting discussion on the question of whether death is a process or an event, see Robert S. Morrison, "Death: Process or Event?" and the response to it by Leon R. Kass in his essay, "Death as an Event," in *Death Inside Out,* P. Steinfels and R. Veatch (eds.), Harper & Row, pp. 63-78, 1975. [Unfortunately, for the presentation, I am unable to incorporate these papers, but these essays must be considered for publication.]

Thus, to those who see, that is for those who rationalize or conceptualize death as an "enemy" or as "chilling wind," there will arise a feeling that death is a very uncharitable, harsh, and abrupt event. However, those who see, that is those who rationalize or conceptualize death as part and parcel of life will have a more detached feeling toward this event. This means that, ". . . death does not have to be a catastrophic, destructive thing; indeed, it can be viewed as one of the most constructive, positive, and creative elements of culture and life" [7, p. 2]. Because we always have understood death and life as separate realities, we have projected a bleak picture on death which it need not have. "If you can begin to see death as an invisible, but friendly, companion on your life's journey—gently reminding you not to wait till tomorrow to do what you mean to do—then you can learn to *live* your life rather than simply passing through it" [7, p. x].

3. THE WAY WE DIE, PLACE OF DEATH, AND TIMELINESS OR UNTIMELINESS OF DEATH

The manner in which one dies, the place where one dies, and when one dies are concerns that occupy most people's mind. However, from a Buddhist perspective, there is no good way, or place, or time to die. For that matter, neither is there a bad way, or place, or time to die. When the causes and condition for death are ripe, death will take place, not otherwise. This principle of causation is known as interdependent origination (*pratī tyasamutpā da*) in Buddhism and this means that whatever takes place (birth, life, or death), or does not take place, can occur if and only if the causes and conditions for its occurrence are present. This principle also holds true for space and time; hence the place where one finds one's self is controlled by the activities one did and does, and the time that any event takes place is controlled by causes and circumstances. This means that terms like "good" or "bad," "timely" or "untimely," "life or death," or "place" are not expressions of reality-as-such, but rather such terms are indicators. By the term "indicator" I am referring to something that gives all the indication of being there, but like the appearance of numbers on a digital clock or letters on a computer screen they are not to be taken as really substantively there. Like the numbers and the letters, the manifestation of death at some time and somewhere is simply an indicator of an occurring change. It is neither good or bad nor timely or untimely.

When death is understood as a natural process, then there is little sense in lamenting about the manner in which one dies or the place where one dies or the time when one dies. However, just as it was in the case of impermanence, the manner, the place, and the time that we die are of major concern to us, because as ordinary people who are bound up in the guilt produced by our desire to live in the expectations of others, we are completely attached to the ideology of manners and behavior. Therefore, even though impermanence implies that there is no substantive reality behind any beliefs about reality we may entertain and even though death is simply part and parcel of life, the very fact of impermanence lies at the very foundation for our loneliness and fear of dying.

According to the Buddhist teaching of interdependent origination, birth and death, i.e., the process of living and dying, is nothing more than the consummation or the fruition of causes and conditions and there is no untimely consummation or fruition of causes and conditions. That fact that birth occurs or that death occurs means that birth occurs because its occurrence is timely and that death occurs because its occurrence is timely. Understood in this manner, birth or life or death is always taking place in their proper time frame. Even though this understanding of causation can be acquired only in the realization of the non-substantiality of reality and of impermanence, still death is a traumatic experience, owing to the fact that we ordinary people are bound up in the delusion produced by our desire to live in the expectations of permanence.

The event of birth, of life, or of death has nothing to do with producing joy or anger, but anyone can be the source of joy if it occurs in a manner that one desires or anyone can be the source of anger if it occurs in a manner that one does not desire. According to this Buddhist principle we can understand anger as arising from the desire to maintain life and not from the fact of death itself. Birth becomes a source of joy, life a source of frustration, and death a source of anger for us, because we are bound up in the ideology of permanence and a substantive reality. That is, we are unwilling to meet the challenge of change, because change implies loneliness and loneliness implies a loss of meaning in life. Hence we speak about the death of a child as untimely, death in isolation in the gutter of the street as a bad place to die, or being involved in a car accident as an unfortunate way of dying.

The discussion thus far may have you thinking that in the Buddhist tradition there is no need for rituals in giving care to the bereaved. Such an understanding probably arises from the matter-of-fact way in which I am presenting the basic teachings of the Buddha. The matter-of-fact presentation of the topics was intentional. It was for the purpose of explicating human experience as the constituent of life just-as-it-is in the manner that an Enlightened being may experience it, that is, to experience reality just-as-it-is. In other words, the matter-of-fact presentation was meant to bring to one's awareness what is just natural. It is as if I am saying to someone who is about to enter a rain storm without an umbrella, "You will get wet if you go out into the rain storm without an umbrella." It is absurd and ridiculous to say something so obvious as "You're going to get wet" to someone who is about to go out into a rainstorm without an umbrella, because under the circumstances, "getting wet" is so obvious. In this case, we have no problem in understanding the obvious, and, in a similar manner, we should also realize the fact that death being the final stage of growth is just as obvious. In the words of Elisabeth Kübler-Ross quoted earlier:

... death is inevitable. We will all die, it is only a matter of time. Death is as much a part of human existence, of human growth and development, as being born. It is one of the few things in life we can count on, that we can be assured will occur [7, p. x].

and further her statement that:

This, then, is the meaning of *DEATH: the Final Stage of Growth*: All that you are and all that you've done and been is culminated in your death [7, p. x].

All that one is and all that one has done is culminated in death. Consequently, there is probably no other event in life, perhaps aside from birth, that should be taken so seriously. It is obvious to me at least that the whole point behind the historical Siddhārtha becoming an enlightened being was to address specifically the question of death. When one understands the significance of death, one will be in a position to confront dis-ease that characterizes one's existence, to confront desire or attachment that causes the dis-ease, to come to some resolution of one's attachments and desires so that one is in control of one's own life and not tossed about by one's fear and uncertainty, and finally to get on with living fully in the moment so that there will be nothing left undone.

To live fully in the moment does not mean to live life superficially as if life had no pain, no distractions, no feelings of loneliness or grief. On the contrary, to live life fully means to live in the very instant (recall my term insta-centric") of pain, distraction, loneliness, or grief so that when death is encountered, whether it be one's own or someone close, one will not have the regret of not having fulfilled one's life fully. The wisdom of Elisabeth Kübler-Ross expressed in the following statement must be respected:

Whether you die at a young age or when you are older is less important than whether you have fully lived the years you have had. One person may live more in eighteen years than another does in eighty. By living, we do not mean frantically accumulating a range and quantity of experience valued in fantasy by others. Rather, we mean living each day as if it is the only one you have. We mean finding a sense of peace and strength to deal with life's disappointments and pain while always striving to discover vehicles to make more accessible, increase, and sustain the joys and delights of life. One such vehicle is learning to focus on some of the things you have learned to tune out—to notice and take joy in the budding of new leaves in the spring, to wonder at the beauty of the sun rising each morning and setting each night, to take comfort in the smile or touch of another person, to watch with amazement the growth of a child, and to share in children's wonderfully "uncomplexed," enthusiastic, and trusting approach to living. To live [7, pp. x-xi].

4. RITUALS, MOURNING AND FUNERAL CUSTOMS, MEMORIAL SERVICES

In the Buddhist tradition, the various rituals, periods of mourning, and funeral service are meant to aid someone (be it that the someone is the one who is dying or is the one who is in the actual face to face encounter with death) to understand the source of sorrow. In order to have the bereaved understand the source of sorrow, as soon as someone dies, the Buddhist priest, if not already present at the place of death, is called to perform a "pillow service." At this time, the priest recites a short sutra, says words of condolence, and reinforces upon the mind of the bereaved the fact that a loved one has died. It may seem unnecessary to reinforce the fact that a loved one has died, but often the bereaved is unwilling to concede to death. The role of the deceased as an Enlightened Buddha, that is one who teaches others the fact of impermanence, is also emphasized.

After the pillow service, the deceased is sent to the funeral home. After the bereaved family returns home, the members of the Buddhist church come to help the family prepare for the funeral service. The members also help the family with cooking and other household chores so that the family members can attend to the preparation of the funeral service. At the funeral service, sutra is chanted, incense is offered, a sermon on the impermanence of life and the importance of the deceased as an enlightened being who, for the benefit of humankind, teaches the reality of impermanence is given, words of condolence are received, and a representative of the family gives words of thanks to the people who attended. A custom that probably originates in East Asia is a practice of bringing money in an envelop to the funeral. This money is given to the family to help cover the funeral expenses. It is not uncommon for the funeral homes to give a 10 percent discount to Buddhist families, because with the money that people bring, the Buddhist family is able to pay for the funeral in full within a day of the funeral. After the funeral, the body is sent to either the graveyard or to a crematorium. There again, a short service of sutra chanting and sermon on impermanence is given. It is also customary for the Buddhist family to meet every seven days for forty-nine days in order to recollect the life of the deceased and to listen to the Buddha's teachings. These services are attended by many of the people from the community and, consequently, these services serve to help and support the family go through the period of bereavement.

It is the caregiver, usually the Buddhist priest, who must direct the bereaved to the source from which the pain of loneliness and of bereavement arises. In the Buddhist tradition the source is understood to be delusion, attachment, and anger, technically known as the "three poisons."

"Delusion," as indicated above, refers to one's inability to confront the impermanence of life. As a result one is "attached" to the idea that death, for example, is not a part of one's life and also that death does not mean the end of one's existence. If one were to find out that one faces an incurable disease such as cancer or AIDS, one will become very perplexed and angry mainly owing to the fact that one feels deprived of life that properly belongs to one. When one becomes perplexed and angry, then perplexity and anger nourishes the deluded mind, and so the endless cycle of delusion, attachment, and anger continues. In order to stop this samsaric existence of going around in circles, one must realize that life is impermanent, is without any substantive permanency, and consequently is not something to which one should be attached. Because attachment is an emotional state which is very difficult to overcome, the caregiver must try to encourage the bereaved person to see or to appreciate the magnificence of the moment or the instant regardless of how difficult the moment or instant may seem. How is one to accomplish this? A few examples from my work as a clergy may help to clarify this.

During my role as a clergy, there were opportunities to assist some in coping with the daily problems of life and to assist others who were completely at a loss because the mother, father, brother, son, or some other member of the family died or ran away to find a new form of life. There were occasions in which I had the opportunity to console a woman whose husband died in a car accident but whose five-year-old daughter and she survived, the opportunity to sit quietly with a mother of a young man whose dream of being an olympic skier was crushed when he rammed himself into a tree and became paralyzed below his hips, and the opportunity to alleviate the pains of the parents who had to come to terms not only with the unexpected reality of their robust son's unforeseen coma but also with having to give consent to remove the life supports that sustained his breathing. In each case, someone was in need of care and I had to depend upon my understanding of Buddhism to respond to these situations. Although I have not been trained as an expert in the field of giving care and palliative care, I would like to share the following experiences with you. (I have refrained from using the names of individuals in order to protect the identity of the people, the whereabouts of whom I no longer know.)

Case I: Giving Care to Those With Worldly Concerns

To find a bride from Japan for many of the available Japanese bachelors was a recurrent event in the Japanese-Canadian experience. Although these events responded to the needs of the young Japanese bachelors, there was always a problem of the Japanese-Canadian spouse not understanding the historical Japanese background that these women represented. The women quickly adapted and absorbed the way of life in Canada. However, because of the long cultural-history of Japan and the terrific technological and scientific advances in Japan, often these ladies were much more cultured, educated, and less old-fashioned than their spouses who were nourished in very ancient Japanese customs. Consequently, although from the Canadian perspective the problem faced in such marriages were seen to originate from the women, I saw my role as someone whose duty it was to point out the mutual interdependence of the two cultures and countries. Consequently, rather than siding with either the husband or the wife, I tried to get both to understand their respect perspectives in the relationship. In clinical terms, I tried not to make one or the other the patient or the savior. Rather, I attempted to bring about an understanding of mutuality. There was, however, one case where, for the sake of the sanity of one of the spouses, I counseled one of them to leave the other.

Case II: Giving Care to the Bereaved

There was an occasion in which I had the opportunity to console a woman whose husband died in a car accident but whose five-year-old daughter survived. This family, on a vacation during the summer, was traveling through Banff National Park. For some reason, the husband had to make a quick decision to avert an oncoming car and turned the steering wheel, out of habit, to the left so that the car slammed head on to another oncoming car. The reaction of turning the steering wheel to the left is a subconscious act that arises naturally in a driver from Japan or any other country, such as England, where the traffic normally flows on the left side of the road. In any event, the husband was killed instantly, and when the wife was brought to the hospital she was still unconscious. The child who was virtually unharmed was in a state of shock and loneliness. Although the husband was conversant in English, neither the wife nor the child had a complete grasp of the English language.

I was called in to arrange the funeral for the husband, because the company for whom the husband worked happened to have a branch office in Calgary and the manager of that branch happened to know about me. Other than the manager of the Calgary branch, everyone else was a total stranger to me. Fortunately, the time I spent during my graduate studies in Japan enabled me to deal with this case totally in the Japanese language. This was somewhat more comforting to me than the time that I was faced with doing a funeral service for a young Chinese man who was killed by a ricochetting bullet or the time I was called to the hospital to perform a service for a Chinese man who died of old age. The Chinese situation gave me concern because, even though I was somewhat familiar with Chinese culture through my reading, I was unfamiliar with the actual customs of a particular Chinese people.

When the woman regained her consciousness, I introduced myself and tried to get her to understand that she was in safe hands and that her daughter was fine. I felt very strongly that, as well as comforting her, she needed to know that someone who spoke her language was near at hand. Often people who can get along in a foreign country even to the degree of shopping and handling the daily affairs of the family are totally at a loss when it comes to an emergency situation. One of the assumptions we make when we visit patients is that because the patient understands English, she or he will be comfortable even in a hospital situation.

From my own experience of being ill in a foreign country, I know that even the ability to speak the foreign language of that country did not bring comfort to me whose mother tongue was English. The reason for the discomfort, I believe, is that to simply know a language even at native fluency does not nourish the cultural and social assumptions of one's own culture. This is something I have learned to keep in mind when dealing with people whose social-cultural background is not grounded in the Canadian soil. However, because the bereaved needs to be comforted, to speak in that person's mother tongue aids the person to gain a sense of comfort more quickly than otherwise.

Case III: Comforting a Mother and a Young Man Who Became Paralyzed

The departure with his companions of an olympic team workout in Canada must have been an exciting moment for this young man from Japan who looked forward to training for his downhill skiing medal. However, human existence is such that one never knows what is in store. He came to Canada with the dream of becoming a olympic star; however, he was not so fortunate. On his way down the mountain slope he lost control and hit a tree. The impact affected his lower spine so that he could not feel anything in his legs nor could he control them any more. My meeting with him was after the accident in the trauma room of the hospital. He was unable to speak English. He knew that the impact was severe, but he was not totally aware of the extent of his injury. He was alone until his mother flew in from Japan to be by his side. The mother, of course, knew no English so my role was to make her as comfortable as possible in a foreign environment and in a situation which did not look too promising for her son. Gradually, the son was given physical therapy treatments so that he could move his arms more easily. The mother was worried that when they returned, her son would not get the medical attention that he was receiving in the Canadian hospital. During my discussions with her, I tried to have her understand how the human situation evolves through the dynamics of causes and conditions and that neither she nor her son needed to feel that the accident occurred as a result of some divine intervention intended to condemn an act that either she or he or some member of the family may have done previously. During the weeks that followed, special Japanese food requested by the son was taken to him. When a Japanese becomes ill, there is a certain kind of plum pickle that often perks up the person and that was what he wanted. The pickle was helpful but what was important for the healing process of the son and the mother was for them to realize and to accept the probable condition of the son becoming disabled. Once they were able to accept the fact, they were able to get on with their life. A letter from the son indicated that he was able to get physiotherapy in Japan and that slowly he was finding new ways to mobilize himself.

Case IV: The Unexpected Reality of the Son's Unforeseen Coma

I received a phone call from the trauma unit of the local hospital because a Japanese person was admitted owing to a stroke. When I arrived at the hospital the man was hooked up to various monitors that indicated his heartbeat, his temperature, and the lack of certain kinds of brain waves. The man was very young and of such a great build that it was difficult for me to believe that someone who looked so healthy and strong could meet such a disaster. Still, the reality of a person lying on the bed attached to life support through all kinds of wires and tubes was confronting me in a manner that could not be denied. I asked the nurse about the family and was told that the parents who lived in eastern Canada were informed and that they would probably arrive by air the next day. I requested the nurse to inform me of their arrival and then left.

When the phone rang, I sensed that it would be the nurse informing me of the parent's arrival. I went immediately to the hospital and found the parents in a state of dismay. They were unwilling to accept that their son was in state of coma and only the life support sustained his life. I was asked by the doctor and the nurse to inform the parents of this situation and to obtain their consent to remove the life support, because the son was brain-dead and there was absolutely no chance of his revival. My task was to alleviate the pains of the parents who could not and would not come to terms with the unexpected reality of their robust son's unforeseen coma and consequently were totally unwilling to give consent to have the life supports removed. The questions that they faced were: How do we truly know that there is no chance for the son to recover? What happens if there should be the slightest chance that the son would have recovered had the life support not been removed? How do we know that the hospital staff had done all that it could to come to such a conclusion?

I could see that the situation was not conducive to a discussion on the removal of the life support. I stayed with the parents in the trauma room for some time and then suggested that perhaps we should retire to another room where we could sit down and relax a bit. We went to the room and sat down. I asked them where they came from, about their life with their son, what kind of a son he was, and so on, so that I could contextualize any comments that I might make at a later time within the comfort of their past experiences with their son. Because they were Buddhist of the Japanese Jodo Shin Shu (True Pure Land Tradition) they were familiar with the teaching of gratitude and appreciation.

It is understandable that to deliver care to someone who has even a negligible understanding of a religious tradition is easier than sharing life's woes with someone who has no religious background at all. But the fact of the matter is that, from a Buddhist perspective, anyone who has an interest in staying alive or an interest in dying already has ample religious background. This means that all sentient beings are already immersed in religion. From this assumption, I began to talk to the parents about the unique occasion of being born as human being. The uniqueness comes from the fact that it is in human existence that each has the opportunity to reflect upon one's own life and to make of it what one will. I asked whether they found their life enriched by the life of their son. They replied how much joy and meaning the son gave them. I asked them to reflect upon what feelings the son might have if he could see the pain that his parents were undergoing. They responded that he would be tormented if he could see their pain. Gradually, I was able to get the parents to understand that life and death are both conditioned states of being. When the condition for life is present then life will take place. When the condition for illness is present illness will take place. When the condition for death is present death will take place. No one is able to escape death. Moreover, when one has not lived in the appreciation of conditioned existence, then each event in life will become a burden and cause pain. Thus, for the parents to truly live in the appreciation of their son, they must live in appreciation of having encountered the life of their son. Further, because each being is in some way a teacher of life's process and because such a teacher can be no other than an enlightened being, i.e., a buddha, they should realize that their son in his state of coma is emanating the reality of impermanence. Gradually through discussions like those that went on for several days, the parents, first the father then the mother, were able to let go of their desire to keep the son in a constant state of coma. On the fourth day, both parents were able to reach a resolution and allow their son to rest peacefully. The life supports were removed and within two hours the son took his last breath.

5. CONCLUSION

To die is not easy. To live is not any easier. Both life and death are difficult to accomplish. I believe that Elisabeth Kübler-Ross makes explicit the ideas discussed above when she states:

> . . . it is those who have not really lived—who have left issues unsettled, dreams unfulfilled, hopes shattered, and who have let the real things in life (loving and being loved by others, contributing in a positive way to other people's happiness and welfare, finding out what things are *really you*) pass them by—who are most reluctant to die [7, p. x].

To this statement by Elisabeth Kübler-Ross, I wish only to add one final Buddhistic comment to those in bereavement. "It is those who have not really lived who are most reluctant to let die."

REFERENCES

1. D. L. Thrapp, Buddhist Helps Solace Sick at L. A. Hospital, *Los Angeles Times,* Sunday, February 23, 1973. Recorded in Aoyama, Tesshi, *OYA-GOKORO KO-GOKORO* (Parental Heart, Child's Heart), Nagata Bunshodo, Kyoto, 1984.
2. D. P. Irish, Multiculturalism and the Majority Population, in *Ethnic Variations in Dying, Death, and Grief: Diversity in Universality,* D. P. Irish, F. Lundquist, and V. Jenkins Nelson (eds.), Taylor and Francis, Washington, D.C., 1993.
3. P. C. Rosenblatt, Cross-Cultural Variation in the Experience, Expression, and Understanding of Grief, in *Ethnic Variations in Dying, Death and Grief: Diversity in Universality,* Taylor and Francis, Washington, D.C., 1993.
4. M. S. Sangharakshita, *The Three Jewels: An Introduction to Buddhism,* Windhorse Publications, Surrey, 1977.
5. B. Ñanmoli and B. Bodhi, Sammaditthi Sutta (Right View), in *The Middle Length Discourses of the Buddha. A New Translation of the Majjima Nikaya,* Wisdom Publications, Boston, 1995.
6. B. Ñanmoli and B. Bodhi, Introduction, in *The Middle Length Discourses of the Buddha. A New Translation of the Majjima Nikaya,* Wisdom Publications, Boston, 1995.
7. E. Kübler-Ross, *Death: The Final Stage of Growth,* Prentice-Hall, Englewood Cliffs, New Jersey, 1975.
8. C. E. Moustakas, *Loneliness,* Prentice-Hall, Englewood Cliffs, New Jersey, 1961.
9. J. B. Long, The Death that Ends Death in Hinduism and Buddhism, in *Death: The Final Stage of Growth,* E. Kübler-Ross (ed.), Prentice Hall, Englewood Cliffs, New Jersey, 1975.

CHAPTER 9

From Mourning to Morning

Rev. Sally S. Bailey

Eleven years following her mother's death a young woman, now seventeen, telephoned me at the hospice to ask if I had a copy of the poem which her mother wrote shortly before her death. I was happy to tell her that I did and that one of her mother's wishes also had been fulfilled in the poem's being published and included in the arts book, *Creativity and the Close of Life* [1].

A time was soon set for the daughter to return to the hospice, where I presented her with a copy of the book containing her mother's poem and picture. We reminisced awhile about the days the daughter had come with her brother and sister to visit their mother when the latter had been a patient and the legacy they had been left. While at the hospice, their mother had created gifts for them in metalsmithing and a variety of crafts. As a family, they enjoyed times together listening to music and stories. Two occasions in particular come to mind.

The first involved a poet in residence who read an English translation of the original Grimm Brothers version *Snow White* to the patient and her children and mother. The poet recounted how they were enchanted with the familiar story of the beautiful Snow White laid to ruin by the jealous and evil queen. The children latched on to the entertainment of the fairy tale story while the patient and her mother began to see a deeper significance in Snow White's death by the poisoned apple. It quickly became a metaphor for the cancer that was taking the young mother's life.

In the original story, when the young prince awakens Snow White, he says to her something on the order of "come and you shall live with me in my father's house," to which Snow White happily accedes. Despite their love for her, the seven dwarfs readily concur. The powerful Christ-like image of the line struck home with those listening to the reading. Tears welled softly in the mother's eyes as she envisioned her daughter, like Snow White, raised from the death of her body. At the end of the story, the patient nodded to the poet knowingly and everyone laughed in a cathartic release at both the comedy and the significance of the tale. I recall that the poet and patient had previously discussed which stories might help her children come to grips with the reality of her dying—hence, the original Grimm Brothers version of *Snow White* was chosen for that particular day.

The second occasion occurred in conjunction with a time when the patient was singing favorite songs with several other patients and their family members in the common room of the hospice. Prior to the young mother's in-patient admission, I had visited her at home and was aware of her gift of writing in the poem she showed me. Therefore, I asked her if she had brought the poem with her so it could be shared with the group. She replied that I could find a copy of the poem at her bedside which I fetched. The poem was untitled and originally written in the masculine gender. However, on hearing it, the group suggested that the poem was more a description of the patient, she agreed, and, in self-affirmation, she changed the gender and retitled the poem with her own name, *Karen*. It became a legacy of the strength of her last days.

It was this poem for which the patient's daughter was looking. Before the patient had died, each member of her family had received a copy of the poem. However, they were a broken family and following their mother's death the three children were taken to live in the homes of relatives. Ten years later, the daughter had gone to live with her father. By this time, she had none of the mementos but only the memories of her mother. One included the poem which she sought as something tangible to remember her by.

I chose to begin this chapter with this patient family story as an illustration of the contribution engagements with art forms can make to people's lives, particularly at a time of dying and bereavement. For the patient, one can see days that were made more meaningful and joy-filled as she created gifts for her family and subsequently for her roommates in the hospice. There were times through sharing stories and music that tears of mourning when anticipating her death, as well as peaks of laughter from spontaneous humorous moments, came forth. And, finally through her poem, the patient was able to say with affirmation:

KAREN

She stands as an entity
A warrior of life
Of freedom
A lover of mankind

Proud and astute
Her world remains
Her own private manifestation

Unforeseen displays of girl-like antics

Emerge intermittently
Creating a surprising revelation
Of her seemingly infallible nature

The depth of her warmth and love

Is so intense
That only with profound perception
Can its existence be recognized

Her unique quality
Her being
The worth of life   [1, pp. 67-68]

The patient's daughter in this story was the youngest of the three children. What became of the others, I do not know. However, when this daughter returned to the hospice so many years later remembering the experiences from her childhood when her mother was dying and remembering there was a special poem her mother had written, I realized even more how significant *every* moment is when we accompany people on their journey to death. I saw anew how important that people who are left behind have "something to remember them by." The mementos or memories of shared experiences become a life-line to root one to the past, to one's history, and to one's identity as a person.

At the same time, one must agree with Dietrich Bonhoeffer who said: "We must take care not to wallow in our memories or hand ourselves over to them, just as we do not gaze all the time at it as a valuable present, but only at special times, and apart from these keep it simply as a hidden treasure that is ours for certain. In this way, the past gives us lasting joy and strength" [2, p. 176]. Hopefully the poem has become for the daughter that valuable present to be read at special times and kept as a hidden treasure which will give lasting joy and strength as she goes forward in life which will be intertwined always with moments of sadness, too, because the daughter is bereft of her mother.

Thus, to understand more fully the role of the arts in relation to dying and bereavement, one can say that engaging in the arts enables persons to mourn, to grieve, and to celebrate life. And, as the above story illustrates, there will be times when it may be difficult to discern the movement from mourning to celebrating or from celebrating to mourning. For the reality is that, that which has brought one much joy in life also can bring one the deepest grief in experiencing the absence of that which brought one joy.

This is another reason why the integration of creative and/or artistic experiences in the lives of all persons, and especially those who are dying and those who care for them, is so essential. Creative expression and/or engaging in the arts, help empty one's pain of heart which may be evoked by the visual images in the arts or sounds in music or nature which call forth tears of mourning when linked to memories of past losses. New works of art are often born out of the times of mourning. One only has to look at compositions of music, literature, poetry, and visual art to see that many of them were birthed through the composer's, writer's, or artist's grief.

What continues to inspire me is seeing the new creations and positive growth which takes place in the lives of persons who are dying when they have been given opportunities and avenues for creative expression. People who are suffering and, particularly, those who are confronting life-threatening illnesses, are longing "to be heard." For some, their statements will come through their words in poems, such as *Karen*, or reflective essays from journals they have kept, or life stories that are passed down from generation to generation. For others, their statements will come through the songs they have sung, dances they have danced, music they have played, or their crafted works of art in a variety of media, photo collections, and/or well-tended gardens.

And what kinds of statements do the dying make? They will include expressions of fear, rage, and anger, as well as faith, hope, and love just like the statements of any person who is living with the realities of life. However, those living with life-threatening illnesses with whom I've worked through the years have focused on developing their innate and unique creative gifts. As one cancer patient, who is an artist, said to me, "I can't do abstract collages anymore. I need to make a statement through my work now." A social activist, her artwork is more powerful at this time, both aesthetically, as well as in the subjects she portrays than before she was stricken. As she has wrestled with the reality that her physical body is temporal, she has also found a new freedom in her life that is reflected in her art.

A particularly heroic example of a contemporary artist's confrontation with her diagnosis of metastatic breast cancer is an exhibit of fourteen paintings by Hollis Sigler, entitled, *Breast Cancer Journal: Walking with the Ghosts of My Grandmother*. This Chicago artist, whose mother and great grandmother died of breast cancer, illustrates through her paintings her own spiritual and emotional journey as a breast cancer patient. Sigler is one of the many artists and writers whose works in the past five to ten years reflect their confrontations with life-threatening illnesses.

It should be noted that there is a growing consciousness, both on this continent and abroad, that the arts contribute to the quality of life of persons as well as help create the environment in which care is given. An increasing number of hospices have included arts programs and/or positions for artists in residence in their hospices. Likewise, major teaching hospitals have begun to develop varieties of cultural and/or arts programs to support patients and families and caregivers. This is further reflected in such organizations as International Arts in Medicine and The Society for the Arts in Healthcare. Hospice Arts along with several arts in healthcare organizations have formed in the United Kingdom. In Europe, the Arts in Hospital movement is sponsored by United Nations Educational, Scientific and Cultural Organization (UNESCO).

An outgrowth of the institutional integration of the arts in the healthcare setting has been the incorporation of the arts in support groups for persons with life-threatening illnesses such as cancer, HIV and AIDS, and for persons who are bereaved. Artists are working in conjunction with therapists with bereaved children, in particular. An increasing number of adult bereavement groups are including opportunities for the bereft to create and engage with the arts. One has only to look at the AIDS quilt as a manifestation of how bereaved persons give expression to their grief as well as hope. This is one of the functions of memorials. They are created to help us re-member.

Much work has been done with Holocaust survivors on this continent and abroad integrating the arts. A vivid example, both in its architecture as well as contents, is the Holocaust Museum in Washington, D.C. Visiting it, one not only relives the horror of the atrocities, which led to the millions of deaths, but also there are spaces designed within the museum where persons may experience comfort and transcendence. Likewise, in Japan, survivors of the atomic bomb have been assisted in processing their grief and losses through their creations. One of the classic stories that has arisen is that of *Sadako and the Thousand Paper Cranes* by Eleanor Coerr [3], which is based on the life of a real little girl who lived in Japan from 1943 to 1955. She was two when the bomb was dropped on Hiroshima and died of leukemia ten years later as a result of radiation from the bomb. Sadako had folded 644 origami cranes believing that if she folded 1,000 cranes, she would be well again. The flock of cranes hung above her bed on strings. Her classmates folded the rest.

Her story continues to inspire people throughout the world. In 1958, a statue of Sadako was unveiled in the Hiroshima Peace Park, standing on top of a granite mountain of paradise. Sadako is holding a golden crane in outstretched hands. In addition to being overwhelmed by my visit to Hiroshima, I will always remember the awe I felt in seeing at the base of Sadako's statue the thousands of strings of a thousand paper cranes which have been brought by visitors from throughout the world who visit her memorial and leave the paper cranes they make in her honor, much like people leave flowers at the graves of loved ones.

Following the Oklahoma City terrorist bombing of the Federal Building where over a hundred innocent adults and children were killed, the survivors and city officials knew that another office building must not be built on the site of the former building. Thus, they have begun to re-claim and design the space as an aesthetic living memorial.

My experience of visiting any kind of a memorial is that they should help us who survive to not run from the pain of the past, but rather weave the experiences of the past into the tapestry of our lives, from which our lives can be transformed.

As previously mentioned, some of the greatest art has been born out of experiences of grief. Throughout history it has been the artists and people of faith who have searched for meaning and wrestled with the issues of dying, death, and bereavement. Therefore, may we look more closely at the function of creativity and engaging with the arts in our lives and how these experiences may assist persons cope with matters of death and bereavement.

The arts help to keep our imaginations alive and maintain our connection to the earth and the created order of the universe. For this is what the arts are all about. They are reflections and expressions of our engagement with our environment, with our surroundings, with our "grassroots." The arts and creativity connect us to the energy and breath of life; that is, the spirit. When we are cut off from the breath of life, we die both literally and figuratively. By staying in touch with our creativity, our imaginations are heightened to be alive to what confronts us, be it a life-threatening illness or the tremendous problems of injustice in our world.

In many ways it is difficult to write or speak about the arts because one can really only understand the arts by experiencing them in every facet of one's being. However, for the purposes of this chapter it might be helpful, broadly and simply, to define the arts as the creative manifestations of a person's response to one's surroundings through a variety of media (i.e., words, music, movement, film, paint, wood, stone, glass, metal, cloth, yarn, plants, etc.).

A creative artistic person works in a particular medium to make order out of what she or he may be experiencing. For, as Simone Weil has stated: "The first of the soul's needs, the one which touches most nearly its eternal destiny, is order" [4, p. 9]. Order is a conduit for truth. Therefore, one might say that the arts function to make truth more real to us, particularly the ineffable truths of life.

You may ask, "What do the arts do?" The arts serve as regenerators of body, mind, emotions, and spirit. The whole person is touched when one engages with an art form. The arts enable people to find meaning for their lives, to become reconnected to their spiritual roots, to the source of life, to overcome the fragmentation of their lives. Engaging in the arts or creative process can enable people to become a more whole person.

How is a person regenerated in body, mind, emotions, and spirit when engaging with the arts? One way to illustrate engaging with the environment and the act of creation may be seen in Figure 1.

We receive images and sounds from the environment through the senses of our body. The images are processed through our emotions, spirit, and mind, and become inspirations/ideas that move through the body and are given form in other images and sounds. Thus, through the creative process, connections to each dimension of one's self are made. All parts of one's being are regenerated. We respond to the images and sounds in a variety of ways, depending on the meanings the images and/or sounds may have for us.

In the examples given earlier in this chapter, we can see that experiences in the arts and creative expression have enabled people to mourn, grieve, and

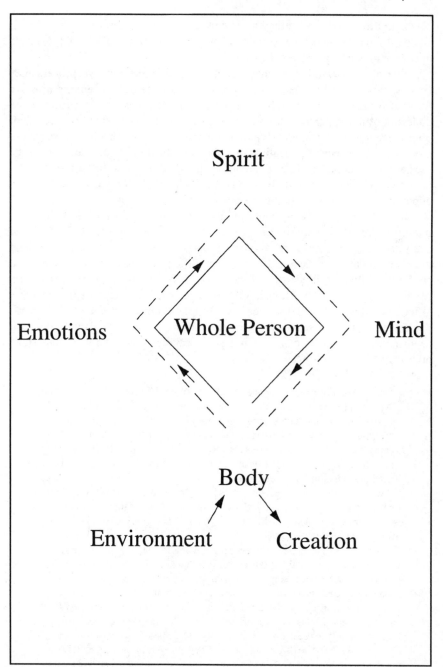

Figure 1.

celebrate life . . . to live as they are dying. Even Zorba clearly understands this when he sings, "Life is what you do, when you're waiting to die . . ." [5], which opens the musical by Ebb and Kander.

I've also observed that when people engage in the creative process they become reconnected to their spiritual roots, the source of their energy to move forward on their journey of life. In the past twenty years, I've accompanied hundreds of dying persons, their families, and caregivers as they've made their pilgrimage toward death, and I've seen the transformations that have occurred in their lives. I've seen that healing from within which is about tuning in to the images and symbols inside us that continually speak to us—calling forth whole-ness and well-being for our lives—can be facilitated by providing people with opportunities to engage with the arts and creative expression.

In addition to creativity and the arts facilitating healing from within, one might say that these experiences also contribute to the growth of the soul and one's quest for a raison d'etre. Accompanying persons as they search for meaning has been one of the richest privileges of my life, particularly when they have to confront debilitating illnesses and have been given so much grace to live with courage and joy in the midst of it. One such person was John, an artist who was gifted in clothes design and fabrication. For me he summarizes why it's impera-tive for all of us to discover our creative centers, claim our creative gifts, and deepen our spirituality to continue living—especially as we enter that "final stage of growth." Listen to John:

> I find that one day someone asked me, "What is it John, that keeps you alive?" And there are a number of possible answers to that, that have to do with the kind of love and support I get from my family and friends which is tremendous. I have the best medical support that money can buy, I have tremendous faith in God, I have a sort of courage to face this. But what really keeps me going is my love of beauty and my desire to see it, witness it, name it, and make it, and I've been blessed with many talents so that my chance to be with beauty, to make beauty, is great and I'm happiest when I'm working. I have worked all my life every day even in the context of this disease which is sometimes completely debilitating, I try to work every day. There is no excuse not to work.
>
> People ask me if I pray. I don't pray in any formal way but I work. My work is praying. Each thing I do is a prayer thanking God for the gifts he has given me. Each time I complete a piece, it's my way of giving thanks. And each prayer, each piece is a question that I ask about how is this possible in such a crazy world, in such a difficult situation with terminal illness and such an intense relationship to my mortality. How can I keep being drawn toward life, toward self-expression, toward beauty? The whole process of living with a disease like AIDS is a very big game of Twenty Questions. Fortunately, it's not limited to just twenty, it's like a million questions and every day I get to ask them and every day that I get to work, as I ask my questions, I'm able to move though life. . . .

Throughout the days of his dying, John indeed "worked" to complete a hooked rug which included his self-portrait and images of things that had special meaning for him. The piece was finished as a wall hanging and gift to his family. This is another observation I've made in working with the dying. They have a deep need to give something to others that is beyond their wanting to be remembered. Infirmed persons become weary of always being cared for. They seek to be able to give to others, too; and opportunities for creative expression can assist them in meeting this need.[1]

Another longing the dying have is the need to feel "normal"—not to be treated as "the patient with this or that disease." Facilitating opportunities for creative expression or engaging with the arts can contribute to the person's feelings of naturalness or normalcy both as a creative person as well as maintaining or creating an environment which is aesthetically comforting.

Do the needs for creative expression or engaging in the arts for bereaved persons differ from those persons who have died? Just as the creations of the dying may also reflect their fears, angst, or grief, as well as transcendence or joy, so too, the creations of the bereft will express a variety of feelings.

The bereaved may seek concrete mementos such as the poem Karen's daughter sought. Others will have no tangible objects that the dead person left or made for them, but only the memories of life shared with the other. This particularly is the experience of persons whose homes and lives have been devastated by natural disaster or war. Thus, the bereft's task will be to create something new out of the loss. This will be more easily accomplished if the bereaved persons have been in touch with their creative centers prior to their loss.

Again, we may turn to the masters in any of the art forms and see the creations that arose out of their losses in life. However, we should not be intimidated by the works of the masters in developing our creativity, because all persons are imbued with a creative spirit that can be expressed in a multitude of ways. Creativity may be seen in ideas to solve problems or create life enriching experiences as well as in works in a variety of media.

From my years of experience, I could cite many examples of creative expressions of the bereaved which range from a wife's designing her husband's tombstone, to a daughter's writing a poignant essay a year following her father's death, to a man composing a symphonic elegy following the death of his orchestra colleague, to parents who facilitated the publication of their artist/author son's book. However, space allows only for details of two of my favorite stories to illustrate how creativity and the arts helped facilitate comfort and healing following the death of their family member.

---

[1] On this subject, see my previous Creativity and the Close of Life, in *Dying, Death and Bereavement*, I. Corless, B. Germino, and M. Pittman (eds.), Jones and Bartlett, Boston, pp. 327-335, 1994.

The first is of a young girl of seven, one of three children, who had a difficult time verbalizing her feelings on losing her mother. The hospice social worker requested that a ceramist on the arts staff accompany her on several home visits to the children. Through working with the artist, the child was enabled to express her fear and sadness surrounding her mother's death through the creation of a large green dragon and a nest of five dragon's eggs (there were 5 members in her family). However, one egg was broken and bleeding. The child's pain of heart became visible through her creative clay work and became a way for her to communicate with others how she was experiencing her mother's death. In addition, clay became a medium in which she continued to work and found comfort and joy for her life in the following months.

The concluding story is of C.J. and her father who was a writer and loved to read and listen to music accompanied by his daughter both at his bedside and in the hospice commons with other patient families. While he was a patient, they crafted pieces in clay and also participated in a joint watercolor project which were facilitated by staff artists. Two brightly watercolored butterflies became part of a collage with a brief Emmet Fox essay entitled, "Worm Gets Ideas" that alluded to metamorphosis. Both C.J. and her father had a delightful sense of humor and easily talked with each other about the reality of his dying and death (his metamorphosis) as they worked on their art projects together.

Following the father's death, I visited C.J. in her home where she took pride in showing me the pieces they had made and which she has "to remember him by." However, the collage was presented to the hospice as one of the permanent works of art. It was sometime later when I removed the collage from the wall to use it as an illustration for a lecture on the topic of death and transcendence through the arts that I discovered that C.J. had written something on the back of the collage. For me the words also summarize the reflections I've presented in this chapter as to the significance of the arts and creativity in enabling people to address issues of death and bereavement:

We all move from mourning to morning.

REFERENCES

1. S. Bailey et al. *Creativity and the Close Life,* Connecticut Hospice, Connecticut, 1990.
2. D. Bonhoeffer, *Letters and Papers from Prison,* Collier, New York, 1971.
3. E. Coerr, *Sadako and the Thousand Paper Cranes,* Dell, New York, 1977.
4. S. Weil, *A Need for Roots,* Routledge & Paul, London, 1952.
5. F. Ebb and J. Kander, *Zorba,* Hal Leonard, Winona, 1968.

CHAPTER 10

The Use of Music as Therapy with the Dying and Bereaved

Lora Koenig Heller and Paul Alexander

The focus of this chapter is to show that music therapy provides opportunities for emotional self-expression, decreases the perception of pain, prepares for and develops acceptance of death, offers quality of life to the patient and family, and assists the bereaved throughout the bereavement process. An historical perspective of music therapy and palliative care are included, as well as definitions and a brief description of specific relevant music therapy interventions. Case examples illustrate effective interventions on the hospital or nursing home units and in bereavement support situations. This is a client-centered, process oriented approach to using music listening/imagery, meditation, active music making, rituals, and song writing with terminally ill patients, their families, and the bereaved.

HISTORY

Although music has been recognized as a healing agent since primitive times, music therapy had not emerged as a recognized discipline until this century. The development of music therapy as an organized profession based on common goals and standards of practice began with "the need to make music applicable to the scientific aspects of medicine in the 20th century . . ." [1, p. 35].

Musician Eva Vescelius, who founded the National Therapeutic Society of New York City in 1903, was a significant influence on many who pursued music as therapy in the early part of this century. She provided music with classifications based on the emotions elicited, and prescribed specific music for various ailments.

The Society dissolved at the time of Vescelius' death in 1917, although the use of music in hospitals continued to increase. In 1926, Isa Maud Islen founded the National Association for Music in Hospitals. A Norwegian immigrant with extensive experience as a nurse, hospital administrator, and music director, Islen saw the need for an organization supporting the therapeutic use of music in hospitals.

Harriet Ayer Seymour, another early advocate of music as therapy, brought live music to New York hospitals and prisons during the 1930s. This work, in connection with the Federal Music Project of the Works Project Administration (WPA), led to her involvement with the classification of songs based on their psychological and physiological effects. In 1941, Seymour founded and presided over the National Foundation for Music Therapy.

The first comprehensive institutional music therapy program was established by Willem Van de Wall in 1923 at Pennsylvania's Allentown State Hospital for Mental Diseases. The components of his program became prototype for music therapy programs across the United States. Ira M. Altshuler, a psychiatrist and composer, founded another significant early music therapy program at Wayne County General Hospital in Eloise, Michigan. Altshuler, who wrote and lectured about music therapy throughout the 1930s, 1940s, and 1950s, is still today one of the most widely recognized founding fathers of music therapy principles and practice.

"During the course of their efforts to care for large numbers of soldiers wounded in World War II, physicians discovered that music could not only boost the morale of their patients, but also facilitate their recovery" [1, p. 38]. This led to an increase in the employment of hospital musicians, training in medical and clinical techniques, and college degree programs in music therapy.

The first music therapy curriculum was established in 1944 at what is now Michigan State University. The University of Kansas offered the first didactic and lab course in 1946. The need to provide standards for training in basic clinical techniques still remained, thus leading to the 1950 establishment of the National Association for Music Therapy (NAMT) for the purpose of "the progressive development of the therapeutic use of music in hospital, educational, and community settings, and the advancement of education, training, and research in music therapy" [1, p. 39]. In 1971, the Urban Federation of Music Therapists, later renamed the American Association for Music Therapy, was founded at New York University in New York City. The National and American Associations for Music Therapy plan to merge in 1998 to provide a stronger, more cohesive code of ethics and standards of practice for the field.

PALLIATIVE CARE

Research and documentation of music therapy programs in hospice/palliative care began in the late 1970s with such pioneers as Susan Munro, Sandi Curtis, Ruth Bright, and Lucanne Magill. The music therapy philosophy of promoting physical comfort, emotional expression, social interaction, and spiritual growth through varying aspects of music extends from the Pediatric Palliative Care Unit to the Nursing Home Hospice Care Program, to the Acute Care Hematology/ Oncology Unit.

Susan Munro writes of the multidimensional qualities of music, allowing it to touch many levels of consciousness, meeting physical, psychological, social, and spiritual needs of the patient [2, p. 105]. "Music nourishes like oxygen. It speaks of the continuity of things. It is a thread from the past, through the present, to the future" [2, p. 89]. Music provides a peaceful avenue for a child to understand her/his illness and related emotions, and for an older adult to reflect on lifetime events.

Although definitions are included in this chapter, it is difficult to define specifically music therapy, as it is unique to each and every patient, each and every therapist. In palliative care, the global purpose of music therapy is to enable the patient to live throughout the dying process. Specially trained clinicians offer music and musical interventions to elicit memories from the past, to provide a quality of life for the present, to develop an acceptance of death and a sense of spiritual existence in the future. This process will be different for each patient, as we all have different musical experiences and connections with music.

Children may show an inner awareness of their illness or terminal condition through play, art, and musical expressions with much more comfort than through direct verbal communications. Elisabeth Kübler-Ross addresses this inner knowing in her book *On Children and Death*.

> If people doubt that their children are aware of a terminal illness, they should look at the poems or drawings these children create, often during their illness but sometimes months before a diagnosis is made. It needs to be understood that there is often a pre-conscious awareness and not a conscious, intellectual knowledge. It comes from the "inner spiritual, intuitive quadrant" and gradually prepares the child to face the forthcoming transition even if the grownups deny or avoid the reality [3, p. 134].

Mary, who will be introduced in the case study section, in her own way let me know that she knew what was happening. My experience with her demonstrates the power of art communication and the benefits of therapeutically utilizing music and visualization for pain reduction. I have learned to trust the use of alternate creative modalities in gaining access to the intuitive and unconscious wellsprings that speak loudly if we listen.

DEFINITIONS

Terminally Ill
One diagnosed with a fatal, degenerative condition [1, p. 109].

Palliative Care

To palliate is "to reduce the violence of; abate." In Hospice Care (care of the terminally ill), it means the reduction or abatement of pain and other troubling symptoms by appropriate coordination of all elements of care needed to achieve relief from distress [2, p. vii].

Music Therapy

The controlled use of music, its elements, and their influences on the human being to aid in the physiologic, psychologic, and emotional integration of the individual during the treatment of an illness or disability [2, p. 104]; The prescribed, structured use of music activities under the direction of specially trained personnel (registered or certified music therapist) to influence changes in maladaptive conditions or behaviour patterns, thereby helping clients achieve therapeutic goals [1, p. 5]; Music Therapy Principles—1) The establishment or re-establishment of interpersonal relationships; 2) The bringing about of self-esteem through self-actualization; 3) The utilization of the unique potential of rhythm to energize and bring order [4, p. v].

INTERVENTIONS

Passive *music listening* provides comfort, reflection, motivation, sleep, music mediated guided imagery, progressive muscle relaxation, meditation to assist in decreasing perception of pain, relaxing mind and body, a sense of peace; preparation for and acceptance of death. Music examples: For relaxation, comfort, imagery—*Pianoscapes,* Michael Jones; *Angel Love,* Aeoliah; *A Child's Gift of Lullabyes Rock-a-Bye Collection,* J. Aaron Brown. For reflection on life—*Four Seasons,* Vivaldi; *Memory,* Andrew Lloyd Webber. Imagery of the dying process—*Adagio,* Albinoni.

Music Making provides active involvement in non-threatening form of expression and interaction, diversion from pain, sense of enjoyment; singing, dancing, instrumental improvisation, musical games.

Song writing uses original or familiar melodies and creating lyrics and/or "orchestration" as a means of self-expression. Songs may be written by the therapist, based on patient thoughts and expressions, for use with the patient (i.e., *Mi Cancion*); written by the patient(s) with guidance from the therapist (i.e., *We All Need Chemotherapy*); written by the therapist as a reflection of the patient's situation, and shared with family members or other care givers (i.e., *A Song for You; Just Fly Away*); songs or musical improvisation by the family member(s) in bereavement therapy.

Lyric analysis occurs when active music listening is followed by analysis and discussion of song content, relating issues in song to personal situation. This can be effective with the dying patient (i.e., imagining heaven with *Free to Be You and Me*, title song) or the bereaved family (i.e., *Goodbye?*).

Additional Songs

Grieving: *The Living Years*, Mike and the Mechanics; *Tears in Heaven*, Eric Clapton; *Mama's Arms*, Joshua Kadison; *The Way We Were*, Barbra Streisand. Growing old: *I Wish I Was 18 Again*, George Burns; *Old Folks*, *Old Man in Our Town*, Kenny Rogers; *Honey*, Bobby Goldsboro.

CASE STUDIES

Music Therapy with Terminally Ill Patients in Acute Care and Hospice/Palliative Care

(Names have been changed for confidentiality)

ROBERTO, a ten-year-old Peruvian boy with leukemia, was actively involved in his music therapy interventions, which took place in Spanish, four days a week in an acute care oncology unit. Goals for Roberto were: to provide opportunities for verbal and non-verbal self-expression; to provide bedside support and mood elevation; to provide quality of life. Together Roberto and I, and frequently his family, sang songs in Spanish and English, helping to expand each other's vocabulary in the other language. Roberto always expressed himself in Spanish, and when a song elicited a relevant emotion, he spoke rapidly. He also enjoyed using instruments as sound effects in stories, and using puppets as characters in songs. His affect was bright, and changed appropriately with his mood.

As Roberto's condition became more and more serious, he became resistant to therapy. So I sat beside him quietly playing guitar and occasionally singing in Spanish. I always left some small rhythm instruments on the bed within his reach, and he almost always decided to join in. I wanted to provide Roberto with relaxation and pain management in pre- and post-operative music therapy when he had his "procedures," yet he was once again resistant. He appeared to fear that I may reject him as his condition worsened, so he began to reject me. Shortly before Roberto died, I wrote for him *Mi Cancion (My Song)*, based on his expression of feelings related to the illness, which became "our song" to sing together during each subsequent session. He realized that I would not reject him, and music therapy was once again his safe haven. My goals were met with Roberto, working with him right until his last day; and his family tucked away some invaluable memories of his humor, his laughter, and his music.

MI CANCION	*MY SONG*
(Spanish)	(English)

MI CANCION
(Spanish)
Algunas veces cuando yo tengo
miedo,
   solamente quiero dormir o llorar
Y entonces necesito un beso o abrazo
   A veces no comprendo por que me siento asi.

Hay mucha gente en mi cuarto que son desconocidos
   Y a veces quiero estar solo
   porque me siento enojado
Yo quiero toda mi salud.

Algunas veces cuando yo tengo meido,
   es dificil porque yo no se como
   decirlo   how to say it
Pues voy a cantar mi cancion.

MY SONG
(English)
Sometimes when I feel scared,
   I just want to sleep or cry
And then I need a kiss or hug
   Sometimes I don't understand
   why I feel like this.

There are so many strangers in my room
   and at times I want to be alone
   because I feel angry
I want my health.

Sometimes when I feel scared,
   it's hard because I don't know

So I'm going to sing my song.

Lora Koenig © 1993

JEREMY, a five-year-old child in palliative care with a diagnosis of AIDS, was a passive participant in his music therapy interventions. The following goals were implemented: to provide opportunity for non-verbal self-expression; to provide mood elevation and decreased perception of pain; to provide quality of life. Jeremy's eyes were almost always alert, and he maintained eye contact for several minutes at a time. He occasionally smiled, however his condition deteriorated rapidly and he was in tremendous pain between doses of meds. Music therapy appeared to provide Jeremy with a sense of comfort, with decreased fear and perception of pain, and with the ability to sleep peacefully.

When he no longer responded to children's songs, rhythmic passive range of motion, and instrumental play, music was provided as a comfort—both for the patient and myself. Soft, instrumental music was playing continuously in my absence. Whenever able, I spent significant amounts of time at his bedside playing live guitar while singing original and improvised songs—and one day wrote *Song for You* while helping Jeremy sleep. This song became a comfort to the family as well, when shared at Jeremy's memorial service a few weeks following his death.

SONG FOR YOU

As I watch you sleeping peacefully,
I can't help but feel relieved
There's so much pain inside you,
it is so hard to believe
That you're still fighting . . .

When you lie awake, your eyes so wide,
I sense your unspoken fear
And I want to help you ease the pain
I want to dry the tears
That you are crying . . .

And I'll sing a song for you
You can count on me to be there
And I will comfort you
As the melody just lingers in the air

There are times when I feel helpless
Because I want to find the cure
To give you freedom from your suffering
And a life that can be yours
With no more fighting . . .

But I'll sing a song for you
You can count on me to be there
And I will comfort you
As the melody just lingers in the air

Lora Koenig © 1995

ROSE, eighty-eight years old, was a long time resident of a skilled nursing facility, and placed on hospice care due to her sudden deterioration. Music therapy goals were to decrease perception of pain and provide quality of life; Rose was not interested in reflecting on her life or expressing emotions related to death and dying. "Who needs all that sad talk . . . I'm gonna die anyway. Now strum that there banjo of yours," she would say.

Our duets consisted of *Amazing Grace, When the Saints Go Marching In, Swing Low, Sweet Chariot, Bicycle Built for Two, If You Knew Susie, My Wild Irish Rose, Shalom Aleichem, Ain't She Sweet,* and other old time favorites. Rose had always wanted to be a singer, and during music therapy, in her last few months of life, that's exactly what she was.

Music as *GROUP therapy* was used on an acute care oncology unit with children ages five to ten in varying stages of cancer. Instrumental improvisations and group singing led to writing the lyrics for *We All Need Chemotherapy.* The following goals were met: to provide opportunities for emotional self-expression; to facilitate musical and verbal discussions related to illness and hospitalization; to establish a supportive, non-threatening environment; to elevate mood and increase social interaction.

WE ALL NEED CHEMOTHERAPY
(to the tune of "We All Sing with the Same Voice," Sesame Street)

When we go to check ups and see the doctor
Sometimes we think we can go home
He says we have to stay, we must put up with it
It makes us feel really sad
We know it's for our good, we must believe it
Even though we wanted to go home
The people here are nice, they become our friends
We all lose our hair and look the same.
We all need chemotherapy
For leukaemia, for a tumour
We all go to the hospital
To get better every day.

Lora Koenig © 1992

DIANA was a sixteen year old suffering from leukemia; she was transferred from acute care to palliative care for comfort and support. Aggressive treatment, such as chemotherapy, was not effective with this patient, but assertiveness on my part was significant. Diana was extremely depressed about her rapidly deteriorating condition, as she had only recently become ill; she wanted to shut out the world. Music was provided for both active and passive involvement, to elicit emotional self-expression, to provide relaxation and pain management, to elevate mood and to provide bedside support.

Diana occasionally banged on the drum when confronted with her fear and anger, she frequently listened to cassette tapes of favorite tunes and relaxing music, and enjoyed the electronic keyboard I had lent to her. A religious, spiritual musical tape was the object of our final interaction. On the Friday before she died, I asked if I could share with her some special music; I sat beside her as she listened, fell asleep, and almost completely relaxed. I later found out that this same music played all day as she died, providing comfort to this patient and her supportive family.

ALBERT, who had suffered a broken hip at age ninety-three, was not recovering due to his age and stage of dementia; he was placed in hospice care in a skilled nursing facility. He had lost both his long- and short-term memory, having forgotten that he was married with two grown children, seven grandchildren, and two great-grandchildren. He did not know where he was or how he got there or that he had eaten lunch; he frequently forgot that he was dying, although he was very uncomfortable. What Albert did remember, however, was that his favorite song was *If I Were A Rich Man*, from *"Fiddler on the Roof."* And he recognized me each day I came in with my cassette player and Fiddler tape.

Goals were not easy to establish or to achieve with this resident, so I settled on providing quality of life and maintaining focus to task. Unfortunately, I could not restore Albert's memory, but the other goals were successful. He loved to listen to the song three or four times while singing along and snapping his fingers until fatigued. Then Albert would tell me stories about how he became a "rich man." His daughter, having overheard one session, told me that his stories were quite accurate, and she thanked me for bringing him life with his favorite song.

MARY was a terminally ill child who drew a picture of an owl a week prior to her death following a visit in which I used music and guided visualization (hypnotherapy) techniques. She was having much difficulty breathing and was in obvious physical distress even with the oxygen mask in place. Gently strumming my guitar I began to create a story inviting Mary to journey to a land where there were beautiful flowers and children playing in sunshine, freely breathing in the spring air. Visibly responding to the imagery and hypnotherapy in conjunction with the music, within fifteen minutes Mary was breathing much more comfortably. In addition to the positive response Mary exhibited, I also had the gift of a song from spending this healing time with her.

BRING RAINBOWS TO THE CHILDREN

Bring flowers to the children, Bring flowers to the children
Bring flowers to the children
Flowers and love
Bring many splendid colors, Bring many splendid colors
Bring many splendid colors
Colors and love

And dance upon the mountains
And skip upon the green grass
Feel the earth beneath your feet
And look up to the sky
And drink in all the sunshine
And feel the breeze that moves the trees
Pick a cloud that has your name
And float on way up high

Bring rainbows to the children, Bring rainbows to the children
Bring rainbows to the children
Rainbows and love
Bring many splendid colors, Bring many splendid colors
Bring many splendid colors
Bring colors and love

Paul Alexander © 1995

With Mary seemingly more comfortable, I asked if she would like to draw a picture: she immediately responded, and within several minutes, handed me her creation. She indicated that she wanted me to keep it. We did not process verbally, as she was unable to speak at this time. Several months following Mary's death I shared the picture with a colleague familiar with art interpretation; he said that the owl is known to be a symbol of death. Through the music and art, Mary was given the opportunity and support to express her awareness of her terminal illness.

ELIZABETH was a fifteen-year-old patient with AIDS in palliative care. Music appeared to be the most effective intervention in eliciting a positive change in behavior—her cries of pain generally stopped, her body relaxed, her breathing steadied, and she frequently smiled. Elizabeth had lost the ability to communicate verbally, however her facial affect and body language clearly expressed confusion and fear related to her condition. Live music was provided to elevate her mood, to assist with deep breathing, relaxation, guided imagery, and to explore the spirituality of God, heaven, and after life. This spiritual reflection led to composing *Just Fly Away*, my interpretation of Elizabeth's thoughts. Recorded music played consistently in my absence; instrumental and spiritual music for comfort, and her familiar favorites for diversion from pain.

JUST FLY AWAY

I thought the pain might disappear
If I closed my eyes, shut out the world
All around me is the enemy
I don't know how to escape from here

Envisioning the "other side"
I sense a comfort, inner peace
The answer to my constant prayer
Yet I always thought that I should hide . . . from there

If I could just fly away
To a place that I don't have to fear
Where my suffering would end
I would gladly go real far from here
If I could just fly away

As I leave you and my short life ends
Remember there's a better place
I'll be relieved of all this pain
I'll miss my family and my friends
But we'll meet again some future day
When you also fly away . . .

If I could just fly away
To a place that I don't have to fear
Where my suffering would end
I would gladly go real far from here
If I could just fly away

Lora F. Koenig ©1995

MUSIC THERAPY IN BEREAVEMENT

The use of music and music therapy facilitates and promotes opportunities for mourning and healing throughout the bereavement process. This section will explore the use of music in working through the tasks of grieving and highlight its significance in ceremony, rituals, and services of commemoration. The appropriateness of music as integrated into the wake and funeral service will also be addressed.

Support is absolutely essential when grieving the illness or death of a family member or close friend. When the loved one was a child, there are additional issues and feelings involved. The following lyrics are an expression of the thoughts and feelings which are common during times of grief and loss.

GOODBYE

It hurts me to watch you, it scares me to see
That what's happening to you could happen to me
I don't want to grow old, I don't understand why
Human beings get sick, they get brittle and die
I want you to stay young, I want you carefree
Can't we live forever, happy and healthy?

I don't think I'll ever be ready to say
"Goodbye . . . I'll see you in heaven some day."
I wasn't prepared to bid you goodbye
It still doesn't seem fair that you had to die . . .

Where do we go when we're no longer here?
Our bodies are left but our souls disappear.
I wonder if heaven is really a place
Or if we just stay buried in a cold, lonely space . . .

It hurts me to watch you, it scares me to see
That what's happening to you can happen to me

I don't want to grow old, I don't understand why
Human beings get sick, they get brittle and die
I want you to stay young, I want you carefree
Can't we live forever, happy and healthy?

Although I'm not sure I'll ever understand why
I have to accept that all living things die . . . goodbye . . .

Lora Koenig (lyrics)
Harvey Greenberg (music) © 1993

Dr. J. William Worden, in *Grief Counselling and Grief Therapy,* delineates four tasks of mourning. *Task I* is to accept the reality of the loss. *Task II* is to work through the pain of grief. *Task III* is to adjust to an environment in which the deceased is missing, and *Task IV* is to relocate the deceased emotionally and move on with life [5]. Music can be a powerful tool for the griever as s/he faces these tasks. Although family, friends, and co-workers tend to support the mourner during the early days following the death and through the funeral, this support does not usually continue in the months when it is most needed. It is not unusual for intense grief to manifest itself at a time when many expect the bereaved "to be getting on" with their lives. Grievers thus often feel isolated and misunderstood as they attempt to integrate their loss into their daily lives.

Music can directly and indirectly acknowledge feelings, thoughts, and behaviors with which one is struggling. Although nothing can take the pain of grief away, music and lyrics can serve as a mirror to the heart of the bereaved individual, opening a door to the healing process. Most people have a familiar or favorite song that reminds him/her of the loved one, or a special moment shared. It may be a wedding song, a children's lullaby, or a song popular during the illness. These special songs are very individual, depending on one's life experiences and music expressive of various eras and generations.

Popular songs of the time can take on a universal appeal due to their frequency of radio air play and poetic meaning. *Tears in Heaven* written by Eric Clapton following his son's tragic death, or *Wind Beneath My Wings* by Larry Henley and Jeff Silbar, for example, may trigger strong emotions and identification with pain as well as with the reality of the loss. These songs thus assist the grievers in accomplishing the first task—the task of accepting and acknowledging the death and absence of their loved one.

Working through the pain of grief is like riding an emotional roller-coaster. As Worden states, "people can short circuit Task II in any number of ways, the most obvious being to cut off their feelings and deny the pain that is present" [5, p. 14].

In counseling the bereaved, hearing and discussing significant songs can facilitate the process of working through the pain. The music and lyrics serve as a natural connection to memories of the loved one, and telling the story is an important activity in grief work. The process of reminiscing and sharing memories is somehow made less threatening when elicited by a special piece of music. Music has a natural way of bypassing barriers we build against feeling various emotions, including pain and sadness. It can catch one off guard and in so doing provide a rich opportunity for healing and accessing these awakened thoughts and feelings.

A song can be the catalyst for acknowledging the difficult and confusing grief reactions often unattended to in daily interactions. Within a therapeutic environment, these responses can be adequately acknowledged and expressed through hearing, singing, and discussing the songs and the memories evoked. Song writing is a tool for further exploration of intimate and specific experiences related to the loss of a loved one.

A safe, supportive environment is essential in taking a step toward healing and facing the emotions encountered in grief. Society frequently sends a message to avoid the subject or not speak the loved one's name. Music can assist in counteracting these negative messages while providing opportunities for healing in ways sometimes unexpected. A song may be heard over the radio or in a place of worship that facilitates emotional release and recall, thus assisting the bereaved person to work through the pain of grief.

Many songs speak of the difficulty of Task III, of adjusting to the environment in which the deceased is missing. The work of this task can take several years to accomplish although it begins soon after the death. Inherent in the work of Task III is the question and struggle "Who am I now?" These lyrics echo the sentiments of the griever searching to find an identity following a loss:

WHO AM I NOW?

You and I were a team, it seems we fought against the odds
You and I, we'd paint
rainbows when
The world would fall apart
We'd laugh and play all day
And make angels in the snow
We were two, you and I
me and you.

Who am I now without you
Who will I turn out to be
I stand alone, I'm broken
in two
Does anyone realize how much
I'm missing you.

You and I, we'd play the music box
And giggle in the sand
You and I, we'd look for
shooting stars
When our tears got out of hand
We'd close our eyes real tight
And make a secret plan
We were two, you and I,
me and you.

You're still with me, like
the air I breathe
And the sun that fills the sky
Forever, you and I

Paul Alexander © 1992

We define ourselves and our place in the world by the relationships, the roles, and the purpose we have in the lives of others, as well as bonds and attachment. Much of the work of grief is not only letting go of the person in our life, but also readjusting and letting go of how that relationship affected our daily expression of self.

A widow no longer has to cook or shop for two, run the bath, or starch the shirts. A widower may have to learn how to balance the checkbook or to defrost the refrigerator. A bereaved parent not only grieves for the present, but also for the future—there will be no graduations, weddings, or grandchildren. They no longer have to shop for birthday presents, walk to the school bus stop, or read a goodnight story. Their child was not supposed to die before they did. A bereaved sibling may feel abandoned, confused, lonely, angry, and misplaced in his/her family. Acknowledging these changes and challenges, and facing the everyday reality without the beloved, is a major task.

Task IV involves the ability to reinvest emotional energy into life. This does not mean forgetting the relationship, but rather moving through the tasks of grief to a point where emotional, behavioral, physical, and spiritual energy is focused on the "here and now" with goals for the future. There has been an integration, and in many cases a transformation, of the surviving person. In some cases Task IV comes through the process of grief and its ebbs and flows. Yet there are times when the bereaved consciously makes a decision to dedicate him/herself to life, even through the devastation of the loss. The song *The Night is Still Young* by John Van Tongeven and Phil Galdstone speaks to the task of reinvesting in life. A bereaved mother spoke with me of how that song triggered in her the will to survive and reconnect to her talents, purposes in life.

She had been struggling with the depression and anguish that often follows the death of a child. Her decision to take experience of loss and grief and use it to help others was the transforming moment for her. Songs of faith and inspiration often speak to transform one's grief and support the griever to reinvest in life. Many people change careers or adopt new belief systems as they integrate and attempt to understand their loss.

Using music to facilitate the process of self-expression and the tasks of mourning is an invaluable tool, both in the individual and group session.

At the wake, funeral, and memorial services for the deceased, music appropriately chosen can serve several purposes:

1. To assist in acknowledging the reality of the death and in releasing the emotions associated with early reactions of grief.
2. To accompany meaningful rituals and to provide comfort in the words of faith and hope, as well as to provide points of opening and closing within the ceremonial structure.
3. To celebrate the life remembered by using favorite and meaningful songs of the deceased and her/his family.
4. To provide times of quiet meditation and reflection, with instrumental music or music representative of the family's culture and religion.

A meeting between the family and the funeral director, clergy, or support staff can facilitate meaningful music choices, while providing comfort and solace. It also empowers the family to contribute to the ceremonies of burial at a time when they are feeling helpless.

Both at the funeral service and in the bereavement process, the use of rituals and music offer significant opportunities for healing and remembrance. Evan Imber-Black states that rituals "mark the loss of a member, affirm the life lived by the person who has died, facilitate the expression of grief in ways that are consonant with the culture's values, speak symbolically of the meanings of death and ongoing life, and point to a direction for making sense of the loss while enabling continuity for the living" [6, p. 207]. Rituals are powerful components of the grieving process, and can bring people together in supportive expression while providing the structure and means to acknowledge the loss. Music further adds significance and a personal touch.

Lighting a candle in memory and in honor of a loved one is a common ritual which can be private or shared. Many support groups for bereaved individuals incorporate candle-lighting ceremonies to acknowledge the love shared in the past relationship. The song *Light a Candle* is frequently used to accompany this ritual while highlighting its power and purpose.

LIGHT A CANDLE

And I will light a candle for you
To shatter all the darkness and bless the time we knew
Like a beacon in the night

The flame will burn bright and guide us on our way
Oh today I light a candle for you.

The seasons come and go
And I'm weary from the change
I keep on moving on, you know it's not the same
And when I'm walking all alone
Do you hear me call your name
Do you hear me sing the songs we used to sing?
You filled my life with wonder, touched me with surprise
Always saw that something special deep within your eyes
And through the good times and the bad
We carried on with pride
I hold onto the love and life we knew.

Paul Alexander © 1993

Planting a tree as a memorial to the deceased person is also a special ritual. Many Hospices and funeral organizations have annual tree planting memorials to honor those who have died, and to foster support within the community. There is tremendous significance in giving life as a memorial for the death of a loved one; the song *Tree of Memory* was written to accompany the tree planting ceremony.

TREE OF MEMORY

And forever this will be
A tree of memory
Growing tall, growing strong
With a promise that all we shared
Still belongs to the flow of life,
A legacy
A living sign that we are part of history, forever

Branches reaching upward
Reaching to the sky
Knowing that there's more to see than meets the eye
The lessons learned, the paths we turned
Are forever etched upon my soul and upon my mind.

I will not forget you though the tides of life will change
And a thousand dreams and thousand nights will take us from this day
But through it all we're rooted deep
In a love that's ours to keep nurtured for all time.

Paul Alexander © 1995

CONCLUSION

Music therapy is a successful client-centered approach in working through issues with a dying patient and/or the grieving family. This chapter provided detailed descriptions of music therapy techniques for encouraging emotional self-expression, for decreasing the perception of pain, for preparation and acceptance of death, and for promoting quality of life for the patient and family.

In summary, music can serve as an invaluable tool in assisting and accompanying the patient through the dying process, and the griever through the tasks of mourning. It can also enrich the power of rituals, funerals, and ceremonies of remembrance. We are emotional, behavioral, social, and spiritual human beings; grief affects us on all those levels. Music, too, has a powerful impact on our emotions, our behaviors, our relationships, and our spiritual connections. It is a natural connection to use the healing power of music and its therapeutic benefits as we face the complexities of loss.

REFERENCES

1. J. S. Peters, *Music Therapy, An Introduction,* Charles C. Thomas, Springfield, 1987.
2. S. Munro, *Music Therapy in Palliate/Hospice Care,* Magna Music Baton, St. Louis, 1984.
3. E. Kübler-Ross, *On Children and Death,* Macmillan Publishing, New York, 1985.
4. E. T. Gaston (ed.), *Music in Therapy*, Macmillan Company, New York, 1968.
5. J. W. Worden, *Grief Counselling and Grief Therapy,* Springer, New York, 1991.
6. E. Imber-Black, Rituals and the Healing Process, in *Living Beyond Loss*, W.W. Norton, New York, 1991.

BIBLIOGRAPHY

Bright, R., *Grieving: A Handbook for Those Who Care,* Magna Music Baton, St. Louis, 1986.
Dailey, A.A. and Goltzer, S.G. (eds.), *Hospice Care for Children,* Oxford, New York, 1993.
Lee, M.H.M. (ed.), *Rehabilitation, Music and Human Well-Being*, Magna, St. Louis, 1989.
Martin, J. (ed.), *The Next Step Forward: Music Therapy with the Terminally Ill*, Magna Music Baton, St. Louis, 1989.
West, T. M., Psychological Issues in Hospice Music Therapy, *Music Therapy Perspectives, 12*:2, pp. 117-124, 1994.

CHAPTER 11

Smashing Pumpkins and Blind Melons: Using Popular Music to Help Grieving Adolescents

Mindy Gough

> To me the alternative rock song sounded like a mix of breaking glass, road construction, and an animal screaming in pain. The lyrics, if indeed there were any, were completely unintelligible to my ears. But to the fifteen year old girl crying in my office, this song was bittersweet, memory-laden, and emotionally provocative. For her it evoked images of time spent with her close friend, killed only weeks before in a car crash. This song, which was for me little more than discordant noise, was for her a connection, an emotional link to a loved person snatched away so suddenly.

As a grief counselor working with children, teens, and adults, I often use music to help bereaved people reach and express their feelings, cope with their losses, and share their memories of the person who has died. I am not a music therapist. In fact, I have no musical skills. I play no instruments. My singing is not something anyone would like to hear. However, I love music and have seen and felt its power to soothe, to comfort, to enliven, and to connect. In this chapter I offer a few ideas to counselors who are not music therapists, but who would like to use music with their bereaved teenaged clients. For our purposes here, I will define "popular music" as country, rock and roll, heavy metal, alternative, punk, rap, and other musical styles commonly found on radio, in music videos, and in dance clubs. For the counselor who lacks musical talent, I have endeavored to offer suggestions that are useful for the non-musician.

WHY USE MUSIC?

In my practice, music fulfills seven main functions. These are:

- to evoke emotions
- to call forth memories
- to stimulate discussion
- to aid coping
- to enhance ritualization
- to enable the bereaved to share the lost person with others, and
- to enable the bereaved to feel the presence of the deceased.

Of course, not all of these functions apply to every client. Counseling activities involving music must be chosen with as much care and consideration of the individual client's situation as any other therapeutic intervention. Of particular importance is the client's place in his grief journey. Counselors should take heed not to rush the client nor push him beyond his ability to cope.

Evoking Emotion

Cook and Dworkin note that music in the counseling context, "can be an intense experience, eliciting powerful emotions as the music stimulates the client to recount poignant moments involving the deceased" [1, p. 125]. Certainly I have observed clients becoming tearful after hearing the first notes of a song that has special meaning for them. One young man of twenty-one had been berating himself for not grieving following his father's death several weeks before, feeling guilty because he had not yet cried:

> I felt numb and distant from everything and I wanted to just feel something, anything. When I put *Cat's In the Cradle* (Ugly Kid Joe) on the CD player, I just bawled. I cried for probably two hours and played it over and over. All I could think of was that my dad wasn't coming back.

For this young man, music helped to reach the emotions that were masked by his feelings of shock and numbness. Music seems to reach beyond our conscious barriers. Segal states that music and other expressive arts "involve tactile, visual, aural, and kinaesthetic senses, most of which are related to the involuntary nervous system" [2, p. 593]. When we hear a piece of music that has special meaning for us, we respond from beyond the paradigm of logic and control that regulates our everyday thinking.

One of Worden's principles for counseling the bereaved reminds the caregiver to "help the survivor to identify and express feelings" [3, p. 43]. By playing meaningful music and giving the grieving client permission to express his feelings openly, we allow him to move forward in his grief journey. Music can help a bereaved person to recognize his feelings and to experience them. A bereaved person can weep, or rage, or sob in response to the feelings elicited by pieces of music. A young woman whose brother died described her emotional response to listening to his favorite music:

> I don't know why I listened to it, because I would always cry. I'd turn it off in public but I'd listen to it at home. It gets the tears out and then you don't have to cry for the rest of the day. It is like therapy.

Calling Forth Memories

Most of us associate certain songs with certain people. I, for example, cannot hear *Old Time Rock and Roll* (Bob Seeger) without envisioning my father in the middle of the dance floor. For the bereaved, songs that are associated with the person who has died take on new and heightened meaning. A teenager whose boyfriend died in a motorcycle crash felt "haunted" by the many songs on the radio that reminded her of her deceased friend:

> I cannot turn on the radio. Every other song was one that John sang, or played in his band, or the one that was playing when I got the phone call that he had been in the accident. He used to write the words to songs out for me and now whenever those songs come on I feel sad and angry all over again.

While some grieving people prefer not to hear songs they associate with the deceased person, many grieving people find, along with tearfulness, some sense of comfort or wistful nostalgia when they listen to these pieces.

A young woman who lost three friends in a single car crash found that listening to songs that reminded her of the good times she'd had with her friends was a healing activity:

> We'd been to Lollapalooza (multi-band outdoor rock concert) the week before the crash, and we had a really great time. We were so happy and excited to be going and met all kinds of people, and felt really close to each other that day. So now I listen to the Tragically Hip when I want to think of them and then I can see them sitting soaked in the rain at 'Palooza laughing and joking. I see all the things we did together and it's kind of like a little movie or a video that goes on in my head. I still cry a lot but I like to remember that day because it was happy.

Another young woman whose newborn child died shortly after his birth listened to songs that reminded her of her pregnancy:

Well, I have been listening to Nirvana songs since my little boy died. The songs have nothing to do with him or about people dying or anything, but they are the songs I heard when I was pregnant. I thought he would be O.K. and I made all kinds of plans and when I hear those songs I remember what it was like when I thought I was going to be a mother.

Worden's principles for counseling the bereaved suggest that grieving people ought to work toward accepting that their loved person has truly died, and that eventually they need to allow themselves to place the deceased person in a new emotional context [3]. In order to make these gradual shifts in perception, a grieving person needs to recall and discuss the life and death of the person who has died. Worden states that "reminiscing is one way to gradually divest the emotional energy tied up with the deceased" [3, p. 48]. By listening to songs that evoke memories of the loved one who has died, a grieving person can begin to realize the reality of his loss and to perceive the deceased person in the context of the past.

Stimulating Discussion

Another function of music is facilitating communication between the counselor and the grieving client. Music can be a starting place, a bridge from unknown territory to warm rapport. In my experience with bereaved teenagers, music has been an almost immediate way to create an accepting and intimate therapeutic environment. By discussing the content of the song or the feelings and thoughts it invokes, the counselor demonstrates her willingness to try to understand the client's world. For teenagers accustomed to having adults dismiss their music as noise, the counselor's willingness to listen respectfully both to the song and to the client's interpretation of it, can develop an atmosphere of mutual trust and regard.

Because familiar music is non-threatening, most clients feel comfortable talking about favorite musical styles and particular songs they enjoy. As trust builds between the client and the counselor, there will be more in-depth discussion about the thoughts and emotions triggered by meaningful pieces of music.

An angry fourteen-year-old girl who had been referred to me by her school vice-principal after her father's suicide, initially refused to respond during our sessions, other than to say "yeah" or "no." When she arrived for her third session, I was playing *No Rain* by Blind Melon, a popular band at the time. She seemed to be struggling to maintain her usual tough, "don't care" demeanor, but began to ask questions about why I was playing the music, if I liked the band, and so on. We were able to talk about music for an hour. When she returned for the next session she brought several compact discs and we talked about songs that held meaning for her. A Blind Melon song, *Tones of Home,* eventually became a focal point in our work together, as we discussed her father's death and her own feelings about suicide.

Communication facilitated by popular music may take many paths. Counselors and clients can discuss the music itself, the song lyrics, or the thoughts, feelings, memories, and images that the music calls forth. Whatever the content of discussion, music provides a safe common ground on which the counselor and client can meet.

Popular music is usually written in the vernacular familiar to teenagers, and may assist the counselor to communicate in language and metaphors consistent with the young client's everyday speech. Hannelore Wass notes that "hate, violence, and murder" are common themes in popular music such as rap and heavy metal [4, p. 100], so it behooves counselors to talk with teenagers about their responses to such material. Examination of song lyrics may enable the counselor to identify themes of suicidal ideation, glorification of suicide, and maladaptive coping strategies, and in turn discuss these with the client.

Aid in Coping

Music can be soothing, comforting, and relaxing. It can help us to achieve serenity and a sense of peace. These calming properties make music an important component of healing. Whether in the form of soft sounds created especially for relaxation or songs that the client especially enjoys, music has the power to create a healing space in the midst of the chaotic feelings that surround a death.

Coping music can be used during a session to help the client feel comfortable, to teach him relaxation techniques, or to introduce music as a healing tool for the client to incorporate into his retinue of coping skills. The most effective use of coping music occurs outside of the office, in the client's day-to-day life. Is he able to find musical selections which help him to feel comforted? Does he take time to play pieces that help him to relax? Can he identify lyrics that help him to make sense of his loss? A young widowed woman spoke about her five-year-old son:

> When he's mad, or upset, or when I've been crying about Dan, the first thing he goes for is his *Lion King* soundtrack (Walt Disney) and he listens to *Hakuna Matata* full blast. I think we all know that song by heart now, and sometimes I want to scream when he puts it on for the four-hundredth time, but I know it's his way of feeling better. And usually when he comes out of his room, he asks for a hug and then he's O.K. again.

A nineteen-year-old girl whose young brother died in a car crash also had a specific song that helped her to feel less sad and more peaceful:

> Peaceful, Easy Feeling (The Eagles) was my cocooning song. When I couldn't deal with everybody crying and moping around, I'd go listen to that and the tight feeling would go out of my chest after a while. My dad had a song, too. He used to listen to it in the barn all the time after Bradley died, and then he'd look a lot less tense.

A fifteen-year-old boy whose mother had died of cancer was surprised by his choice of coping music:

> I thought I must be going crazy. The only thing that made me feel better right after my mom died was listening to church music. We aren't big churchgoers in my family, so I don't know where that came from. But my grandma had this tape and for some reason it just hit me. I don't listen to it anymore, but it helped a lot at the time.

Many clients have benefitted from listening to recordings such as the *Solitudes* series (Dan Gibson) which combines soothing music and nature sounds. However, I find that teenaged clients are not as keen on this kind of music and may find it irritating instead of calming. The approach that seems to be most effective is to encourage the bereaved young person to seek out music that fits his emotional needs, and to offer suggestions if required. Do not discount the calming properties of music by bands with names such as Smashing Pumpkins and Blind Melon. Though the counselor may find such music to be noisy and unpleasant, the grieving teenaged client may find comfort in the familiar sounds.

Enhancing Ritualization

Music is a natural supplement to ritualization following a death, whether funeral, memorial service, or private ritual. While most funerals and memorial services use traditional religious music, in recent years families have begun to make use of more personal musical selections. For bereaved teenagers, popular music adds a familiar and meaningful element to death rituals. This is not to say that popular music ought to be included in all rituals. Some popular music, despite its meaning for the bereaved teenager, is inappropriate for funerals or memorial services attended by family members of all ages. However, personal good-bye rituals can use whatever creative elements the client desires.

Many of my teenaged clients have expressed dissatisfaction with the death rituals organized by adults in the family. One fourteen-year-old boy whose friend died in a car crash made a tape of the deceased boy's favorite songs and placed this in the casket, along with a marijuana cigarette:

> I figured that somebody should say good-bye the way he would have wanted it. That suit they buried him in was just stupid. He never wore a suit in his life. And that canned music at the funeral home made me want to puke. It was like they were having their own little party and didn't even know who was in the coffin. They should have put him in jeans and a Pearl Jam shirt and played *Garden* (Pearl Jam).

Other teens have held informal gatherings of their own to say good-bye to friends who have died:

After the accident (in which 3 teenagers died) we went to the funerals but you couldn't cry much, you know? One guy's priest talked about him and it was obvious he didn't know him at all. At the other (funeral) they didn't talk about her at all. At the end I asked my other friend, did they say her name even once? So we did our own funeral. There's a shack in the back of our property that we all used to go to together, so about twenty of us went there and had a fire and played all their favorite songs and talked about them. That was the real funeral.

Music plays a large role in ritualization. It allows time to remember, to think, to grieve, and to say good-bye. Bereaved teenagers need to be given permission to use familiar music—at funerals and memorial services, where appropriate, and in personal good-bye rituals.

Sharing the Deceased With Others

Lang and Caplan state that, "telling the story of our relationship with the lost loved one" is an essential part of the grieving process [5, p. 1]. Songs that remind the bereaved person of their deceased loved one or songs that were favorites of the deceased person are effective ways for the grieving person to share stories and memories of the deceased. The grieving client can use special songs to explain the life of the person who has died to a counselor, grief support group, or friend. Songs not only evoke memories for the grieving person, but also convey some of the feelings of the bereaved person to his or her listener.

A seventeen-year-old boy whose deeply loved grandfather died suddenly was able to talk about his grandfather's life by bringing tape recordings of his grandfather's favorite tunes to the session.

Like, I'm listening to Guy Lombardo! When grandpa was alive I used to nag him about how stupid that music was and try to get him to listen to my music. Now I actually listen to that stuff because it reminds me of who he was. I can go through each song and I've got another story to tell about him. I bet he's in heaven laughing his ass off because I'm listening to his old crap.

A twenty-one-year-old woman used the song *Guardian Angels* (The Judds) to tell the story of her grandmother's life. She made slides of old family photographs and played the song while displaying the slides:

Initially I just did this for me. I loved that song and it just told the story of her life so well. After a while I thought, why don't I show this to my mom and dad, or my cousins? So I did and we all cried and laughed. I'm so glad I shared it with them because I didn't feel so lonely and sad afterwards.

Feeling the Presence of the Deceased

Not every bereaved person wants to feel that the deceased is nearby. For some, the concept of the deceased being present in some way is frightening and unpleasant. For many clients, though, a feeling that their deceased loved one is nearby in some way is a great comfort. My grieving teenaged clients have described experiencing a sense of the presence of a loved person after listening to meaningful music. A twenty-five-year-old woman whose brother died in a car crash six years before, described feeling his presence:

> I listened to music so much after he died—I listened to Pink Floyd because it was the music that he loved. It wasn't that I liked it, but it was his music. When I listened to it I actually felt like he was there. You put yourself in his place.

A seventeen-year-old boy spent time in the bedroom of his young brother who had died after a long illness:

> You know, you feel pretty stupid listening to Sesame Street songs and Barney and that stuff. But when I'm in his room I can smell him and when I listen to his tapes I can almost feel him in the room with me. You probably think I'm nuts but that's what happens.

Once, while listening to Deanna Edwards perform her song, *Walk In The World For Me,* I too felt that my deceased sister was somehow close by. For me, this was a positive experience. However, many teenaged clients have prefaced their discussions about feeling the presence of a loved one with statements like, "Don't think I'm crazy, but . . ." or, "You probably won't believe this, but . . ." The grief counselor should assure the bereaved client of the normalcy of this kind of experience. Many of my young clients have described feeling peaceful or relieved following the experience of feeling a loved one's presence. Meaningful music may facilitate this experience.

MUSIC IN THE COUNSELING SESSION

How, then, does one go about actually using music to help a grieving person? What equipment is required? Must a counselor add Iron Maiden, Smashing Pumpkins, and Led Zeppelin to his or her musical collection? Does one need to be able to decipher the screams and wails seemingly so prevalent in today's popular music? How does one introduce the topic?

Getting Started

My office is equipped with a portable stereo capable of playing tapes and compact discs. Because collecting music is a hobby enjoyed by my husband and me, I have over five hundred albums of music from which to choose. However, as my husband is fond of alternative bands such as Smashing Pumpkins, and I prefer Elvis and gospel, I do not necessarily have clients' preferred selections on hand. While I believe it is helpful for the counselor to have some musical selections available, it is not necessary or possible to have an extensive, varied selection of music in one's office. Clients will almost always own copies of the music that is most meaningful to them.

It is also helpful, though not necessary, to familiarize oneself with the popular music prevalent in one's geographic area. Though this familiarity will come with time, some extra research will be beneficial. MuchMusic and other music video television stations are an excellent source for counselors wishing to learn about the personalities, images, and culture of popular music. Many libraries also lend newly released compact discs, many of which contain printed lyrics. In addition, most teenagers will be happy to teach you about the popular music that they enjoy.

The Music

It is important to start where the client is. Cook and Dworkin note that "many adolescents when sad or depressed almost automatically turn on their radio or stereo" [1, p. 124]. Certainly most of the teenagers who come to my office are attached to portable stereos of some kind. A simple query such as, "What are you listening to today?" can be enough to lead to a therapeutically useful conversation. It is for this reason that counselors do not need an extensive music library to be able to use music effectively in their work. Counselors need only to ask, and bereaved teenagers will guide them to the appropriate musical selections.

While the majority of music used in the counseling session will be selected and provided by the client, the counselor may wish to collect some selections to have on hand. Songs about death, the afterlife, sadness, despair, suicide, and the meaning of life often hold special meaning for bereaved people. Memorial songs created by recording artists in memory of deceased family, friends, or public figures, such as *Empty Garden* (Elton John) written for John Lennon, or *Tears In Heaven* (Eric Clapton) written for the artist's five-year-old son, may also have significance for the bereaved. However, counselors must keep in mind that teenagers tend to be loyal to one style of popular music and may not find meaning in music that is unfamiliar to them. Practically speaking, musical anthologies and compilations such as *Oh What A Feeling: A Vital Collection of Canadian Music* offer a large selection of songs at relatively little cost. An appendix of therapeutically useful songs is included at the end of this chapter.

Although not in the popular music realm, there are several recording artists that deserve mention here. These are musicians who record songs that focus on death, dying, and grieving. Deanna Edwards, Paul Alexander, The Monks of the Western Priory, and others have created music meant to reflect the feelings and thoughts of grieving people. Some of my teenaged clients have rejected this music when I have offered it, finding the musical style too distant from their familiar music. Others, though, have connected deeply with the lyrics of songs such as Edwards' *You're Going Home* and Alexander's *Light A Candle*. An appendix of grief and bereavement musical resources is included at the end of this chapter.

The Method

Using music in grief counseling can take several forms: listening to music provided by the client or the counselor, talking about music or the feelings it evokes, or using music in conjunction with another creative intervention. For the counselor, competency in grief counseling is required, as is comfort with music as a medium. The most important principle of using music in grief counseling is, in my view, to allow the client to guide the process. Encourage him to share songs that he likes or dislikes, that make him feel sad or happy, that evoke warm memories or melancholy ones. By inviting the grieving client to share music that is meaningful to him, the counselor gives him the opportunity to share his memories, his feelings, his thoughts, and his tears.

There are many musical activities that can be used to assist the bereaved client in his grief journey. In addition to those listed here, the creative counselor can adapt traditional counseling techniques and activities to include music in some way. The following activities are listed according to their relevance to the seven functions of music in grief counseling detailed earlier in this chapter.

To Evoke Emotions

The musical self-portrait is an assignment that is useful for developing rapport and for gaining insight into a bereaved client's sense of self. The client is asked to make a tape recording (or a list, if recording equipment is unavailable) of songs that, when taken as a group, represent a portrait of who he is. The resulting musical portrait can be played aloud and song lyrics and themes can be examined.

To Call Forth Memories

The musical biography is similar to the musical self-portrait assignment, but the client creates a musical portrait of the person who has died. Playing and discussing this musical biography allows the client the opportunity to tell the story of their loved one's life and to examine them as a person. Again, song lyrics and themes can be discussed.

To Stimulate Discussion

Counselors can encourage bereaved clients to bring with them to the next session music chosen to express selected feelings or thoughts. For example, grieving clients can be asked to find a song that shows:

- how they feel today
- their philosophy of life
- what their grief feels like
- what the afterlife is like
- what death means to them
- how they will feel in five years
- how angry (sad, empty, etc.) they feel
- what their loved one would say if they were here.

In the session, the counselor and client can listen to the client's selection and use it as the basis for discussion. The counselor can ask the client to select songs that are relevant to the client's place in his grief journey—reflective songs to call forth memories, hopeful songs to encourage faith in the future, and so on.

Counselors can offer musical selections from their own collection as well. It is imperative that the counselor examine the lyrics in some depth before attempting to use a piece of music in the counseling session. If I believe that a piece of music might be relevant to the work I am doing with a client, I first listen to determine what themes and messages the song conveys. This may be more easily said than done due to the lack of verbal clarity common in current popular music. However, many compact discs contain copies of song lyrics. If the lyrics are relevant and suited to my client's intellectual and emotional needs and capacity, I prepare a written copy of the lyrics and present these to the client when I play the song during the counseling session. We then talk about the grieving client's cognitive and emotional responses to the music.

To Aid Coping

Deanna Edwards advises all people to have a musical first aid kit [6]. Clients can be encouraged to create a tape recording of songs that give them comfort and peace and help them to make sense of the loss. The musical first aid kit may help grieving people to feel more peaceful and may lessen their emotional pain.

I have found it valuable to assign clients to seek an anthem or guiding song that becomes their rallying tune as they journey through grief. Clients have reported feeling empowered and strengthened by finding and playing this piece of music. An example of this kind of song is *The Dance* (Garth Brooks) which includes these lyrics:

And now I'm glad I didn't know
The way it all would end, the way it all would go
Our lives are better left to chance
I could have missed the pain
But I'd of had to miss the dance [7].

To Evoke Emotion, To Enhance Ritualization

Complementary techniques such as journaling, photo therapy, drawing, painting, sculpting, creative movement, and dance can be added to enhance a client's experience of the musical selection, depending on the level of trust established and the aptitudes and interests of the client. Examples of complementary activities are:

- sculpting to music
- drawing or painting to music
- writing a journal response to music
- writing lyrics or music of one's own
- writing a poem or story in response to music
- making a photographic collage in response to a song
- creating a dance or creative movement piece to music
- creating a personalized good-bye ritual that includes music
- making a photograph or photo story in response to a song

To Enable the Bereaved to Share the Lost Person With Others:

Music can also be used in the context of the grief support group. Members can be asked to introduce themselves by playing a favorite piece of music or a song that describes how they are feeling that day. When trust is established, members can be asked to share a song that reminds them of the person who has died, or a song that was a favorite of the deceased person. Members can also share songs that reflect their feelings of grief, or songs that help them to find meaning in the midst of grief.

To Enable the Bereaved to Feel the Presence of the Deceased

If the grieving client is to sense that the deceased loved one is nearby, it is best that this should occur naturally, without the counselor's urging. However, it is advisable for the counselor to give the client permission to talk about such an experience if indeed it occurs. The counselor might introduce the topic by sharing the story of someone who has experienced the presence of a loved one while listening to music, and reassure the client that such experiences are normal following a death.

DOES MUSIC MAKE A DIFFERENCE?

During an eight month social work internship at a large high school, I encountered many students who were grieving the losses of parents, siblings, grandparents, and friends. When I think back to that time I am always reminded of a song by a popular band called R.E.M., that included the lyrics:

When your day is long
And the night is yours alone
And you're sure you've had enough of this life
Hang on
Don't let yourself go
Cause everybody cries
And everybody hurts sometimes [8].

Students brought this song to our counseling sessions time and time again. The students in a grief support group adopted the piece as their theme song. One eighteen-year-old student reported that the song had "saved (his) life":

I was just about at the bottom of my barrel. I felt like you (the counselor) were the only one who gave a shit if I lived or died. I wanted to be with Shelley (girlfriend who had ended her own life). I thought I was like Kurt Cobain, this lonely, tragic loser who might as well just give it up. But when I was going home on the bus I was listening to my walkman and *Everybody Hurts* came on. I felt like it was a message to keep going. If I hadn't heard that song at that moment I was planning to walk in front of a truck.

I have no doubt that music makes a difference.

APPENDIX A
Therapeutically Useful Popular Music

<u>Songs About Death:</u>

<u>Leader of the Pack</u>, (Shangri-Las)
<u>Honey I Miss You</u>, (Jim Nabors)
<u>The Crossroads</u>, (Bone, Thugs N' Harmony)

Drive By, (Neil Young)
Seasons in the Sun, (Terry Jacks)
At My Funeral, (Crash Test Dummies)
In My Time of Dying, (Led Zeppelin)
The End, (The Doors)
Fiddler's Green, (Tragically Hip).

Songs About an Afterlife:

Tears In Heaven, (Eric Clapton)
Spirit in the Sky, (Kentucky Headhunters)
Friends, (Michael W. Smith)
Silver Thunderbird, (Marc Cohn)
Angels Among Us, (Alabama)
Guardian Angels, (The Judds).

Songs About One's Philosophy of Life:

Castles in the Sand, (Jimi Hendrix)
Tonight, Tonight, (The Smashing Pumpkins)
Stand Tall, (Burton Cummings)
Learning to Live Again, (Garth Brooks)
Desperado, (Eagles)
Flying on Your Own, (Rita McNeil)
Circle of Life, (Elton John)
Turn, Turn, Turn, (The Byrds)
The Dance, (Garth Brooks)

Songs About Sadness and Other Emotions:

Shout, (Tears For Fears)
Sunshine on Leith, (Proclaimers)
Tracks of My Tears, (Smokey Robinson and the Miracles)
Everybody Hurts, (R.E.M.)
Comfortably Numb, (Pink Floyd)

Songs About Despair and Suicide:

Jellybelly, (Smashing Pumpkins)
Settle For Nothing, (Rage Against the Machine)
You're Only Human, (Billy Joel)
Grip, (Rollins Band)
Tones of Home (Blind Melon)

Memorial Songs:

Superman's Song, (Crash Test Dummies)
Empty Garden, (Elton John)
Tears In Heaven, (Eric Clapton)
They Dance Alone, (Sting)
One Tree Hill, (U2)
Unforgettable, (Natalie Cole)
Guardian Angels, (The Judds)

APPENDIX B
Grief and Bereavement Musical Resources

Deanna Edwards—Rock Canyon Publishers, 777 E. Walnut, Provo, UT 84604

Paul Alexander—The Crossroad Publishing Co., 370 Lexington Ave., New York, NY 10017

Centering Corporation—1531 N. Saddle Creek Rd., Omaha, NE 68104

Compassion Books—477 Hannah Branch Rd., Burnsville, NC 28714

REFERENCES

1. A. S. Cook and D. S. Dworkin, *Helping the Bereaved,* Basic, New York, 1992.
2. R. M. Segal, Helping Children Express Grief Through Symbolic Communication, *Social Casework, 65,* pp. 590-599, 1984.
3. J. W. Worden, *Grief Counseling and Grief Therapy,* Springer, New York, 1991.
4. H. Wass, Appetite for Destruction: Children and Violent Death in Popular Culture, in *Factors Influencing Children and Adolescents' Perceptions and Attitudes Toward Death,* D. Adams and E. Deveau (eds.), Baywood, Amityville, New York, 1995.
5. G. Lang and S. Caplan, *Grief: The Courageous Journey,* CorAge Books, London, Ontario, 1993.
6. D. Edwards, Personal communication, London, Ontario, 1995.
7. T. Arata, The Dance, performed by Garth Brooks on the album *Garth Brooks,* Morganactive Music, Pookie Boy Store, 1989.
8. Berry, Buck, Mills and Stipe, Everybody Hurts, performed by R.E.M. on the album *Automatic For the People.* Nightgarden Music/Unichappell Music, Inc. (B.M.I.), 1992.

CHAPTER 12

The Use of Humor, Art, and Music with the Dying and Bereaved

Gerry Cox

Dying and death touch the lives of everyone. As a sociologist and educator, it has become clear that many approaches are needed to aid those who are dying or grieving. Humor, music, art, story-telling, literature, spirituality, and play are all methods that can be used to aid those who are dying or grieving.

FUNCTIONS OF HUMOR

The word humor has been used historically to mean sickness. The bodily humors were thought to be symptoms and causes of illness [1]. Henri Bergson has suggested that humor is inherently social. Its main social benefit is to shame those who are unwilling or unable to fit with the demands of a flexible social order [2]. For those who are not well, humor can be used to help them accept their condition. All people who live long enough will eventually get an illness. Humor may allow them to face the illness with a better emotional state. If the illness is severe or life-threatening, humor can have great value. One of the root causes of humor is fear. The relaxation of humor can allow one to escape from that fear [3]. The idea of using humor to overcome fear was a major part of Gothic fiction [3]. Humor allows one to establish a temporary sense of normality, relaxation, and security to allow the person to cope with or at least minimize the fear and to rise above the physical pain that he or she might be experiencing [3].

Humor and laughter can also promote wellness and health. A humorous outlook can both prevent and help to cure diseases [4]. How much pain people experience is influenced by their state of mind. The more one concentrates on pain, the greater the discomfort. As many athletes have discovered, if the contest is close or one's team is winning, minor injuries may go unnoticed. If one's team is losing badly, minor injuries quickly become noticed. Laughter helps the person to think about something other than their pain whether the pain is physical or emotional. The dying child faces both. Grieving people may forget their pain for a few moments when given reasons to laugh.

In dealing with most pain, laughter does have a therapeutic effect and promotes confidence and hope. Laughter is good medicine, because it gives people opportunities for diversion and freshness. Humor will facilitate the lessening of fear and anxiety. Humor will contribute to the acceptance of the reality of the death.

Certainly, relaxation and anxiety reduction are also important before examinations. Poor mental attitudes and emotional stress can cause physical deterioration. It is amazing how many students become physically ill on exam days. Emotional stress such as fear, anger, and anxiety do have degenerative and debilitating effects on the body. These effects, which are evident and must be medically treated, can be inhibited by humor [5], which inhibits and counters fears that constitute the basis of despondency and depression.

Humor conveys messages, facilitates social relations, diverts aggression, and manages "touchy" situations by producing a feeling of social solidarity. It serves as a coping mechanism to deal with and to neutralize external pressures and to reduce internal stresses. Leming and Dickinson suggest that the child needs to be taught that it is okay to express one's feelings through laughter [6].

One generally is able to take oneself and one's situation less seriously when one is able to laugh and to smile. No matter how bad things may seem, if one is able to laugh at oneself, one is generally able to cope. Nothing is so sacred, so taboo, or so disgusting that it cannot be the subject of humor [7]. By developing coping strategies, one can manage acute and prolonged stress [8]. Stress management requires that an adjustment be made. Cold, heat, sorrow, joy, drugs, or hormones may provoke an identical biochemical reaction in one's body [9]. The goal is not to eliminate the stress. It cannot be eliminated. The goal is to make the stressful situation tolerable without disruptive anxiety or depression [10]. Humor is created because it allows us to do many things that we need to do. It allows us to cope openly with problems, with anxieties, things that are frightening, and allows us to release tension [11]. The joking of the dying person liberates the individual from piety and passive acceptance of the impending death [12]. Laughter will not keep one from dying, but one will often not die as suddenly nor with as much pity. Just as wine changes some people, laughter changes others [13].

Besides coping with anger and aggression, humor and laughter may also function as a coping mechanism when people face a death by allowing them to avoid or deny feelings too frightening to face. For example, humor will allow people to approach a topic that is both personal and serious with a degree of liberation that will not trivialize their losses. Serious illness, the threat of death, and even death itself can be temporarily avoided or more readily dealt with through the use of humor. People enduring a crisis may laugh or humor one another in order to boost morale, even when they are not in a playful state of mind. Humor provides the individual with an avenue to deal with suffering whether his or her own or someone else's. The very topic of dying and death typically induces fear. In such conditions, one can cope with the fearfulness of the situation by the use of humor [4]. Often, from a self-preservation point of view, finding some humor in overwhelmingly painful or depressing situations can not only make such situations seem less so, but can also help to preserve the positive energy needed to cope with the crisis. While humor may be used to relieve anxiety and fear, people should not be encouraged to use humor to avoid facing painful situations.

Humor and laughter can reduce nervous tension. An individual in a moderate state of stress can laugh even when common sense tells him or her that nothing is funny. Laughter is associated with hope, the will to live, trust, faith, joy and love—all of which can mobilize the natural defense mechanisms of the body and have a biochemical effect upon the immune system and endrocrines, respiratory, cardiovascular, neurological, and musculo-skeletal systems [15]. For example, when stress is present in the vigil or wake and following funeral, humor may relieve or reduce the tension. Perhaps the adult could play a game with the child. On a scale of one to ten, rate each person's performance as a grieving individual, or rate their style of dress, or any other topic that seems to be appropriate for the child and his or her age. Whatever game is chosen, the game should be thoroughly thought out before playing it. Adults can play games with children that can lead to an understanding of death through humor. Marshmallow charades has children act out some common phrase that relates to the theme of death. If no one guesses the phrase, the child suffers the torture of being pelted by marshmallows. Having an adult explain the feeling suffered by "losers" and the meaning of the terms is essential to the success of the game. Writing one's epitaph or planning one's funeral offer a potentially humorous way to introduce a difficult topic. Parents or teachers can use this technique. As a parent and as a teacher, it has been quite effective in my work. Developing commercials for funeral homes, casket makers, or cemeteries can be a fun-learning experience. A life after death or a reincarnation party may be a humor learning experience as well. The options chosen should be planned carefully and be consistent with the leader's beliefs and developed under adult supervision. It is difficult to teach with humor if one does not agree with the tenets of humor. The leader must be able to laugh with the children. A funeral director who feels that others dislike him will not laugh at their jokes about his or her profession.

When one is seriously ill or dying, humor can facilitate the individual's ability to cope. Laughter is a bodily thing that can have physical effects [16]. Like the performer, the seriously ill or dying are on stage. They can perform for their visitors. Many perform without humor and may make their visitors feel uncomfortable. Some provide humor that uplifts the visitors. A friend who recently died illustrated this point. He responded to long, sad faces by asking, "Did someone die around here?" He also planned his own funeral and requested that it be a happy occasion with much singing and laughter so that people might remember him with a smile. Such people are the good. Everyone has a choice to define himself, herself, one's family, and so forth. Each person has the ability to define one's world as a dirty, miserable place, or one can define the world as a challenge to make better, or any other definition that one chooses. The choice belongs to each person.

Most have a friend or family member that no matter what one does, it is never good enough. If one visits, it is never long enough. These relationships are the miserable. Each probably also has a friend or family member that accepts your presence and gifts with love and caring. No matter what is offered, it is accepted as a gift of love. These people are the good. One cannot help but smile when one thinks of them even when they have died. Their death is a gift to the living. It can help the living to know better how to live and to discover what is important. In all of this it is important to remember that we all learn by example.

Everyone is a teacher. Does one teach others to complain and to prophesy doom? Does one teach others to love their children as one loves his or her own? Does one teach others about dying and death by the way one faces his or her own death? By designing a cheerful wake service, an uplifting funeral, and by encouraging humor throughout dying and death, my friend taught others how to face their own dying and death. His approach to humor could also uplift the seriously ill or dying.

Humor helps survival. Even in Auschwitz, humor made the situation bearable. While humor cannot counteract the sentence of death, it can allow one to manage. Elie Wiesel argued that humor became a defiance against the death camps and that defiance was a victory [17]. Dying people have a death sentence. Humor will help many of them to cope.

Humor does help people to overcome their illnesses. Norman Cousins used humor therapy to overcome a terminal illness [17]. While there is little scientific evidence of the power of humor over terminal illness, there is considerable evidence that it could at least be helpful. Humor is clearly useful in dealing with stress. According to Steven Kelly, humor allows one to manage and to cope with stress [18]. Humor therapy has been documented to aid asthma patients [19]. It has been shown to aid those who have experienced heart attacks [18]. Why is it helpful? One explanation is that humor is a source of energy that can be channeled in a positive or in a negative direction [18]. It may also be helpful because it benefits blood circulation, which mediates cardiac effects that can be harmful [18]. Part of the positive effect of humor may also be attributed to its ability to dispel clouds of unrest and fear. Humor is moisture. Surely, you have heard someone say, "I laughed so hard that I cried." The power of humor to influence is great. It takes the clouds away [20].

FUNCTIONS OF MUSIC

Music also effects one's mind and body with a remarkable similarity to humor. Historically, the shaman used music to heal. Music has been thought to be spiritual in nature. The shaman used music to heal the sick by the Navajo, Cherokee, Apache, and many other Native-American groups. Like most other Native-American religions, the Navajo religion centers on curing ceremonies and a system of sympathetic, imitiative magic [21]. The chants, dances, and healing are art forms in themselves. Music heals in much the same way as humor. Music stimulates laughter and elevates one's mood [22]. The power of music is strong. Music has been used in hospitals as therapy since World War II [23]. It was used from the time of the Greeks through the Renaissance in the Western world as a part of the healing process of both body and soul. It was viewed as a part of holistic care that has reemerged today [24]. It has been used as therapy succesfully with both children and adults. As a therapeutic device, it has a predictable and measurable effect upon human behavior. It has a physiological base to its effect [25].

Music heals in much the same way as humor. Music can relax those in morbid states and aid their mental health [22]. Music helps the patient to react better to medical treatment and to be in a more receptive mood to receive the treatment [22]. Like humor, music makes tensions manageable and may even reduce or eliminate tensions [26]. The effects of music are even greater when experienced with others [23]. Music does play an important role in health [27].

To help the grieving or dying person manage his or her feelings and to gradually begin to grasp the reality and finality of death, one can learn to listen to the tune rather than the words of what is being said [28]. The person will develop slowly and change his or her perceptions over time. Often people may feel the obligation to be strong or brave for others. Children, in particular, are very inquisitive. The child will certainly have feelings, but no two children will react in the same way to an impending death, including their own [29]. Each child will try to not only understand what is happening to them, but they will also try to understand why it is happening to them [30]. Adults can help the child to learn his or her own tune. What is the meaning of the child's life for the child? What is the meaning of the child's life for the adult? Both the child and the adults will better be able to face the death with a willingness to accept suffering as a part of life [31]. The same processes will aid adults in their struggle to understand and develop meaning from dying and death situations.

Like the other arts, music has rarely been given a fair hearing in the social sciences. The social aspect of music and the other arts is often ignored. Music and art are normative and are part of the value structure of a culture. Some groups, like Native Americans, do not separate the esthetics of art and music and religion. Their focus for music is not how does it sound nor how it will it sell, but rather what is it for? The chant-like music has text that reflects the values and spirit of the mores of the people. The Navajo use songs to heal as with the Enemy Way or the Mountain Chant ceremonials [32]. The healing ceremony contains the values and norms of the people. Christian songs, Jewish songs, and Native-American songs may all hold some healing value to those who hear them. Music is typically combined with other art forms. In Canada, music therapy is used with dancing, physical exercise, group games, acting, painting and drawing, and so forth [33]. The drypaintings of the Navajo combine all of the major arts using chants, music, poetry, songs, drama, dance, and prayers [34].

FUNCTIONS OF ART

Like humor and music, art also can be used to aid those faced with dying. Art Therapy aids in facing denial and reduces fear in the dying [35]. Fear increases pain and causes reflections about death [36]. Like humor and music, art can help diffuse the fear and lower the pain. Art facilitates the relaxation of the defenses and leads to greater self-awareness [37]. Art therapy is particularly effective with children or the severely traumatized. Art therapy has been successfully used with the terminally ill and their families [38].

As a sociologist, I have used art to allow elementary school children to vent their feelings and frustrations about the Gulf War, a teacher's untimely death, and the deaths of other students [39]. It frees the child to say through the art what he or she does not feel free to say with words. It allows them to do the impossible. It allows them to fulfill both their negative impulses and positive wishes without fear of consequences [40]. Even the most alienated child can express his or her most hidden feelings without repercussions. Creative art brings out experiences that allows the alienated child to communicate and be understood that could not occur otherwise [41]. Children who are in pain or have great anxiety can relax and even strengthen their immune system responses [42].

FUNCTION OF THE ARTS

Other art forms serve the same or at least similar functions for children who are faced with dying. Dancing, drama therapy, poetry, and storytelling are only a few that can be used with children faced with dying.

Dancing has always been a means of exercise and pleasure. All dancing was originally sacred. Historically, dances often personate the dead [43]. The Hopi Kachina is one such example. Dance has been a part of the traditions of most peoples. In the Western world, there are many rich traditions involving the use of dance. The Catholic Church has a long history of Liturgical dance [44]. A Christian healing dance was used in the 1300 and 1400s [45]. Dance has been a strong part of the Hebrew tradition [46]. Dancing as a form of creative expression can allow one the freedom to move, to create, and to feel free.

Dramatherapy has also been found to be important in the healing process for children [47]. Goldman and Morrison have used dramatherapy to succesfully help students deal with Kübler-Ross' stages of the dying process and to work through grief and issues of facing death [48]. Kellerman found that drama aids with unresolved grief and to say good-bye to the deceased [49].

Storytelling can clearly aid people to face crises and traumas. Why do we read stories to children? Why do we take children to theme parks? By reading to children or taking them to theme parks, we as adults get to enjoy as children. As parents and adult caregivers, the use of children's stories is a part of your normal activity with children. Many excellent children's books are available to help children with dying and death issues. These same books are also quite helpful for the adults who read them to the children. Stories can be used to access emotional states and attitudes of children [50]. One can then begin to tell stories that can lead to understanding. Helpful children's books do exist. For example, *Charlotte's Web* by E. B. White [51] is a beautiful story about a spider, the narrative is a suspenseful, humorous, witty account of death and new beginnings. *The Happy Funeral* by Eve Bunting [52] is the story of the death of a Grandfather that illustrates how funerals can be happy for those who have lived a happy life. Jack Kent's story, *There's No Such Thing as a Dragon* [53], is a wonderful example of how one needs to keep things in perspective. It is an excellent book for those facing death. Therapists have used photos, poetry, sculpture, and many other creative forms of expression to aid those facing the death process or grief. Weiser has found that photos can be used to aid both children and adults to face the death process and grieving [54]. Phillips [55] and Morrison [56] have found that poetry is therapeutic and healing for both the dying and the grieving. Laidlow has found writing to be useful with healing loss and grief of death [57]. Sally Bailey has found that the most alive patients are those who are in touch with their own creativity. They are able to pour forth rage, fear, and anger. She has been able to enliven hundreds of dying people with art [58]. Creativity aids in the struggle for mastery over trauma. It works for both children and adults. Elie Wiesel and others used writing to survive the grief of the death camps [59]. As adults, we try to protect our children. Somehow we seem to think that if we are not straightforward with them about their impending death that we are protecting them. Our very protection of our children may increase their fears. Children are not born with fears [60]. We, as adults, live what we learned as children.

For most, a death leads to a focus upon what was lost rather than upon what one experiences in a relationship. In every relationship, there are good times and bad times. A child needs to remember the good times and to accept the bad times.

One way to approach this lesson is to reminisce with the child, and one way to begin is to bring out photo albums.

THE ARTS AND THE DYING

When a child faces a life threatening illness, humor, music, art, and other fine arts can perform many important functions. They can become a safety-valve for releasing hostility and discontent and otherwise unacceptable feelings [61]. The arts can be used in sacred situations to make the participants seem more human. Showing the "bloopers" from the latest Superbowl allows those fans and players who may take the game too seriously as a "sacred" event, to begin putting the game in perspective when viewing the mistakes of such excellent players in a game.

The arts can allow the participants to deal better with the anonymous bureaucracy and maze of technical jargon that surrounds the seriously ill in institutions. Humor, music, and art can also be an expression of individualism which could enhance one's feelings of self-control in the face of a situation where one seemingly has no control. Such activities also allow the individual to maintain his or her own value when dealing with the elites of the medical world. Doctor jokes, music, or even drawings of doctors, can make medical people seem less imposing to the dying. Lastly, humor, music, and art can allow the seriously ill or the dying to deal with the paradox of life and death.

CONCLUSION

We can use humor, art, and music to allow ourselves to grow and to learn, as well as to understand the more important uses of humor in facing what fate life has to offer. The use of humor, music, and art as a therapeutic agent is possible. Humor, music, and art can function to relieve anxiety, stress, tension, anger, hostility, and allow one to cope with crises. They can temporarily neutralize emotionally painful situations.

REFERENCES

1. L. Pirandello, *On Humor,* University of North Carolina Press, Chapel Hill, North Carolina, 1960.
2. J. Palmer, *The Logic of the Absurd: On Film and Television Comedy,* BFI, New York, 1987.
3. P. Lewis, *Comic Effects: Interdisciplinary Approaches to Humor in Literature,* State University of New York, Albany, 1989.
4. G. Cox, *Sociology of Death and Dying: Theory and Research,* Fort Hays State University, Hays, Kansas, 1990.
5. L. Peter, *The Laughter Prescription: The Tools of Humor and How to Use Them,* Ballantine, New York, 1982.

6. M. Leming and G. Dickinson, *Understanding Dying, Death, and Bereavement*, Holt, Rinehart & Winston, Forth Worth, 1994.
7. C. Powell and G. E. Paton (eds.), *Humor in Society: Resistance and Control*, St. Martin's, New York, 1988.
8. K. Mogg and B. P. Bradley, Attentional Bias to Threat: Roles of Trait Anxiety, Stressful Events, and Awareness, *The Quarterly Journal of Experimental Psychology*, 47A:4, pp. 841-864, 1994.
9. H. Selye, *Stress without Distress*, J. B. Lippincott, Philadelphia, 1974.
10. A. Monat and R. S. Lazarus, *Stress and Coping: An Anthology*, Columbia University, New York, 1977.
11. A. Ziv, *Personality and Sense of Humor*, Springer, New York, 1984.
13. H. Mindness, *Laughter and Liberation*, Nash, Los Angeles, 1971.
14. L. Joubert, *Treatise on Laughter*, University of Alabama, Alabama, 1980.
15. V. M. Robinson, Humor and Health, in *Handbook of Humor Research*, P. E. McGee and J. H. Goldstein (eds.), Springer, New York, 1983.
16. N. Holland, *Laughing: A Psychology of Humor*, Cornell University Press, Ithaca, New York, 1982.
17. A. R. Eckardt, *Sitting in the Earth and Laughing: A Handbook of Humor*, Transaction Publishers, New Brunswick, New Jersey, 1992.
18. L. E. Mintz (ed.), *Third International Conference on Humor: Conference Abstracts*, Conference Committee, Washington, D.C.
19. M. Grotjahn, *Beyond Laughter*, McGraw-Hill, New York, 1957.
20. S. S. Cox, *Why We Laugh*, Benjamin Blom, New York, 1976.
21. B. P. Dutton, *Indians of the American Southwest*, Prentice-Hall, Englewood Cliffs, New Jersey, 1975.
22. J. Alvin, *Music Therapy*, Basic, New York, 1975.
23. E. T. Gaston (ed.), *Music in Therapy*, Macmillan, New York, 1968.
24. B. Cole, *Music and Morals: A Theological Appraisal of the Moral and Psychological Effects of Music*, Alba House, New York, 1993.
25. K. M. Higgins, *The Music of Our Lives*, Temple University, Philadelphia, 1991.
26. L. Bunt, *Music Therapy: Art Beyond Words*, Routledge, New York, 1994.
27. D. M. Schullian and M. Schoen, *Music and Medicine*, Henry Schuman, New York, 1948.
28. D. M. Moriarty (ed.), *The Loss of Loved Ones: The Effect of a Death in the Family on Personality Development*, Warren H. Green, St. Louis, 1983.
29. E. H. Schneider, *Music Therapy*, Allen, Lawrence, Kansas, 1961.
30. R. Coles, *The Spiritual Life of Children*, Houghton Mifflin, Boston, 1990.
31. C. Pregnant, *When a Child Dies*, Ave Maria Press, Notre Dame, Indiana, 1992.
32. L. C. Wyman, *Sandpaintings of the Navajo: Shootingway and the Walcott Collection*, Smithsonian, Washington, 1970.
33. V. S. Lombardo and E. F. Lombardo (eds.), *Kids Grieve Too!*, Charles C. Thomas, Springfield, Illinois, 1986.
34. W. Matthews, The Night Chant, A Navajo Ceremony, in *Memoirs of the American Museum of Natural History*, Vol. VI, The Hyde Southwestern Expedition, 1902.
35. D. R. Henley, *Exceptional Children: Exceptional Art: Teaching Art to Special Needs*, Davis, Worchester, 1992.

36. E. R. Hilgard and J. R. Hilgard, *Hypnosis in the Relief of Pain,* Brunner & Mazel, New York, 1994.
37. E. Kramer, *Art as Therapy,* Schocken, New York, 1971.
38. M. F. Levick, *They Could Not Talk and So They Drew,* Charles C. Thomas, Springfield, Illinois, 1983.
39. G. R. Cox, B. Vandenberk, R. J. Fundis, and P. McGinnis, American Children and Desert Storm: Impressions of the Gulf Conflict, in *Beyond the Innocence of Childhood,* D. Adams and E. Deveau (eds.), Baywood, Amityville, New York, 1995.
40. J. A. Rubin, *Child Art Therapy: Understanding and Helping Children Grow Through Art,* Van Nostrand Reinhold, New York, 1978.
41. G. H. Williams and M. H. Wood, *Developmental Art Therapy,* University Park Press, Baltimore, 1977.
42. E. L. Feindler and F. R. Kalfus, *Adolescent Behavior Therapy,* Springer, New York, 1990.
43. W. O. E. Oesterley, *The Sacred Dance: A Study in Comparative Folklore,* Cambridge University Press, Cambridge, 1923.
44. R. Gagne, T. Kane, and R. VerEecke, *Introducing Dance in Christian Worship,* Pastoral, Washington, 1984.
45. E. L. Blackman, *Religious Dances in the Christian Church and in Popular Medicine,* George, Allen & Unwin, London, 1952.
46. M. Daniels, *The Dance in Christianity,* Paulist, New York, 1981.
47. S. Jennings, *The Handbook of Dramatherapy,* Routledge, London, 1994.
48. E. E. Goldman and D. S. Morrison, *Psychodrama: Experience and Process,* Kendall & Hunt, Dubuque, 1984.
49. P. F. Kellerman, *Focus on Psychodrama: The Therapeutic Aspects of Psychodrama,* Jessica Kingley, Philadelphia, 1992.
50. G. Combs and J. Freedman, *Symbol, Story, and Ceremony: Using Metaphor in Individual and Family Therapy,* Wm. Norton, New York, 1990.
51. E. B. White, *Charlotte's Web,* Harper and Row, New York, 1952.
52. E. Bunting, *The Happy Funeral,* Harper and Row, New York, 1982.
53. J. Kent, *There's No Such Thing as a Dragon,* Gooden, New York/Western, Racine, Wisconsin, 1975.
54. J. Weiser, *Phototherapy Techniques: Exploring the Secrets of Personal Snapshots and Family Albums,* Jossey-Bass, San Francisco, 1993.
55. E. L. Philips, *Love, Poetry, and Psychotherapy,* Irvington, New York, 1985.
56. M. R. Morrison, *Poetry as Therapy,* Science, New York, 1987.
57. T. A. Laidlaw, *Healing Voices: Feminist Approaches to Therapy with Women,* Jossey-Bass, San Francisco, 1990.
58. S. Bailey, Creativity and the Close of Life, in *Dying, Death, and Bereavement: Theoretical Perspectives and Other Ways of Knowing,* I. B. Corless, B. B. Germino, and M. Pittman (eds.), Jones & Bartlett, Boston, 1993.
59. D. Aberbach, *Surviving Trauma: Loss, Literature, and Psychoanalysis,* Yale University Press, New Haven, 1989.
60. K. J. Doka, *Disenfranchised Grief,* Lexington Books, Lexington, 1989.
61. A. J. Chapman and H. C. Foot (eds.), *Humor and Laughter: Theory, Research, and Applications,* John Wiley & Sons, New York, 1976.

CHAPTER 13

The Arts and Story: A Source of Comfort and Insight for Children Who are Learning about Death*

Sandra L. Bertman

Death education is in many ways a misnomer. There is little we teachers can tell children or adults about death. There is, of course, information to share and research to be considered. But this knowledge serves primarily as a foundation or framework; death education really means permission to share attitudes, fears, and concerns. The classroom provides a conducive yet structured setting in which to become aware of varied views of life and death, different styles of coping with loss, and the grieving process.

The expressive arts convey a rich variety of human experience. Who of us has not wondered what it feels like to be dead nor pondered the significance of being? Who of us has never felt afraid, alone, uncomfortable, or at a loss for words? The realities of coping with loss perceived by the artist can elucidate those of students. Fictional images can serve to reduce the individual's sense of isolation and open the mind to previously unconsidered ideas and behaviors. This aesthetic language of the human spirit is not the exclusive province of professional artists. It exists within us all. Expressions in the form of dialogue and drawing, for example, give focus and vision to deeply felt feelings and concerns present in the student of any age.

---

*This chapter is based on a version published in *Omega, 10*:2, 1979-80 © 1979, Baywood Publishing Co., Inc.

Working with the visual and literary modalities (story, song, painting, film), this chapter:

1. identifies sources of concern and consolation;
2. presents materials and techniques for eliciting and expressing emotion; and
3. underscores the "mutuality"—the university and yet individuality—of each subjective experience.

THE LIFE CYCLE:
A NON THREATENING "GRABBER"

Life Cycle, an abstract animated film, is an involving, non-threatening instrument that can help students focus on perceptions of life and death [1]. The animation, restricted to blobs which move to a musical soundtrack, presents a framework; a structure devoid of verbal exchanges or much in the way of human characterizations. However, emotional connotations and intent are quickly ascribed to the pulsating blobs of the viewers. Details of individuality such as age, sex, and values are debated. The responses range from being moved by the blobs ("they seem so real") to being affected ("they seem so generalized, non personal"). One of the blobs dies—"at home," "with husband," and "is the grandmother," or "in the hospital," "alone," and "is the grandfather." The students' experiences of/and fantasies about death emerge in giving the animation personal definition.

THE LIVED VS. THE UNLIVED LIFE

Students are concerned with whether the blob which dies had a "full" life; a life marked by warm relationships, a loving marriage, children, and grandchildren. But not all students evaluate the blobs' lives with such tenderness. The blob that dies is ascribed an "empty" life—one of form: born, schooled, married, grandparented, and died. This unlived life assessment is reminiscent of the Solomon Grundy of the nursery rhyme ("born on Monday . . . married on Wednesday . . . died on Saturday") [2].

Some people conclude (and console themselves) that the blob which dies had a "good" life. If death occurred any other place along the life cycle, far earlier or far later, could it appropriately be called "a good life?" Is it merely a matter of number of years, or is it, rather, what one does with those years? When faced with the diagnosis of acute leukemia, Ted Rosenthal concludes in the biographical film, *How Could I Not Be Among You?*, that it is not death people fear, it is the "incompleteness" of their lives [3, p. 45]. "Completeness" to Rosenthal, has nothing to do with living out one's four score and ten; it has to do with not having lived fully "in the moment," with not having lived those years well whatever their number. In *The Magic Moth*, a children's story, the mother recounts how special and happy her daughter's short life was for the family [4]. When questioned by her son about his sister's death, she answers that some people do not seem to be meant to live very long:

"Then why was Maryanne born?"
Mother smiled, "Maryanne was like the plants in our garden," she said. "They only last a short while, but they make us happy while they are here" [4, p. 56].

In *Annie and the Old One*, another story for children, an Indian grandmother feels her time has come and prepares the family for her death: "When the new rug is taken from the loom," she says, "I will go to Mother Earth" [5, p. 41]. Annie tries to hold back time by undoing the weaving each evening, her mother completed during the day. But Annie eventually comes to understand—and accept—the appropriateness of a timely death:

The cactus did not bloom forever. Petals dried and fell to the earth. She knew that she was a part of the earth and the things on it. She would always be a part of the earth, just as her grandmother had always been, just as her grandmother would always be, always and forever. And Annie was breathless with the wonder of it [5, p. 41].

No matter what their individual ideas of afterlife or death, most readers come to appreciate Annie's feeling that all living things are intimately connected with each other.

It is not always easy to die in one's time. Others may not understand, especially people who work in highly structured institutional environments. In *Dying in Academe*, an intern is no more able than Annie to accept an old person's readiness to give up life [6]. The patient, Mr. Kahn, explains metaphorically to the young physician, "you see . . . the engine is broken down; it is time for the engineer to abandon it." His more direct statement of intention to die leads to the following discussion:

". . . it's not allowed. You are in a hospital, a university hospital, equipped with all the latest technology. Here you must get well."
"My time has come."
"Time is measured differently here" [6, p. 56].

Violating the old man's wishes by resuscitating him as she's promised not to do, is simply a sophisticated way of unraveling the weaving, of undoing the careful arduous work of dying. Unfortunately, for the young physician, the consequences are more far reaching than the awareness that death is no enemy. The intern is left with a sense of tension between certain taught professional roles and the inherent human value of honoring another's autonomy.

WHAT DOES IT FEEL LIKE WHEN YOU DIE?

The last vignette of *Life Cycle* slowly freezes and the animated blob becomes, quite literally, in-animate [1]. This is the first time the pulsating blob is seen not moving. What is death? In fact, "your heart stops beating." BUT DOES THE DEAD PERSON STILL FEEL? This question often becomes an obsessive one for younger students.

Children's drawings and accompanying explanations reveal a continued concern for the comfort and safety of the body. One six year old explains what's in the picture he constructed; the men are carrying the dead body to the cemetery high over their heads: "she shouldn't be dragged; that would be bad" [7]. A bit later, examining why a river of tears is coming from one figure whose mother died, he says, "That was his mother and she's watching them. She feels sorry." He quickly corrects himself, "I mean, he (the grieving son) feels sorry."

Children's literature deliberately addresses this concern. In the *Magic Moth,* after burying William, the guinea pig, Mark-O is thinking about how uncomfortable his pet must be under the wet, heavy dirt. A conversation with his mother reveals this worry and his continuing doubt in spite of her reassurances:

> "Momma, do you think William is cold out there?"
> "No, I don't" she answered.
> "Why?
> "Well, because after guinea pigs die, the don't feel anything anymore."
> "Are you sure?"
> "I am very sure" [4, p. 24].

In another novel, *Growing Time,* a mother comforts her son, Jamie, with the consolation that their pet dog is no longer feeling the aches and pains he suffered in his aged life: "his teeth don't hurt him and his legs don't hurt him anymore" [8]. Unfortunately, she prefaces these words with "He is happy now," a statement which causes confusion in the classroom. Students, even the youngest ones, pick up the contradiction. If he is not able to *feel hurt,* how can he *feel happy?*

It is not only children who wonder whether the dead body might feel pain or discomfort. A recently bereaved nursing student confessed an affinity to Mark-O when she told the class of her overwhelming urge to run out during a rainstorm in order to cover her dead sister's mound. Rationally, she "knew" her sister was immune to cold. Nonetheless, she was haunted by the thought that her sister was cold and getting wet. In *Gifts,* the speaker exhibits concern when the funeral people come to collect her mother's body [9]. Reminiscent of the six year old who insisted a body not be "dragged," she and her father actually rearrange heavy furniture so the corpse can be removed without being twisted or discomforted in any way:

> ... Daddy was horrified, and he said, we'll have to move the bookcase, but it's heavy, because he was worried about how they'd get her out on the cot, if they had to fold it to get it in [9, p. 68].

WHERE DO YOU GO WHEN
YOU'RE DEAD?

Not only might the dead one still feel, but where is he now? What happens after death is a major question. In the children's book, *The Tenth Good Thing About Barney,* one youngster envisions his cat in the ground helping flowers grow and he consoles himself with the thought, "you know...that's a pretty nice job for a cat" [10]. His sister pictures Barney "in heaven with lots of cats and angels, drinking cream and eating cans of tuna" [10].

The confusion with place, with literalness, is voiced by Mark-O (*Magic Moth*) who is trying to make sense of the sister's death. In this story, an adolescent brother tries to respond to Mark-O's insistence that Maryanne will come back:

> "Well, no, she won't. But where she is going it will be nice."
> "Is she going to China?"
> "Creepers! Don't you know anything? Of course she's not going to China. When people die they go to heaven."
> "Is heaven under the ground?"
> "Of course not. Quit asking questions" [4, p. 17].

Using this conversation as a focus for role play in the classroom, a ten-year-old girl responded to Mark-O's next question, "Do you think she's in heaven?"

> Well, I really don't think so. I think that she goes in the ground and goes to little pieces of the soil but the heart goes to the family and makes them think about the good times with the person who dies and finally they feel better and go out and just have a good time. And the person who dies stays in the other people so they don't forget her and always think of the good times [7].

In another classroom setting, a fifteen-year-old adolescent picked up on the conversation by composing a dialogue:

> "No, not exactly. Maryanne is not alive anymore. She's not with us here on earth. There is only one part of Maryanne that is alive, and that is her mind."
> "You mean her brain?"
> "More than her brain—her other thoughts and what she believed about the people and things on earth. Her ideas are alive."

"Yes, but where did she go? I saw her go into the ground."

"Her body went into the ground, but where do you think her mind went?"

"I bet it went to the place Dad used to take us to on the cape. You know, the place with the flowers!"

"That's probably what Maryanne's mind is thinking now. Wouldn't that be nice for her to think about forever?"

"Yes, cause that was her favorite place! I'm glad she's happy now. When I die, will Dad let me have a new bike?"

I laughed and said, "Why don't you ask Dad for a new bike now?" [7].

The concern with where the being is, where that self, that spirit of a person or animal has gone, is not so easily dismissed. The issue frequently arises both in the literature and in the classroom. If King's old worn out body buried beneath the apple tree is "nothing to him anymore" (*Growing Time*), then what is something to him? What and where is the "him" that once was? In much the same way as the nine year old and fifteen year old explained to Mark-O that Maryanne still existed in memory and essence, Jamie's grandmother (*Growing Time*) [8] helps him understand how King's spirit did not get buried with his body underground but remains alive and at home with them:

Well, look here child, I can't see a thing, without my glasses. I can't see the stove over there, but I know it is, all right. I can't even see my own shoes right now, but I know my feet are in them, don't I? Well, I know what's in the heart, too. And I know King still has a home to come to [8, p. 23].

Not having the benefit of exposure to the nine-year-old and fifteen-year-old students, or to Jamie's grandmother, Mark-O (*Magic Moth*) again raises the question when the minister consoles his family with a prayer voicing the concept that life never ends it just changes:

"Is that really true?"

"That is what I believe," replied the minister. "I believe that when people die they step through the door into another place that we can't see with our eyes."

"Could they go through a window, too?" Asked Mark-O, remembering the moth.

"Yes. Windows let in light, and I believe there is light where people go. But not the kind of light you see with your eyes. It is more like the kind you feel inside when you love someone, like Maryanne" [4, pp. 45-46].

Just such warmth, love, and presence is felt by the speaker in *Gifts* when she is uncomfortably cold and puts on one of her dead mother's sweaters and thinks "its like having her arms around me" [9, p. 69].

COPING: STAYING IN TOUCH

Responding to the assignment "describe in picture or words someone dead," one third grader wrote the following letter to his (dead) grandmother:

Dear grandmother

Where did you go? Will you come back, please come back. I will give you a cake a car as much gold as you want and a lot of house and everything you want. Are you in havin or in your grave or are you a ghost.
If you are in havin I will send you a letter if you are in you grave I will put the letter on your grave and if you are a ghost I will be scared [7].

The letter reveals how badly the boy misses his grandmother and how much he wants her back. It does not deny the fact of death; rather, it tries to make sense of where the grandmother is now in actuality or in essence. The letter is a way of feeling the strength of being in touch with the lost person, just as is wearing a piece of clothing and gaining the comfort of "having her arms around me" [9].

This youngster's letter is in spirit much like Maxine Kumin's poem in which she tells her dead friend how it is without her:

Shall I say how it is in your clothes?
A month after your death I wear your blue jacket.
The dog at the center of my life recognizes you've come to visit, he's
    ecstatic. . . .
I think of the last day of your life,
Old friend, how I would rewind it . . . [11, p. 58].

In the story, *Dusty Was My Friend,* the main character resolves his sorrow and emptiness after his friend's accidental death, by the same vehicle: a written communication directly to (dead) Dusty, despite parental challenge:

"You can't do that."
"Yes I can."
"But Dusty is dead. He couldn't read it," Mom said.
"I know that." Of course I knew that. Sometimes mothers act dumb [12].

and symbolically, delivering it

. . . I wanted to put it on Dusty's grave . . . But he is buried where the accident happened, far away. Maybe someday I'll go there. I'd like to. I have the letter in my secret treasure drawer in case I ever do. Otherwise, I'll just keep it [12].

This is an explicit illustration of the healthy working out of one's grief, no matter what the age.

COPING:
PARTICIPATING IN THE LAST RITES

In a book for the very young, *The Dead Bird,* a group of children experience sadness when they happen upon a newly dead bird. The thought of performing a ritual makes them feel better:

> The children were very sorry the bird was dead and could never fly again. But they were glad they found it, because now they could dig a grave in the woods and bury it. They could have a funeral and sing to it the way grown-up people did when someone died [13].

In the classroom, it becomes apparent that quite a large percentage of students have never attended a funeral. Nervous laughter punctuates the discussion as students of all ages identify with Mark-O (*Magic Moth*) whose stomach hurts when he thinks about his sister's funeral ("He had never been to a funeral and knew he would not like it") [4, p. 48]. In this novel, the mother does not heed Grollman's advice of allowing the young child to attend the burial "if he chooses" [14, p. 32]. Explaining the details of what to expect from the event and well aware of the value of family participation, she insists five year old Mark-O attend:

> "Do I have to go?" he asked Mother.
> "Yes you do," she replied firmly. "Anyway, it will not last very long. You will feel better if you go. Remember how you always bury Guinea Pigs when they die? You read poems when you put them in the ground, and you say a prayer. Then you feel better. This is like that" [4, p. 49].

In *Gifts*, the relevant rite which arouses anxiety for the author precedes the funeral. The father does not insist on participation:

> . . . Daddy had taken me out on the porch and said: there's a tradition of our people. We wash our own dead. It's a last act of loving kindness. I plan to do that for your mother. Would you like to help me? I was stunned into silence. Then, I said hesitantly, I want to do it, but I don't know if I'm able. He was silent. Finally I said: yes. You don't have to if you don't want to, he said. I can do it alone [9, p. 69].

Seeing her mother dead initially overwhelms this young adult:

> I was stunned and terrified that I would scream or cry; fail him, and her. I stood there, clutching the prayer book and praying for strength not to fail him . . . [9, p. 71].

The participation in washing her mother's body transformed a "distasteful chore" into a "last act of loving kindness." Even more, the act of participation is perceived as a reciprocal gift showering the giver with unexpected feelings of contentment and mastery:

> . . . I feel a certain strength in myself that I never thought I'd be capable of, just because I helped . . . [9, p. 71].

REMEMBERING AND ALLOWING ONESELF TO FORGET

> . . . and if thou wilt, remember [15].

Remembrance, and the solace and contentment it brings, is a concern of many students. This issue is addressed, in part, in *Where is Dead*, a film exploring the ramifications of an accidental death of an older sibling [16]. The younger sister Sara tests her mother's explanation of what memory is with both her grandfather and Anne her best friend. Anne's mother had warned Anne not to remind Sara of David (the dead brother). In the classroom, we freeze the film in these two instances (after the friend's revelation of her mother's admonition and before the grandfather's healthy answer about the value of memory) and students role play their responses. The ensuing conversation graphically exposes the discomfort of the consoler, the horrors of not mentioning painful memories, and ultimately the benefits of sharing. It becomes apparent that the burden of small talk widens the gulf between bereaved and friend, and even may evoke anger.

Role playing the grandfather's explanation of memory to Sara, an eleven year old said:

> Your brain keeps on thinking of him even though he's not a physical being. In the mind there has been a place set aside for him and you usually don't think of it until he dies (then it stands out) [7].

To Sara's (role played) response, "I don't want to remember David because it makes me sad," the same youngster explained:

> Well the more you don't think of him the sadder you'll get. Because in this place in the mind (it's like water leaking out of a dam—if you don't stop it it will leak out more and more until it will all come out and it will explode the dam). Well, that's sort of like a person. If you don't think of him you'll get sadder and sadder and finally it has to all come out. Some way or other [7].

In strikingly similar imagery, Shakespeare acknowledges the value of sharing grief and the danger of repressing painful memories:

> Give sorrow tounge
> The grief that does not speak
> Whispers the o'erfraught heart
> And bid it break [17, p. 1212].

The film *Where is Dead* opens at the playground with David's encouraging Sara to attempt the slide. Positioning himself at the foot of the slide, he reassures his sister, "Don't worry, I'll catch you." In the final scene, once again at the playground, the film demonstrates the positive incorporation of memory. Sara pauses, briefly, at the top of the slide and relives the time David was there to assist her. The memory is not so painful that she is unable to complete the slide. To the contrary, recalling how her brother made it safe for her to come down, Sara slides and then positions herself at the foot of the slide exactly as David had done. She reassures another child with his words, "Don't worry. I'll catch you."

> "And if thou wilt, forget" is the concluding line of Rosetti's couplet [18, p. 1245].

After the ritual burial of a dead bird in Margaret Wise Brown's book *The Dead Bird*, we find the following description of the children's behavior:

> And every day, until they forgot, they went and sang to their little dead bird
> and put fresh flowers on his grave [13].

The illustration on the following page focuses not on the grave in the woods (though it is visible in the distance), but on the children happily involved in a ball game. Both the parenthetical phrase, "until they forgot," and this pictured scene declares, unjudgmentally, it is O.K. to forget. Forgetting is in the natural order of things. And one does not have to feel guilty for enjoying ongoing life.

In the film *The Day Grampa Died*, the rabbi consoles young David with the idea that "Grampa doesn't die as long as we remember him" [15]. The discomfort in the classroom exposes an unintended implication of the rabbi's words. Students infer from this that the grandson now has the responsibility of remembering. As long as he does so, grandfather is "alive" somewhere—in limbo or a waiting place of some sort. The minute David forgets him, his grandfather will really be dead. And David, then, would be saddled with the guilt of having caused the death.

As in the final scene of *Where is Dead*, the filmmaker demonstrates that one needn't be preoccupied with the sadness of loss, and that memories aren't always painful. The suggestion of time lapse is indicated by the details of season change—foliage, birds, and lighter weight clothing. David is playing with a friend. Seeing a man that resembles his grandfather, David pauses from his play. But he is only slightly distracted. He smiles to himself at the reminiscence, and continues playing.

COPING: ALLOWING ONESELF TO CRY

The idea that giving way to tears is a sign of weakness, especially for males, is directly voiced in Hamlet when Claudius rebukes a grieving son for "obsequious sorrow." "'Tis unmanly grief" [19, p. 889].

To the student, letting go means quite literally, "crying our eyes out." The fear of giving way to tears seems to be connected to losing control and the possibility of never being able to stop. In the six-year-old's picture, grief is overwhelming. Lest the viewer miss the young artist's intention, the word "CRY" is incorporated into the composition (see Figure 1).

Being overwhelmed by grief is depicted somewhat differently in the eleven-year-old's set of drawings. The first picture (Figure 2), quite Duchamp-like in technique, focuses on the process of the boy becoming memory to his parents. While this is happening the parents are crying profusely. The extent of their sorrow is indicated by the number and detail of tears flowing from the parents eyes accumulating in a puddle at their feet.

In the second drawing (Figure 3), no tears are visible. But circles under their eyes, the occupation ("making sad balloons"), and the protruding stomachs signify greater desolation. The youngster explains that the parents have big stomachs because they are still "eating to feel better" and are consumed with their sadness "a long time later."

This youngster's final drawing did not indicate that all those tears had succeeded in washing the sadness out of the grieving parents. Grief is so overwhelming in its early stages, so all encompassing, that is hard to believe the pain will be mitigated with time and that life will again hold meaning. Quite incredulously, poet George Herbert writes "Who would have thought my shrivel'd heart could have recover'd greeness?" [20, p. 1088]. Giving way to tears and to whatever other discomfort one is feeling, is the strange mystery of the healing process.

Some people don't cry. A person might wonder, as she looks around and realizes that no one else has dry cheeks, "Am I some kind of monster?" Being under-whelmed by grief is also cause for anxiety. Students fear being exposed as less than human, as callous and unfeeling, if expected behaviors (such as crying after a death or a funeral) are not displayed. As Mark Twain, tongue in cheek, guides us:

> Where a blood relation sobs, an intimate friend should choke up, a distant acquaintance should sigh, a stranger should merely fumble sympathetically with his handkerchief [21, p. 152].

Twain's satire brings a smile to one's face, for we all recognize the pressure of the expected response. Peter Ivanovish felt it (and behaved accordingly) when he visited Ivan Ilych's widow in Tolstoy's novel, *The Death of Ivan Ilych*:

Figure 1.

And (he) knew that, just as it had been the right thing to cross himself in the room, so what he had to do here was to press her hand, sigh, and say, "Believe me . . ." [22, p. 99].

Priority has little to do with sincerity, and students sometimes feel that the *shoulds* should be eliminated: grief work is not etiquette. Yet, it also should [sic] be remembered that expected, recognized forms of behavior are very comforting in time of unusual stress. Although manners are sometimes used hypocritically, they remain the currency of concern, and they are an indispensable mode of expression for many.

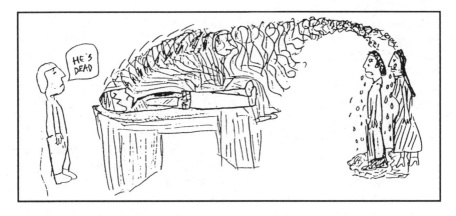

Figure 2.

Figure 3.

The intense mood swings and inconsistency of feelings that accompany loss are acknowledged with a tinge of guilt by the mother in the short story, *The Bad Baby:*

> You know, she says, her face suddenly troubled, there are days when I think it would be a relief to rend our clothes and walk around with ashes on our heads—when I want no part of my sanity, when I don't want to function at all. And there are other times, like today, when I want to skate and make lunch and laugh, even though . . . [23, p. 31].

Poet Helga Sandberg comments on her own behavior at the news of her father's death, "When they told me to come, I could not weep." Again, after the wake, she mentions leaving the funeral parlor "unweeping" [24, p. 96]. Similarly, in a children's novel, *The Taste of Blackberries* [25], Chuck notes that he was unable to cry at his friend's funeral. Feeling guilty, he tries to make the tears come by pressing his face into his father's coat buttons.

The classroom responses to Chuck's dry eyes range from logical explanation ("What good is crying? It's not going to bring his friend back"), to empathetic statements ("I couldn't cry either. I'd be too shocked"), to intimations of what does, indeed, happen ("It's O.K. not to cry now. At one point he'll cry. If it's not now, later, Maybe tonight"). If a class member does judge or berate Chuck for not caring (e.g., license to forget, not crying, or not displaying the expected behavior), tolerance for a multiplicity of responses and styles warrants special consideration.

Tears are not the only way for pain to be relieved. Sadness and tenseness may be handled by surprising and unusual responses. Young Mark-O's behaviors after Maryanne's funeral (*Magic Moth*) were frenetic physical activity and displaced anger:

> When he got out on the playground at recess, he ran faster, yelled louder, and played harder than he had ever done before. When he went home he was happy until he got on the porch. There were more people in the house! How he hated all these people! It was his house. Why wouldn't they leave him alone? He could hear them laughing, too. . . . He went in and stomped loudly up the stairs. When Mother called him down to lunch, he did not answer [4, p. 46].

Concern may even be expressed by bizarre outbursts, such as a sacrilege or a piece of macabre, "sick" humor. The anxiety at the time of President Kennedy's death was addressed in the high school classroom by such *MAD* comic jokes as "What did Caroline get for her birthday? A jack-in-the-box." To an assignment to describe death, a thirteen year old boy responded with this drawing (Figure 4). This adolescent's grandfather had recently undergone open heart surgery.

Crying is sometimes for oneself. In her poem *Death*, one sixth-grade girl reveals a tolerance for the range of responses exhibited by her family when faced with the illness and death of her grandfather. With remarkable clarity and not a tinge of guilt, she attributes her own tears, not to sadness at her grandfather's death, but to the awareness of her own vulnerability:

> My Grand father's gone
> Never to return.
> He was in the hospital
> Getting better.
> He died though I
> Knew he would.

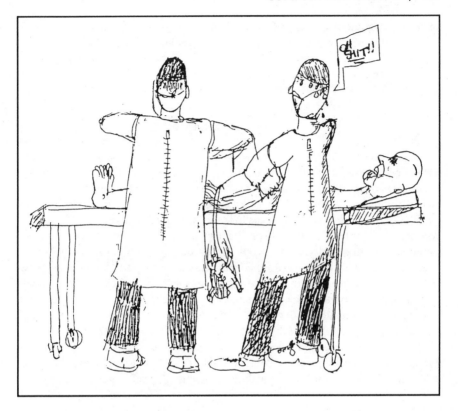

Figure 4.

My mom hated it.
  He was her dad.
  She kept saying
"I wish I could cry."
  She never cried.
I didn't either except
  When I thought
THIS will happen to
  Me too.   [7]

In *A Taste of Blackberries*, Chuck, who had not cried at his friend's funeral was surprised to find his "tear faucets" turned on by the sight of his mother tucking him in that evening. "The strange thing is I wasn't crying for Jamie," he confesses. "I was crying for me" [25, p. 47]. Gerard Manly Hopkins points out in the poem *Spring and Fall: To A Young Child*, that when meditating on any loss, one is intimately confronting one's own mortality [26]. Hopkins affirms the experiences of the sixth-grade poet and of Chuck when he, gently but directly, concludes to Margaret, weeping over the passing seasons ("Goldengrove unleaving"):

> It is the blight man was born for,
> It is Margaret you mourn for.

CONCLUSIONS

The classroom can be a repository of death experiences, anxieties, and feelings. Art expressions in the form of film, story, dialogue, and drawing can give focus and voice to deeply felt concerns that are present in the student of any age (which, of course, applies to any one of us infant to octogenarian, and then some). The use of one art form quickly leads to identification of similar themes in another form. The stimulus of pictorial or literary media—including the now classic children's literature cited here—prods us to articulate sentiments that may have been previously unsharable. Death education is not group psychotherapy; nonetheless, open expression in a once taboo area can ease feelings of fear and loneliness. As important as any content that gets generated in the discussion is a community of mutuality with one another as well as a kinship with the artists and published authors. Provoked by classmate or artistic image, "the ease and discharge of the fullness and swellings of the heart" can occur in the classroom. Francis Bacon succinctly phrased it in his essay *Of Friendship:* "Friendship works two contrary effects, for it redoubleth joys and cutteth grief in halves" [26].

REFERENCES

1. *Life Cycle,* film animation created by E. Zinn, production pending, Program of Medical Humanities, UMASS Medical School, S5-100A, Worcester, Massachusetts.
2. S. Grundy, *The Real Mother Goose,* Rand McNally, Chicago, 1916.
3. T. Rosenthal, *How Could I Not Be Among You?,* Braziller, New York, 45, film distributed by Benchmark Productions, Scarsdale, New York, 1973.
4. V. Lee, *The Magic Moth,* Seabury, New York, 1972.
5. M. Miles, *Annie and The Old One,* Little Brown, Boston, 1971.
6. N. Caroline, *Dying in Academe, New Physician,* American Medical Student Association, Virginia, pp. 654-657, 1972.
7. S. L. Bertman, *Death Education: A Primer For All Ages,* collection of student work, unpublished manuscript, Program of Medical Humanities, UMASS Medical School, S5-100A, Worcester, Massachusetts.
8. S. S. Warburg, *Growing Time,* Houghton Mifflin, Boston, 1969.
9. D. Linett, Gifts, *MS. Magazine,* pp. 67-71, March 1978.
10. J. Viorst, *The Tenth Good Thing About Barney,* Atheneum, New York, 1972.
11. M. Kumin, How It Is, *New York Magazine,* New York, March 3, 1975.
12. A. Clarly, *Dusty Was My Friend,* unpublished manuscript.
13. M. W. Brown, *The Dead Bird,* Young Scott, New York, 1958.

14. E. Grollman, *Talking About Death,* Beacon, Boston, 1970.
15. *The Day Grampa Died,* Bailey Film Association, California, 1970.
16. *Where is Dead,* Encyclopedia Britanica Films, Chicago, Illinois, 1975.
17. W. Shakespeare, Macbeth, in *Shakespeare: The Complete Works,* Harcourt Brace, New York, 1948.
18. C. Rossetti, Song, in *An Anthology of World Poetry,* M. Van Doren (ed.), Reynal & Hitchcock, New York, 1928.
19. W. Shakespeare, Hamlet, in *Shakespeare: The Complete Works,* G. Harrison (ed.), Harcourt Brace, New York, 1948.
20. G. Herbert, *Anthology of World Poetry,* Reynal & Hitchcock, New York, 1928.
21. M. Twain, At the Funeral, *Letters from the Earth,* Fawcett, New York, 1932.
22. L. Tolstoy, *The Death of Ivan Illych,* New American Library, New York, 1960.
23. R. Silman, The Bad Baby, *New Yorker Magazine,* New York, 1973.
24. H. Sandberg, Father, Once You Said That in the Grace of God, *McCalls Magazine,* New York, October 1968.
25. D. Smith, *A Taste of Blackberries,* Crowell, New York, 1973.
26. G. M. Hopkins, Spring and Fall: To a Young Child, *Immortal Poems of the English Language,* O. Williams (ed.), Pocket Books, New York, 1952.
27. F. Bacon, Of Friendship, *Oxford Anthology of Prose,* New York, 1935.

CHAPTER 14

Children, Death, and Fairy Tales*

Elizabeth P. Lamers

HISTORICAL BACKGROUND

There is a history behind each of the familiar stories that parents read at their children's bedsides. Many of what have now become common fairy tales had their origin in an oral tradition intended as adult entertainment, replete with ribald humor and sensational events. As these tales began to be transcribed and considered more specifically as material intended for children, they began to contain incidents and behavior that reflected the customs of the place and period in which they were written down and that were intended to provide children with a moral education. Especially in the earliest versions, death had a place in children's stories because of its ubiquity and drama. There have been significant transformations to fairy tales, and to the content of children's stories in general, since a literature for children first appeared. Until recently, topics that have come to be considered disturbing to young people, concerning issues that adults would wish to protect them from, have been diluted, softened, and removed from the literature for children. In our modern generations, children have been insulated from an awareness of mortality.

Particularly in the last hundred years, a significant movement away from issues of morality and mortality has taken place. This has reflected the tremendous changes in attitudes concerning children and death over the last century. These changes have coincided with the shifting of the demographics of

---

*This chapter has also appeared in *Omega, 31*:2, pp. 151-167, 1995, and in *Awareness of Mortality*, J. Kauffman (ed.), Baywood, Amityville, New York, 1995.

death in this time period and with the changing of attitudes toward children and their upbringing.

Up to the end of the nineteenth century, the highest mortality rate was to be found in children under the age of fifteen; today the highest rate is found in adults of far more advanced years. In the past, children were exposed to dying because it occurred almost exclusively at home after a short illness; death now occurs almost exclusively in some sort of healthcare institution following a prolonged illness. Although in recent years hospice programs have sought to return dying to the home, the majority of elderly persons still die either in a nursing home or a hospital. As a result, children and even young adults today are commonly separated from the reality of death [1]. This isolation is reinforced by a scarcity of material that would introduce children to the universal experiences of dying and death.

The changing composition and structure of the modern family has also had an isolating effect on the young person's awareness of mortality. At the end of the last century, it was common for children to grow up as a member of an extended family, consisting of parents, grandparents, aunts and uncles, who all lived in the same rural area. A child today is more likely a member of a "nuclear" or one parent family, living in an urban area, often separated from relatives by hundreds of miles. Children in rural areas once were exposed to dying and death in their families, in their communities, and among farm animals. They had repeated opportunities to be close to death, to ask questions about death, and to participate in healing religious and social bereavement ceremonies and rituals.

While once the loss of a relative was an occasion for ceremonies that emphasized and reinforced family coherence, today the death of a relative, especially an elderly or distant one, may pass with little or no observance. Many parents have come to believe that children should be shielded from dying and the facts of death, and it is common today for children not to attend funeral services [2].

Although children may be exposed to literally hundreds of deaths in television programs and cartoons, these are a different kind of death, typically of a "bad" person, who because of some evil actions "deserved" to die. Children's cartoons consistently present to children a distorted view of mortality, even fostering the especially erroneous conclusion that death is somehow "reversible." With little contradiction, beliefs like these can continue to influence and pervade perceptions of death [3]. They come to stand in place of substantial experiences with dying and death, giving rise to difficulties and misunderstandings in later years when the child, as an adult, has real experiences with mortality. Beliefs like these have been fostered by the isolation of the child from the experience of death as a part of life, an isolation that can be traced in the transformation that has occurred to the stories and fairy tales that have been read to children since such tales first appeared in written form in the early 1700s.

BOOKS ABOUT DEATH FOR CHILDREN

The removal and glossing over of incidents of dying and death from material that children are exposed to has been occurring regularly since about the 1920s. At the same time religion was being removed from school books. It is only in the last twenty years that this tendency has begun to be reversed, and children's books now often contain topics that were previously taboo, including, feelings, divorce, sex, and even death. Religion is still taboo in school books.

From the early 1800s until the 1920s, American children were commonly taught to read with a series of textbooks, such as those by Lyman Cobb, Worcester, Town, Russell, Swan or McGuffy. In *McGuffy's Eclectic Readers,* the subject of many of the selections and poems was the death of a mother or child [3]. These deaths were typically presented as a tragic but an inevitable part of life. The manner in which death was portrayed can be found in such representative examples as William Wordsworth's poem *We Are Seven* [4], in which a little girl describes her family as having seven children, even though two are dead and buried in the churchyard near their house. The experience of the death of an older sister is also described in this poem. Other selections from the *Readers* in which death is a theme are: *Old Age and Death* [5], by Edmund Waller, *The Death of Little Nell* [6], by Charles Dickens, *Elegy in a County Churchyard* [7], by Thomas Gray, and *He Giveth His Beloved Sleep* [8], by Elizabeth Barrett Browning.

A selection in the Fourth *Reader* by an anonymous author, entitled *My Mother's Grave* [9], provides an emotional account of a young girl's experience with her dying mother. The story aims to make children polite and obedient to their parents, by giving the example of a young girl who didn't realize how fleeting life can be. The author of the story recaptures her thoughts while revisiting the grave of her mother, who had died thirteen years previously. She remembers how she had been unkind to her mortally ill mother after coming home from a trying day at school. Realizing her lapse in manners later in the evening, she returns to her mother's room to ask forgiveness, to find her mother asleep. The little girl vows to awaken early to "tell how sorry I was for my conduct," yet when she rushes to her mother's room in the brightness of morning she finds her mother dead, with a hand so cold "it made me start." The author relates how even thirteen years later, her remorse and pain are almost overwhelming. This is not the type of subject matter and emotional content that is generally considered appropriate for today's basal readers.[1] The basal readers commonly used today in classrooms rarely contain any references to death or dying. They might contain a chapter from a book such as *Charlotte's Web,* by E. B. White [10], but the chapter would not be the one in which Charlotte dies.

---

[1] A basal reader is a text with which reading is taught. There are many different series, each usually having one book per grade level.

Insight into the fashion in which scenes of death and dying were typically portrayed in the nineteenth century can be found in the book *Little Women* [11], written by Louisa May Alcott in 1869 and still widely read by young readers today. Alcott wrote of the death of young Beth in a straightforward manner that was especially uncommon for her day. Recognizing that her depiction was at odds with the melodramatic scenes that were current in more romantic literature, Alcott added in the paragraph following Beth's death: "Seldom, except in books, do the dying utter memorable words, see visions, or depart with beatified countenances . . ." [11, p. 464].

The elements that Alcott took exception to were all common in death scenes in the literature of 1830 to 1880, where they reflected the expectations of an audience that was accustomed to being given a romanticized picture of death and its consequent "final reward" in what was known as "consolation literature." A preoccupation with death and a glorification of the afterlife was evident in the popular literature from both England and America in this period. Much of this literature was written either by Protestant clergy (especially Congregationalists and Unitarians), their wives, or pious women of the congregation [12].

Between 1940 and 1970 only a few children's books contained references to death. Two that have become classics are *The Dead Bird* [13], by Margaret W. Brown and *Charlotte's Web*, by E. B. White [10]. White's publisher initially refused to publish *Charlotte's Web* unless the ending was modified to allow Charlotte to live. White refused [14]. The book was criticized by reviewers who said that death was not "an appropriate subject for children." *Charlotte's Web* is still a best seller, and often is one of the books which second or third grade teachers choose to read to their classes.

The separation of children from death has diminished somewhat in the last twenty years. Elisabeth Kübler-Ross' early work [15] helped make death a subject that could be discussed and studied. Children's books in the late 1960s began to discuss subjects that had previously been neglected, such as death and divorce. During the 1970s and 1980s, over 200 fiction books were written for children with death as a major theme. Unfortunately very few measured up to the standard set by *Charlotte's Web* [10], *Little Women* [11], *The Yearling* [16], or *The Dead Bird* [13]. During the same period some very good non-fiction books about death were written for children of various ages. (See resource list at end of chapter.)

This cornucopia of books on death has helped to begin to make death a more acceptable topic for discussion. The hospice movement has also helped by reintroducing home care for dying persons to many communities. Even so, many children are still insulated from death and often are discouraged from attending funerals. It is not unusual to find adults in their forties who have never attended a funeral [17]. The diminished awareness of mortality that begins in childhood, then, is often carried on into adulthood.

THE DEVELOPMENT OF CHILDREN'S LITERATURE

Prior to the development of a literature intended specifically for children in the middle of the seventeenth century, there were two characteristic ways in which children were considered. The first was a holdover from the age of the Greeks and Romans, in which children were perceived as miniature adults. Another manner of perceiving children, as something infra-human, was distinguished by Michel de Montaigne, the French humanist and essayist of the sixteenth century. It is difficult, however, from a modern perspective, to be sympathetic to Montaigne's assertion that children possessed "neither mental activities nor recognizable body shape" [18, p. 229].

Authors writing children's literature in the eighteenth century were primarily interested in educating children and assisting them to become socially acceptable human beings. Beyond providing just a certain amount of book learning, they also sought to teach the correct ways to behave. For this reason, all the tales of Perrault had an emphatic moral at their end. They were cautionary tales of what could happen to a child if he or she didn't act in a proper fashion. Some of Perrault's titles were: *La Belle au Bois Dormant* (Sleeping Beauty) [19], *Le Petit Chaperon Rouge* (Little Red Riding Hood) [20], and *Les Fées* (Toads and Diamonds) [21]. As pointed out by Maria Tartar in, *Off With Their Heads!*:

> From its inception, children's literature had in it an unusually cruel and coercive streak, one which produced books that relied on brutal intimidation to frighten children into complying with parental demands. This intimidation manifested itself in two very different forms, but both made examples of children. First, there were countless cautionary tales that managed to kill off their protagonists or make their lives perpetually miserable for acts of disobedience. Then there were stories about exemplary behaviour which, nonetheless, had a strange way of also ending at the deathbeds of their protagonists [22, p. 9].

In 1658, John Amos Comenius's *Orbis Sensualium Pictus* (A World of Things Obvious to the Senses Drawn in Pictures), a Latin school book, was published. This teaching device was the first picture book for children [23], and it was also the first to respond to the recognition that children needed their own literature because they were not scaled-down adults. It was still almost a century, however, before children's literature began to come into its own. In 1744, John Newbery wrote *A Little Pretty Pocket Book* [24] for children. This book is credited as signifying the "real" start of children's literature in England.

FAIRY TALES

Fairy tales provide an excellent example of the fashion in which themes that came to be considered distressing to children have been moderated over time, and insulation of children from an awareness of mortality can be traced through the progression of different versions of typical stories. A generalization can be made about fairy tales as they came to be thought of specifically as children's stories: the sexual content was diminished and the amount of violence tended to be increased. This process can be seen in successive editions of the Brothers Grimm's Fairy Tales. To understand this evolution, it is necessary to have a picture of the environment in which it took place. According to the perception of children's needs current at the time that the Brothers Grimm were writing, children did not need to be protected from portrayals of violence.

William Jordan [25], in *Divorce Among the Gulls*, provides a dramatic context for the state of life that was not untypical for children in London a mere one hundred years after the time that a children's literature came into being:

> I doubt that any of us can comprehend how brutal the fight for survival has been throughout evolution. We ignore our prehistoric, evolutionary legacy, a world in which most children died in infancy or childhood, where teeth rotted out by the age of twenty, where gangrene took the lives of the injured, where thirty-five was foul old age. Even as recently as 1750 in London, the toll of disease staggers the mind: Of 2,239 children born that year, only 168 were still alive five years later [25, p. 169].

From its inception, literature for children has been motivated by a belief that children needed written material not so much for entertainment but to prepare them for life. The majority of books published and intended for children up through the 1800s can be compared to James Janeway's *A Token for Children: Being an Account of the Conversion, Holy and Exemplary Lives, and Joyful Deaths of Several Young Children (1671-72)* [26]. The London Bills of Mortality for the period shortly following the publication of Janeway's book show that the mortality rate of children age five and under was running as high as 66 percent [22]. Writers of this era commonly concurred with Janeway's position that they held a sacred duty to salvage the souls of those who were "not too little to go to Hell." The exemplary stories in *A Token for Children* were also designed to provide comfort to children faced with the tragedy of a sibling's death or confronted with their own mortality when visited by some dread disease [22].

The violence and death in stories written for children takes on a different light when put in the context of such high rates of mortality. The practice of abandoning unwanted children either at the Foundlings' Hospital or on church steps was increasing in the 1700s. It was not just the poor but all classes who contributed to the ranks of abandoned children. The foundling institution was established to make it possible to dispose of infants without leaving any record. Buffon [27] noted in 1772 that about one-third of all children born in Paris that year were abandoned. Jean-Jacques Rousseau (1712-1778) claimed to have turned his five children over to the state, leaving them at the Foundlings' Hospital at birth [28].

A high mortality rate for children was reflected in children's literature. As Freud noted in *The Interpretation of Dreams*, half the human race failed to survive the childhood years [29]. The characteristically romanticized depiction of an afterlife that was superior to the life of this world was seen as a way to help children cope with the brutal facts of the life they had no choice but to lead. In the seventeenth and eighteenth centuries, children were routinely required—not just encouraged—to attend public executions so that they could see the price of criminal behavior. This says much about the methods of child rearing believed appropriate in this era [22].

The Brothers Grimm's story *Aschenputtel*, or *Cinderella*, shows an emphasis on punishment that was lacking in the earliest oral versions, and that increased in intensity in subsequent editions. In the early version, taken by Perrault from the oral tradition, Cinderella forgave her step-sisters for mistreating her and introduced them at court. Grimm's first version has Cinderella's sisters turning pale and being horrified when Cinderella becomes a princess, but in the second edition the sisters are punished by being blinded by pigeons that peck out their eyes [22].

In the Brothers Grimm's *Hansel and Grethel* there is a description of how horribly the witch howled when Grethel pushed her into her own oven and how ". . . Grethel ran away, and therefore she was left to burn, just as she had left many poor little children to burn" [30, p. 57]. The use of violence as punishment for bad behavior is typical in fairy stories. And violent occurrences were frequently shown to be the result of even minor misdeeds. This tendency is evident in the collection of stories found in Struwwelpeter [31]. In these short tales, Little Pauline plays with matches and goes up in flames, and Conrad the Thumbsucker gets his thumbs sliced off. As Tartar points out, the interesting point here is that ". . . the weight is given to the punishment (often fully half the text is devoted to its description) and the disproportionate relationship between the childish offense and the penalty for it make the episode disturbing" [22].

The removal of sexuality from books intended for children was a development that paralleled the evolution of housing in Europe. In the Middle Ages houses were rarely more elaborate than was necessary. Few homes had more than one room. The poor had hovels which were little more than a shelter for sleeping. Family life tended to be compromised. Because there was no room for children, only for infants, the older children were commonly sent away to work as apprentices or servants.

The living quarters of the bourgeois would typically be above a store or artisan's shop. It generally consisted of a single large room in which the household cooked, ate, transacted business, entertained, and slept. Households of up to twenty-five people were not uncommon. Privacy was unknown [32], and children were not sent to bed in their own rooms so that racy stories could be told to adults only. Beds were generally large because they were intended to hold more than one or two people. Children lived and worked alongside adults and listened to the same stories. Since children were in the company of adults who were not their parents, but were employers or other servants, there was not the same concern about what children were exposed to that parents of today have.

By the seventeenth century, this living arrangement had evolved into one in which there tended to be a greater segregation between the quarters allocated to working, food preparation, and sleeping. There still tended to be a main room used for dining, entertaining, and receiving visitors, but servants and children began to be separated into smaller rooms adjacent to the central, common areas [32]. It was at this time that fairy stories began to be transformed into works intended more strictly for children. This transformation of living spaces coincides with other changes that had great impact on children, including attitudes about how children should be taught about proper behavior and about death and dying.

By looking at the changes in one fairy tale, *Little Red Riding Hood,* we can observe the changes in attitudes toward death, children, and their education. The earliest known oral version of the tale of *Little Red Riding Hood,* for example, would not generally be considered suitable entertainment for children today. In the version of the story traditionally told in Brittany, Little Red is unwittingly led by the wolf to eat her grandmother's flesh and drink her blood, and she performs a provocative striptease for the disguised wolf before climbing into bed with him. Little Red later escapes from the wolf when she goes outside to relieve herself. As this tale was originally told, its primary purpose was to entertain adults, so it was not as heavily encumbered with the admonitions and advice that later came to distinguish versions of this tale intended for children.

The earliest written version of Little Red Riding Hood was recorded in French by Charles Perrault in 1696-97. The title of the story in French was *Le Petit Chapeon Rouge.* The "chapeon" was a hat worn in the Middle Ages, which suggests an even earlier oral tradition [33, p. 22]. One of the fullest texts faithful to the traditional, oral versions of *Little Red Riding Hood* was also recorded in France at the end of the nineteenth century [22].

Perrault's first version of the tale was published in *Histoires ou Contes du Temps Passé* (Stories [Tales] of Times Passed), subtitled Contes de Ma Mère L'Oye (Tales of My Mother Goose). Perrault included seven other tales along with the tale of *Little Red Riding Hood.* Each of these tales had a moral in verse at the end. In this version of Little Red's tale, the grandmother and Little Red are both eaten by the wolf, and both perish. Although Perrault did not have Little Red's mother giving her any initial warnings before she departed for her grandmother's house, he did conclude the story with a moral suitable for the intended audience of children: Do not speak to strangers or you, too, may provide a wolf with his dinner. The violence of this story is later moderated in the Brothers Grimm retelling by the introduction of an additional character, a hunter or woodcutter, who is able to rescue Little Red and her grandmother by slicing open the wolf and letting them out.

The version of Little Red's tale as told by the Brothers Grimm also gives an expanded role to Little Red's mother, who gives Little Red many warnings and much advice before sending her off through the forest to Grandmother's house. Little Red is admonished to "make haste . . . go straight . . . behave prettily and modestly . . . do not run . . . and do not forget to curtsy and say 'good morning' to everyone who knows you" [30]. These initial admonitions served to educate the young audience of the story in the manners that were expected of them, and they provided a framework in which the resulting action of the story would be played out. The Brothers Grimm vividly portrayed the consequences of not heeding Mother's advice. Interestingly, in this version, the hunter refers to the wolf as "old sinner" [30, p. 109], perhaps as an oblique reference to risqué incidents excised from the children's version but remembered from the oral tradition.

In a popular nineteenth-century retelling of Little Red's tale found in *Old Favorite Fairy Tales*, Grandmother still gets eaten by the wolf, but Little Red survives and learns to pay closer attention to her mother's words: "For she saw the dreadful end to which/A disobedient act may lead" [30, p. 112]. This version of the tale has an interesting emphasis on avoiding any unnecessary suffering of the characters. Here is the depiction of the wolf putting an end to Grandmother:

> He jumped up on the bed, and ate her all up. But he did not hurt her so much as you would think, and as she was a very good old woman it was better for her to die than to live in pain; but still it was very dreadful of the wolf to eat her [33, p. 20].

The editor of *Old Favorite Fairy Tales* was apparently undecided about whether Grandmother's fate was good or bad. When the woodcutter arrives on the scene to rescue Little Red, he advises her that one shouldn't "tell one's affairs to strangers, for many a wolf looks like an honest dog" [33, p. 20]—an interesting way of warning a young girl that looks can be deceiving!

In later versions the hunter arrives in time to shoot the wolf before he eats either Little Red or her grandmother, and in still other versions, even the wolf is spared to escape through an open window, or to become Little Red's pet. The moral or message of the story also evolves with the transformation of the events depicted in the story. In the traditional, oral version of *Little Red Riding Hood*, Little Red was not forewarned by her mother about the dangers of talking to strangers, therefore Little Red cannot be seen as naughty or disobedient. In Perrault's original written version the mother does not give Little Red any cautions, either, while in later versions the mother often gives many instructions and admonitions to her daughter. Upon rescuing Little Red from the dire misfortune she brings upon herself, the hunter/woodcutter inevitably gives her a lecture on obedience and points out to her that she now knows what can happen if she disobeys her mother's warnings. The role that mortality plays in the changing tale of Little Red Riding Hood is seen to diminish as the tale evolves; rather than being the graphic and unmourned event as Perrault depicted it, it becomes unrealistically softened in the later versions, eventually being banished to the periphery of the young audiences' attention.

WHAT IS A FAIRY TALE?

To understand better the significance of the place that fairy tales and other tales told to children have in determining the formation of attitudes relating to death and dying, it is helpful to become familiar with some of the different definitions that these tales have been given. Fairy tales have been defined in various ways by different people. Rollo May considered fairy tales to be ". . . our myths before we become conscious of ourselves" [34, p. 196]. Bruno Bettelheim wrote,

> The figures and events of fairy tales . . . personify and illustrate inner conflicts, but they suggest ever so subtly how these conflicts may be solved, and what the next steps in the development toward a higher humanity might be . . . presented in a simple homely way . . . Far from making demands, the fairy tale reassures, gives hope for the future, and holds out the promise of a happy ending [35, p. 26].

Madonna Kolbenschlag writes:

> Fairy tales are the bedtime stories of the collective consciousness. They persist in cultural memory because they interpret crises of the human condition that are common to all of us. They are shared wish fulfilment's, abstract dreams that resolve conflicts and give meaning to experience [36, p. 2].

Edwin Krupp makes a distinction between fairy tales and the rest of children's literature,

> The term "fairy tale" is sometimes used for all children's stories, but the fairy tale really has its own special character. It involves or takes place in another realm or world, not in the one in which we usually reside. Fairy tales are really stories of the supernatural. Other laws prevail in them, and the creatures that inhabit them do not belong to ordinary reality [37, p. 11].

All of these definitions are good and even have merit in their own context, yet they are unsatisfying in their failure to consider the origin of these tales in adult entertainment and the purposeful manner in which they were converted into tales intended for children.

There is an easily confusing overlap between fairy tales, folk tales, and myths.

Myths are the most easily distinguishable, as they are mainly stories intended to provide explanations for the occurrence of natural phenomenon, generally by personifying a natural effect as an animistic or anthropomorphic deity. The depiction of the sun in its course as Apollo driving his fiery chariot, and winter being caused by Demeter mourning for the six months of Persephone's captivity in Hades, are typical of mythological stories. Even though in their later elaborations myths might come to deal with models of behavior and other topics commonly found in fairy tales, their origins can be found in the earliest explanations of natural phenomena. Broad definitions like Rollo May's [34] seem to apply more clearly to myths than to fairy tales.

Folk tales and fairy tales are not as easily distinguished, as indicated by the fact that published collections of folk tales and fairy tales may very well contain some of the same stories.

A characteristic of fairy tales is the flexible way that they have been perceived by authors. Authors in different times and places have recognized that fairy tales are capable of carrying a message that can be tailored to fit their particular needs. Existing as they do in the common domain, fairy tales and their characters provide an easily accessible medium for both writers and their audience. The task of the audience is eased by the familiarity of the characters and situations with which they are presented, and the writer's burden is lightened as he brings stories from an earlier time into conformity with the standards he is trying to represent. The subtle or obvious manner in which a fairy tale departs from its audiences' expectations while still fulfilling their desires is a measure of its successful telling. A current example of this phenomenon is the bestseller *Women Who Run With the Wolves* [38], in which many fairy tales are retold with an emphasis on their pertinence to the modern female experience.

Fairy tales are also significant in the wide range of characters and situations that may be found in them. Children are presented with characters that they can identify with in fairy tales, commonly in the guise of a child not so unlike herself or himself who is faced with an adverse situation in which he or she is called upon to make new judgments and exhibit mature behaviors. Children can be exposed to a range of novel situations through the fairy tale, and exposed to models for their own behavior to fit a variety of their needs. The most popular fairy tales, especially, have always been adapted as adult perceptions of children's needs have changed and adult needs to communicate various lessons to children have changed [39].

In distinction to fairy tales, folk tales often concern the actions of pseudo-historical or typical personages who are engaged in activities that represent cultural standards that children are expected to aspire to. The unerring accuracy of William Tell is related in a folk tale, as is George Washington's chopping down of the cherry tree and his precocious, unwavering honesty. The adventures of Paul

Bunyan and his gigantic blue ox, Babe, are folk tales that recast popular stories from the era of the westward expansion of the United States as "tall tales" with a common main character.

It cannot be maintained, as Bettelheim's definition suggests, that a fairy tale invariably holds the promise of a happy ending. *The Little Mermaid* [40], which is a definite fairy tale, has been subjected to a great deal of distortion, or "artistic license," to produce a happy ending. At the conclusion of the tale as Hans Christian Anderson originally wrote it, the Little Mermaid chooses death for herself rather than murdering the Prince, which would have enabled her to regain her form as a mermaid. The only consolation for the Little Mermaid, who had already sacrificed her home, family, and voice to pursue her love for the mortal, human Prince, is that after performing deeds of kindness for three hundred years as a "daughter of the air," she might gain a human soul and join the Prince in heaven. The very morning that the Little Mermaid sacrifices herself and spares the Prince, he marries a princess from another land whom he mistakenly believes had rescued him from drowning, when actually the Little Mermaid had saved him. Only in Disney's version does the Little Mermaid manage to displace the "other woman" and marry the Prince. Disney justifies this alteration by casting the evil sea-witch in disguise as the other princess.

The classic fairy tale *Bluebeard* [41] also presents a problematic ending. In this fairy tale, one of three sisters marries a wealthy but mysterious man, distinguished primarily by a beard of blue color. After the wedding, the wife is given access to all Bluebeard's possessions, but she is forbidden to use one small golden key. When she inevitably opens the door the key closes, she discovers the bloody bodies of Bluebeard's previous wives. When Bluebeard discovers his wife's transgression, he prepares to add her to his collection. At the last moment, the wife is saved by the sudden appearance of her brothers, who hack her husband into pieces before her eyes. The happiness of the ending of this tale must be considered more one of degree; although the latest wife did not meet the fate of her predecessors, is it really a happy ending to have your brothers murder your husband? This tale also leaves unresolved the dilemma of the wife's part in the action. Her disobedience is a necessary part of the story, yet there is no clear resolution to this issue. The fast and easy way to conclude a fairy tale is to recite "and they lived happily ever after," yet when one takes a close look at fairy tales there are many which do not have a "perfect" ending.

THE FUTURE OF FAIRY TALES

When folk and fairy tales existed solely in an oral medium, every story teller was able to tell a version of a story that was personalized by the demands of his or her time, place, and audience. When stories came to exist more exclusively in printed form, they began to reflect more enduringly the nature of the time and place in which they were recorded. For this reason, it is especially odd that we continue to read to our children—often without the slightest degree of critical reflection—unrevised versions of stories that are imbued with the values of a different time and place. L. Frank Baum, the originator of the tales of the land of Oz (1900), recognized this predicament, and recommended that it was time for a new set of "wonder tales," and that previous fairy tales should be classed as "historical" [22].

There is a growing perception that children are capable of having an understanding of dying and death as natural processes, and that the lifelong relationship a person has to dying and death is based in no small measure on the experiences of childhood. In the last twenty years, there has been a revolution in the practices and perceptions surrounding dying and death, yet little has been effectively done to transmit these changes to children. Adults are beginning to recognize the difficulties they have experienced as a result of being sheltered from an awareness of mortality and the need is felt for a way to transmit a realistic awareness of mortality to children.

Denoting traditional fairy tales as "historical" would help distinguish the changes in values and behaviors that have occurred in the many years since they were recorded, and would encourage parents and teachers to more critically examine just what they are presenting to children. Modern editions of fairy tales have enormous appeal, demonstrated by the lavishly illustrated editions that have been offered recently by some of the large publishing houses. It is interesting to note that reviews of these books have concentrated on the beauty of the illustrations, the size of the book, the quality of the paper . . . in other words on everything but the content. The assumption seems to be that the buying public already knows what the content is and that no explanation is necessary.

But it is important to consider the implications of fairy tales in our modern world. Perhaps it is time to begin transforming them to reflect the tremendous changes that have occurred in a world increasingly forced to accept the limits of medical technology, where death is being acknowledged again as a necessary and inevitable counterpart to life.

Reading with a child is a wonderful activity; introducing someone to the world of books is to offer them the promise of a greater and better world. Fairy tales can be an important part of this process, because their "real" existence is in the imagination of a child, and through the action of a fairy tale a child can learn that he or she can confront circumstances that are new or frightening and be able to do the right thing. It is important that the tales we tell to our children reflect what we ourselves believe; rather than continuing to insulate children from the realities of death and dying, especially by providing the unsuitable types of messages that Saturday morning T.V. provides, fairy tales can provide a medium for children to be introduced to the types of situations that they will encounter all their lives.

One of the few activities that haven't changed since the eras of our parents and grandparents is tucking a child into bed with a story, even down to the story we might choose to read. There is a comfort in this nostalgia, and a sense of continuity to this activity that can make all involved believe in the truth of the final ". . . and they lived happily ever after." A cartoon in a recent edition of the *New Yorker* magazine illustrated this [42], while also showing the capacity fairy tales have to portray facets of the world that are not necessarily easy to explain. The cartoon showed a mother reading a bedtime story to her daughter with the caption "She married and then divorced, and then she married and divorced, and then she married and lived happily ever after."

Although this cartoon was certainly intended to be ironic, it still points out the purpose of providing moral instruction that fairy tales can fulfill. With the expanding use of hospice programs, and the corresponding increase in opportunities for children to be exposed to meaningful death experiences, and with the increase of the awareness of the lethalness of AIDS, it is important that even the tales told to children come to reflect current perceptions of dying and death.

BOOKS ABOUT DEATH FOR CHILDREN AND YOUNG ADULTS

The following list of books is a sample of general books (fiction and non-fiction) about death available for children.

Non-Fiction

J. Bernstein and S. J. Gullo, *When People Die*, Dutton, New York, 1977.

E. J. Le Shan, *Learning to Say Good-Bye: When a Parent Dies*, Macmillan, New York, 1976.

E. Richter, *Losing Someone You Love. When a Brother or Sister Dies*, Putnam, New York, 1986.

E. E. Rofes, and The Unit at Fairweather Street School, *The Kids' Book About Death and Dying*, Little, Brown and Co., Boston, 1985.

O. Segerberg, Jr., *Living with Death*, Dutton, New York, 1976.

H. Zim and S. Bleeker, *Life and Death*, Morrow, New York, 1970.

Fiction

L. M. Alcott, *Little Women*, Gossett and Dunlop, New York, 1947 (originally published 1869). (Sister—illness)

S. Alexander, *Nadia the Willful*, Pantheon, New York, 1983. (Brother—accidental)

Aliki, *Two of Them*, Greenwillow, New York, 1979. (Grandfather—old age)

J. Bartoli, *Nonno*, Harvey House, New York, 1975. (Grandmother—natural death)

J. Blume, *Tiger Eyes*, Bradbury, Scarsdale, New York, 1981. (Father—murdered in robbery)

M. W. Brown, *The Dead Bird*, Addison-Wesley, Reading, MA, 1965. (Wild bird—natural death)

E. Buntin, *The Empty Window*, Frederick Warne, New York, 1980. (Friend—illness)

E. Coerr, *Sadako and the Thousand Paper Cranes*, Putnam, New York, 1977. (Hiroshima—leukemia caused by radiation)

M. Craven, *I Heard the Owl Call My Name*, Doubleday, New York, 1973. (Young priest—illness)

T. de Paola, *Nana Upstairs and Nana Downstairs*, Putnam, New York, 1973. (Great grandmother and grandmother—natural death)

E. Douglas, *Rachel and the Upside Down Heart*, Price, Stern, Sloan, Los Angeles, 1990. (Father—heart attack)

M. Gerstein, *The Mountains of Tibet*, Harper and Row, New York, 1987. (Reincarnation)

P. Hermes, *You Shouldn't Have to Say Good-Bye*, Harcourt, New York, 1982. (Mother—illness)

M. W. Hickman, *Last Week my Brother Anthony Dies*, Abingdon, Nashville, 1984. (Infant brother—congenital heart condition)

M. Kantrowitz, *When Violet Died*, Parent's Magazine Press, New York, 1973. (Pet bird—natural death)

P. Mann, *There are Two Kinds of Terrible*, Doubleday, New York, 1977. (Mother—illness)

M. Miles, *Annie and the Old One*, Little, Brown and Co., Boston, 1971. (Navajo Indians—grandmother—natural death)

K. Paterson, *Bridge to Terabithia*, Crowell, New York, 1977. (Friend—accidental death)

A. de Saint Exupery, *The Little Prince*, Harcourt, New York, 1943. (Death—general)

D. Smith, *A Taste of Blackberries*, Crowell, New York, 1973. (Friend—bee sting allergy)

M. Talbert, *Dead Birds Singing*, Little, Brown and Co., Boston, 1985. (Mother, Sister—car accident)

T. Tobias, *Petey*, Putnam, New York, 1978. (Gerbil—illness)

S. Varley, *Badger's Parting Gifts*, Lothrop, Lee and Shephard, New York, 1984. (Personified animals—remembering someone after death)

J. Viorst, *The Tenth Good Thing About Barney*, Anteneum, New York, 1971. (Pet—natural death)

S. S. Warburg, *Growing Time*, Houghton Mifflin, Boston, 1969. (Pet Dog—natural death)

E. B. White, *Charlotte's Web*, Harper and Row, New York, 1952. (Death as a natural consequence of life)

H. Wilhem, *I'll Always Love You*, Crown, New York, 1985. (Pet Dog—natural death)

C. Zolotow, *My Grandson Lew*, Harper and Row, New York, 1974. (Grandfather—remembering him)

REFERENCES

1. L. A. De Spelder and A. L. Strickland, *The Last Dance,* Mayfield, Palo Alto, 1983.
2. E. P. Lamers, The Dying Child in the Classroom, in *Children and Death,* G. H. Paterson (ed.), King's College, London, Ontario, pp. 175-186, 1986.
3. *McGuffy's Eclectic Readers,* Vols. 2-6, Van Nostrand, New York, 1920.
4. W. Wordsworth, We Are Seven, in *McGuffy's Eclectic Readers,* Vols. 2-6, Sixth Reader, Van Nostrand, New York, p. 163, 1920.
5. E. Waller, Old Age and Death, in *McGuffy's Eclectic Readers,* Vols. 2-6, Sixth Reader, Van Nostrand, New York, p. 95, 1920.
6. C. Dickens, The Death of Little Nell, in *McGuffy's Eclectic Readers,* Vols. 2-6, Sixth Reader, Van Nostrand, New York, p. 96, 1920.
7. T. Gray, Elegy in a Country Churchyard, in *McGuffy's Eclectic Readers,* Vols. 2-6, Sixth Reader, Van Nostrand, New York, p. 108, 1920.
8. E. Barrett Browning, He Giveth His Beloved Sleep, in *McGuffy's Eclectic Readers,* Vols. 2-6, Sixth Reader, Van Nostrand, New York, p. 195, 1920.
9. Anonymous, My Mother's Grave, in *McGuffy's Eclectic Readers,* Vols. 2-6, Fourth Reader, Van Nostrand, New York, p. 253, 1920.
10. E. B. White, *Charlotte's Web,* Harper and Row, New York, 1952.
11. L. M. Alcott, *Little Women,* Gossett and Dunlop, New York (originally published 1869), 1947.
12. A. Douglas, The Domestication of Death, in *The Feminization of American Culture,* Anchor, New York, pp. 200-226, 1988.
13. M. W. Brown, *The Dead Bird,* Addison-Wesley, Reading, Massachusetts, 1965.
14. D. L. Guth, *Letters of E. B. White,* Harper and Row, New York, p. 531, 1976.
15. E. Kübler-Ross, *On Death and Dying,* Macmillan, New York, 1969.
16. M. K. Rawlings, *The Yearling,* Charles Scribner's Sons, New York, 1938.
17. F. I. Newton, *Children and the Funeral Ritual: Factors that Affect Their Attendance and Participation,* master's thesis, California State University at Chico, 1990.
18. F. I. Newton, *Children's Literature,* Encyclopedia Britannica, Britannica, Chicago, 1976.
19. C. Perrault, La Belle au Dormant (Sleeping Beauty), in *Favourite Fairy Tales,* J. Mulherin (ed.), Granada Publishing, London, p. 12, 1982.
20. C. Perrault, Le Petit Chapeon Rouge (Little Red Riding Hood), in *Favourite Fairy Tales,* J. Mulherin (ed.), Granada Publishing, London, p. 22, 1982.
21. C. Perrault, Les Fees (Toads and Diamonds), in *Favourite Fairy Tales,* J. Mulherin (ed.), Granada Publishing, London, p. 52, 1982.
22. M. Tatar, *Off With Their Heads! Fairytales and the Culture of Childhood,* Princeton University Press, Princeton, New Jersey, 1992.
23. C. Johnson, *Old-Time Schools and School Books* (reprint of 1904 Macmillan edition), Dover, New York, p. 16, 1963.
24. J. Newbery, A Little Pretty Pocket Book, 1744, in *Children's Literature,* Macropedia, Vol. 4, Encyclopedia Britannica, p. 231, 1976.
25. W. Jordon, *Divorce among the Gulls,* HarperCollins, New York, 1991.
26. J. Janeway, A Token for Children: Being an Account of the Conversion, Holy and Exemplary Lives and Joyful Deaths of Several Young Children (1671-72), in *Off With*

Their Heads! Fairytales and the Culture of Childhood, M. Tatar (ed.), Princeton University Press, Princeton, New Jersey, p. 14, 1992.

27. Buffon, in B. J. Boorstin, *The Creators,* Random House, New York, 1992.

28. B. J. Boorstin, *The Creators,* Random House, New York, 1992.

29. S. Freud, The Interpretation of Dreams, Vol. 4 of the Standard Edition (trans. James Strachery) (Hogarth, London, 1953), p. 254, in *Off With Their Heads! Fairytales and the Culture of Childhood,* M. Tatar (ed.), Princeton University Press, Princeton, New Jersey, p. 46, 1992.

30. L. Owens (ed.), *The Complete Brothers Grimm Fairy Tales,* Avenel, New York, 1981.

31. Struwwelpter, in M. Tatar, *Off With Their Heads!, Fairytales and the Culture of Childhood,* Princeton University Press, Princeton, New Jersey, p. 37, 1992.

32. W. Rybcznski, *Home: A Short History of an Idea,* Penguin, New York, 1987.

33. J. Mulherin (ed.), *Favourite Fairy Tales,* Granada Publishing, London, 1982.

34. M. Rollo, *The Cry for Myth,* Delta, New York, 1992.

35. B. Bettelheim, *The Uses of Enchantment,* Vintage Books, New York, p. 26, 1977.

36. M. Kolbenschlag, *Kiss Sleeping Beauty Goodbye,* Bantam, New York, p. 2, 1981.

37. E. Krupp, *Beyond the Blue Horizon: Myths and Legends of the Sun, Moon, Stars and Planets,* HarperCollins, New York, p. 11, 1991.

38. C. P. Estés, *Women Who Run With the Wolves,* Ballantine, New York, 1992.

39. N. Tucker, *The Child and The Book,* Cambridge, New York, p. 80, 1982.

40. H. C. Anderson, *The Little Mermaid.*

41. C. Perrault, La Barbe Bleue (Bluebeard), in *Favorite Fairy Tales,* J. Mulherin (ed.), Granada Publishing, London, p. 38, p. 1982.

42. *New York Magazine.*

CHAPTER 15

Children's Exposure to Sudden Traumatic Death: Bereavement, Post Traumatic Stress Disorder, and the Case for Early Intervention

David W. Adams

Billy, age eight, ran to his neighbor's house. He was "white as a sheet" and sobbing so much that he could not speak. When he clung to the neighbor, Mrs. Watson, she knew something was drastically wrong. Finally Billy blurted out "Daddy." Mrs. Watson gently led Billy back to his house where he balked at entering. She went through the house, ending up in the basement where Eric, Billy's father, was slumped over and hanging by a lamp cord. Billy's mother was out of town, so in a state of shock, Mrs. Watson had to deal with the emergency. It was much later when she found Billy lying in a fetal position on his bed crying uncontrollably. In Mrs. Watson's words, "I had never seen anyone cry like that, I did not know how to help him." The discovery of his father's grotesque, lifeless body plunged Billy into the depths of a numbing shock and a mourning reaction that unfolded like an unending nightmare for months to come.

His mother returned home immediately and relatives rallied to her side. With great difficulty she tried to comfort and support Billy. However, she was so distressed herself that during the time of the funeral she sent him to be cared for by a neighbor. Billy became increasingly mute and withdrawn during the next several months. This led his mother to seek professional help for him.

As a clinical social worker, grief therapist, and death educator, I have been concerned about the tendency of society in general, and of health professionals in particular, to overlook the needs of bereaved children. The impact of such an oversight is especially apparent following sudden traumatic deaths when much of the care is focused on the medical problems of the deceased and the provision of short-term emotional support for the adults who are in attendance at, or immediately after, an unexpected death. At best, ambulance, hospital, and law enforcement personnel provide brief support and, in some instances, follow-up debriefing and linkage to clergy or bereavement counseling resources in the community. Usually these resources are focused on the surviving adults. Surviving children are often dependent on the care given by grieving family members who are in shock and may communicate limited or incorrect information in order to shield children from the impact. Such protection is the natural response of parents in the face of any threat to the well-being of their children. Unfortunately, children like Billy cannot be totally protected and even the temporary buffering of the impact of tragic deaths due to homicide, suicide, disaster, accident, and other unexpected causes is frequently limited. Children are vulnerable, and the experience of the loss and subsequent memories vary in intensity and are revisited throughout their lifetime.

Bereaved children are "disenfranchised," "disadvantaged," or as I would prefer, "forgotten grievers." "Disenfranchised" because they are frequently overlooked and their needs discounted by adults [1]. "Disadvantaged" due to the fact that children are compromised by:

- limitations in their ability to conceptualize death
- thought processes that may be primitive, literal, concrete, and lacking in abstraction
- the use of imagination and magical thought processes that lack the balance of strong reality-based judgment
- limited communication skills
- a lack of life experience
- dependency on adults for control, nurturing, and protection
- emotional immaturity reflected in their capacity to tolerate uncertainty and ambivalence
- a tendency to somatize anxiety which is difficult to communicate in words or actions [2, 3].

THE REACTIONS OF BEREAVED CHILDREN TO SUDDEN TRAUMATIC DEATH

Children's understanding of death, their general reactions during bereavement, and some problems encountered are described in other chapters within this volume. This chapter will examine the specific area of the impact of sudden, unexpected tragedy and will focus on children's reactions that are severe and difficult to manage. These reactions have been delineated by various authors as "distorted," "complicated," or "disabling" [4-6]. Rando states that there are five risk factors associated with traumatic death that increase complications for mourners. These are equally applicable to children and adults and include:

1. "suddenness and lack of anticipation;
2. violence, mutilation, and destruction;
3. preventability and/or randomness;
4. multiple deaths;
5. the mourner's personal encounter with death, where there is either a significant threat to personal survival or a massive and/or shocking confrontation with the death and mutilation of others" [6, pp. 568-569].

Rando suggests that when death is traumatic, "violence, mutilation, or destruction" are the most complicating factors and differentiate this type of death from other types of sudden, unexpected death [6, p. 569]. These factors arouse the mourner's feelings of horror, shock, helplessness, vulnerability, and threat [6]. Other clinicians and researchers agree with Rando and point out that when humans are the perpetrators, the impact of a sudden traumatic death is most intense and lasting [7-9].

At the time of a tragedy, children are extremely vulnerable. They are subject to the same elements of surprise that affect their parents and other family members. The world as they have known it is disrupted without warning or preparation; their lives are permanently changed. Sudden traumatic death tends to be accompanied by heart rending emotional pain, in addition to the shock of the trauma. When family members die, parents upon whom children depend for role modeling, protection, and guidance are frequently unavailable or compromised by the necessity to attend to their own needs, let alone those of their children. This is particularly true when parents have difficulty communicating, are overwhelmed by intense emotion, and have trouble reconnecting to their roles within the family. The absence of this support means that for children, grief may be doubly isolating. They are deprived of their association with the loved person as well as the comfort and guidance that they need from adults in order to cope with the death.

Critical Incident Stress

In recent years, emergency response personnel have been taught to recognize that when adults are involved in or witness a sudden traumatic event, they are prone to intense emotional and physical shock and its sequelae including psychic numbing, denial of the death, impulsive and aggressive behavior, extreme anxiety, guilt, sadness, and occasionally physical collapse. They have also been taught to implement a specific debriefing process within twenty-four to forty-eight hours after the event. This process is based on crisis intervention techniques and the recognition that critical incident stress (CIS) impacts with a vengeance on cognitive, affective, and psychomotor systems. Victims, and in many instances emergency personnel themselves, are emotionally supported in groups and are guided through a short-term debriefing process that includes:

- stabilization of the situation. Others take control in order to reduce stimulation and confusion
- mobilization of resources and creating an awareness of what is available
- recognition that others are experiencing similar cognitive, affective, physical, and behavioral responses
- continuing assistance as needed [10].

Since children may require longer than adults to adapt to sudden traumatic death due to their lack of cognitive and emotional maturity and the impact of violence, mutilation, and destruction, they are less amenable to the structured CIS group debriefing process commonly used with adults.

However, early assistance can be provided to help children in two ways. I believe that the combination of these two interventions has the potential to lessen the severity of children's grief reactions and facilitate mourning.

First, families can be given practical guidance in order to help traumatized children find respite from the commotion and intensity of the traumatic event. Parents or other adults can be coached to help children re-establish a sense of safety and security, as well as assist children in coping with the physiological and emotional reactions to trauma. These adults can:

- Allow children to rest and sleep as needed.
- Reduce stimuli that may be linked with the death. Children of all ages are easily startled and vulnerable to the impact of sudden and loud noise as well as excessive activity and confusion around them. Their environment should be as quiet as possible for a day or two following the trauma and longer if needed. However, siblings should not be prevented from seeing, comforting, or playing with each other.
- Give children love, hugs, and comforting as needed in order to reassure them and make them feel safe and secure.
- Help children when feasible to be in familiar surroundings with their own toys, books, and other treasured objects.
- Encourage children to relax by using music and simple relaxation techniques such as deep breathing.
- Facilitate children's reconnection with their imaginations by telling them favorite stories and using diversionary techniques to create positive imagery.
- Screen the watching of television and videotapes so that content is familiar, innocuous, non-violent, and humorous.
- Ensure that children receive proper nutrition and hydration.

• Allow children to engage in physical play and active exercise as appropriate. This can be especially helpful if they are agitated and need to release pent-up energy and emotion.

The second way to assist children is through age-appropriate expressive psychological techniques that can be applied after the initial shock. These will help children to gradually express their grief. To wait for twenty-eight days to elapse so that a post-traumatic stress disorder (PTSD) can be formally diagnosed prior to commencing psychiatric treatment or other therapy seems unreasonable. Early intervention is in harmony with the perspective of Frederick who states that:

> The longer the symptoms continue, treated or untreated, the poorer the prognosis. When PTSD is present but missed, which is a frequent occurrence in younger age groups, inappropriate treatment is given, if any at all [11, p. 89].

The application of psychological techniques in treating PTSD is more complicated than the provision of practical guidance. How we assist traumatized children can be enhanced through our knowledge of PTSD as well as knowledge of the "red flags" or distortions signaling complications in children's mourning. The balance of this chapter discusses pertinent concepts from the PTSD literature and describes the role of parents and family in affecting how children cope. It closes with the recognition that psychological techniques introduced immediately following children's exposure to sudden traumatic death should be similar to those applied in the individual treatment of children who are diagnosed with PTSD after twenty-eight days have elapsed. Treatment should be continued as needed.

"Red Flags" Signaling that a Bereaved Child is in Difficulty

It has been suggested by Boyd Webb that "when the child's social, emotional, or physical development shows signs of interference, the grief process can justifiably be considered to be 'disabling' and the deliberate use of that term indicates that something is wrong" [5, p. 21]. The behaviors that point to children in difficulty have been described as warning signs or "red flags" or distortions in the grieving process [4, 5, 12, 13]. These may include:

• continuous denial of reality
• intense mood swings
• lack of emotion and flattening of affect
• extreme anxiety and panic attacks
• apathy
• extreme guilt feelings and self-blame
• destructive thoughts or actions toward themselves or others

- prolonged insomnia, interrupted sleeping patterns, and night terrors
- psychosomatic disturbances

Many of these symptoms are present in varying degrees in most bereaved children. Intervention should take into account the intensity, duration, and apparent significance of these reactions, taken either individually or in combination. Parents, teachers, and other significant adults should be taught to recognize, monitor, and communicate with children about their thoughts and feelings, and seek assistance from professionals as needed.

POST TRAUMATIC STRESS DISORDER (PTSD)

Since 1980, it has been formally recognized that when children are exposed to traumatic events that are outside of the usual range of human experience, they may develop symptoms which can be collectively categorized as a post-traumatic stress disorder (PTSD) [5-8].

In the literature, PTSD has been identified as a major consequence of death and destruction associated with homicide, suicide, disaster, and war. It has also been found in adults and children subjected to molestation, rape, abuse, incest, or life-threatening illness [7, 8, 11].

Criteria for PTSD

There are three major criteria within the PTSD category delineated by the American Psychiatric Association [5, 8]. These are as follows:

1. *Re-experiencing the traumatic event* through recollections that are intrusive and distressing. These may include dreams, illusions, hallucinations, and flashbacks or dissociative sudden recall.
2. *Avoidance of stimuli associated with the trauma* or a *numbing of general responsiveness* as a new experience. This must include at least three of the following components:
   - avoidance of memories or feelings linked to the trauma;
   - keeping away from activities or events that trigger recall of the traumatic event;
   - failure to remember specific details of the event;
   - a reduction of interest in important activities;
   - detachment or feeling estranged from others;
   - limitations in affect.
3. *Persistent increased arousal* including at least two of the following:
   - problems going to and remaining asleep;
   - irritability and being prone to outbursts of anger;
   - inability to concentrate.

Although this diagnostic category contains many similarities to the symptomology of acute and complicated grief reactions and major depressive disorders, the clustering of symptoms has value because it facilitates specificity in identification, documentation, and treatment [5, 6]. Its application to the reactions of children who face situations that are outside the usual range of human experience and have symptoms in place for longer than twenty-eight days has increased awareness in the mental health community that children are prone to suffering from the consequences of tragedy. It has helped mental health professionals to recognize that children are vulnerable to long-term psychological and physical reactions and that intervention can facilitate the mitigation of symptomology and potentially limit the consequences. Researchers such as Frederick have also demonstrated that children have a greater tendency to develop PTSD than adults. In his study of 150 children including fifty victims each of disaster, physical abuse, and child molestation, 77 percent of all children were diagnosed with PTSD. Only 57 percent of 300 adults in situations associated with hostage-taking, human induced tragedies, and natural disasters measured with the same instrument developed PTSD [11].

Terr suggests that there are two distinct predisposing categories of PTSD [14-16].

1. A single violent action such as a suicide or homicide resulting in a readily definable PTSD reaction.
2. Repetitive acts associated with war, terrorist attacks, or natural disasters which affect communities.

I am convinced that the first category may be expanded to include unusual incidences such as witnessing a mutilating accident or sudden death. The second category can generate numbing and overwhelming sadness. It may be more apt to cause what Harris Hendricks and her associates describe as "chronic intractable PTSD" [8, p. 17]. This phenomena affects at least one-fifth of all PTSD victims. Terr suggests that repeatedly traumatized children make major continuing attempts at self-protection using denial, repression, and a variety of other defense mechanisms in order to isolate themselves from the terror of their experience. They often identify with the perpetrator of their distress and may become homicidal or suicidal [14-16].

PTSD in Childhood

Terr, Pynoos and Eth, and Frederick have independently determined that when children suffer from PTSD, their reactions may differ from adults in frequency and intensity of specific symptoms [7, 11, 14, 15]. When matched closely with the three major criteria in the PTSD diagnostic category, these differences are as follow:

1. *Re-experiencing the traumatic event* includes the reality that:
   - pre-verbal memory of a tragic event in young children may lead them to exhibit in their play, mannerisms, and feelings, symptoms of distress that are traceable to infancy or very early childhood;
   - children, particularly from the toddler stage on, are often subject to recurrent nightmares and night terrors;
   - sudden visual flashbacks are usually absent. Unlike adults, children tend to fantasize and may integrate their thoughts or visions of the tragic event into their play activities or into the natural process of daydreaming;
   - some, but not all children, particularly those in latency and pre-adolescence, may experience visual hallucinatory episodes or feelings of presence and are often reluctant to discuss these with parents, perhaps due to the fear of their reaction. Sometimes these experiences add to children's anxiety and become an additional burden that they feel compelled to retain [5, 7, 11, 14, 15].

2. *Avoidance of stimuli associated with the trauma* or a *numbing of general responsiveness* includes:
   - the potential absence of psychic numbing. This reaction may be manifested in other ways such as displaying a lack of feeling in communication or relationships;
   - the presence of residual psychic phenomena in their play including re-enactment of the tragic event. However, children may either avoid or be unable to verbalize their thoughts and feelings;
   - an absence of the vegetative or nervous symptoms displayed by adults. Instead, children may exhibit physical distress as a component of phobic reactions or chronic anxiety;
   - regression and behavior common to earlier developmental stages such as clinging to a parent, thumb-sucking, enuresis, and sometimes encopresis;
   - an absence of disavowal or traumatic amnesia. However, I believe that some details of the tragic event may be suppressed by traumatized children. These may surface later on in adulthood—a delayed and partial traumatic amnesia resulting in symptoms such as increased arousal, hyperalertness, and panic that are characteristic of anxiety disorders in adult life;
   - hints about a shortened future. These may be made more frequently and openly by children than adults;
   - differences in interpretation of time. Children, especially in prelatency, lack the historical perspective of adults, and young children in particular, may have their sense of time skewed due to confusion or their indulgence in magical thinking [5, 7, 11, 14, 15].

3. *Persistent increased arousal* is a common problem that may be manifested through:
   - hypervigilance, especially when children are fearful of a recurrence of the traumatic event or are suffering from chronic anxiety;
   - problems getting to and remaining asleep, as children frequently engage in reflection at bedtime. Memories of the deceased may be aroused through discussions with a surviving parent or adult, sharing thoughts with siblings, listening to stories, prayers, or experiencing the loneliness of a darkened room. In some instances, children who wake up in the night may gravitate to unusual places.to sleep such as on a mat with the family dog or beside a parent's bed or outside of the room of a deceased sibling as they seek comfort and a sense of safety;
   - irritability aggravated by sleeplessness, emotional fatigue, or other elements of the mourning process, a parent's behavior, the absence of the deceased, or changes in their lives. Underlying rage, accumulation of frustration, and inability to perform regular activities or control peers may result in aggressive outbursts, especially on the playground;
   - concentration difficulties are frequently manifested in children's restlessness and inability to focus at school. Although Terr suggests that school difficulties are usually short lived, I believe that for some bereaved children concentration problems are prolonged or delayed. When children remain untreated for PTSD reactions, they may be misdiagnosed by school officials who believe that they have learning deficiencies or attention deficit disorders (ADD) [5, 7, 11, 14, 15].

Factors Influencing PTSD in Children

Research has revealed that children's reactions to a catastrophic event are closely related to their phases of cognitive and emotional development; their perceptions of the reactions of their family, especially their parents; and their direct exposure to the trauma [7, 8, 17, 18]. In one situation involving a sniper attack in a Los Angeles schoolyard in which fifteen persons were shot and a young girl died at the site, children who were most vulnerable to PTSD were those who believed themselves to be in the greatest jeopardy or who witnessed the event [16, 17]. Researchers suggest that the extent of these children's reactions had little to do with previous exposure to violence or other traumatic experiences, recent events, gender, or age. However, for other children who were on the periphery of this violent tragedy, these factors played a distinct role in the timing and extent of their grief reactions [7, 8, 17, 18].

In their classic work, Pynoos and Eth offer useful observations concerning the response of children to trauma. They differentiate between children's reactions to witnessing a violent act and being physically traumatized themselves.

They suggest that witnessing trauma includes heightened passivity, helplessness, and a sense of being unable to control what has transpired. Children are without protection from the emotional impact. On the other hand, when children are injured themselves, they are more apt to be preoccupied with their own pain, suffering, and the process of recovery. When physical trauma is internalized, instead of experiencing PTSD symptomology in the short term, children may be prone to developing dissociative symptoms and other psychopathology in later developmental stages [7]. I believe that children's reactions are closely linked to the severity and intrusiveness of the trauma; their perceptions of the danger it caused and losses experienced; and the nature of ensuing intervention and emotional support provided by family, peers, other adults, and professionals. Peer support assumes increasing importance with age.

How do Children Cope Following a Sudden Traumatic Death?

Lazarus defined coping as a process that is "activated when threat is perceived, intervening between threat and observed outcome, aimed at regulating emotional distress and eliminating the threat" [19, p. 52]. He also suggests that the overall decrease in negative affect is the "measurement of the effectiveness of the coping" [19, p. 52]. Children prone to PTSD have been found to be compromised by lack of control and difficulty coping in at least four areas:

1. *behavioral* because they have been unable to modify the stressful event
2. *cognitive* due to their developmental immaturity and the impact of the trauma on their thinking
3. *informational* because details of violent or mutilating deaths are often hidden from them
4. *decisional* as adults may deny them the opportunity to see any part of the deceased person's body or participate in death related rituals due to the needs of adults who wish to protect them. When children are devoid of ways to control, they have great difficulty dealing with the devastation of any death, especially a sudden, traumatic, violent death. They must use their own perceptions, primitive thought processes, and imaginations to find some way to comprehend what has transpired and try to regain some measure of control [20].

When children are severely traumatized, Pynoos and Eth describe four common psychological methods that children use to control traumatic anxiety [7, p. 25]. I have incorporated a case example to illustrate each method.

1. *"Denial-in-fantasy"* requires children to use their imaginations to reverse the outcome of the event and reduce the severity of the impact.

When seven-year-old Jennifer's sister Betsy, age eleven, was killed while the two girls stood at a bus stop, Jennifer kept replaying the accident using her favorite doll. She frequently changed the outcome in her play and talked with her doll about school and future plans. Sometimes she emerged from her imaginary world believing that Betsy was still alive only to become tearful again when Jennifer remembered the blood on the ground beside her. Other memories of the event had been temporarily blotted out.

2. *"Inhibition of spontaneous thought"* is achieved when children avoid reminders of the event.

Tom was twelve when he returned home early from school and found that his father had committed suicide by connecting a hose to the car exhaust. Tom was very tearful and angry. He avoided discussing the event and refused to go near the garage. He begged his mother to move somewhere else. It was several months before he described his reaction to his father's cyanotic face and extremities and the shock of seeing his lifeless eyes.

3. *"Fixation to the trauma"* concerns children's efforts to make the traumatic event more tolerable through the use of an incomplete, unemotional journalistic recounting of the event or, in my experience, repetitive partialization of the severity of the experience in play or artwork.

This behavior was present in Jennifer's play as well as "denial of fantasy." It was also part of five-year-old Ben's repetitive recounting of the death of his mother, Susan. She was a single parent who was strangled by a male intruder in the middle of the day. Ben was playing in the next room when he heard a male voice and his mother cry out and fall to the floor. Ben froze and a few hours later was found by his maternal grandmother huddled behind a chair in his bedroom. Ben struggled with his confusion about the event and the finality of his mother's death. He had great difficulty conceptualizing the reality of the homicide, and each time he told his story or drew pictures of the event, his communication lacked an emotional connection to his loss.

4. *"Fantasies of future harm"* may preoccupy children and enable them to deal with the trauma by "supplanting the memories of the event with new fears" [7, p. 25]. This process can impact severely on their ability to function.

When nine-year-old Mark was being driven to school by his parents, he was alone in the back seat. His six-year-old sister, Cindy, was in the front seat between his parents. At a busy intersection, their car was demolished by a dump truck. His father died instantly, his mother sustained multiple injuries, and his sister was in a coma for several weeks. Mark, who was usually a happy, easy-going boy, was devastated. Initially, he withdrew to his room and would come out only when his grandmother coaxed him. Gradually, with the support of both grandparents, he returned to school and the neighborhood playground. His anxiety was manifested in panic related to going to the hospital, walking alone to school, and riding his bicycle. However, to everyone's surprise, he rode in his grandfather's car without any apparent apprehension.

When children grapple with the impact of violent trauma Pynoos and Eth also note that children may identify with:

- the perpetrator and play out the violent act. This is common in situations such as those studied by Harris Hendricks and her associates in which a mother was murdered by the father. For male children in particular, such a homicide generates extreme internal conflict and, at times, results in uncontrollable rage and aggression. In addition, I believe that it may also intensify fears of retribution and recurrence, especially if play is not properly guided;
- the victim in a process of identifying and expressing feelings about what has transpired including fantasies of revenge;
- the mediator or rescuer in which the child identifies with third party interveners such as firemen, ambulance attendants, or police. In many instances, at least initially, children may change the outcome in therapeutic play or other expressive interactions with the therapist [7].

How Do Parents and the Family Influence What Transpires?

Children are in great need of parental support throughout the normal course of life events. When children are traumatized by a sudden death, especially one that involves violence, mutilation, or destruction, their need intensifies markedly. Parents need to be able to manage the family. They should be able to promote clarity in communication, acceptability of rules, role consistency, task delineation, and understanding of differences of opinion. They should also be able to resolve conflicts and be in harmony when nurturing, protecting, and controlling their children. They should be positive role models and identity figures. When parents are in control of family life, children are able to develop and maintain their self-esteem, self-image, and self-confidence [21].

Unfortunately, in many cases the needs of children may be compromised within the family, and their ability to deal with the severe impact of traumatic bereavement may be restricted by family behavior that includes:

- exclusion of the child from visitation, the funeral, the burial, or memorial services;
- lack of communication about the tragic event and the time following,
- parental preoccupation with the deceased so that the child is neglected physically and emotionally;
- destructive communication that in a small number of families makes the child feel rejected and guilty. The child may be held accountable for the death by one or more family members, or be viewed as a contributor to it;
- lack of explanation, clarification, and reassurance concerning parents' feelings;
- parental mood swings, irritability, unpredictability, and, at the extreme, rage and physical punishment of the child;
- manipulation of the child so that the child is forced to be the parents' protector or caregiver, or required to take on unreasonable or inappropriate responsibilities;
- demands for secrecy and collusion so that information and feelings are blanketed and maintained within the home;
- moving physically and uprooting the child from school, friends, and the neighborhood.

Each of these factors may complicate the mourning process and impact upon the treatment methodology described in the section that follows.

THE TREATMENT OF PTSD IN CHILDHOOD

When it comes to trauma, most clinicians who have never suffered through a traumatic experience can scarcely intuit what horror a child victim may have endured. For that reason it can be hard for a therapist to realize that he or she may be inflicting some measure of "therapy trauma" . . . a therapist may have no idea what the child's limits of tolerance are and may press blindly on until forced to stop [9, p. 132].

Treatment Methodology

In the literature, there are varied opinions concerning the timing, methodology, and duration of treatment. One clearly articulated approach involves a ninety-minute interview for the assessment and treatment of children ages three to sixteen years who suffer from PTSD and have witnessed severe violence [7, 22]. This includes three phases.

1. An engagement or validation phase in which children draw a picture and recount a story. This process provides a linkage to the child's inner

concerns about the traumatic event. In some situations, this linkage may be subtle and a series of drawings may be required to gently help the child identify the connection.

2. In-depth exploration of relevant issues in order to pay specific attention to "the child's perceptual and affective experiences" [7, p. 9]. The child's story is carefully linked to the trauma, this time by the therapist, in order to facilitate a release of emotions. The therapist then guides the child through a process in which the child talks about, enacts, or draws each aspect of the traumatic experience. The interview gradually shifts from the general to the specific and incorporates the child's description of what was witnessed, the child's perceptions, and the worst moment. During this phase, the child is encouraged to:

   • confront issues associated with accountability for the event
   • fantasize about actions that might have prevented or modified the outcome
   • express apprehension regarding retaliation and punishment
   • acknowledge fear of recurrence
   • discuss previous traumatic experiences and dreams
   • examine feelings about controlling their own impulses.

3. Closure which involves a review of the session; acknowledgment of normalcy and legitimacy of the child's emotions; an outline of what to expect in the future; reinforcement of the child's self-esteem; and the child's evaluation of the interview.

By applying this methodology, Pynoos and Eth found that the interview brought immediate relief and improvement to traumatized children. Children were also more amenable to further assistance from other caregivers as needed and were helped most by being able to articulate their fantasies of revenge [22, 23].

There are many similarities between this approach and those used by other clinicians. Most interventions stress the need to reduce children's use of avoidance and the need to help them identify strategies to effectively deal with future stress [23]. Unique aspects can be identified in most approaches. For example, Pynoos and Eth enable the child to describe the details of the trauma [22]. Ayalon, and Galente and Foa incorporate the use of rituals and structured activities [24, 25]. Ayalon also makes a concerted effort to intervene in the child's system of appraisal of the trauma and its consequences, uses puppets and drama, and applies systematic desensitization *in vivo* [24]. One such application involved traumatized children being accompanied by their parents to a beach where terrorists had landed. There they were gradually exposed to noises associated with the traumatic event.

In contrast to Ayalon, Everstine and Everstine caution against the use of desensitization, as this process may return children to the role of victim in fantasy and result in psychic numbing. This reaction may also be misinterpreted and viewed as a step to recovery as opposed to "blunted affect" [9, p. 131]. They focus their work on helping children to master symptoms in order to dilute the impact of the trauma and increase their confidence. In whatever methodology is used, children need to work through the process in a manner that does not overstimulate them or rekindle the effect of the trauma.

In my work, I tend to extend intervention over several months on a weekly or bi-weekly basis, using a combination of the above methodologies and also concentrating on helping children to identify and manage the triggers that can precipitate sudden outbursts of aggression. This is especially relevant to male children who are grappling with their emotions following the suicide or homicide of a family member. This focus is in tune with the Everstines who advocate the need for safety and security in therapy and recognition that children who release rage through aggressive play may have "a magical fear of consequences of those displays" [9, p. 132].

In addition, I believe that violent acts may be repeated on the playground or in the neighborhood by traumatized bereaved children, as in Mark's case.

> Ten-year-old Mark became extremely aggressive several months after he witnessed the strangulation of his mother by a former boyfriend. Mark had to be forcefully removed to stop him from choking a classmate during recess. Just prior to the incident, unbeknownst to his father and stepmother, Mark had made many drawings of people being strangled. He had also engaged in mock stranglings of close friends. Later, in treatment, Mark admitted that he was frightened when he tried to strangle himself, quickly explaining that it was just an experiment. The attempt to choke the classmate was not really meant to hurt the other boy. In fact, Mark was afraid of doing so, and said: "My anger took over."

IN CLOSING

Early Intervention

The psychological techniques that are part of early intervention are closely linked to the beginning of the three phase treatment methodology for PTSD. Traumatized bereaved children should be helped to express their feelings on their own terms using therapeutic play, artwork, and story in an environment that is safe and secure. In most instances, they should be seen individually, be accompanied by significant adults as needed, and be guaranteed privacy and confidentiality as appropriate and within legal limitations. This process should begin as soon as children emerge from the initial shock. It breaks the ice and can lead to an in-depth exploration of children's perceptions and feelings concerning the death, similar to phase two in Pynoos and Eth's approach, but extended over several weeks. Closure of the process may be viewed either as a point of respite or the end of individual therapy. In future encounters, my preference would be to continue individual therapy on its own, or to combine it with a bereavement support group operated by other professionals. In some instances, however, only a bereavement support group may be the treatment of choice.

Points Worth Remembering

In our approach, we must recognize that:

- families play a key role in CIS and in facilitating children's comfort, well-being, and sense of safety
- children are less tolerant of pain and anxiety than adults
- the natural anxiety that accompanies cognitive and affective development— separation anxiety in pre-school children, mutilation anxiety in the middle years, and suffocation anxiety in pre-adolescence—may be amplified due to the traumatic event or its sequelae
- children, especially young children, tend to use their imaginations and may distort their perception of traumatic events and their role in them
- evasive behavior is a common defense measure children use to avoid re-encountering the horror of what transpired. Counteracting this behavior requires skill and caution
- regression is another defense mechanism common to children of all ages. Its presence may govern intervention, and the extent of regression may be a barometer of the fragility of a traumatized child
- children look to parents or other adults for guidance and approval. In any therapeutic interaction, children may mask their feelings in order to protect adults, or as a response to fear of blame or retribution
- a favorite doll or stuffed animal is an invaluable partner in any interaction with children. Experiences can be shared with this partner, and many feelings and actions can be expressed indirectly through it
- pets, especially cuddly animals, provide additional comfort and reassurance for severely distressed bereaved children and make few demands in return
- trust, familiarity, routines, and forewarning are all key ingredients in helping these children. When feasible, continuity of professionals involved in CIS intervention should be encouraged until the time of initial closure.

What is Needed in the Future

In order to effectively meet the needs of severely traumatized bereaved children who witness a sudden traumatic death, urban pediatric trauma centers and emergency services in smaller communities need to ensure access to skilled pediatric mental health and bereavement counseling practitioners. Additional research is required concerning the timing of intervention and to determine if early intervention combining practical approaches and expressive psychological techniques can modify or prevent the development of PTSD. I believe that this is possible and that early intervention in the mourning process is absolutely essential.

REFERENCES

1. R. R. Ellis, Young Children: Disenfranchised Grievers, in *Disenfranchised Grief: Recognizing Hidden Sorrow*, K. J. Doka (ed.), D. C. Heath and Company, Lexington, Massachusetts, 1989.
2. T. Rando, Anticipatory Grief and the Child Mourner, in *Beyond the Innocence of Childhood: Helping Children and Adolescents Cope with Death and Bereavement, Volume 3*, D. W. Adams and E. J. Deveau (eds.), Baywood, Amityville, New York, 1995.
3. D. W. Adams, Understanding Sibling Grief and Helping Siblings to Cope, in *Children and Death*, G. H. Paterson (ed.), King's College, London, Canada, 1986.
4. E. A. Grollman (ed.), *Explaining Death to Children*, Beacon Press, Boston, 1967.
5. N. Boyd Webb, Assessment of the Bereaved Child, in *Helping Bereaved Children: A Handbook for Practitioners*, N. Boyd Webb (ed.), The Guilford Press, New York, 1993.
6. T. A. Rando, *Treatment of Complicated Mourning*, Research Press, Champaign, Illinois, 1993.
7. R. S. Pynoos and S. Eth, Children Traumatized by Witnessing Acts of Personal Violence, in *Post-Traumatic Stress Disorders in Children*, S. Eth and R. S. Pynoos (eds.), American Psychiatric Press, Washington, D.C., 1985.
8. J. Harris Hendricks, D. Black, and T. Kaplan, *When Father Kills Mother*, Routledge, London, 1993.
9. D. S. Everstine and L. Everstine, *The Trauma Response: Treatment for Emotional Injury*, W. W. Norton & Company, New York, 1993.
10. J. T. Mitchell and G. S. Everly, Jr., *Human Elements Training for Emergency Services, Public Safety and Disaster Personnel: An Instructional Guide for Teaching Debriefing, Crisis Intervention and Stress Management Programs*, Chevron, Ellicott City, Maryland, 1994.
11. C. F. Frederick, Children Traumatized by Catastrophic Situations, in *Post-Traumatic Stress Disorder in Children*, S. Eth and R. S. Pynoos (eds.), American Psychiatric Press, Washington, D.C., 1985.
12. S. Fox, *Good Grief: Helping Groups of Children When a Friend Dies*, New England Association for the Education of Young Children, Boston, 1985.
13. D. W. Adams and E. J. Deveau, How the Cause of a Child's Death May Affect a Sibling's Grief, in *Bereavement: Helping the Survivors*, M. A. Morgan (ed.), King's College, London, Canada, 1988.
14. L. Terr, Children Traumatized in Small Groups, in *Post-Traumatic Stress Disorders in Children*, S. Eth and R. S. Pynoos (eds.), American Psychiatric Press, Washington, D.C., 1985.

15. L. Terr, *Too Scared to Cry*, Basic Books, New York, 1990.
16. L. Terr, Childhood Traumas—An Outline and Overview, *American Journal of Psychiatry, 110*, pp. 10-20, 1991.
17. R. S. Pynoos, C. Frederick, K. Nader, and W. Arroyo et al., Life Threat and Post-Traumatic Stress Disorder in School-Age Children, *Archives of General Psychiatry, 44*, pp. 1057-1063, 1987.
18. R. S. Pynoos, K. Nader, C. Frederick, L. Gonda, and M. Stuber, Grief Reactions in School-Age Children Following a Sniper Attack at School, *Israel Journal of Psychiatry and Related Sciences, 24*, pp. 53-63, 1987.
19. R. Lazarus, Positive Denial: The Case for Not Facing Reality, *Psychology Today, 13*, pp. 44-60, 1979.
20. F. Worchel, Adjusting to Childhood Cancer: A Model for Psychosocial Care, in *Teaching More than Medicine: Psychosocial Considerations in Pediatric Oncology*, J. Van Eys, D. R. Copeland, and E. R. Davidson (eds.), M. D. Anderson Cancer Center, Houston, Texas, 1992.
21. M. Massey, Cause or Effect: Today's Child, *EAP/Extra, 46*, p. 4, 1995.
22. R. S. Pynoos and S. Eth, Witness to Violence: The Child Interview, *Journal of the American Academy of Child Psychiatry, 25*, pp. 306-316, 1986.
23. K. C. Peterson, M. F. Prout, and A. Schwartz, *Post-Traumatic Stress Disorder: A Clinician's Guide*, Plenum Press, New York, 1991.
24. O. Ayalon, Coping with Terrorism, in *Stress Reduction and Prevention*, D. Meichenbaum and M. Juremko (eds.), Plenum Press, New York, 1983.
25. R. Galente and D. Foa, An Epidemiological Study of Psychic Trauma and Treatment Effectiveness After a Natural Disaster, *Journal of the Academy of Child Psychiatry, 25*, pp. 357-363, 1986.

CHAPTER 16

Why Have a Funeral?: Hindu Funerals in England: Past, Present, and Future

Pittu Laungani

Since everyone has funerals, the question, why have funerals, seems rather pointless. As a rejoinder, one might be tempted to add: but why *not* have funerals! Everybody has them! However, the fact that everybody has funerals and people all over the world express the loss of their loved ones by having a funeral, simple or elaborate, does not in itself justify having a funeral. A universal practice does not by itself become a self-justificatory practice. There is no axiomatic reason why funerals ought to be held. So the question why have funerals is not as pointless as appears at first sight. The question in fact is extremely difficult to answer.

FUNCTIONS OF FUNERALS

Funerals, as Houlbrooke points out, have several functions and purposes, both religious and social. "They are intended to benefit in some way both the living and the dead" [1, p. 163]. There is also a sense of duty performed well. The bereaved may derive some benefits from the funeral and the gathering of mourners may provide the required moral support. Perhaps a better way to approach the question would be to consider the functions a funeral serves from three perspectives:

1. the deceased
2. the family of the deceased
3. the community

1. The Deceased

The dead have no awareness of their being. Thus, whether the funeral for a given person was lovingly planned, lavishly or simply executed, or whether the deceased was buried, cremated, or unceremoniously disposed of in other ways, with a minimum of fuss and attention, makes no difference to the deceased, because the deceased, as was said above, have no awareness of their being. No one, as far as one knows, has attended his or her own funeral.

The deceased, while they were alive, may have made elaborate plans and may have left explicit instructions in their last Will about the nature and type of funeral ceremonies they would desire upon their demise, trusting the heirs and beneficiaries of their estate to carry out their instructions and fulfill their legal, familial, religious, and social obligations. However, this still does not answer the question, why have a funeral?

As has been argued elsewhere [2], one of the strangest aspects about death is the fact that none of us can ever experience our own death. We can visualize it in our minds in its meticulous detail, we can imagine it, we can even role-play it, we can "witness" our own funeral, we can fantasize the effects of our death on those we leave behind, but we cannot experience our own death. To experience an event it is necessary for the person to be conscious and, therefore, alive. Although we shall *never* experience this final event, we are nonetheless terrified of its occurrence. Shakespeare encapsulates the fear of death thus:

> Of all the wonders that I have yet heard,
> It seems to me most strange that men should fear,
> Seeing that death, a necessary end,
> Will come when it will come.
>
> (Julius Caesar, II, 2.)

Although the fear of death is widespread, it would seem, according to Kübler-Ross, that the fear of death is universal [3]. Why the idea of one's death should strike such universal terror in us all remains a mystery. Whether the dread of death, or something after death, is due to the "undiscovered country from whose bourn no traveller returns" or whether it is due to other unexplained factors, which include ideas of extinction, hell and damnation, extinction and annihilation, permanent severance of oneself from one's loved ones and from the material world in which one has lived, etc., one cannot say with any degree of certainty.

In the West the fear of death can be attributed to several factors. Most Western societies have witnessed a decline in the status of established religion. At a psychological level this has resulted in diminishing beliefs in an after-life, rebirth, heaven, and hell [4]. This, along with the gradual dissolution of the extended family and community networks, has meant that the beliefs and practices, as well as the institutional structures which would have supported the bereaved, are now often unavailable or inadequate. In addition, the socio-political processes of humanization and secularization have shifted our attention away from the destiny of the deceased toward the fate of the bereft. Sadly, the individual is left on his/her own to cope and come to terms with this fundamental human problem.

However, we each have our own *private* reasons for fearing death: reasons which often remain unvoiced. There are some, like Tony Walter, who argue that the acceptance of a humanist philosophy prepares its adherents to face death without fear [5]. He argues that death equals extinction and therefore it is not to be feared. Because we can never know of any life beyond the grave there is no point in worrying about it now. Therefore one learns to accept the inevitable with a sense of equanimity. What matters is not one's death, for that is inevitable and unavoidable, nor what lies beyond death (which of course one does not know), what matters most is *how one lives one's life*. A humanist is more concerned about living and life than about death and dying. It should be pointed out that a humanist view is a *rationalist* view of life and death, to which only a small minority is likely to be attracted. Rational behavior, as Freud points out, is, to a large extent, a myth. According to Freud, people merely find rational explanations for their largely irrational behaviors. Consequently, the majority of the people—not just in Western societies, but all over the world—are unlikely to acquire the immunity from all the primeval dreads and terrors associated with death and extinction, which an adherence to a humanist philosophy claims to equip a person with.

Therein lies the first clue to understanding the functions of funerals. There is within society, all societies, a social, cultural, and, in many instances, a religious expectation that upon death one will not be alone and that one will be accompanied in one's final journey by one's survivors, well-wishers, and mourners. Intertwined with these social and cultural expectations are one's psychological expectations that one's funeral, attended by one's family members, relatives, and a large contingent of friends and well-wishers, bears testimony to a life well lived. One believes that one will be remembered by those one has left behind, and in the process, "survive" one's death.

In India, as indeed in most other cultures, the number of people attending a funeral is often seen as a measure of the quality of life lived by the deceased. The virtues of the deceased are often assessed by the magnitude of mourners attending the funeral. Although a person may not rationally plan for his or her funeral, the cultural expectation that upon one's death one will be accompanied by a large contingent of mourners emphasizes one of the functional values of funerals all over the world. It is hardly surprising that in many societies extremely elaborate, extravagant, and lavish funeral arrangements are made to ensure that the deceased "goes out in style."

2. The Family of the Deceased

Family members of the deceased, in general, have their own agenda, part private and covert, part public and overt. Among Indians, Hindus, and non-Hindus, death in the family provides an opportunity for the extended family members who, over the years, may have spread out to different parts of India or to different corners of the earth, to meet together. As a result of staying together for several days, at least until the last rites related to the deceased have been performed, they are able to share their lives, renew old relationships, heal past hurts (even open fresh wounds), and thereby succeed in sustaining the structure of the extended family network, which is one of the most unique and significant features of Indian society. The extended family needs to be seen not merely in its structural terms but also in terms of the psychological functions which it serves, the main one being the emotional binding of people within the familial structure. Funerals, particularly of a significant member within a family, cannot be missed. Not to attend a funeral is an act, by omission, of extreme impiety; it is likely to incur the wrath of the family which, in extreme cases, might lead to the deviant being ostracized. Funerals draw families together and perpetuate the extended family network.

There is also the desire among the family members of the deceased to ensure that the funeral will be attended by large groups of people comprising their *jati*, sub-caste, members within their community, and other friends and well-wishers. As was said earlier, a vast gathering of mourners is often seen as a measure of the superior status of the deceased and, by implication, of the family. The family may thus go to great lengths to extol the virtues, acts of charity and piety, which the deceased may have performed when they were alive and may have decreed to be performed upon their death. Feeding of mendicants in their hundreds, if not in their thousands, offerings of clothes, sweets, gifts, and money to Brahmin priests, the distribution of *pedas,* sweets, and such other ostentatious public displays become emblems of piety, charity, and philanthropy. (In passing, it might be mentioned that among Indians, acts of charity are seldom performed anonymously: they are often performed with due pomp and ceremony. One must not only be charitable but one must be *seen* to be charitable. Virtue, in the context of Indian religious philosophy, is not its own reward.)

The family members may also participate in expensive, time-consuming, and elaborate rites and rituals during the twelve to fourteen days of mourning. It is here that deeply ingrained religious beliefs provide the necessary means by which covert agendas are transformed into overt agendas. It is therefore important to see the ceremonies, the rites and rituals observed by the bereaved in the context of such beliefs.

Let us take one example. There is a strongly held belief [6-8] that upon death the dead, referred to as *preta*, undertake a voyage, a journey which takes them through several kingdoms of Yama, King of the underworld, until a year later they reach an abode referred to as *pitr-loka*. It is a temporary abode of the ancestors, and it is here that it is decided by Yama, Lord of death, whether the deceased shall go to *svarga* (heaven) or to *narka* (hell).

The decision is made on the basis of the nature of actions (*karma*) performed by the deceased during their life. To ease the passage of the *preta*, during the year's journey it is expected that the survivors of the deceased will perform all the required ceremonies, *sraddha*, observe all the rites and rituals with zeal and faith. Failure to do so will result in the soul of the deceased (which, upon death is painfully torn from the body of the deceased by the *yamadutas*, helpers to Yama, King of the underworld) to remain in a state of acute torment. Lapses, intentional or unintentional, in the faithful performance of these sacred duties may also result in adverse consequences which befall upon the survivors. The family of the deceased may be tormented, haunted by the presence of *Bhutas*, or malevolent spirits, which manifest themselves soon after the death of the person and the rapid dissolution of the body. These *bhutas*, on occasions, are said to exercise such a malevolent and powerful influence over the lives and fortunes of the survivors that the bereaved may feel compelled to call upon experts to exorcise these evil spirits. However, the zealous performance of all the rites and rituals related to the death of a family member will (so it is believed) lead to the eventual repose of the soul of the departed and ward off the evil influences of the *bhutas*.

It is not always recognized that funeral rites are dedicated to the control, neutralization, and destruction of the *bhutas*. Even cremation does not always guarantee the total destruction of the *bhutas*, or the psychic corpse. It now becomes clear why cremations in India are performed with such speed: first, because of reasons of hygiene, second, because of caste-related factors of "contamination." A corpse in the house has a contaminating influence on the house and on the members of the household. It is therefore important for the members of the household to remove the body post-haste so that the bereaved are able to engage in purification rites and ceremonies and wipe out the blot which such contamination brings upon the family. The final function of the cremation is to ensure the destruction of *bhutas* [9].

3. The Community

Indian society, as has been extensively argued elsewhere, is a community-based society [10-12], where one's immediate family, one's extended family network, *baradari*, one's sub-caste, *jati*, and, to a certain extent, one's friends and well-wishers, all of whom play a significant role in the lives of the bereaved family. Funerals are by no means "private" affairs, as they might be construed in the West. They are public events. Anyone who is or was associated with the bereaved family may attend the funeral. To miss a funeral, as was stated earlier, is seen as an unforgivable violation of communal norms, to attend one is an act of grace. Thus, it is evident that funerals fulfill a variety of communal functions, which may be summarized as under:

1. In the process of sharing a significant event with the members of one's community, the family is drawn emotionally closer to the community.

2. The nature and the type of funeral arrangements which follow serve to establish in an extremely subtle way the hierarchical position of the family within the family's immediate sub-caste, *jati*, and above all, within one's *baradari*, extended family network. The caste-system, it should be noted, does not operate on a system of parity. The members of the family comprising a sub-caste compete to rank themselves on a hierarchical position. Such a position is fluid. The generosity or otherwise with which a given family is perceived as performing the rites and rituals related to major social and religious events such as births, marriages, and funerals, may result in a shift in the corresponding ranking position.

3. The "correct" performance of all the funeral rites by the family members also helps to sustain and perpetuate the cultural traditions whose roots can be traced to the early Vedic period [13].

4. From a psychological point of view the involvement of the community members in the actual participation of the funeral rites and in the performance of all the communal duties may have immense psycho-therapeutic benefits upon the bereaved family. The realization that one's joys—and in this instance, one's griefs and sorrows—are shared and will continue to be shared for several days, if not weeks, by one's community may assist the bereaved family to cope with and come to terms with the loss of their loved one. It may even speed up the process of recovery and rehabilitation into an altered state of life. Since empirical evidence on this issue is not available, it is premature to draw any firm conclusions.

5. Finally, the correct performance of the funeral rites confers grace upon the bereaved family, and, by reflection, upon the community [1].

HINDU FUNERALS IN ENGLAND

Over the years, striking changes have occurred between the funeral practices of Hindus in England and those living in India. Let us examine some of the significant changes that have taken place and then tease out the social, cultural, and policy implications of such changes.

1. In India, when a person dies or is about to die, he/she is lifted from the bed and is placed on the floor. The symbolism of "earth to earth" is in keeping with the teachings of the Shastras. Upon death, a drop or two of Ganges water dipped in *tulsi*, basil leaf, is sprinkled on the lips of the dead person. The windows in the room are also thrown wide open to allow the soul to escape from the body

unhindered. It is important that the passage of the soul to escape from the body is unimpeded. Since most people in India die at home and not in hospitals it is possible for the relatives of the deceased to place the body on the floor, settle around it and grieve and chant devotional hymns and engage in the initial rites and rituals related to the immediacy of death [14]. Soon the family priest is summoned and arrangements for the funeral are set into motion.

Such a practice does not occur in England. Since most people die in the hospital, it would seem unreasonable to expect the hospital authorities to permit the body to be lifted out of bed and placed on the floor. Nor would it seem appropriate to allow the relatives of the deceased to gather round the body and express their grief and sorrow openly and copiously.

2. In India, *all* the funeral arrangements—from the laying of the body to its final cremation—are made by the family members of the deceased. Undertaking is seen as a polluting occupation in India. Since only the untouchables, *sudras*, deal with the final disposal of the dead, to allow an undertaker into one's house would result in the pollution of one's house and of the members of the household. It would also create serious and insuperable complications with regard to the performance of religious ceremonies accompanying the preparation of the body [12, 15]. Therefore the notion of undertakers is alien and even quite repulsive to Indian thinking. In England, however, the funeral arrangements are entrusted to undertakers, leaving it to them to make all the funeral arrangements, to transport the body, keep it in their chapel until the day of the funeral. Occasionally a culturally enlightened undertaker may invite the families of the deceased to wash, anoint, and dress the corpse, but in general even that important function is left to the undertakers.

3. In India, corpses are *never* placed in closed coffins. They are carried on a bier and the face of the deceased, more often than not, is kept uncovered. This is done in order to allow the mourners to have a last glimpse of the deceased.

In England, the deceased are placed in closed coffins. The coffin is then transported in a hearse on the day of the funeral. At the request of the mourners, the hearse may stop outside the house of the deceased; the coffin is brought into the house, the lid is unscrewed, the face is exposed to view, and the mourners, their hands folded in silent supplication, file past the coffin. When all the assembled mourners have had their last *darshan,* sacred glimpse, the lid is screwed back on, and the closed coffin is once again transported in the hearse to the crematorium.

4. The crematoria in India do not bear even a faint resemblance to the crematoriums in England. In India, crematoriums—referred to as "ghats"—may be found on open ground, by the river, and in specially designated areas by the Municipal Authorities. Cremations are performed on open log-fires. In some large cities, e.g., Bombay, electric crematoriums have also come into service. Some of the mourners may sit and wait until the body is reduced to ashes; this may take several hours.

In England, the disposal of the dead is done "behind closed doors." The coffin is brought into the chapel, which for the purposes of a Hindu funeral, is turned into a make-shift temple by the introduction of framed pictures and/or statues of God Shiva. The mourners, instead of squatting on the floor as they would do in India, sit in pews. An Anglican style service is held, the Brahmin priest who, in all probability had never met the deceased in his life, recites a rehearsed eulogy, and twenty or thirty minutes later (that is the time allotted by the crematorium authorities for the service), the funeral guests are ushered out. This marks the end of funeral. The coffin is quietly and efficiently moved to where the electronic cremators are placed, and at the press of a button, the coffin slides into the enveloping flames of the cremator. Occasionally, a few close relatives are allowed to push the coffin into the cremator. The gesture is symbolic and bears no resemblance to what transpires in India, where the funeral pyre is set alight by the immediate members of the deceased's family.

5. It has already been mentioned earlier that there is among Hindus in India a sense of urgency with regard to cremations. There is an expectation that funerals will be held within twenty-four hours of death. Delays in funeral are deemed to be inauspicious, and every attempt is made to avoid such inauspicious occurrences.

This is seldom the case in England. Several days may go by before a funeral is performed. There are several reasons which may account for this delay. The person concerned may have died over the weekend, thereby making it difficult for the relatives of the deceased to obtain a death certificate during the week-end. Delays may also occur because of the inability of the undertakers to appreciate the urgency of Hindu funerals.

CULTURAL, ETHICAL, AND POLITICAL IMPLICATIONS

We need now to consider the implications of some of the major changes in the funeral practices which have been described briefly. They can be examined from at least two competing perspectives:

1. CHANGE IS INEVITABLE
2. CHANGE IS AVOIDABLE

Let us consider each of these perspectives briefly.

1. Change is Inevitable

The pre-Socratic philosopher Heraclitus, who proposed a theory of a state of continuous flux, was reputed to have remarked that "the only thing that does not change is change itself" [16]. Everything changes. Nothing ever remains.

Consequently the changes which have taken place in the funeral practices of the Indians living in England were unavoidable.

Such a view is tautological. It leaves several questions unanswered. Apart from the inevitability of change, it does not tell us why, for instance, the changes which have occurred are more in keeping with the accepted norms and practices of British society, and less with the norms and traditions of Indian society. Why is it that all the changes in funeral practices which have been referred to have been made by the Indians living in England and hardly any by the host community? Is it that the norms and standards of practice set by British society are construed as being the "gold standard" and that there is an expectation that all immigrant groups (regardless of whether they happen to be first, second, or third generation Indians or Pakistanis, or whoever, living in England) will attempt to abide by and conform to the established norms?

Critics viewing the situation from a Western perspective would perhaps be right in contending that although the funeral practices of the Hindus might well be true of Indians living in India, they do not have the same meaning or relevance for Indians living in England. They would point out too that the situation in England is vastly different from that in India. The Thames is not the Ganges. Open *ghats*, crematoria, here are as real as leprechauns. The dead are not tied to hastily assembled biers and paraded through the streets before reaching the crematorium. It would be difficult, if not impossible, to create situations which would permit a replication of the Indian experience. Even if such conditions were to be created here, would the second and third generation Indians living here follow them and wish to perpetuate them?

The above arguments, at first sight, seem quite robust. A closer examination reveals that some of the arguments are specious. Let us consider just one point. Whether the second generation or third generation Indians living here follow the ancient Indian practices related to funerals is not the point. The point is that there is an assumption that all those who live in England must conform to the normative expectations related to certain kinds of behaviors. This takes away from the individuals the vital element of choice and forces them to conform to practices which may seem alien to their fundamental religious beliefs, attitudes, and values.

It should of course be recognized that many of the changes and adjustments expected of the members of ethnic minorities may in fact be peripheral—even cosmetic—and would not in any way affect the core values of their own unique culture. They may then be seen as having a nuisance value, a heavy price which an ethnic group is expected to pay by virtue of living in another culture.

If, on the other hand, the expected changes were those which struck at the very root of their cultural values and led to a gradual but permanent erosion of their customs and traditions and consequently the demise of their culture, then it would be difficult to justify those changes. It would then become necessary to question and even challenge the demands for such changes. For if such changes were to be allowed to continue, and the members of ethnic minorities willingly or unwillingly submitted to such changes, they would over time transform the cultural values of the Indians living in England, and in a subtle, if not insidious way, bring their values in line with those of the British culture.

Such changes, were they to occur, would become manifest not just in Hindu funerals, which may become indistinguishable from Anglican funerals, but would be reflected in most of the traditional beliefs, attitudes, values, and social practices of the Indians living in England. This form of homogenization of cultures, which sociologists refer to as the "coca-colonization" of cultures, although it may contain certain practical advantages, will take away the variegated richness and the wisdom from old cultures. Such a course of action is likely to lead to the dilution, if not the eventual erosion, of the values which comprise a given culture.

2. Change is Avoidable

It is evident that changes which are likely to affect the core values of a given culture and transform it in ways which are considered undesirable need at all costs to be avoided. This can be achieved in several ways:

1. The host culture would need to learn to respect the core values, traditions, and customs of other minority cultures living in England.

2. Vital and accurate information about cultures would need to be actively and regularly promoted through the media, the press, through conferences, workshops, and governmental and non-governmental agencies.

3. Important members of various cultural groups, e.g., religious leaders, community elders, health professionals, bereavement counselors, social workers, local councilors, politicians, academics and scholars, etc., would need to meet on equal terms and as equal partners and express a genuine willingness to learn from each other. It is only then that one might find ways of preserving the uniqueness and the sanctity of different cultures. But for one culture to assume that there is little or nothing of any value which they might profitably learn from another culture, some of which have sustained and perpetuated themselves for over four thousand years, is precisely the kind of attitude which is inimical to a genuine cross-cultural understanding and the creation of multi-cultural society. Besides, the hallmark of a civilized and enlightened society is the extent to which it tolerates and permits and fosters the perpetuation of a heterogeneity of cultural and religious beliefs.

It should be recognized too that some changes are unavoidable. Cultures are like living organisms. They are subject to growth, development, change, decay, and regrowth. Some cultures decline, die, and, over time, become extinct. Others are more robust and are able to withstand and/or assimilate the forces of change. But no culture is totally immune to changes. Technological innovations, medical advances, rapid growth in population, cataclysmic disasters, internal insurrection, external invasion are some of the well known and powerful factors which may lead to rapid changes in the core beliefs and values and social behaviors of people in a given culture. In that sense, therefore, all cultures are subject to change and such changes to a large extent are unavoidable. To avoid the breakdown of a culture it becomes necessary to pre-empt the major changes and attempt to implement measures which would prevent disruptions and dislocations in cultures, precipitated by sudden changes.

CONCLUSION

Cultures may also die of neglect. People in a given culture may even have a hand in their culture's demise. In the author's personal view, Hindu culture in England—unlike Islamic culture—is in danger of dying because of the insensitivity, the inaction, and the indifference of the majority of Hindus living in England. What one sees instead are the external manifestations of Hindu culture, such as the grand and opulent temples which have been built in London, Leicester, Birmingham, and several other cities. The construction of a temple and the ritualistic worship does not necessarily lead to the perpetuation of a culture. An ostentatious display of external artifacts, without a genuine internalization of cultural values is unlikely to promote a culture. It is form without substance, ritual without meaning, worship without understanding.

If the efforts of the few are not to be frustrated by the indifference of the many, urgent steps need to be taken to find viable ways of promoting Indian cultural values. If not, Hindu culture, notwithstanding its grand temples, will decline. The forthcoming generations of Indians in the process of assimilating into the mainstream of British society may fall between two cultures, becoming members of neither one nor the other, developing, instead, fractured cultural identities.

REFERENCES

1. R. Houlbrooke, "Public" and "Private" in the Funerals of the Later Stuart Gentry: Some Somerset Examples, *Mortality, 1*:2, pp. 163-176, 1996.
2. P. Laungani and F. Roach, Counselling, Death and Bereavement, in *Handbook of Counselling,* S. Palmer (ed.), Sage, London, 1997.
3. E. Kübler-Ross, *On Death and Dying,* Tavistock Publications, London, 1969.
4. C. M. Parkes, P. Laungani, and B. Young, *Death and Bereavement Across Cultures,* Routledge, London, 1997.
5. T. Walter, Secularization, in *Death and Bereavement Across Cultures,* C. M. Parkes, P. Laungani, and W. Young (eds.), Routledge, London, 1977.
6. N. N. Bhattacharya, *Ancient Indian Rituals and their Social Contents,* Manohar Book Service, Delhi, India, 1975.
7. W. A. Borman, *The Other Side of Death: Upanishadic Eschatology,* India Book Centre, Delhi, India, 1990.
8. S. G. Filippi, *Mrtyu: Concept of Death in Indian Traditions, Reconstructing Indian History & Culture No. 11,* D. K. Printworld, New Delhi, India, 1996.

9. H. Aguilar, *The Sacrifice in the Rg Veda,* Bharatiya Vidya Prakashan, Delhi, India, 1976.
10. P. Laungani, Cultural Differences in Stress: India and England, *Counselling Psychology Review, 9*:4, pp. 25-37, 1994.
11. P. Laungani, Patterns of Bereavement in Indian and English Societies, *Bereavement Care, 14*:1, pp. 5-7, 1995.
12. P. Laungani, Death and Bereavement in India and England: A Comparative Analysis, *Mortality, 1*:2, pp. 191-212, 1996.
13. A. J. A. Dubois, *Hindu Manners, Customs and Ceremonies,* Rupa & Co., Delhi, 1906/1993.
14. S. Firth, Approaches to Death in Hindu and Sikh Communities in Britain and Cross-Cultural Perspectives on Bereavement, in *Death, Dying and Bereavement,* D. Dickenson and M. Johnson (eds.), Sage, London, 1993.
15. P. Laungani, Death in a Hindu Family, in *Death and Bereavement Across Cultures,* C. M. Parkes, P. Laungani, and W. Young (eds.), Routledge, London, 1997.
16. B. Russell, *History of Western Philosophy,* George Allen & Unwin, London, 1946/1961.

CHAPTER 17

Creating Rituals for the Non-Religious

Rev. Lloyd D. Smith

A primary function of ritual and ceremony is to create "sacred space," i.e., a place where our deepest feelings and beliefs can be experienced fully, honored honestly, and expressed without fear of condemnation. To create such rituals requires sensitivity and an accepting non-judgmental approach.

That the social and cultural context for creating and conducting death and bereavement rituals has changed goes almost without saying. Institutional chaplains are frequently called upon to preside at funerals for folk who have little or no connection with mosque or temple, church or synagogue. Community clergy, too, occasionally are asked to provide rituals for the "non-religious" of their area. Even within our own congregations, there have been shifts in outlook. The ritual prescriptions which once provided support and consolation, in many cases, are becoming irrelevant to the faith of members and adherents. The attitudes which characterize Western society are shared by a growing proportion of those within religious institutions.

This shift has come within my own experience. Although born into a "non-religious" family, i.e., a family with no formal connection to any religious institutions, I was raised within Christendom. Religious instruction was given, weekly, in the public schools. Memory work was assigned from the Christian scriptures. I have witnessed and experienced the shift to a more "secular" society in which a declining minority express their faith in traditional, institutional ways.

CONTEXT AND GENERAL OUTLOOK

Three main themes can be identified in this "modern" outlook which will affect our shaping of rituals for the "non-religious" folk of our society. The first is a widespread *skepticism*. The Western world has become, by and large, more literate and better educated. With this has come a disillusionment with "experts" and institutions. The "war to end all wars" did not bring about global peace. Major technological disasters—from "thalidomide babies" to "The Love Canal" to Chernobyl—have contributed to a growing distrust of science. Political and business leaders have been exposed as less than trustworthy. We want some assurance that comes from "beyond" experts or institutions. Despite this general skepticism, belief in God—whatever form that may take—has become stronger than it was immediately following World War II.

"Modern" folk express, second, a high level of *anxiety*. Our lives are often frantic in pace and sometimes leave us with a sense of chaos. We feel we have no control over the future, that we are victims of forces beyond our power. Much of our lives, especially in our work, has become a grinding routine. Further, technology is changing so rapidly that we may feel increasingly inadequate and unable to cope. So, we yearn for meaning, a sense that our lives make a difference. And we long for some assurance of personal destiny. This often takes the form of a belief in some kind of "afterlife."

A quick walk through a bookstore offers evidence of the third theme of our "modern" outlook, viz., our *religious fascination*. In some ways, we have become quite gullible and unthinking, accepting without question the pronouncements of each new *guru* to publish a book and appear on one of the "talk shows." In part, this may be the result of our romantic hopes regarding relationships. We yearn for intimacy with other people. We long to feel accepted, that we have a place of importance in some "bigger" plan.

MOURNERS' NEEDS

With these "world-view" yearnings in mind, we can begin to create death and bereavement rituals for the "non-religious" which can help participants move into a healthy process of grief [1]. Clearly, even the best rituals or ceremonies will not lead to a completion of these bereavement needs. However, well-crafted ones lead to positive first steps and can be a prophylactic against subsequent difficulties.

In general, the first need for mourning is to *acknowledge the death*. Whether it is the sudden death of an accident or cardiac arrest, or the "expected," and perhaps welcomed, demise of an elderly relative or a person who has suffered a prolonged illness, the reality of the death must be recognized. To some extent, the very fact that we start to work with the family, planning and preparing the liturgy, offers a first step in this process. Gathering at the house or at the funeral home for a time of public visitation is a ritual of acknowledgment. This reality can be stated at the beginning of the service itself with simple and direct words such as: "We have gathered here as family and friends, co-workers and neighbors, to acknowledge the death of *NM* and to celebrate *her/his* life and all that *s/he* means to us." Euphemisms should be avoided as they tend to deny the reality of the death. But speaking the names of the deceased can help to keep mourners grounded in actuality.

It is common in our society to use euphemisms, and to avoid mentioning the name of the deceased lest we cause pain. However, for "healthy" grief, mourners need, secondly, to *enter the pain* and, thirdly, to *remember the deceased*. In grieving, we do not "cure" or remove pain, but find pathways through the pain to new life. By creating "sacred space," we help mourners in that process by providing a safe and non-judgmental context for experiencing, honoring, and expressing their pain. Whether this is at the time of the visitation, within the service itself, or during the social time afterward, mourners can be encouraged to speak honestly of their experiences and feelings.

We remember the deceased by telling the stories which reflect the effect that person had on those who gather in grief. Readings and musical selections can be chosen which reflect the attitudes and beliefs of the person who has died. The "eulogy" or "words of remembrance" needs to be honest. A falsely glowing apotheosis is neither an accurate remembrance nor an aid in entering the pain.

In the fourth place, mourners need to *develop a new self-identity*. They have to enter a new social order. Accepting the consolation of visitors can begin this process. At the social time following the service, the mourners can make the first steps at finding their place in their social circles without the presence of their loved one. Within the service, words can be chosen which underline the inter-relatedness of the gathered community.

The service also helps with the final need of mourners: to *receive support from others*. Grief can be a very isolating experience. So, opportunities need to be provided for mourners to experience their inter-relatedness with others.

COMMON PATTERNS

All rituals follow a general pattern of community-building, opening, link with the past, action and closing; ceremonies for death and bereavement are no exception. Even so, to be "sacred," i.e., to express accurately and honestly the feelings of the gathered community and their sense of meaning, no single ritual can be the prescribed pattern for everyone. "Fill in the blanks" ceremonies are only serendipitously helpful.

The *community-building* begins as the family gathers to make plans for the service, or to review and implement the plans and wishes specified previously by the deceased. While families may want to honor the wishes of the person who has died, it is important to remember that the rituals of bereavement are for the bereaved and the communities to which they belong. Hearing and affirming their feelings and beliefs helps to create the "sacred space" which will help them in the grieving process.

It is important, also, in our fragmented society to have a time of visitation before the service itself begins. Whether this takes place the evening before or immediately prior to the service will depend on how many people might reasonably be expected. Friends, neighbors, and co-workers are both mourners and comforters. Gathering to acknowledge this fact helps to deepen the bonds of inter-relatedness. It can be helpful, for this gathering, to assemble a collage of photographs of the deceased, or a table of remembrances where there can be placed items of special significance to the one who has died and to those who are grieving.

The *opening* of the service may consist of a simple and clear statement of the fact of death and the purpose of gathering. As noted earlier, it is a time for acknowledging the pain of the gathered mourners and for remembering the one who has died. Where appropriate, as well, mention may be made of the anxiety felt by some at finding a new self-identity, e.g., a widow/er who may feel apprehension at managing without a partner.

There may follow some form of "invocation." For those mourners who express a belief in God, this may take the form of a prayer acknowledging divine presence and seeking comfort and strength in grieving. When the gathered community is more diverse, it would be appropriate to offer invitations and then allow silence for personal "prayer." Silence is a necessary part of good ritual, allowing the gathered individuals to be nourished by what has just been spoken.

Where the mourners' beliefs have been shaped by Christendom, the *link with the* past might include reading(s) from the Bible. In all situations, other readings which reflect the attitudes and characteristics of the deceased and the mourners would be appropriate. Poetry, carefully chosen and meaningfully read, can be especially helpful for mourners. Here, as well as during the community-building and the closing, music is particularly apt, and most homes and all funeral homes are equipped with music systems.

An important part of this link with the past are "words of remembrance" or the "eulogy." Often the person conducting the service will speak these words, gathering together the stories of the deceased which have been told during the visitation time. Sometimes a close friend or family member may wish to speak. Since emotions can play havoc with the greatest self-control, I have adopted a practice of encouraging them to have their words written out, and assuring them that they will not be condemned for being emotional and that, if they wish, I would finish reading their words for them in the event that they cannot continue.

A variety of elements form the *action* portion of the ceremony. Prayers, giving thanks for the life of the deceased, and asking for help in the grieving process can be suitable, especially if offered as invitations, allowing those who have gathered to provide their own detail in silence. Some words of commendation and committal can be spoken, whether or not the people actually gather at the graveside. Also, the ritual action of pouring some sand on the casket helps to acknowledge the reality of death.

When all is completed in the service, the leader may speak some words which summarize what has been done. In this *closing*, there may also be brief words of encouragement, and the participants are dismissed with an invitation to share a meal and social time. The "funeral lunch" offers an opportunity for establishing the new social order and for further remembering the deceased.

PERSONAL MYTHOLOGY

In an attempt to make rituals personal, and thus more helpful, I have developed a simple device for acknowledging the differences in the way people view reality. Based on the literary typology of Northrop Frye [2], this tool helps the person shaping the ceremony to use images and language which more accurately reflect the diverse beliefs and attitudes of the deceased and the mourners. It is important to remember that all people use all these patterns when telling their stories. And no one style is "better" than any other. Further, the names I give them are drawn from literary criticism and do not reflect the popular usage of these words.

For some, life is a kind of awakening process. Hidden meanings are gradually revealed, and the expectation may be that in death all will be revealed. For such people, whose stories are *comedy*, each "plot twist" establishes a new era, leading to an ultimate resolution. The song "Somewhere Over the Rainbow" from *The Wizard of Oz* expresses this "springtime" way of looking at life.

Others experience life as a quest for transformation. In this adventure, each challenge or disappointment is accepted as an obstacle to be overcome or a test to be completed. Somewhere, at the core of the quest in which death is seen as the greatest adventure, lies a dream. Such "summertime" stories of *romance* are summed up in "Dream the Impossible Dream" from *Man of La Mancha*.

A third worldview regards living as the submission to principle or to the fate of a hidden fault. Devotion to duty figures strongly in this way of looking at things. For such "autumn" folk, submission is the proper response to death. Like Tevya in *Fiddler On the Roof*, these people whose stories are *tragedy*, these folk live according to deep principles to which they submit.

The practical and intellectual outlook, reflected in the music of Vivaldi, are pragmatic and realistic. They do not pretend to be heroes or heroines, but simply "get on" with life. These are the "winter" folk and their style of speaking of life is *irony*. For them, death is simply the last thing to be done.

CONCLUSION

At the end of the day, each ceremony for death and bereavement will be different. With the changed attitudes of people in "Western" society, the former religious rituals hold less and less meaning. There is, then, an opportunity to accept and acknowledge the beliefs and attitudes of mourners and create ceremonies which will help them take the first steps in a "healthy" process of grieving.

REFERENCES

1. A. Wolfelt, Practical Ideas for Creating Meaningful Funerals, *Thanatos,* pp. 4-9, Summer 1995.
2. N. Frye, *Anatomy of Criticism,* Atheneum, New York, 1969.

CHAPTER 18

Hospice Care of Formerly Abused Individuals

Patricia Zalaznik

Formerly abused individuals constitute an unrecognized and under-served population, a minority group who may have special requirements and need special
understanding and compassion during their hospice care. Their abuse may have
been physical, emotional, sexual, and/or neglectful. There is a dearth of literature
about providing hospice care for formerly abused people. This exploratory report
provides information based on interviews with professionals and formerly abused
individuals. Numerous quotations are from confidential interviews with these
respondents; consequently, the respondents are identified only by their roles. The
questions, responses, and some tentative conclusions will be discussed as well as
suggestions for future research and training.

One expert on hospices asserted, "This is a new hospice piece. There is so
much abuse that we only see the tip of the iceberg, especially around loss and
death issues." Others said, "Death is our greatest teacher; this is not recognized.
During the time of dying, the learning may be [either] stuck or accelerated. Dying
often speeds up learning"; and, "The fact that a person is dying may lead to
increased trauma around unresolved issues and makes them more pressing." "The
spiritual struggle at the end of life is about making meaning of life. Sometimes
there are issues that get resolved, sometimes not. The [fact of] limited days pushes
people to deal with it."

According to one respondent in health care knowledgeable about hospice and
health care at end of life, "The public is taking back their dying. There is a gaping
hole in medical training especially the psychological and spiritual piece. . . . *This
process can be a spiritual treasure chest for caregivers in terms of meaning-
making and questions before death.* Dying is processing and meaning-making

about one's self, one's relatives, life experience, and God. Many people have found their new spirituality or God from trying to come to terms with a great deal of pain. Where do I find God in the midst of my pain?—exploring the spiritual questions."

A therapist who is also a formerly abused person explained, "There is the need to interview nurses, doctors, volunteers—staff people who have been abused and *dealt* with it. They have stronger values about giving back, especially if they have done their healing work. Their motivation to help others is part of *their* healing too."

A few statistics underscore the need to examine this topic. Reportedly, one in four females is abused, and one in six to seven males is abused. Abuse is underreported; some say only one in four is reported. Abuse of males is reported less frequently than female abuse. Reported in the United States in 1994, the alleged abuse per thousand was 41.5; the determined abuse per thousand was 13.1. The total estimated population in the United States under age eighteen was 68,024,000 [1].

The National Hospice Organization indicated that, in 1995, approximately one out of every seven deaths (14.8%) in the population of the United States were tended to by a hospice program. There were 390,000 patients served by hospices. In 1995, the average length of stay was 61.5 days [2].

SEEKING ANSWERS

An exploratory questionnaire was constructed to interview professionals with experience pertinent to this investigation, such as researchers in abuse and people with extensive experience in hospices and/or hospitals. This questionnaire was conducted with people from all over the United States. While the original goal was to interview relevant professionals, some of them later disclosed that they, too, had been abused. Furthermore, after the interviews began, formerly abused persons offered to participate. While none of these people were terminally ill, several had been hospitalized for an extended period, and made useful observations about their experience. One victim of ritual abuse even postponed the interview until after her surgery so that she could give more insightful answers.

Interviews were conducted face-to-face when possible; the remainder were by telephone appointment. The interview typically lasted sixty minutes, although ninety minutes was not unusual. Respondents generally were very cooperative. One strength of this interviewing research was that it allowed sufficient time during the interview to pursue different facets of the topic. Another strength was that the descriptions and examples were in the respondent's own words. Having respondents from a variety of orientations gave more scope to the replies. The quotations for this report were selected either to show typical responses or to show the range of responses. Italics indicate respondent's emphasis. A possible weakness of this exploration is that the biases of the author may be reflected in the emphases, and selection of the examples and quotations, as well as in the organization of this information.

These interviews questioned whether hospice care for a formerly abused individual would differ from care for any other person, and whether the various *types* of abuse would make any difference. The interviews also inquired about different approaches to hospice care, what specific caregiving behaviors would be identified as appropriate, and to which care-providers could be of the most service. Finally, it questioned what issues might arise for hospice personnel as well as issues facing the survivors and next of kin. For the Interview Format, see the Appendix.

Forty-four respondents were questioned during this exploration, including medical personnel, hospice experts, abuse experts, social service and mental health workers, and victims of abuse and of ritual abuse. Totals by occupation or status as victims were sixty-two, a number greater than forty-four interviews because, in many instances, victims of childhood abuse pursued adult careers in caregiving occupations such as nurse or therapist. Some respondents changed careers but remained within the groups interviewed. This questionnaire was used to elicit a broad range of responses, not quantifiable answers. The questions were intentionally broad to set the stage for discussion. The categories of respondents are listed in the Appendix. No hospice patients were interviewed in this exploration.

WHO ARE THESE FORMERLY ABUSED PATIENTS?

Logically there are five ways to know that the patient is a victim of abuse:

1. The patient tells someone.
2. The family tells the caregiver(s).
3. The abuse is common knowledge (e.g., survivor of the holocaust).
4. The patient's medical records indicate past abuse.
5. The patient exhibits behavioral cues similar to those of Posttraumatic Stress Disorder (PTSD).

Many formerly abused patients do not disclose their abuse. The patient's behavior and reactions, however, may be recognized by those knowledgeable about victim's responses to abuse.

According to one abuse expert, "There are three criteria for PTSD. All three must be met in order for a patient to be defined as such." Respondents repeatedly mentioned these behaviors. First is "hypervigilance" or the need to be aware continually and "on duty" to protect oneself. Second is the wish to distance oneself from "triggers" and reminders of the abuse, such as sounds, locations, and odors. A trigger is defined as anything that causes the formerly abused person to feel as if they were back in the abusive situation again. As Stedman says, a trigger is a "term describing a system in which a relatively small input turns on a relatively large output, the magnitude of which is unrelated to the magnitude of the input" [3, p. 1853]. One victim of childhood ritual abuse explained that *anything*—a piece of furniture, a food, a color, a pillow—could be a trigger for a given person, depending upon the individual situation of abuse. The third criterion is the frequent experience of reliving the event as though it were occurring right now, also called "flashbacks."

An abuse expert explained, "The literature indicates that most people are basically okay after abuse, but a lot do end up with serious problems." Posttraumatic Stress Disorder (PTSD) is common in this population. According to The Diagnostic and Statistical Manual of Mental Disorders (DSM IV), Posttraumatic Stress Disorder has the following diagnostic features:

> The essential feature of Posttraumatic Stress Disorder is the development of characteristic symptoms following exposure to an extreme traumatic stressor involving direct personal experience of an event that involves actual or threatened death or serious injury, or other threat to one's physical integrity; or witnessing an event that involves death, injury, or a threat to the physical integrity of another person; or learning about unexpected or violent death, serious harm, or threat of death or injury experienced by a family member or other close associate. . . . The person's response to the event must involve intense fear, helplessness, or horror (or in children, the response must involve disorganized or agitated behavior). . . . The characteristic symptoms resulting from the exposure to the extreme trauma include persistent reexperiencing of the traumatic event, . . . persistent avoidance of stimuli associated with the trauma and numbing of general responsiveness, . . . and persistent symptoms of increased arousal. . . . The full symptom picture must be present for more than 1 month, . . . and the disturbance must cause clinically significant distress or impairment in social, occupational, or other important areas of functioning.

> Traumatic events that are experienced directly include, but are not limited to, military combat, violent personal assault (sexual assault, physical attack, robbery, mugging), being kidnapped, being taken hostage, terrorist attack, torture, incarceration as a prisoner of war or in a concentration camp, natural or manmade disasters, severe automobile accidents or being diagnosed with a life-threatening illness. For children, sexually traumatic events may include developmentally inappropriate sexual experiences without threatened or actual violence or injury. Witnessed events include, but are not limited to, observing the serious injury or unnatural death of another person due to violent assault, accident, war, or disaster or unexpectedly witnessing a dead body or body parts. Events experienced by others that are learned about include, but are not limited to, violent personal assault, serious accident, or serious injury experienced by a family member or a close friend; learning about the sudden, unexpected death of a family member or a close friend; or learning that one's child has a life-threatening disease. The disorder may be

especially severe or long lasting when the stressor is of human design (e.g., torture, rape). The likelihood of developing this disorder may increase as the intensity of and physical proximity to the stressor increase [4, p. 424].

Furthermore, abuse is socially defined in many ways. What a younger generation may view as abuse, many of today's elderly grew up viewing as a way of life. Verbal abuse was and still is common. However, interpretations of what constitutes abuse can vary immensely among cultures of the world. In addition, the definition of abuse may be modified by the family itself, their religion, and perhaps other variables.

Many respondents, both professionals and victims of former abuse, suggested that the following signs or cues could indicate a history of former abuse:

low self-esteem	hyperalert responses
absence of eye contact	pronounced startle-response
cognitive impairment	reactions to triggers
delusions	inability to be close to anyone
dissociation	withdrawal
projection of issue(s) onto caregiver	difficulty in group situations
learned helplessness, passivity	sensitivity to group dynamics
heightened anger	fear
heightened sensitivity	emotional vulnerability
super-controlling behavior	guilt
defenses not in place any more	anxious
regression	reactions that never fully go away
problems with sleep	challenges in doing life-review
hypervigilance	more time needed to resolve

In the words of one hospice physician, "People blame themselves for their abuse—that they deserve it." Finally, said another, "If the abuse nearly caused death before (such as the holocaust), expect it would be more heightened at actual time of death. Some patients may deal with their impending death instead of their old issues."

WOULD CARING FOR FORMERLY ABUSED PEOPLE BE DIFFERENT?

In response to the question asking whether care for a formerly abused individual would be any different from care for any other person in hospice, one expert said, "Not all people who have been abused have problems. However, adults with a history of abuse may have *consequences* in mental health such as trust, attachments, development of relationships, and difficulties in accepting empathy and care." A physician responded that this care is "not different in hospice care *in theory*," and added that hospices need flexibility in areas which people want to work on. They also need a skilled, trained staff to work with this population.

Responses to the question of whether care for formerly abused people would be different generally noted patients' behaviors, patients' characteristics, family qualities, and issues concerning patient treatment. Some possible variables in abuse also emerged from answers to this question.

One professional caregiver claimed, "Sometimes abused persons blame themselves for being abused and have deep feelings of guilt and being unworthy. A few months before this ninety-seven-year-old resident died, she attempted to take her life. It was only after that, she shared [with me] her unhappy childhood of incest. I was with her *many hours* listening and helping her. She said, '*I have to tell this to someone before I die.* As a child, whenever I needed something such as new shoes or a dress, my father would make me engage in sex with him. This went on for years. I never told anyone ever, not even my husband. Now that I have told you, it is all right for me to die.' The woman died peacefully within two days."

Another professional described the following case. "Be sensitive and know past abuse. For example, a male survivor died a few months ago. He was a refugee and had been in a holocaust concentration camp. [Even though it was prescribed], he would not use a face mask for oxygen because it reminded him of the gas chamber; no way was anyone putting anything on his face! Psychologically, he was a loner and kept his distance. [Earlier, as a nursing home resident] this patient wouldn't wear stripes or stand in lines because these also caused flashbacks to his concentration camp experience."

Responses of Formerly Abused Patients May be Different

For the formerly abused, patient care takes more time, more patience, and requires the development of trust and communication. When a patient takes medications, the abusive experience(s) may come back. Patients may have issues around being touched or examined; this applies to bathroom care and oral hygiene. As one expert respondent explained, "Treatment may lead to unexpected reactions, flashbacks, and revictimization. This means suffering *twice* for the same procedure; this also results in *twice* the anguish."

"The patient's self-esteem may be pretty shot," said one hospice expert. He continued, "They may turn down offers of a back rub or a can of pop, etc. because it's hard for them to accept people being nice to them." Some patients need to express their rage and tears. One abuse expert asserted: "Formerly abused people are either stuck in rage and anger or have gone as far as transformation. There is not much in between."

Several professionals maintained that one should expect reactions to specific care procedures that don't seem logical (i.e., the throat being swabbed and patient's reaction is out of proportion to the procedure). In the words of one expert, "Staff need to understand that their formerly abused patients have low levels of trust, intimacy, communication skills, ability to express their feelings, and that they may close down. Often these people die emotionally alone. Also, patients don't believe they are worthy."

Families of Formerly Abused Patients May Be Different

Several respondents working in health care stated that there may be differences in the families of formerly abused patients. Generally, a family in which abuse has existed is a closed family system and lacks the capacity to nurture its members. Asked one professional, "If the abuser is a family member, and if the family has managed to face the abuse issue(s), how will that affect the patient now?" The abuse, however, may have occurred outside the family, and the family may either be unaware of it or may lack the ability to cope with it. In any event, the entire family is the unit of care in hospice, not just the patient. Therefore, trying to manage effectively interactions with the entire family is important and may be complex.

In summary, "When caregivers know the history of abuse, they can give better and more appropriate care," according to a respondent.

WILL DIFFERENT TYPES OF ABUSE MAKE A DIFFERENCE IN HOSPICE CARE OF FORMERLY ABUSED PERSONS?

One expert questioned, "How does the victim of sexual abuse from a family member process and deal with issues at the end of life? What about forgiveness and anger? There may be problems during the final hours. Does the patient want the perpetrator there at the time of death? Females who have always hidden this information—how do they deal with abuse issues at the end of life?"

Most respondents said the type of abuse *would* make a difference. One expert clarified this by saying, "Not just types of abuse but *consequences* of abuse as well. *If it became PTSD, that is not curable; you learn to live with it.*" In fact, repeated abuse as a child leads to more complex reactions later. A history of abuse for many years contributes to the patient being hyperalert and hypersensitive.

"Sexual abuse is a category all to itself: trauma, lots of anger, its own set of needs," according to one professional. Sexual abuse leads to psychological issues. In one example, a young female patient had been the victim of sexual abuse and was very preoccupied with sex during her hospice stay. She was also very angry and demanding. The staff learned the importance of setting and enforcing boundaries and limits. Victims who have handled difficult situations by being seductive or by not having boundaries may show both of those behaviors in hospice.

Within the category of sexual abuse, there is abuse by a member of the clergy. If that was the abusive situation for the patient, there may be a problem in hospice with having a chaplain or other clergyperson present.

"The identity of the perpetrator also makes a difference; it is worse if it is a family member," claimed one respondent. Patients who have suffered trauma of sexual abuse associations with the smell of an assault, and this may trigger extreme reactions. Sexual abuse will make a difference in dental, oral, pelvic, and rectal care, during exams, and in receiving treatments. In general, victims of sexual abuse will have the most psychological and social differences. As one professional discussed, "Sexual offenders will have confused their child victims with love and sexual abuse [occurring together]; this leads to the child becoming more messed up."

Physical abuse is easier to address. With a history of physical abuse, however, patients will flinch whenever you come near them. With physical abuse, some of the issues are about touch, privacy, and modesty. Psychological abuse results in depression issues. Verbal abuse is not as recognized because you cannot see the scars. "However, any abuse victim is emotionally abused and emotional abuse is the worst, the hardest to overcome," claimed one expert. In general, more abuse issues lead to the need for more work later. That is why personnel should know about abuse, the psychological responses to abuse, and some desirable methods of handling difficult situations with patients.

"Child abuse in a family affects the victim's concept of God because parents symbolize authority," stated one expert. "The formerly abused patient needs spiritual support; they have a sense of expectation of bad stuff. 'Shit happens to us; we deserve to be victims.' They feel responsible for illness."

Finally, very few interviewees responded "no" to the question of care for a formerly abused patient being different. "Probably not if you follow good care principles," said one. However, they qualified their responses with comments such as, "These patients need compassion, love and respect because boundaries have been so violated," and "They also need listening, witnessing, and the chance to tell their story."

The complexity of the issue of abuse and the responses to this abuse may create multiple variables. *The possible variables* on abuse that emerged from this investigation include:

age	culture
nature of abuse	where the patient is, in life-review
intensity	education
severity	how far in the past the abuse occurred
duration	degree to which patient has addressed the abuse
repetition	meanings the patient assigns to the abuse
nature of perpetrator	threat of death occurring with abuse
(family, clergy)	relationship of abuse to cause of death
site of abuse (bed?)	

HOW DO WE DELIVER APPROPRIATE CARE TO FORMERLY ABUSED PEOPLE?

The most common responses to this question were: give as much control as possible to the patient, carry out a thorough assessment, anticipate the likelihood of dissociation, and prepare the patient. See Appendix for list of key concepts.

Control

Control was the most frequently mentioned concept in this entire exploration. It is desirable for those working with formerly abused patients to be "super-aware and give every choice possible to the patient," according to one professional. These may be major choices such as the location where care is provided, to some relatively minor choices such as color of bedding or the time at which personal care procedures are most comfortable. Respondents underscored the importance of these processes being *patient-led*.

Because the patient's bed becomes an extension of themselves, it may be intrusion if someone sits on the bed. Avoid touching without the patient's permission. "This is a dignity and respect issue and is further complicated in people that have been incested or abused in their own bed. Their wheelchair is also part of their personal space," said one expert. The element of control also allows the patient some *time* for decision-making whenever possible, especially for things such as having a massage. If the patient cannot speak, there needs to be an agreement on hand signals that indicate to "stop" or other vital communications. Likewise, it is very important to knock before entering the patient's room.

One example of lack of control was the case of a formerly abused mother staying in a hospice who wanted her reading glasses. The nurse refused to give them to her saying that she no longer needed them. Not only did the patient want them, but the family was used to always seeing her wearing glasses, so they were distressed.

"All abused females have sleeping issues and trust issues with males especially when prone or being cared for—except maybe for physicians," said one formerly abused respondent. She suggested, "I need you to tell me what you are going to do, particularly when I'm sleeping. Don't touch me without doing that. I need more time to adjust to change, and I need explanations more than once. Also, I need to be able to bring from home my pillow and blanket that nurture and shield me. It would be helpful to have someone do a ritual to clean the space for [my] occupancy. I need to bring items that protect me such as a picture of the virgin mother, a shield, and warm decorative objects that help." This respondent had been a childhood victim of ritual abuse.

One respondent advised, "Watch your *voice* of authority. Don't tell me what to do. [I am vulnerable], so don't put your face in my face, especially when I'm in pain or disoriented. Avoid hugs, arms, touching."

Another way of giving control to the patient would be to ask, "Are there any family members who you would like to have help you or not help you?" One respondent suggested, "Offer the family counseling, time to see the patient any time twenty-four hours a day so their chances [of dealing with their issues] are maximized."

Promote Touch Being Controlled by the Patient

As one formerly abused therapist claimed, "Hospice workers often do not know what is intrusive. Do not give hugs without permission. Never reach over and pat someone on the leg; that's too vulnerable a spot, especially for sexually abused patients." Touch can be a trigger; touch can be what patients need the most, but touch can be what they fear the most. In the words of one abuse victim, "Some patients do not like being touched because they fear this closeness; some patients keep their thoughts of being abused ever in their mind. They find it hard to forget." In summary, one interviewee requested, "Control your boundaries, especially in a hospital room. Hospitals are run for the convenience of the nursing staff, but *this* needs to be controlled by the patient whenever possible."

Prepare the Patient

"It would help if hospital [personnel] could tell you what you can expect down the road," said one former abuse victim. "For example, a doctor arrived to remove [my] drainage tubes. He came in and did not introduce himself—just wanted to remove tubes. I felt as though I had no control. Strangers doing strange things to me was very depersonalizing." An introduction, an explanation, and some element of choice may have prevented this reaction.

Describe procedures to patients in advance and, whenever possible, give warnings to patients. This could be "In a few minutes, you will be given a _____ (procedure or care)," or "Somebody will be in to check on you at 2 A.M." Ask questions privately and treat patients carefully. Do not intrude, as the patient may jump or scream or may even have a panic attack. If the patient is startled, there may be a need to identify what is startling. In response to a patient's reactions, the staff can respond with open-ended questions such as "Did I frighten you?," "Did I hurt you?," or "Does something about this bother you?"

Assessment

While some patients may not even know what they need, one expert reported that a focus group of abused clients stated they *want* experienced personnel to assess for abuse. Awareness of any history of abuse is essential. One professional questioned, "Will patients identify themselves as having been abused? Many females don't see they've been abused." Another respondent suggested asking specific questions about abuse *behaviors* to get around this issue. Privacy issues were mentioned by respondents as well as the fact that people may not want to disclose or discuss their abuse.

A patient's mental health may sometimes make it difficult to discern a history of abuse such as in cases of psychosis, schizophrenia, Alzheimer's, delusions, and inaccurate memory. One respondent described a patient who was thought by the staff to be demented. This caregiver, herself aware of the consequences of abuse, recognized that this patient was clearly describing a date-rape [flashback], and was not delusional at all.

Although assessments are completed upon admission to the program to assist in the development of a care plan, the hospice may learn about abuse only after the person has been a patient for a while. Therefore, it is important to continue to assess the situation for information as well as *support*. One professional recommended interviewing protocols that could provide guidelines in such cases. The assessment will also need to question whether the patient is suicidal.

Dissociation

It may be necessary to take into consideration the likelihood of the patient's "dissociation," a patient behavior frequently mentioned by respondents. Dissociation is the "separation of a group of related psychological activities into autonomously functioning units, as in the generation of multiple personalities" [5, p. 539]. Stedman defines dissociation as "an unconscious process by which a group of mental processes is separated from the rest of the thinking processes, resulting in an independent functioning of these processes and a loss of the usual relationship; for example, a separation of affect from cognition" [3 p. 510]. Dissociation may result from abuse, according to one abuse victim, "when the victim cannot control their body, the mind goes elsewhere." Dissociation was also described as "going back into the flashback images." As one formerly abused respondent describes, "A patient who has repeatedly been abused may dissociate and not be in the body. This is a safety device so you do not feel the abuse. There is safety and comfort in doing that. Actually a *positive* quality of dissociation is the ability to dissociate at will; this has become a gift; I now can direct it and be safe with it and with boundaries."

The staff needs to learn how to recognize and cope with patients when they dissociate. One way to prevent dissociation is by describing a procedure in advance, and then by talking through the procedure to orient the patient. Give them control, especially with people who have been traumatized sexually. It helps if the caregiver knows how to assist the patient to come back when dissociation does occur by saying, "Listen to my voice." Have someone else present as a witness or advocate.

The staff may find that development of a repertoire of skills will assist in this effort. For example, one respondent offered, "Don't touch a person without permission." For grounding a patient who has a tendency to dissociate, one patient found that when the therapist simply touched her toe, it was sufficient to stay in the here and now." A therapist summarized, "Gently talk to the patient who is dissociating about what is going on so they feel safe and will stay present and not dissociate."

Flashbacks

In preventing or dealing with flashbacks, be gentle, respectful, and reassuring. It is essential to develop a sense of trust that cannot be violated.

Medications and Substance Control

One formerly abused individual gets very concerned if hospitalized and "drugged" [medicated] because being drugged was part of her former ritual abuse as a child. In daily life she avoids any chemicals that are mood-altering because she is terrified of having "too much and losing control." This was specified by several of the abuse victims interviewed.

Personal Care

With many formerly abused patients, difficulty in undressing is common, so patient care and exams must be treated cautiously and with respect. Train doctors and nurses to give care to *abused* patients. Physicians need to have a nurse in the room during procedures. Give patients affirming statements and choices. Discover procedures that made the patient most comfortable before. Some possible problems may be treatments such as use of suppositories or the selection of clothing. "You may want to avoid anything tight around neck like hospital gowns," recommended one social worker.

Mouth care for sexually abused people may be problematic. There is evidence of difficulty with the dentist if there was sexual abuse involving the mouth. One respondent described a female victim of sexual abuse as never having gone to a dentist during her entire adult life. In hospice care this may translate to use of the thermometer, tongue depressors, swabs to clean the mouth, and oral examinations.

In delivering appropriate care to formerly abused patients in hospice, the respondents again identified the importance of being aware of the family system and dynamics.

WHAT CAREGIVING BEHAVIORS MAY BE HELPFUL TO FORMERLY ABUSED PATIENTS?

One hospice expert declared that it is important to "Accent faster growth and resolution, sensitivity, and the physical . . . incorporate therapeutic touch and massage." Because each person's dying is unique, it is essential to respect the patient's timetable and individuality. Another respondent said that it is important to address *behaviors* but not label the patient. By incorporating flexibility and respect and allowing patients to lead us, it is possible to create opportunities for these patients to complete their lives according to their needs. It is also fundamental to honor the patient's struggle with God. Another professional summarizes, "Patients need behaviors that build trust."

Individual Case Unique

Each case has its own dynamics. In every case there is the opportunity for change or transformation, for resolution, but respondents warn not to expect it. Although the process is different for each patient, it is always important to create safety, comfort, and respect. Acknowledging the patient is essential, also.

Relaxation Techniques

Expect that patients will be hyperalert, so create a quiet, comforting, and cheerful environment. "Any kind of special nurturing acceptable to a patient such as a less threatening kind of massage—hand, arm, foot massage—or maybe a warm, scented bath," suggested one victim of former abuse. It may be relaxing to have books read to them or to hear books on tape. Relaxation tapes with ocean sounds or other pleasant sounds would also be relaxing. Consider teaching the patients techniques for meditation. "On the other hand," as one formerly abused person added, "any of the above may be triggers. *There is nothing that is neutral.* Anything has the potential to be a trigger: a color, a furnishing, a sound, or a smell—*anything.*"

It was suggested that the patient might be more relaxed in a single room. Conversely, another respondent discussed a formerly abused patient who did not interact with roommates but always wanted to be in a three-bed room. This is, again, an example of the need to be mindful of the individual patient's preferences.

Issues of Sexual Abuse

The consequences of caring in a hospice for a former victim of sexual abuse include precautions in care involving the mouth, procedures for personal care, and the sex of the caregivers. If possible, select caregivers of the same sex if the perpetrator was of the opposite sex. Handle these on a case-by-case basis.

Visitors

Visitors may or may not be understood by the hospital staff. Further, there is the question of how to handle the perpetrator or family members as visitors. What about the issue of someone coming to visit whom the patient does not wish to see? "No one should be shocked at this. Give the patient control over who visits and what hours they visit," offered one hospice professional. The patient may need assistance from the staff in enforcing this or help with setting limits.

Spiritual Needs, Preferences

It is crucial to respect the patient's spiritual journey and to let them determine this. For example, a crucifix on the wall may be a symbol of support to Christians, but it could be very painful to a person formerly subjected to ritual abuse. Respect the request to remove it. For spiritual connections, offer access to therapists, clergy, spiritual advisors or directors, but if the individual is the victim of ritual abuse or abuse by clergy, he or she may have different preferences.

Emotional State of Well-Being

Hospice workers need to build relationships of trust with formerly abused patients. Said one hospice worker, "People may have defined themselves as selves of shame. They didn't allow for their *own* divinity." Regardless of how long it's been since the abuse, patients need reassurance that they are good people, and they did not cause the abuse. Patients need statements from caregivers like, "I care about you and you are a good person." Reaffirm them as persons who "did not deserve it." Accept them just as they are and be supportive. With a terminal condition, the patient may be depressed and anxious. During the last six months of life, patients may have mood disorders and increased potential for suicide. The concern about suicide is complicated by a history of severe abuse. One professional said that perhaps the patient may consider suicide as a means to retaliate at the abuser, as in having the perpetrator find the body.

Avoiding Revictimization

"Avoid revictimizing the patient. This is huge and vitally important!" declared one formerly abused person. Being told information by staff in an abrupt, uncaring way may lead to an abuse reaction occurring again. The patient may feel re-victimized, scared, alone, and vulnerable in dealing with this. The pitfall is that the patient will believe; as one professional said, "*I'll* have to take care of me." That patient may need more individual support and may not have any support in place.

Staff also need to be exceedingly alert to avoid blaming the victim. More than one formerly abused respondent alleged that formerly abused people are re-victimized constantly. They may be asked questions like, "So, why didn't you *leave* the abuser?" which very inappropriately trivializes and blames. Just one sentence like this alerts the patient that the caregiver does not understand abuse. At the same time, staff need to avoid blaming the family; treat the family with respect, the same as other families.

Life-Review Opportunities

This is an important aspect of what is often called "closure." A general yet time-consuming approach would involve open-ended questions and patient-led interactions. If the patient is willing to participate, ask questions such as, "Will you tell me your life story?" or "What could other people benefit from knowing about your experience?" and "How could you pass this on?" Bring up the patient's accomplishments as well as things the patient might do differently. The social worker, or whichever caregiver is involved, listens and facilitates this process for the patient. It was suggested to produce memories on paper in a journal or album. Finally, do not expect that problematic situations are going to be *healed* during hospice. This is a time of *opportunity,* but the process should be patient-led.

CAREGIVERS

Respondents readily discussed the qualities of desirable caregivers for formerly abused persons. They also addressed some behaviors of caregivers such as giving clear descriptions of procedures to be performed, warning of procedures whenever possible, and avoiding labeling the patient. One hospice manager described having contracts with their patients.

The most common responses were that caregivers should be sensitive, empathic, respectful, patient, cheerful. One victim of traumatic abuse reminded us that patients "need to laugh, and the staff needs to acknowledge that people are still alive and live in the *now*." Other qualities identified were kindness, gentleness, ability to communicate, being even-tempered, trustworthy, non-judgmental, understanding, good at listening, and, finally, the ability to ask gentle questions. "Sympathy, empathy, understanding; develop personal rapport; just be with them. Caregivers do not understand," claimed one formerly abused professional. Reenactment makes the caregiver into a perpetrator in the interpretation of the patient. "It's all mixed up together. . . . Staff needs to have good parenting skills . . . be a person first, then a professional to avoid re-victimizing. Help patients find a place of peace and closure. This is not simple or easy. They may want to finish this big life issue."

It is important to validate the patient's experiences and feelings. As one respondent observed, "Validation and normalization are great ground levelers. The patient will pick up cues from staff because their antennae are continually out; their comfort level depends on how you ask." "People then feel they are not a freak. If you make the patient feel more anxieties, their antennae go up." "It is natural to have an anticipatory pain reaction; don't make pain into a behavioral issue because that *may cause patient to relive the abuse as though it's happening all over again* . . . (twice the anguish)," stated one professional.

Another professional described a contract their hospice has with each patient. The patient can fire a single hospice worker or the entire team if they are not satisfactory. This gives the patient ultimate control.

WHAT PROBLEMS MAY THERE BE WITH FAMILIES AND OTHERS?

When asked if there were issues with next of kin, one professional replied, "Absolutely! Issues that remain." Their hospice has family sessions facilitated by a very skilled therapist. "People can share the good, the bad, and the ugly. People can say what they want to say. It requires a skilled clinician to guide family members through this. Some men would have died without saying, 'I Love You' to relatives. In many situations, the issues probably don't get dealt with."

Reactions to Abuse

Survivors include friends, family, siblings, children, and perhaps even parents. Experts on abuse question their reactions to the abuse. Do the next of kin have knowledge of the specific abuse in this case? What is their level of denial? How relevant or appropriate would it be for them to know? Who was the perpetrator? Do they need education about it? They may lack general knowledge about abuse and may not understand the cycle of violence or relevant issues such as guilt. It may be important to find a way to get them to hear the patient's concerns.

There may be different perspectives on specific abuse and, at the same time, the desire of the family to be considered normal. Is there a need or desire for therapy or counseling now? Where are next-of-kin with processing and forgiveness? There could be a continued denial leading to an impasse of resolution. The family dynamics can be huge and can include denial, rejection, condemnation, ostracism, and lack of support. In contrast to the expectation of healing issues of abuse during hospice, there may be splits in families, as well as guilt, feuds, power struggles, personal insecurities, and trust issues. One hospital professional claimed, "You could *feel* the tension in the room."

Not only does this affect the current next of kin; it may affect survivors in the next generations. This needs to be handled on a case-by-case basis; issues at the end of life depend on what that earlier experience was. These issues also need to be managed with confidentiality and privacy.

The Perpetrator

Is the perpetrator still active in the life of the patient? According to one professional, "Perpetrators can be cunning and may seem socially charming; however, they are psychopaths or sociopaths." Sometimes the mother is the perpetrator, or the father is the perpetrator against his sons. There may be issues with the mother if she colluded in some way, especially if the mother is now the caretaker. One abuse expert explained, "Females having experienced sexual abuse by their father seem to carry it for the rest of their lives. . . . There are issues of forgiveness both from victim to perpetrator and from perpetrator to victim. Even if the abuse is resolved, there may still be problems around the perpetrator. All their old issues have the potential of coming up again."

Another issue may be visitors to patients and the need for boundaries. The patient may desire visitors to avoid discussing certain subjects. The staff may need to support the patient actively on this. Finally, all of the above may contribute to complicated or ambivalent grief even before death occurs.

WHAT ISSUES MAY ARISE FOR HOSPICE PERSONNEL AS A RESULT OF WORKING WITH FORMERLY ABUSED PATIENTS?

In general, the greater the former abuse of the patient, the greater the likelihood that there will be issues for staff. Responses to this question focused on the personal issues of the staff, the possible current job issues, and the need for training the staff.

As one expert observed, "Greater obstacles are accented here. The patient may have resistance to intimacy even though that has the potential for greatest growth at end of life. Therefore, hospice workers need to show up *every day* to establish trust with a non-communicator."

Another professional in the area of abuse stated, "Staff may suddenly recall their own buried abuse. It makes a big difference if you've dealt with your own abuse; otherwise it will be a big issue. People who have *not* been abused will have trouble 'getting it,' may *not* be able to do the sharing." Lack of education may lead hospice personnel to be less therapeutic and more judgmental. He continued, "Many do not understand the dynamics of abuse. Staff training will help to increase their tolerance, empathy, and willingness to get help for things they do not understand."

The staff may have personal issues concerning their own former abuse. First, "Is the personal history of abuse resolved or not resolved? This work may cause their own unresolved issues to surface. They may feel frustrated, as in grieving. Many caregivers are 'wounded healers,' and this work may compound their stress." They need to discuss their personal issues one on one with supportive staff members and may need to be referred to mental health providers. Second, it is important for staff not to project their experience, desires, needs, or interpretations onto the patient's situation. And, finally, the caregiver needs to prepare spiritually with their own higher power to be a supportive person for the patient.

When it comes to the current job and the consequent needs, experts described the emotional toll on hospice workers and the need for acknowledging and validating the caregivers' feelings. "Hospice staff is supposed to *feel*—to be empathic. They [then] have a need to debrief," said one. Because a case may trigger things in a hospice worker's life if previously abused, the worker may either withdraw or get closer to the patient. Several respondents described cases in which the hospice personnel themselves were concerned about their need for processing afterwards. This can sometimes feel overwhelming, as in a case where a woman was dying of AIDS that she had contracted from her abusive husband. One pastoral counselor described how her work with an abusive situation caused her a secondary victimization reaction that lasted for years.

Another issue for hospice personnel working with formerly abused people is workers who believe "It's not my job. [They] don't see it as part of health care. [They are in] denial and refuse to ask questions," reported one hospice professional.

This leads to the question of how much work the hospice staff should do with a given patient and how much unfinished business needs to be referred to another resource such as a consulting therapist. Clients do shift and have trouble being heard. The most important thing we can do is *hear* their stories, but that "hearing" may be challenging. A formerly abused patient could be very antagonistic instead of passive—could be very demanding. This situation may be more adequately addressed by a therapist.

Besides experiencing what Larson calls "compassion fatigue" [6], workers may ask themselves, "Can I handle this with perspective, or will I get sucked into their pain?" In fact, this may motivate someone to leave a case or to ask for special consideration.

WHAT ARE THE RECOMMENDATIONS ON TRAINING CAREGIVERS OF FORMERLY ABUSED PEOPLE?

"Most staff haven't got a clue about abuse," according to one expert, who continued, "Personnel may not be aware of signs of former abuse or emotional responses of these patients." Also, another expert stated, "There is a gaping hole in medical training, especially the psychological and spiritual piece." The objective of training is to help physicians and nurses become less threatening and more effective.

Training should incorporate not only information about abuse, but also how that may apply in the hospice context. Specifically mentioned were: good boundaries, appropriate touch, body language, behavioral cues, an awareness of triggers, and letting the patient know of procedures in advance. Patient care could be improved by conference discussion early in the case of the possibility of abuse history and appropriate treatment. Also, volunteers need training on hospice care of the formerly abused.

Becoming non-judgmental as well as avoiding the interpretation that the victim must have done something to invite abuse are both essential. In general, this society supports the commandment "Honor thy mother and thy father." In cases of abuse by parents, however, if the caregivers insist on this commandment, the former abuse probably will *not* be dealt with and the patient is less apt to heal.

While some hospices have minimal training, others do training of all staff and volunteers twice a year. One hospice expert requested, "Educate staff with real experiences; don't minimize, especially with the older population. Most caregivers are assistants with little education. They need to learn how to validate the patient's reality and definition of the situation. Nursing orientations in mental health are hit-or-miss in-services during the year. We may get only 30 out of 500 workers attending. [In our state] assistants need only twelve CEUs per year including all areas of health issues."

Because many of our newer immigrants come from situations of abuse or violence (Cambodia, Bosnia, African nations, etc.), education on how to provide culturally sensitive care will be increasingly needed in addition to the training about abuse. One hospice even sent their workers to a holocaust museum so they would understand and increase their empathy for their patients who were survivors of the holocaust.

"There are some excellent training videos that illustrate [such things as] dissociation. Having formal training in abuse and in trauma *may* be useful but is *no* guarantee," one respondent claimed. She continued that, "Lots of formerly abused women are *not* supportive." However, most respondents shared the belief that "those with training, those who have been abused themselves and have been through their own therapy, they would really understand."

In addition to training on hospice care of the formerly abused, respondents cited the need for advocacy and advocacy training. Many hospitals have programs for advocacy in the emergency room, urgent care, and perinatal units. While not everyone may become skilled at this, psychologists and social workers are some of the professionals who have trained to be patients' advocates.

WHO COULD BE OF THE MOST HELP TO FORMERLY ABUSED PATIENTS?

While respondents identified job titles, qualities, and advocacy, they consistently recommended formerly abused caregivers who have resolved their own abuse issues. Among job titles mentioned were: physicians, nurses, chaplains, social workers, counselors, volunteers, pastoral counselors, and home health aides who are carefully selected. Also suggested were child life workers trained to play with children in a hospital setting. "A case manager or person who would know most, one person who understands and has continuity of care and could consistently follow through," was recommended. The interdisciplinary team conferences that are normal procedure in the hospice could be even more helpful in cases involving former abuse.

Bereavement following abuse is sometimes associated with complicated grief. Therefore, having the bereavement coordinator, clergy, social workers, or a grief counselor involved before the death of the patient could be beneficial in working with other family members or friends later on.

Qualities of caregivers that were discussed by respondents included: pleasant, uplifting, good at boundaries, adaptable, compassionate, non-judgmental, supportive, respectful, and possessing professional integrity. Also mentioned were people who can provide comfort and a level of safety, and are good listeners. Again, the essential ingredient is the ability to develop and inspire trust.

In summary, one stated, "[It] doesn't matter the *initials* after the name. What is important is listening, communication skills, and the willingness to make an investment in this person."

WHAT OTHER FACTORS ARE IMPORTANT TO INCLUDE IN THE STUDY OF HOSPICE CARE OF FORMERLY ABUSED INDIVIDUALS?

Recovery

One therapist observed, "Survivors of former abuse tend to fall into two camps. They are either stuck in rage and anger or have achieved some transformation and desire to make it better for someone else. There doesn't seem to be much middle ground." One victim of fifteen years of abuse asserted that she expects to work on recovery for the rest of her life.

The Value of Disclosing Former Abuse

In answering this questionnaire, some people indicated that they, too, have been abused. One respondent discussed her own abuse by a brother and the later consequences for her, her brother, and her family. Another participant said, "I've had serious abuse in marriage and as a teenager. Although I've been through therapy for years, it still brings memories and tears, but that's all right. I feel *better* after discussing it."

The Spiritual Factor

Two expert respondents discussed the importance of the spiritual component in providing hospice care for formerly abused individuals. They suggested that the moral, religious, spiritual component is often missing or inadequate. One of the respondents continued, "Most people are dying without the psychospiritual guide to the other side." Reasons for inclusion are the huge fear of sin, death, hell (3 respondents), as well as the fact that victims of former abuse have issues with God and often a negative image of God. "There may be spiritual issues, a struggle with God; a question of needing to pay God back, or not interpreting God as a loving God." Because victims feel responsible, steps in their healing include the need to get beyond their anger and hostility and the belief that they somehow asked for their abuse.

Disagreement on Assessment

There was less general agreement on assessment at intake. One stated, "Do not have question(s) about abuse on intake; ask *only if* you see red flags." Others recommended a sensitive, caring, non-judgmental approach in universal screening to discover former abuse such as, "Everyone feels victimized sometimes. In what ways in your life did you feel treated unfairly?" "Because we are very concerned about violence in our society, I'm going to ask you a couple of questions. Does anyone control your behavior by emotional abuse or have you had this experience in your past? Have there been big secrets about or involving loneliness, isolation, or pain?"

Time Remaining for the Patient

How much time the patient now has in hospice was also a concern. "System-wide in the United States now, the average hospice patient is only served three weeks. Not time or energy for much work on this," claimed one professional. However, "There is another alternative called 'Care Options' which is for patients with terminal diagnosis but a prognosis allowing two years. There would be more opportunity to work on these issues during that time."

Intergenerational Effects

Intergenerational effects were mentioned such as the victimization of the second generation of survivors of the holocaust. Responses and behaviors get passed down from one generation to another. For example, a female victim of emotional abuse described, "That went back two generations, actually three generations of saying at birth 'It's *only* a girl.' " With assistance, there is the possibility of understanding and healing to prevent intergenerational transmission of abuse.

Financial

As one respondent claimed, "Interventions are less likely with HMOs today. Federal programs are less likely to support a patient 'who is not deteriorating fast enough.' Financial assistance is lost due to Medicare not being available for the long term. This is system-wide; [only] 10 percent of clients may be reached in help with abuse due to financial barriers."

WHAT OTHER AREAS OF LITERATURE MAY BEGIN TO INFORM US ABOUT DELIVERING HOSPICE CARE CARE TO FORMERLY ABUSED PEOPLE?

Respondents participating in this exploration suggested that the following areas of literature may provide information applicable to the population of formerly abused individuals as well as give suggestions to consider in offering hospice care for these vulnerable people at the end of their lives.

Veterans from World War II, the Korean War, Viet Nam, and the Gulf War
Victims of torture
Holocaust survivors
Posttraumatic Stress Disorder
Victims of domestic violence
Refugees and new Americans from locations involving significant abuse
Prisoners of war
Responses of abused women during labor
Information on discerning the accuracy of disclosure
Disaster victims

CONCLUSION

The purpose of this exploration was to report on hospice care of formerly abused persons. This is a new area of investigation with no specific body of literature. Other areas of literature which may inform us were identified, as well as numerous variables. This information was assembled from forty-four interviews with professionals and formerly abused individuals. There is potential and need for research in this area. Such research will contribute to understanding in patients, staff, and professionals of more effective, compassionate ways to serve this vulnerable population at the closure of their lives.

Some of the major questions in this exploration were:

- How will we identify formerly abused persons who are now patients in hospice?
- How and why might care of formerly abused patients be different?
- Will different types of abuse call for differences in hospice care?
- What may be the salient family issues?
- What are the consequences for hospital personnel in serving formerly abused people?
- What are recommendations for training staff about this population?
- What literature may inform us about delivering hospice care to formerly abused people?

Some of the key concepts emerging in this new sphere of hospice serving formerly abused people are: confidentiality, assessment, dissociation, control by the patient, the process being patient-led, the sensitivity of caregivers, and the need for training staff. The spiritual component also needs to be investigated for supporting this particular population.

There are increasing levels of violence in our culture and worldwide; abuse is escalating, according to Rando [7]. The consequences for hospice will be challenging. While we might prefer to focus on the prevention of abuse, our efforts to cope with abuse will need to escalate. As one hospice expert reminded us, "Abused people fear abandonment in general plus abandonment as part of health care. Dame Cicely Saunders, the renowned advocate of hospice, said 'We will not abandon you.'"

The economic costs and trade-offs of this care will need to be considered. What about this newly-identified need in the face of diminishing health care funding? One very experienced hospice professional claimed that, "Good care and peaceful dying are also more cost effective."

It seems important to avoid pressure on patients like that experienced with the Kübler-Ross "stages" in the 1970s when some caretakers regarded the "stages" as prescriptive rather than descriptive. They tried to motivate and move the patient through all of the "stages." Respondents in this study reaffirmed that serving formerly abused patients needs to be a more patient-led, gentle investigation with the patient deciding what and how much unfinished business he or she wishes to work on. This will vary depending upon how much energy the patient has and how much intensity this unfinished business will demand.

Research is needed in several areas such as obtaining information from other bodies of literature. Other investigations could be on patient assessments, patient cues, the avoidance of re-victimization, and how best to meet the needs of formerly abused patients. Research on the related reactions of families and close friends would be fruitful also. Explorations about staff should include the staff's responses to this formerly abused population, the most effective aspects of staff training, the occurrence of secondary victimization of staff, and staff burnout or dedication in this area [8]. There are overarching questions about the challenge of conducting ethical and compassionate research on the patients themselves. How can research on such a vulnerable and dying population be managed appropriately? Would the findings warrant the intrusions?

What is discovered about hospice care of formerly abused individuals will be valuable for training in medicine, nursing, mental health, and pastoral care. Such training will also be useful for nursing assistants and volunteers who routinely see these patients. It certainly will be applicable in other settings such as hospitals, senior residences, and nursing homes.

In conclusion, formerly abused hospice patients may have had a difficult, challenging journey. This investigation, however, suggests some ways to create a hospice experience which is less threatening and more comfortable for them. When this has happened, patients may then be better able to complete what Byock calls, "Five things [that] have been communicated to one another: "Forgive me." "I forgive you.". . . "Thank you." "I love you." and "Good-bye" [9, p. 188].

The distinction between *healing* and *curing* may be especially relevant in the hospice care of formerly abused people. While this process is patient-led and may be facilitated by staff, we should never underestimate the possibilities of transformation!

APPENDIX:
Interview Format

The following questions were included in this interview:

1. Have you ever known a formerly abused person who received hospice care?
2. Do you know of anyone else who has served such an individual who is or was dying?
3. Do you know of any experts in the field of abuse or hospice or other relevant professions who may be able to answer questions about serving formerly abused individuals?
4. Do you have any suggestions of literature pertinent to this topic?
5. Can you suggest any one else, local or national, whom it would be helpful to interview?
6. In your experience in caregiving, do you think that care for a formerly abused individual would be any different from care for any other person in hospice? If "no," why not? If "yes," why do you think so?
7. What problems do you think may be encountered in doing this research?
8. Are there ways if approaching hospice care with formerly abused individuals that would be useful to consider?
9. What care-giving behaviors may be helpful to these patients?
10. What issues do you think there might be with survivors, next of kin, others?

11. Will different types of abuse make any difference in hospice care of these persons?
12. What issues may arise for hospice personnel interacting with such patients?
13. In a hospice, what individuals could be of most service to formerly abused patients?
14. Now that you have heard or read the initial questions, what other questions need to be addressed?
15. Can you think of any other information you would consider important to include in the study of hospice care of formerly abused individuals?

Types of Respondents

physician, palliative care	1
hospice experts	4
nurses	10
hospice nurses (not included in above)	4
abuse experts	9
hospice social workers1	1
abuse victims	6
victims of ritual abuse (not included above)	2
pastoral chaplains or counselors	3
pastoral care assistants	4
therapists	5
psychologists	7
total by occupation or victim status	62

Key Concepts Reported On for Formerly Abused Patients

individual case unique
control, control, control
touch
    control by patient
    always permission
    therapeutic touch
spiritual needs
techniques for relaxation
dissociation
flashbacks
prepare the patient

sexual abuse issues
    care involving mouth
    care of genital area
    caregivers of same sex as abuser
medications
visitors
emotional issues
    sensitivity
    aggression, assertiveness
opportunities for life-review
avoid re-victimization

REFERENCES

1. Minnesota Department of Human Services, St. Paul, Minnesota, 1997.
2. National Hospice Organization, *Hospice Fact Sheet* (Updated June 1, 1997).
3. *Stedman's Medical Dictionary* (26th Edition), Williams & Wilkins, Baltimore, 1995.
4. American Psychiatric Association, *Diagnostic and Statistical Manual of Mental Disorders*, Fourth Edition, Washington, D.C., 1994.
5. *The American Heritage Dictionary of the English Language* (Third Edition), Houghton Mifflin, Boston, 1995.
6. D. G. Larson, *The Helper's Journey: Working with People Facing Grief, Loss, and Life-Threatening Illness*, Research Press, Champaign, Illinois, 1993.
7. T. A. Rando, *Sudden, Traumatic and Violent Deaths: Interventions in Complicated Types of Bereavement*, presented at Minnesota Coalition for Death Education and Support, St. Paul, Minnesota, May 24, 1996.
8. B. C. Harper, Growth in Caring and Professional Ethics in Hospice, *The Hospice Journal, 12*:2, pp. 65-70, 1997.
9. I. R. Byock, Caring for the Dying, in *Readings in Thanatology*, J. D. Morgan (ed.), Baywood, Amityville, New York, 1997.

BIBLIOGRAPHY OF RELATED READINGS

Besharov, D. J., *Recognizing Child Abuse: A Guide for the Concerned*, The Free Press, New York, 1990.

Bertman, S. L., Bereavement and Grief, in *Introduction to Clinical Medicine*, H. L. Greene et al. (eds.), Mosby Yearbook, Philadelphia, pp. 681-684, 1991.

Caldwell, M., Kernel of Fear, *Discover*, pp. 97-102, 1995.

Corr, C. A., A Task-Based Approach to Coping with Dying, in *The Path Ahead*, L. A. DeSpelder and A. L. Strickland (eds.), Mayfield, Mountain View, California, pp. 303-315, 1995.

Corr, C. A., Morgan, J. D., and Wass, H., *International Work Group on Death, Dying, and Bereavement: Statements on Death, Dying, and Bereavement*, 1994. [IWG Secretariat, King's College, 266 Epworth Avenue, London, Ontario, Canada N6A 2M3.]

Figley, C. R., *Helping Traumatized Families*, Jossey-Bass, San Francisco, 1989.

Flannery, R. B., Jr., *Post-Traumatic Stress Disorder: The Victim's Guide to Healing and Recovery*, Crossroads, New York, 1992.

Gilbert, K. R., "We've Had the Same Loss: Why Don't We Have the Same Grief?" Loss and Differential Grief in Families, *Death Studies, 20*, pp. 269-283, 1996.

Hobbs, C. J., Hanks, H. G. I., and Wynne, J. M., *Child Abuse and Neglect: A Clinician's Handbook*, Churchill Livingstone, New York, 1993.

Jordan, J. R., *Coping After Traumatic Loss: What the Counselor Needs to Know*, presented to Association of Death Education and Counseling, Washington, D.C., June 25, 1997.

Lattanzi-Licht, M. and Connor, S., Care of the Dying: The Hospice Approach, in *Dying: Facing the Facts*, (3rd Edition), H. Wass and R. A. Neimeyer (eds.), Taylor & Francis, Washington, D.C., pp. 143-162, 1995.

Lefley, H. P. et al., Cultural Beliefs About Rape and Victims' Response in Three Ethnic Groups, *American Journal of Orthopsychiatry, 63*:4, pp. 623-632, 1993.

Lynn, C., *Does Incest Hurt Worse than Grief?* presented at Association of Death Education and Counseling, Boston, March 6, 1992.

Lynn, C., *How Close Is Too Close? How Far is Too Far?: The Establishment and Maintenance of Personal Boundaries Between Therapists and Trauma Survivors,* presented at the Association of Death Education and Counseling, Memphis, March 6, 1992.

Matsakis, A., *I Can't Get Over It: A Handbook for Trauma Survivors,* New Harbinger, Oakland, California, 1992.

McCartney, J. R. and Severson, K., Sexual Violence, Post-Traumatic Stress Disorder and Dementia, *Journal of the American Geriatric Society, 45,* pp. 76-78, 1997.

Murburg, M. M., *Catecholamine Function in Posttraumatic Stress Disorder: Emerging Concepts,* American Psychiatric Press, Washington, 1994.

National Hospice Organization, Standards of a Hospice Program of Care, *The Hospice Journal, 9:*4, pp. 39-63, 1994.

Rhodes, N. and Hutchinson, S., Labor Experiences of Childhood Sexual Abuse, *Birth,* pp. 213-220, December 1994.

Rosenblatt, P. C. and Fisher, L. R., Qualitative Family Research, in *Sourcebook of Family Theories and Methods: A Contextual Approach,* P. G. Boss, W. J. Doherty, R. LaRossa, W. R. Schumm, and S. K. Steinmetz (eds.), Plenum, New York, pp. 167-177, 1993.

Rosenblatt, P. C. and Fisher, L. R., Sexual Assault Victims: A Protocol for Health Professionals, *Physician Assistant,* pp. 123-130, 1990.

Trolley, B. C., A Bridge Between Traumatic Life Events and Losses by Death, *Omega: Journal of Death and Dying, 28:*4, pp. 285-300, 1993-94.

Zupanick, C. E., Adult Children of Dysfunctional Families: Treatment from a Disenfranchised Grief Perspective, *Death Studies, 18,* pp. 183-195, 1994.

CHAPTER 19

The Dream Catcher and the Universality of Grief

Thomas O'Neill

GRIEF, MOURNING, AND THE USE OF SYMBOLS

Grief cannot be understood, only felt. Grief, the experience of loss, is universal. Mourning, the way in which an individual or group expresses that loss, is cultural. It is important to understand this distinction when working with bereaved people and reflecting on our own experiences and expressions of grief and loss.

Grief is not an intellectual concept, one that can be neatly dissected and labeled. Every statement we make about grief, every explanation that we give to someone in pain, is a distortion of a truth which only they can name. In order to work with people who are grieving we must, in a sense, enter into their pain. We talk about our grief, not because it becomes more comprehensible in the process, but because we have a story that must be told. It is this universality of grief that allows us to walk with all manner of people who have experienced or are experiencing a loss.

The grief groups that I have facilitated have been diverse in every respect: age, sex, race, economic means. But it is the shared experience of grief that brings a group together and helps healing to begin. Grief is one of the most common of all human experiences, matched only by love. They are, in fact, two sides of the same coin. You cannot have grief unless you have love, since grief can only be experienced in relationship to someone or something that is valued. Without love there is no grief, which explains why grief groups are so powerful and cohesive: Participants are not only sharing the devastating experience of grief, but also the inspiring story of love whose absence is so keenly felt.

277

Understanding the second concept, that mourning is cultural, is also very important. We process or mourn our grief based on a number of factors: age, sex, religious beliefs, family rituals, etc. It is essential that we understand where a person is "coming from" in order to accompany him or her on the journey toward healing.

When I deal with families, I emphasize that it is very important for them to acknowledge and allow for differences in how each family member deals with grief. In group work, you often deal with people from a variety of backgrounds, which must be taken into account. In one-on-one situations, it is important to remember that you are working as a "group" of two; that you have to include yourself and your own background because you cannot work with another's grief without it in some way touching your own. It is the very nature of grief, its universality, that permits it to tap into our humanity on the most elemental level.

Robert Fulghum, in his book *All I Really Need to Know I Learned in Kindergarten* [1], tells about a newspaper account of a Russian soldier in Africa who is captured in a hostile military action as the result of refusing to leave the body of his wife who had been killed. This story really impressed Fulghum because, at the time, Russia was viewed as the "evil empire" by the American public, and the depth of the soldier's love and grief indicated that the enemy shared our basic humanity.

I remember my father telling me about an incident that occurred when he was a soldier in World War II in Germany. The war was drawing to a close, and he was riding in a jeep through a German city. Along the road some elderly German women were walking, praying the rosary for the deliverance of their sons who had gone to war. He thought of his own mother back in Ohio who was also praying the rosary daily for his safe return. Almost immediately the women along the roadside became "mothers" instead of "Germans." The soldiers he had been fighting were no longer "the enemy," but rather became sons and husbands. Shared experiences of grief are very strong bonding mechanisms. And it is through this sharing, this coming together, that healing begins.

The ability to accompany a person or group of people on a grief journey comes from combining the two concepts: grief and mourning, the universal and the cultural. Different cultures provide us with the tools that help us grieve. The universality of grief allows us to use the beautiful treasure of stories, rituals, and symbols from the various cultures in ways that enable healing for all of us, and in doing so, bring us closer together in the human family.

Symbols seem to cross cultural boundaries more easily than other metaphorical elements, and there are some symbols which are found in almost all cultures. One of these symbols is the circle.

A few years back, while I was in the process of preparing for a rather diversified grief group, I found myself searching for a unifying theme around which I could build the group activities. The group members represented a wide range of cultures, ages, religions, races, education, and economic classes. This group of family members ranged in age from five to eighty-three and had experienced a variety of losses. The symbol and theme that kept coming to mind was that of the dream catcher.

I had first seen a dream catcher the summer before at a camp we ran for children who had lost a loved one. I had tried at the time to find out more about the dream catcher, whether or not is was a Native-American symbol, what it represented, but was unsuccessful. But I continued to find myself drawn to the combination of the circle and the web, and felt that it had promise as a powerful symbol around which I could structure my wide-ranging grief group. Attracted and inspired by the dream catcher, I shaped my own interpretation of its meaning, and wrote the following story:

THE DREAM CATCHER

Long ago, there was a young man who was the best hunter in his nation. He was very proud of his strength, his quickness and his ability to provide food for his people. His father and the other elders in the nation had spent many years teaching him the skills of the hunter, for the life of the nation depended on those skills.

One year, the nation faced the harshest winter anyone could ever remember. Food became very scarce. The old and the very young were starting to die. A council was called by the elders. The hunters were brought into the council where they were told that food was needed soon or the nation would not survive. The life of the nation was placed in the hunters' hands, and they were sent out in search of game.

Before he started on his hunt, the young man went to a grove of trees where he built a small fire. He threw some sweet grass on the fire, and as the smoke and sweet smell rose to the sky, he prayed that he might be successful in his hunt.

The young man was gone for many days. He found that all his skills as a hunter were useless before the harsh winter which fought him. Finally, when he was almost too weak to go on, he found an old elk trapped in a deep snow bank. He killed the elk and prepared it to be taken back to the nation. Before he started home, he once again built a small fire and threw in the sweet grass. As the incense rose, he thanked Wakan Tanka for success in his hunt.

After a long hard journey, the young man was able to bring the much-needed food to the nation. Upon his arrival, he saw that some of the other hunters had also been successful and that the nation would survive. But the young man soon learned that though the nation would survive, there were many losses—including his own father.

Upon learning of his father's death, all life seemed to drain out of the young man. He kept to himself, spoke to no one. He continued to hunt for the nation to help it through the last of the winter, but when spring finally arrived and his people were out of danger, he left.

The young man was very confused and angry as he wandered aimlessly through the wilderness. He could not understand or accept what had happened. He had done everything he was supposed to do. He had used all his skills, said all the right prayers and offered the sweet grass to Wakan Tanka—but still his father had died along with many of his friends and family.

In his anger, the young man decided to go in search of Wakan Tanka and demand some answers. He headed for the sacred mountain of his people where, at the summit, he intended to confront Wakan Tanka.

After many trials, the young man reached the mountain. He decided to camp that night and to start his climb the next morning.

A short distance away he saw the light of a camp fire. He decided to investigate the camp to make sure he would not be in danger. In silence, he crept through the shadows to the place where he could see the fire but remain hidden in the darkness himself. From his hiding spot, he could see a lone woman tending the small fire. He could tell that she had seen many winters. In fact, he could not recall ever seeing anyone as old as this woman. He decided to wait to see who would be joining her.

After lying motionless for over an hour, the young man was startled when the old woman called out to him to come and enjoy the warmth of the fire. At first the young man did not move. He was too good a hunter to let his presence be known and was surprised that this old woman seemed to sense he was there. Again the woman called out to him telling him that he had stayed in the dark long enough and that it was time to come into the light.

Warily, the young man came into the light prepared to be attacked by the woman's hidden companions, but nothing happened. Upon reaching the fire, the old woman welcomed him and offered him food and drink. Still distrustful, the young man refused the offer and kept his hand on his knife. The old woman smiled at him and told him that he had nothing to fear, that she was the guide to the mountain. At this, the young man started to laugh at the thought of this old woman even attempting to climb the mountain, let alone guiding a strong hunter like himself.

It had been a long time since the young man had laughed and the feel of it was strange, but pleasant. The old woman just smiled and took his hand. At the touch of her hand, the young man felt something he had not felt in a long time, safe and peaceful. The young man slept well that night.

Before dawn the next day, the old woman woke the young man and started up the mountain. The climb was hard and dangerous. As they got closer to the summit, it took all the young man's strength to put one foot in front of the other. Many times, he would have fallen except for the help of the old woman who seemed tireless.

When they reached the summit, the young man collapsed to the ground. He lay there a long time. As he gasped for breath in the thin air, he thought back upon his journey: the arduous climb up the mountain, the many hardships he faced getting to this sacred place, back to the long winter and the death of his father, and to the small grove of trees where he made his offering to Wakan Tanka before his hunt. And as he traveled back with his thoughts, the anger in him began to grow. In his anger he found strength. He stood up with clenched fists raised to the sky and shouted his question, "Why?"

The question seemed to explode from him. The sky around him was filled with it. But in response there was only silence. His anger spent—the young man collapsed back to the earth, his mind filled with confusion. Why were his skills not enough? Why didn't his prayers work? Why did his father die? Why had he gone on this long journey and climbed this mountain only to find silence?

Looking up through his tears and confusion, the young man saw the old woman quietly sitting on a rock nearby. With his eyes, he pleaded for help. The old woman came over and reached out her hand to him. The young man took her hand and in her touch again found peace and strength.

He stood up and she said, "My son, there are no answers here. Your answers are below with the people." With that she pointed down to the plains below and he could see his nation. The tepees were formed in a circle with each entrance facing the east and the rising sun. All the people of the nation were standing in a circle facing inward. Among the people, the young man could see his father and mother and many friends who had died during the harsh winter. He did not understand. He looked to the old woman for guidance. She told him, "My son, that is the sacred circle. All are a part of the circle. It has no beginning and no end."

Suddenly, the young man could see lines of light that connected all the people. These strands of light filled the circle to where it looked like a huge spider web. Again, he looked to the old woman.

"What you see is the web of life. Every action, every thought connects you with another person."

In looking again, the young man could see that the lines of light coming from his father seemed old, not as bright as others. The old woman explained that when a person dies, he no longer actively participates in building the web of life, but does not leave the sacred circle. Those with whom he was connected during life he remains connected with, through the memories which the lines in the web store. As time passes through the holes in the web of life, the web catches the memories and the dreams.

Again, the young man looked down and saw the plains below filled with circles of people connected with webs of life. The brilliance and the beauty of his .vision overwhelmed him, and he covered his eyes. He felt the old woman's hand on his shoulders and again peace flowed over him. He opened his eyes and saw that in his hand was a circle held together by string forming a web in the center. The old woman said to him, "In your hand you hold a symbol of the sacred circle, the foundation of the web of life, a dream catcher. It speaks of your relationships, your memories, your dreams."

But the young man said, "What of my question?"

"You hold the answer in your hand. Take the dream catcher and teach your people." With that, the old woman vanished.

The young man built a small fire. In it he placed the sweet grass in memory of his father and in gratitude for the teaching he had received. He hung the dream catcher around his neck and, with a light heart, started the journey back to his people.

*   *   *

After the writing of the story, I had an even stronger need to find out whether or not the dream catcher was really a Native-American symbol. The many different cultures on this planet are treasure troves of stories and symbols that can be used by all of us on our journeys of growth, but it is important to treat these treasures, these gifts, these cultures, with respect.

I contacted the head of the local Native-American organization, and told him that I had written a story about the dream catcher that I wanted to use in a grief group. He informed me that the dream catcher was indeed a Native-American symbol and that he would like to read the story before I used it. With some apprehension, I met with him and was delighted when, after reading the story, he stated that it captured the spirit of the dream catcher symbol and would have no objection to my using it. After gratefully receiving his endorsement, the task then became to weave the activities of the group around the dream catcher.

ACTIVITIES WHICH COMPLEMENT THE DREAM CATCHER SYMBOLISM

In planning the activities, I made a conscious effort to select those that would enhance the dream catcher symbol, among them the knots game, the island game, and the making of a family dream catcher including a pouch containing the good-bye letter.

The knots and island games are played in small groups divided according to age. The knots game is played by having the group (8 to 10 people) stand in a circle. Each person puts his left hand in the circle and loosely holds the hand of another group member who is not standing next to him. Each person then puts his right hand in and takes the hand of a different person, again someone not standing next to him. They now have a knot of hands and arms which must be untangled without letting go of the hands that are being held. The group quickly realizes that it looks like a living dream catcher, and the symbolism is discussed.

To play the island game, the group again stands in a circle. In the middle of the circle is a small platform. The object of the game is for the group to be able to stand together on the small platform all at the same time. The group reaches into the circle and takes another by the hand. Again, a dream catcher is formed. In order to complete the game successfully, it is essential that each member of the group both give and accept help. Without both cooperating and relying on others, the group will not be able to balance itself on the platform.

The dream catcher is made by each family using a metal ring with a 9-inch radius and a long length of cord. While making the dream catcher, the members of the family tells stories of their loved one—the stories that were woven during their lifetime. Once the dream catcher is completed, the families attach small mementos of their loved ones. At the end of the group, a small leather pouch containing good-bye letters is attached to each dream catcher.

USING THE DREAM CATCHER IN A GRIEF GROUP FORMAT

The group I was to lead was designed to meet for four consecutive Saturdays, two hours each day. The outline for the group is as follows:

Grief Support Group

Day 1

9:45 A.M. – 10:00 A.M.
- Refreshments

10:00 A.M. – 10:30 A.M.
- Welcome participants
- Introduce staff
- Read the Dream Catcher story

10:30 A.M. – 11:45 A.M. — Small Groups (age appropriate)
- Have each individual introduce themselves apart from their loss
- Activity: Knots
Make the connection between the activity and the dream catcher
- Have each participant share their loss
- Begin work on the Mural (Each group draws a mural during the first three meetings which will be shared during the Memorial Service.)
- Grief Education—Loss Process
- Tell participants to bring mementos
- Closure activity: Make a circle and hold hands. This forms the "Sacred Circle" which is the foundation of the dream catcher
- Select a volunteer to report to the large group

11:45 A.M. – 12 Noon — Large Group
- Volunteer from each group reports
- Inform participants that they will be making a family dream catcher next week
- Remind them to bring in mementos of their loved ones
- Validate their courage
- Acknowledge their pain
- Encourage return
- Emphasize the importance of their energy in making up the group energy. Everyone is essential to the group. They are not here by accident. They each have come together on this particular day, at this particular time, for a reason. We are each here to help and learn from each other.

Day 2

9:45 A.M. – 10:00 A.M.
- Refreshments

10:00 A.M. – 10:30 A.M. — Large Group
- Welcome participants back
- Review symbolism of the dream catcher
- Make family dream catchers in family groups—include stories of the loved one with the making of the dream catcher

10:30 A.M. – 11:45 A.M. — Small Groups
- Welcome back group—see where they are at—any reaction from past week
- Activity: Island
As we experience loss, there is a need for an increase in support which we receive and give.
- Grief Education: normal grief reactions
- Share mementos of loved one
- Mural
- Introduce good-bye letter to loved one
- Closure Activity: Again form the "Sacred Circle"—review the symbolism. Then have people reach out and take the hands of others not next to them creating the "Web of Life" and completing the dream catcher.
- Select a volunteer to report to the large group

11:45 A.M. – 12 Noon — Large Group
- Volunteer from each group reports

- Acknowledge their pain
- Encourage return
- Explain that we will hold on to their dream catchers until the end of the program
- Bring in small mementos to incorporate into the dream catcher
- Write a good-bye letter to your loved one and bring it in next week

Day 3

9:45 A.M. – 10:00 A.M.
- Refreshments

10:00 A.M. – 10:30 A.M. — Large Group
- Welcome participants back
- Review the first two weeks
- Work on dream catchers in family groups incorporating the small mementos into the dream catcher; tell stories about the mementos

10:30 A.M. – 11:45 A.M. — Small Groups
- Mementos shared by anyone who did not have an opportunity last week
- Touch base with everyone—see where they are, their reactions from the last two weeks
- Share good-bye letters
- Grief Education: managing stress
- Mural
- Closure Activity: Again form the "Sacred Circle" then create the "Web of Life." Once the symbolism is reviewed, start to unravel the knot. Once someone is "outside" the "Web of Life," stop. Talk about the symbolism of someone leaving the "Web of Life" (dying) but still being connected to the "Sacred Circle."

11:45 A.M. – 12 Noon — Large Group
- Re-form family groups and have them place good-bye letters in pouch and tie pouches to the dream catcher
- Symbolically link all the groups by having everyone stand in a circle holding hands creating the "Sacred Circle".
- Remind them that next week is the last week. Talk about the importance of the last week. We will be starting with a Memorial Service and then the groups will come to closure.

Day 4

9:45 A.M. – 10:00 A.M.
* Refreshments

10:00 A.M. – 11:00 A.M. — Memorial Service (outside if possible)
* Include mural and dream catchers

11:00 A.M. – 11:45 A.M. — Small Groups
* Deal with any issues resulting from the Memorial Service
* Give everyone an opportunity to come to closure with the group
* Fill out the evaluations
* Affirm individual participants
* Closure Activity: Create the dream catcher and untie the knot
* Select a volunteer to report to the Large Group

11:45 A.M. – 12 Noon — Large Group
* Volunteers from each group report
* Thank everyone for caring enough about themselves and the children to come to the groups. Encourage them to continue to work with their grief.
* Have everyone stand in a circle holding hands (Sacred Circle). Have everyone reach out creating the "Web of Life"—Closure

MY PERSONAL IDENTIFICATION WITH THE DREAM CATCHER

After preparing the design of the group, and assembling the staff, we decided to do a dry run of the reading of my story which would occur on the first day of the group. I started to read my story aloud and found that, after only a few sentences, I was unable to continue. I was overwhelmed by emotions that were both intense and completely unexpected. I sat there in silence as the tears flowed from my eyes. Someone else finished the story as I tried to figure out what was going on. I had read that story dozens of times. I had written it! What was happening?

Then I realized that I had never read the story aloud before. I had never given voice to it. I became aware that it really was my own story, the story of the pain that I felt when I lost my father eighteen years before; the anger that I had carried as I wandered looking for some meaning to that devastating loss. I had begun to face my own grief through the symbol of another culture. All the pain had come back, but with it growth and healing. I saw the dream catcher as a gift that was given to me, and I had made it my own.

GROWING THROUGH GRIEF

As I said earlier, all cultures contain treasures of stories and symbols. These treasures can be gifts to people who approach them with respect and an open heart. We have much to share with each other, and in the sharing will come healing and growth for all of us.

How can we grow through grief? It is so easy to get overwhelmed and buried in our pain. In our mourning we can become isolated and imprisoned by the very walls we put up to protect ourselves. But when we bring people together and encircle those individual walls with the universal element of grief, those walls become strands in the web of life that we use to connect with each other.

We can use our differences to teach and learn from each other. The key to using our grief to help heal each other is communication. We have to talk with each other. The group becomes a dream catcher. Through the unifying element of grief, we can use our differences to help each other heal and grow. We tell adults that they are the role models—and they are—but they can also learn from the children. The adolescents are a bridge: They are close enough to the child to really get in touch with their feelings and they have the vocabulary to express them. Men can learn from women, and women can learn from men. Our cultural backgrounds give us valuable coping skills to share. We must allow for the differences and learn from them.

There are excellent manuals available on religious beliefs, practices, and rituals to assist the caregivers of dying patients and their families. They have useful information, but the best information you can receive is from the patient and families themselves. You have to be open. Talk to your families, and especially listen. We have to communicate.

As incredibly painful as grief is, I sometimes wonder if it is not as great a gift as love. Perhaps through our universal experience of grief and pain, we may be able to look past all our differences and come to realize that we are truly one people.

Postscript: In further researching the dream catcher, I found that there are many Native-American stories and legends about spiders and webs, but the Ojibwe originated the dream catcher. The Ojibwe (or Chippewa as they are also known) had their traditional homeland around the Great Lakes region. The dream catchers were traditionally hung over sleeping children. It was believed that the dream catchers would filter out all the bad dreams and allow only good thoughts to enter their minds. The bad dreams, which were caught in the web, perished with the first rays of the morning sunlight.

REFERENCE

1. R. Fulghum, *All I Really Need to Know I Learned in Kindergarten*, Ivy, New York, 1992.

CHAPTER 20

Hope and the Caregiver: A Journey Toward Self-Awareness

Darcie D. Sims

One out of one dies. Nothing—no one—lives forever. In an age of medical miracles, we have not yet eliminated death. We have some new and interesting choices concerning the when, where, and how of death, but we still have not conquered the whether. All things end at some point.

Regardless of how much energy or emotional commitment we invest in a relationship, it cannot last forever. Because one cares, because one invests a certain portion of one's self into the cycles of others, one learns what it is to hurt and to grieve when those cycles are complete in one way or another.

Grief accompanies our constant round of hellos and good-byes. Yet we are often unaware or unresponsive to the losses we experience. We may not even realize we are grieving. We may only experience an "unsettled feeling"—a common companion when change brushes against our life's fabric.

The people caregivers help every day are dealing with lots of hellos and good-byes. They are coping with changes that can and often do shatter the illusions of their world. Caregivers are also coping with their own hellos and good-byes. It's a miracle that we ever hear each other, because we are so busy saying hello and good-bye to people, places, and events in our own worlds.

Change is never easy, but when it occurs in your settings—crisis centers, hospitals, emergency rooms, hospice rooms, funeral homes, and street corners— change takes on a new and terrifying hue. We react to change in many ways. Some of us immerse ourselves in work while others become passive and disinterested. Some become angry and argumentative. Expressions of grief can be subtle or dramatic. Adaptation to change can be challenging or devastating.

If we have, then we are in danger of not having, and that loss, whether through death, divorce, abandonment, or mutual dissolution, can be the most painful and devastating experience of one's own life cycle. Or it can be a point of growth and expansion of the spirit. But, regardless, loss hurts.

> There were no happy sounds in our house any more and the sun cast only shadows of sadness. Joy had been buried one afternoon in late fall and winter came to reside within our hearts. Would we ever be happy again? Would I ever laugh or dream or sing again?
> If I could just see Hope. If I knew what to look for or how to act or feel. If I knew where the end was, maybe I could find the beginning. If only the pain would stop. Help me, please [1, p. 8].

And so you come, a caregiver, wanting to ease the pain, wanting to comfort the aching heart. Who are you? Where do you come from? And what magic will you bring to ease the troubled spirit?

We come with good intentions, a pocketful of skills and an outstretched hand. We define ourselves as caregivers, taking care and giving care to those who are hurting, sick, injured, dying, lost in grief, and to those who are struggling to find themselves. We come because we care . . . because we cannot do anything less. But caring is hard. It is extremely difficult to watch someone in great pain. Every instinct says stop the pain! Yet, truly effective caregivers understand their task is not to eliminate the pain, but to give the client/family skills and tools to deal with the pain themselves. It is not a matter of pain or no pain, but how we manage the pain we have.

You have made a commitment to be available, to be there when someone is hurting, dying, grieving. We seek to enter the lives of others and bring to them a message of hope and joy. But what are you and how can you help those grieving the death of a loved one? What do you bring to this place of pain and grief? What light can you bring to this darkness? How can you find hope in the midst of such pain, trauma, grief? Who are you who dare to speak of hope in the midst of despair?

PERSONAL EXPLORATION

Before we can begin helping others, we must spend a few moments thinking about ourselves. It is an important first step, yet very often overlooked. However, if you will take the time to explore yourself a bit before you begin something, you may discover all kinds of information that will help you. If we can begin to understand what motivates us, we may be able to understand what motivates others and we just might be able to allow everyone to have their own agenda, needs, and ways of meeting those needs.

Every time we experience a hello or a good-bye in our life, we must ask and attempt to answer the question of who am I now? Who am I now that some of my dreams aren't coming true as I had planned? Who am I now that someone I love has died? Who am I right now?

INTRODUCE YOURSELF EXERCISE

1. Introduce yourself to someone near you. If you are alone as you read this, then think about how you would introduce yourself. You only have ten seconds. What would you say? Most of us would begin an introduction with a greeting of some kind immediately followed by our name. It is the most common way to begin a conversation, particularly with someone you may not know.

2. Introduce yourself to someone else (or the same person or just think this through if you are alone) without using your name. What would you say this time? When we can't use our name, we often move on to other ways of identifying ourselves such as occupation, title (Mr., Mrs., Doctor, etc.). We may also use a relationship (mother, son, spouse, etc.).

3. Now think about how you would introduce yourself if you could not use: name, title, occupation, relationship. It is beginning to get harder and harder. Perhaps you might think of telling something about your hobbies or interests, where you are from, a physical description (I'm tall) or an emotional state (I'm happy).

4. Think now, one last time, how you would introduce yourself without using your name, title, profession, location, relationships, hobbies, likes/dislikes, interests—without using any kind of adjectives or descriptors of any kind! What is left to tell about ourselves when all of these labels and descriptions are no longer available to us?!

Perhaps you thought of simply saying: "Hello, I'm me." And you would be right. For no one else can be you, so you described yourself as being a unique individual, distinguished from all others. But, in grief, in times of traumatic or dramatic change, we often feel that even the "me" part of ourselves has been destroyed. So, take away the "ME" and introduce yourself.

The hard part, the really hard part of this exercise is that just as soon as I figure out what to say, I lose that part of me, too! And in grief, all that I have known and cherished may be gone as well as the easy ways to identify myself. The awful part is that, even though all that I hold dear and true to myself is gone, I am still here. I didn't disappear with everything and everyone else. I am still here, now alone and without means to know who I am. And now, you, as a caregiver, wish to talk about hope?

Where is hope when everything I know and trust and believe in is gone? Where is hope when I do not even know if I exist any more?

We have many ways of introducing ourselves. We use our name, our professional titles, our relationships, our hobbies, skills, our expectations of ourselves. We see ourselves in particular ways and we base our lives on these perceptions. We don't often think consciously of all these factors when filling out a name tag, but we are influenced by others' perceptions and reactions to us. We are who we think we are.

Our self-image begins its definition from the very moment we are born. We react to the reception we receive from others. Over time, we change our self-image. We define ourselves from the outside in. Each time we experience a hello or a good-bye in our life, we add or subtract from our self-image.

We become very good at redefining ourselves as we grow up. We build our lives around our perceptions of ourselves and how we think others see us. We are either secure or insecure about who we are and where we fit into the scheme of things. We grow expert in "Self Talk" and we can convince ourselves of just about anything: from being too fat, too dumb, too worthless, to being too sick, too young, too old, too everything. We rarely see ourselves as being too right! We always count what we're not first.

We build our lives around our perceptions of ourselves and how we think others see us. We are either secure or insecure about who we are and where we fit into the scheme of things. We are always in process of becoming someone else.

The only way left to introduce one's self is ultimately "I am." And how many of us know that we do exist even when there is no label to define us? How many of us have stood that naked, that exposed, and learned the truth of ourselves? We simply are, even when there are no words to describe us. Even when there is no one to know us, we still are. How raw, how exposed, how honest is this introduction! Do you know the "I am" part of yourself or do you still hold tightly to some labels, some identifiers that are dependent upon others' opinions, acknowledgments, or judgments? Have you ever met your "I am" part of yourself?

"I AM"—the ultimate in an introduction—the very core of who we are. It is from the core, this essence that truly effective care and help begin. Your toys and tricks, words and wisdom will fall far short of hope if you do not live and breathe and speak from the heart. The head knows facts and theory, skills and words. But it is the message of the heart that heals the shattered places.

Speak only from this place—where you and I are real, where God lives and is heard through your voice.

We also have expectations of ourselves as well as of others. And these expectations also influence how we manage to live our lives. We either endure, survive, or live our life. We can sit in the dark and moan or we can struggle forward, learning to dance in the dark as best we can. We can dare to speak of hope or we can list all the reasons why hope cannot exist. The choice is ours.

EXPECTATIONS OF SELF

List three expectations you have of yourself as an *individual;* three expectations you have of self as a *helper;* three expectations you have of those you are trying to help; three expectations that you think those you are trying to help have of *you.*

These expectations can be grand and glorious or simple and ordinary. But be honest with yourself. There is no one here to look over your shoulder. Only you, at your core, will read and learn from what you have written.

Look at your first set of expectations (of self as an individual). You probably wrote down things you think you should be doing or qualities that you think you should have. If you did, then add to your list some of the expectations you have of yourself that are yours alone, not someone else's thoughts about you. This is the time for being real to yourself.

Now look at the second list of expectations you wrote down (of self as a helper). Do any of the expectations on the second list also appear on the first list? If you had to write down ten expectations or even twenty, then probably the lines between these two categories would begin to blur. We often see ourselves as care providers at the core level of our being so it is not unusual or "wrong" to find the line between what one expects of one's self as an individual and those expectations one has in the care provider role to become almost invisible. If, however, there are no similarities, it might mean it would be a worthwhile exercise to examine more closely your intent in being a care provider. Those who are most successful at providing care for others do so from the core part of themselves, giving from the heart rather than the head. When caring comes only from the head, burnout and stress reactions are far more prevalent than when there is a good "match" between expectation and experience.

Would it make any difference in your responses if we changed the word "expectation" to the word "demand"? To demand somehow seems more forceful, more authoritative, less "kind." Yet, it is only a change in a word that creates such a shift in thinking. What do you demand of yourself, both as an individual and as a care provider? Begin to listen carefully to yourself and perhaps the answers will become clear.

Now look at the list you prepared for question number 3 (expectations of those you are trying to help). Most of us have been taught it is not polite to expect things from others and that we should offer our help freely, without hope or expectation of any "reward." Yet, in our humanness, we live with the hope of being recognized, acknowledged, and perhaps even appreciated. So, many of our expectations have to do with being acknowledged, well received, liked. We often expect those we are trying to help to participate with us in the process. It is much harder to help someone who is not involved in the change process than it is to work with someone who is motivated, willing, and eager to change.

What kinds of things do you expect of those who receive your care? Write down these expectations and hold on to them. They will become important in a moment. It is valuable to become aware of our "demands" or expectations we hold for others. At least then we know when to be disappointed!

The last list is the most difficult and often completely overlooked as care providers begin to assess their own strengths, skills, knowledge, willingness to share, to relinquish, to grow. It is also the place we often get into "trouble." "What do you think others want of you" gives us lots of information about our perceptions of others and what we think they think of us. It can become confusing and resemble psychological "double talk," but we often base our entire actions upon our own impression of what others are thinking and doing. Many times we create our own sense of reality without bothering to check it out with those we are making assumptions about.

Often we think others want us to have the answers to their problems. All of us are looking for answers and, many times, the caregiver is bombarded with questions that reflect a desperateness to secure an answer—the right answer, of course! Many times care providers are asked to provide not only the right answers, but the answer we want to hear as well!

The world may come to your door, bearing an armload of broken toys, asking you, the care provider, to fix them. We hand over to you the shattered pieces of our lives and expect (demand?) you to reassemble the puzzle, to repair Humpty Dumpty, with no cracks showing, please.

The world is asking you for help, to be supported, to be rescued, to be healed of this terrible pain of grief. And many times, the world is impatient with the speed of healing and so demands of you the magic potion. It may seem as though everyone believes you have the answers and the magic wand, which will restore joy, peace, love, and hope to all. It is a big request and an even greater expectation. It is the hope of all who knock on your door . . . to be relieved of pain and sorrow and grief.

ARE YOU A CARE GIVER OR
A CARE TAKER?

Do you give care or take care? The difference is quite important. The issue of being a care giver or a care taker is as old as giving and taking care of others. But we are only now beginning to recognize it as something more than a play on words. We talk a lot about care giver burn-out and stress management and how to help ourselves help others, but it goes back to our earlier questions—what are your expectations of yourself?

Are you trying to eliminate pain? Are you trying to make it alright? Are you trying to make it easier? Or are you trying to make it less lonely, less frightening?

Are you trying to help with the panic instead of the pain? Are you trying to restore control, or are you trying to support?

What if the person you are trying to help doesn't do it right? Do you measure your effectiveness by the success or lack of success of your clients? We measure success by how close we come to meeting our own expectations. What do you expect of each encounter with life? How you define yourself will always be influenced by your expectations, your demands upon yourself, others and upon life. Our expectations influence our daily reactions to everything that happens to us. We create our own success, our own failure, our own hope.

Do you give care and concern or do you take care of—are you needed or wanted? Do you want to help or do you need to help? Is your intent to make them feel better or be better at feeling? The intent of the help is strongly influenced by the expectations of the helper and the helped.

Be careful that you do not fall for the "magic wand" syndrome. We are not in the business of "fixing broken toys." We do not have the answers or the magic potion. We can help more with the panic than the pain. It is standing beside someone in times of adversity, not walking through the fire for them! In that moment of being there when someone cries out in pain, in fear, in grief, you become a symbol of HOPE. Caring is the first part of hope.

SELF-AWARENESS
AS A SYMBOL OF HOPE

By taking the time to do some self-exploration, we begin to understand our motives, our strengths, weaknesses, and our skills. Become aware of yourself, not only as a care provider, but as a human being as well. Remember the "I am" and continually be in search of that inner self where wisdom, peace, fulfillment, and love reside. It is the only way to survive, thrive, and grow.

And then, find someone to share your journey. We are like wandering storytellers, searching for someone who is willing to share our journey, to listen to our story, to take us seriously. For it is in the telling of our narrative that we discover ourselves and the touchstones of our lives.

If we are to be heard, however, we must also be ready to listen. Our gift to ourselves and to each other is to listen to the songs of the human spirit, struggling not just to survive, but to live! Take care to give care and learn to receive it as a gift from another fellow struggler.

DO I HAVE TO CARE LESS IN ORDER
TO CARE MORE?

Caring for someone who is hurting, regardless of the source of his/her pain, is a difficult yet wonderful task. There are few helping situations that are more rewarding or more demanding of a caregiver's skills. Caregivers who work with the sick, the injured, the dying, the bereaved, the disabled, the addicted, or with anyone who is in pain, must address not only the client's issues, but their own fears, pains, losses, concerns, and questions as well. It is most difficult to watch someone in deep emotional or physical pain. Every instinct says stop the pain. Yet, truly effective care providers understand their task is not to eliminate the pain, but to give the client the tools and skills to deal with the pain themselves.

Care-providing is truly an emotionally exhausting task, yet one filled with rich rewards and personal satisfactions. One of the most difficult parts of becoming a helper is walking that fine line between outside observer and participant in the drama of another human being's life. We must remain separate enough from others' distress to avoid being downcast by their depression, frightened by their fears, or disturbed by their anger.

There must be space in our closeness to one another. Because our heart knows no bounds, we must learn to set the boundaries between us and to integrate wisdom into our caring. We must tap into our own inner source of wholeness in order to help others find their own wellspring of strength, compassion, and capability. Caring for others can be a source of tremendous stress or tremendous reward—the choice of what we see and experience is up to us.

We have chosen careers that demand sophisticated listening skills. We listen to others, but do we ever listen to ourselves? And if we do take the time to listen to ourselves, what do we hear?

Listen to yourself. Do you walk, talk, or move rapidly, even when you don't have to? Are you always in a hurry? Are you constantly trying to get more and more done in less and less time? Does your mind keep going long after you have settled down to rest? Are you losing things, forgetting appointments, always feeling "behind," frantic, or just plain lost?

Do you know what day today is (without looking at a calendar)? How many watches do you have and are some of them set five to ten minutes ahead of schedule so you won't be late? Do you wave to other drivers with certain fingers or daydream about painting graffiti? Do you pray you will be taken hostage by some nomadic tribe or Betty Crocker? Do Twinkies and a diet soft drink make up your fiber content for the day?

Do you wish you didn't have a beeper? How many telephones do you own? Do you have a phone in your bedroom, bathroom, car? Do you know your home phone number or is it on speed dial? Do you know where your home is, and when was the last time you actually visited?

Can you identify the names of all of your children and the dog and the fish. Did you even know you had a fish?

Do you wish there were more than twenty-four hours in each day so you could catch up? Are you tired just thinking about all of this? If you have read this far, how far behind are you with your other work?

BURN-OUT AND COMPASSION FATIGUE

If you found yourself nodding your head in agreement with any of the above statements, then you could be a candidate for burn-out or compassion fatigue.

It is easy to define burn-out as being a combination of physical exhaustion and unfulfilled expectations. When, over and over again, we do not get what we need and/or want, we begin to harbor resentments. These may accumulate for days, weeks, even months until these resentments become concrete, a barrier between ourselves and our real feelings. Add to this ever building wall of resentments, sheer physical exhaustion and we have the ingredients for burn-out or compassion fatigue.

We find ourselves hating to hear the phone ring, not wanting people to contact us, especially if they have problems! We become slow in responding to the needs of others and we may even become deaf to our own needs. We find ourselves growing numb to the pains of the world and may not even recognize our own hurts and wounds. We can sink into depression or find our feet running faster and faster, in an ever widening circle of nothingness. The faster we seem to go, the less we get done. Eventually, we can collapse into the "I Don't Care" syndrome and become lost in despair. Hope eludes us, the keeper of the light, and we begin to wonder if there really ever was a light.

Coping with stress, especially with compassion fatigue, is an integral part of your job. You do not have to become a victim of stress or burn-out. It is more effective to learn to become a partner with life's stresses, to roll with the punches, and to take care of yourself. Look in the mirror. We are our own greatest source of stress and fatigue! Stress is a natural and normal part of life, but we often make it worse by worrying.

Stress is a response to a stimulus and we can gain some measure of control over how we react. Stress is an individual matter, defined differently by all. It depends upon one's physical health, emotional and psychological states, socio-economic status, spiritual connections, and experiences. Stress is the distance between expectation and experience. We measure success by how close we come to what we expect and when the distance between our expectation and our experience is great, the level of stress increases. When we expect a bad day and we get one, the level of stress is actually not as high as when we expected a great day and we experienced a less than wonderful one!

We alone determine the positive or negative effects of what happens to us. We can think ourselves into a deep hole or learn to become flexible and pliant. Perhaps our greatest weapon against the destructive power of unrelenting stress is our attitude. We cannot always control what happens to us, but we can control what we do with what happens to us.

When we give the gift of ourselves, we risk being used, being consumed by an ever-needy world. Yet, it is precisely that gift of self that is the most valuable of all treasures. In order to give that gift of self, we must first know what it is that we intend to give and then make sure there is enough to go around. We must find ways to refill the empty well whenever it runs dry. We must learn to build support systems for ourselves as well as for our clients.

What can we do, in the space of a few minutes, on a daily basis, to help re-connect and re-energize ourselves? How can we learn to live with what we've got instead of what we want? How can we find hope for ourselves so that we may give it to others?

CREATIVE COPING TECHNIQUES FOR DEALING WITH STRESS

1. Acknowledge Your Expectations

Become aware of what you are expecting of yourself. We define success by how close we come to our own expectations. What do you expect of yourself? What do you expect of others? What do you expect of your job? Be honest with yourself!

2. Breathe

Learn to breathe deeply, bringing a fresh supply of oxygen to your body. Inhale through your nose and exhale through your mouth. Become aware of your breath and practice. Breathe in peace, blow out tension. Breathe in joy, exhale sadness and despair. Breathe in love and let out loneliness and emptiness. Breathe into the calm. Create safety within yourself. Listen to the quiet that resides deep within your being. Breathe into yourself. You can get together with a group of coworkers and just breathe. With practice, you can learn to control the internal atmosphere, regardless of how chaotic it is on the outside. Breathing is the first step. Without it, nothing else much matters.

3. Exercise and Take Care of Yourself

Have you ever seen a happy jogger? Find something you love doing and do it. If nothing else, buy the shoes and walk around in them. Be realistic about what you can and are willing to do. No one said you can't put a few chocolate chips in the oat bran. Lighten up a bit . . . one cookie won't hurt. A box might . . .

4. Be Realistic

Figure out what you ought to do, what you should do, and what you can do. Then compromise.

5. Create a Supportive Network of People

Identify those with whom you feel great and hang around them more often. Some people drain us and others enrich our feelings of value and self-worth. Find those who add to your sense of well being and re-energize you.

6. Banish "Ought" and "Should" from Your Life

Never again let those two words dictate your life. Listen to your inner self and learn to trust the wisdom of the self. You already know what to do, when to do it, and how to do it. Ought and should never accomplished anything but increasing the pain and the stress of living. Let them go.

7. Put the Motion Back in Emotion

Find some creative, personally non-destructive, healthy ways to express the full range of your emotions. Talking about emotions, especially anger, is not always the most effective way to deal with those emotions. Sometimes we just need to DO SOMETHING. We often let the emotions "build" inside us until they simply "explode" into illness, injury, depression, withdrawal, or violence. A nerf brick that can be tossed or pounded without doing any harm works well. You might also try throwing marshmallows at twenty paces, breaking garage sale china in the backyard, or hitting a pillow with a plastic bat. Do something to get the intensity of the emotions outside you. Put the motion back into the emotion. Otherwise you may turn to drugs, alcohol, or withdrawal as ways of trying to cope.

8. Be Compassionate and Forgiving of Yourself

Send yourself a love note. Write it, stamp it, and mail it. When it comes, read it and then put it in your personal applause file. If you do not have a personnel applause file, make one. Any time anyone says something nice to you, jot it down and toss it in the file. Cards, notes of praise, and thank you's go in there too. It sometimes becomes a lifeline during the really dark moments.

9. Love What You Do

Match expectations with experiences as often as you can. Be fulfilled as often as you can. If this is not the work you love, search for the work that makes your spirit sing. Only when you and your profession are a good match can you truly know and share hope.

10. Listen to Others

The greatest gift you can give to yourself and to others is a pair of ears. Listening is a skill and a gift. It is a new and challenging experience every time we do it—always be fresh in your wonder of the creativeness of the human spirit! Listen to everyone, but follow your own music!

11. Have a Smile-on-a-Stick

Sometimes we do not have the energy to be what others need us to be, so carry a paper smile-on-a-stick with you to hold up when asked "How ya doin' today?" Few want to know how we are really doing so the universal answer has become "I'm fine" even when we're not. Wearing a mask is okay as long as we know it is a mask and that we can remain true to our core self. Acknowledge to yourself your true feelings and then decide which ones you will share with others. You can always appear to be "fine" on the outside as long as you listen to the "real you" and take appropriate steps toward really being fine.

12. Groan

Sometimes we just need to release the pain, the sadness, the grief that accumulates within us. Take a deep breath in, hold it for a few seconds and then release it, sending it out of yourself with whatever sound accompanies the breath. Don't be surprised if it sounds more like a groan than a giggle. Working with death and dying issues on a daily basis is hard work and can tax even the most centered and grounded person. It is your right to hurt and your privilege to be able to feel. Acknowledge those feelings and release them.

13. Do Something Nice for Yourself Every Twenty-Four Hours

It doesn't have to be a big something. Maybe it's not answering the phone when you are in the bathroom or snatching ten minutes alone to read a chapter in a new book or taking a fifteen-minute walk. Whatever you love doing, do it as often as you can. You deserve a small treat today. Don't wait until you can afford it, have the time or the energy. If you can't get to Hawaii today, you can, at least, stand next to a pineapple in the grocery store and daydream a bit!

14. Ask for What You Need

Make a help-on-a-stick sign to carry with you at all times. Wave it whenever you feel you could use a little help. Don't wait for others to see that you need help. As caring as we may be, we often become "blind" to the needs of others. We become so self-focused that we may even miss the most obvious clues. It does not necessarily mean you are not cared for, but may just mean no one "saw" your distress (are you very good at hiding your needs from others, from yourself?) Learn to ask and receive help. Don't deny others the opportunity to help you and for both of you to grow in spirit. How hard it is to ask for assistance, but what a gift you give to others when you allow them the pleasure of helping you!

15. Insist on Joy

Demand joy in your life every day. Fly a paper airplane, send a chocolate kiss to someone, tell a joke, smell a flower, hum a bit.

16. Find a Pair of Rose-Colored Glasses

They help you see things in a different way and I've noticed that others look at me differently, too. Rose colored glasses are nothing more, but nothing less than a change in perspective. If I cannot control what happens to me, I can control what I do with what happens to me. It's not disrespectful to claim the absurdity of something in order to see beyond the pain, the trouble, the despair, the hopelessness. It is believing in the possibilities of tomorrow.

17. Make a Personal Plan for Survival

We are always looking for the answers in the wrong places. We look in books. We listen to speakers. We ask each other in hopes of finding the perfect answer. Instead of looking for answers around us or from others, we need only listen to ourselves. The wisdom is within. Make one small change each day. It only takes a moment to find the magic within.

Let it both rain and snow on you instead of always having an umbrella. Discover the joys of living with the unknown, the challenges of simply being in the now instead of always worrying about what was and what will be. Don't lose today because of a poor yesterday or an uncertain tomorrow.

Learn to take care so you can give care. Take care of yourself so you will be able to make the responses you wish to make, and be as capable as you choose to be. We cannot always protect ourselves from the rain, but we can go together in search of the parade.

THANK YOU–THE WORDS OF HOPE

Thank you. Such simple words yet they carry with them the spirit of hope and, without that, we are little more than a collection of molecules. Without hope, who would be there to pull up the sun every morning? Without hope, who would collect the stars and redistribute them every evening? Without hope, who would hear the songs of the broken hearts and dream of being the weaver of mended threads?

For what and for whom are you thankful? Do you have a long list or is there only one for whom you are grateful? How many hurting hearts have you heard? How many empty hands have you held? How much did you give away and what did you receive from someone who received your care?

What "gifts" did you receive from someone for whom you were providing care? It doesn't matter in what capacity you were the helper, what did you receive in exchange for your help? Or did you think you were the only one "working"? Did you think it was only a one-way exchange? Even when it feels as though we are the only one contributing to a relationship, an exchange is taking place. What did you receive as you were giving? What did you learn from your contact with those you were helping? What "gifts" did you receive in exchange for your help?

When you can begin to realize that giving help is also receiving help, the balance scale is equalized and the exchange becomes mutual. You may, of course, feel you are giving more than you are receiving and often your clients may feel they have nothing to share with you. But, hope is born when you can actualize the exchange and help your client realize he, too, is of value and worth.

Do you know what your true value is? Do you fully understand what you are giving when you stretch out your hand to find those struggling in the dark? Do you think it is your words of wisdom that bring light to a world gone dark? Do you think it is your action or perhaps your knowledge that brings hope to those who cannot imagine the horizon of another day?

Do you know all of your words, thoughts, knowledge, and action pale in comparison of your true gift? Go back to the beginning of this chapter when you were asked to strip away all of the facades we wear, all the labels we hold to be true about ourselves. What did you find when you finally reached that seemingly empty place where you had no name, no title, no profession, no relationships, no likes or dislikes, no hobbies, no descriptors of any kind? Striped of everything familiar and sacred, discovered you still exist—that core place was still intact, in spite of the terrible wind storms of life.

It is from that place, from that core of wholeness, that hope springs. You and you alone are the gift you give to others. That's why we call you a present—you and your presence are the hope you bring. It's not your words, your actions, your knowledge—it's you. It is being there when the rest of the world shudders in horror, recoils in terror, flees in fright. It is being there when there are no words left to say, when there are no actions to be taken, except to move closer to one another and find the hands searching in the darkness. You are the light at the end of the tunnel—you are the hope for a world grown silent with grief.

When you can dare to live from your core, your essence, when you dare to reach out across your own pain and grief and find the hands searching for the light, you become the voice of hope. Do not be afraid of the grief or the intensity of the pain. It is the right of the bereaved to hurt so deeply as they have loved so greatly.

The human spirit has an infinite capacity to endure, survive, and to grow. It requires laughter and tears to flourish. It requires love and faith, strength and support as well. It requires you and me and all of us together.

Hurt and pain have their lessons and we cannot rob ourselves of the richness of the tapestry that hurt and love weave together. To eliminate one from the loom is to break the thread and steal away the fabric.

The gifts within love are obvious. We do not dispute them. Yet, the gifts within hurt are as equal. I could not understand light if I had not known darkness. I could not sing sweet if I had not tasted bitter. I could not laugh if I had not cried.

Hope isn't a place or a thing. Hope isn't the absence of pain or fear or sadness. Hope is the possibility of renewed joy. It's the memory of love given and received. Hope is that magical moment when we reach out across our own hurt and pain and find each other, all searching in the darkness.

Hope is here. Hope is you when you live and speak from that inner core, that essence of "I am." You are the voice of the spirit. You are the voice of hope!

Hope is you and me and the person next to you and across the room and down the street and in your dreams. WE ARE EACH OTHER'S HOPE.

REFERENCE

1. D. D. Sims, *If I Could Just See Hope,* Big A and Company, Wenatchee, Washington, 1994.

BIBLIOGRAPHY

Harbaugh, G. L., When the Caregiver Needs Care, *Lutheran Partners,* September-October, 1991.

Sims, D. D., *Why are the Casseroles Always Tuna? A Loving Look at the Lighter Side of Grief,* Big A Company, Wenatchee, Washington, 1990.

Sims, D. D., Creative Coping when Caring Becomes Commonplace, *The Director,* LXVII:8, pp. 26-30, 1995.

Sims, D. D., *Tips for Creative Coping* (audio-cassette), The Compassionate Friends, Oak Brook, Illinois, 1988.

Wolfelt, A., Bereavement Caregiver Burn-Out: Signs and Symptoms, *Thanatos,* pp. 6-8, 1988.

Wolfelt, A., Caring for the Caregiver, *Thanatos,* pp. 16-18, 1989.

Contributors

David W. Adams, M.S.W., C.S.W., is a professor, Department of Psychiatry, Faculty of Health Sciences, McMaster University and Executive Director, Greater Hamilton Employee Assistance Consortium. He has authored and co-authored books, contributed numerous chapters and articles and is internationally known as a speaker, program consultant, and workshop facilitator.

Paul Alexander, M.S.W., is a social worker in private practice and musician who combines the two skills to work with dying children and grieving adults.

Victor Baez, Ph.D., is associate professor of social work at Colorado State University. He teaches courses in ethnic identity and social work policy.

Rev. Sally S. Bailey, M.A., is an ordained Christian minister as well as a professional musician. She uses the two backgrounds to work with the dying. For several years she was director of the Arts Program at Connecticut Hospice in New Haven.

Sandra L. Bertman, Ph.D, is professor of humanities at the University of Massachusetts School of Medicine. She is the author of numerous articles and chapters and has authored and edited numerous books.

Gerry Cox, Ph.D., teaches courses in Social Theory, Racial and Ethnic Minorities, Criminology, Death, Grief and Bereavement, and Social Problems. His research is primarily in the areas of death and dying, sociology of sport, and criminal justice. He has authored, co-authored, or edited five books and over twenty-five articles and chapters in books. He is a member of the International Workgroup on Death, Dying, and Bereavement, secretary of the Midwest Sociological Society, serves on the Executive Committee for the Center for Death Education and Bioethics Research, and serves on the American Sociological Association's Education Committee.

Rev. Fr. Richard B. Gilbert, M.Div. is executive director of the World Pastoral Care Center, and Founding Director of Connections—Spiritual Links. Based in Valparaiso, Indiana, he travels extensively to present on grief, pastoral care, and spiritual assessment. He has over 100 articles and reviews published, is the author of two books, and with John Morgan, co-edited *Health Care and Spirituality: Listening, Assessing, Caring.*

Mindy Gough, B.S.W., is a social worker at a community mental health center in Clinton, Ontario. She also has a private practice called "A Gentle Place for Grieving Children. Mrs. Gough's practice and research focus on using creative methods such as photography, music, and art to help grieving people of all ages.

Lora Koenig Heller, M.S., R.M.T., is a music therapist and special education teacher specializing in deafness, speech/language delays, and autistic-spectrum disorders. Currently in private practice in New York City, she has worked extensively in pediatric medicine and early intervention. At St. Mary's Hospital for Children, where much of the research for this chapter took place, her work was designed to meet the needs of terminally ill children and their families.

Glennys Howarth, Ph.D., is associate professor of sociology at the University of Sydney, Australia. She has been researching and publishing in the field of death and dying for many years and is author of *Last Rites,* (Baywood, 1996) and co-founding editor of the journal *Mortality.*

Leslie Kawamura, Ph.D., is professor of religion at the University of Calgary, and chair of the department.

Elizabeth P. Lamers, M.A., is credentialed both as a classroom teacher and a reading specialist. She has worked with terminally ill and bereaved children for the last ten years, and has conducted workshops and lectured extensively on the dying child and return to the classroom, children and grief, children's literature and death.

Pittu Laungani, Ph.D., is an associate professor in psychology at South Bank University, London, England. His main research interests are in the field of cross-cultural psychology. He has published over fifty research papers in the area, and has written and edited six books, which also include a play. His most recent book (with Colin Murray Parkes), *Death and Bereavement Across Cultures*, was published by Routledge, London, in 1977. His latest book, *Counselling in a Multicultural Society* is published by Sage, London.

John D. Morgan, Ph.D., holds a doctorate from the University of Southern California. Dr. Morgan has spoken in Canada, the United States, Australia, New Zealand, England, Sweden, Russia, China, and Japan. He is professor of philosophy at King's College, University of Western Ontario, and coordinator of the King's College Centre for Education about Death and Bereavement

Kevin Ann Oltjenbruns, Ph.D., is an associate professor in the department of Human Development and Family Studies at Colorado State University where she has taught both undergraduate and graduate courses in loss and grief. She has co-authored a textbook entitled *Death and Grieving: Lifespan and Family Perspectives* (Harcourt Brace, 1998). Dr. Oltjenbruns also serves as coordinator of the university's diversity curriculum infusion project.

Thomas O'Neill has worked for over twenty years as a counselor with a variety of clients ranging from people with disabilities in Ohio to runaways in New York

City and troubled youths in Kansas. In the mid-90s, Tom was a bereavement counselor at a hospice where he developed programs for grieving children and adults. He has a Masters Degree in rehabilitation counseling from Bowling Green University (Ohio) and is a licensed social worker.

Eleanor G. Pask, Ed.D., has a professional background in pediatric nursing. She has completed her doctorate in the field of bioethics. Dr. Pask has held a number of positions in the field of pediatric health care and is currently executive director of The Childhood Cancer Foundation Candlelighters Canada.

Sam Silverman, Ph.D., is a researcher who contributes in several disciplines. Trained as a physical scientist and as an attorney, he has published papers in various aspects of bereavement as well as, recently, a discography of the music of Moise Vainberg, a Polish-Russian composer and friend of Shostakovich.

Darcie D. Sims, Ph.D., is a bereaved parent, licensed psychotherapist, hypnotherapist and grief management specialist. She is the Director of Training and Program Development for Accord Grief Resources and Consulting of Louisville, Kentucky. She is a Diplomate in both the American Psychotherapy Association and the National Board Certified Clinical Hypnotherapy Association.

Rev. Lloyd D. Smith, B.A., M.Div., Ph.D., a native of London, Ontario, is a graduate of Western, Queens, and Glasgow (Scotland) Universities. Ordained in the United Church of Canada in 1967, he has served parishes in southern Saskatchewan and southwestern Ontario. His current specialty is ritual and spirituality.

Patricia Zalaznik, M.A., is a workshop leader, publisher, author of *Dimensions of Loss & Death Education Curriculum and Resource Guide, Stone Soups & Support Groups,* and *Bibliography on Grief.* Besides facilitating grief groups at North Hospice, she is a founder of Eva House Children's Hospice in Minnesota. Zalaznik is completing a doctorate at The Union Institute.

Index

religiosity, 4, 91
religious music, 156
Rilke, 19
ritual, 81, 147, 148, 156, 162, 184, 186,
    243-247, 250-252, 257, 260, 262,
    273
ritualization, 152, 156, 157, 162
role, 38, 68, 74-76, 81, 82, 84, 91, 95-97,
    115, 116, 118, 125, 157, 171, 181,
    185, 203, 204, 215, 217, 221, 224,
    226, 228, 232, 235, 287, 293
Rosenthal, 178

sacred, 79, 81, 168, 172, 200, 235, 237,
    280, 281, 283-286, 302
safety, 96, 97, 99, 180, 216, 221,
    227-229, 259, 261, 268, 298
Schweitzer, 20
secular, 41, 79
security, 1, 14, 167, 216, 227
self, 4, 13, 14, 17, 18, 21, 22, 27, 31, 32,
    51, 53, 78, 81, 83, 91, 96, 98, 101,
    102, 110-112, 124, 128, 130, 131,
    133, 136-140, 146, 147, 160, 169,
    172, 182, 217, 219, 224, 226, 231,
    245, 246, 250, 253, 254, 289, 292,
    293, 295, 297, 299, 300
semantic, 39
Shostakovich, 7, 29, 30, 32-34
Singer, 28, 139
song, 17, 28, 29, 31, 92, 133, 136-141,
    144-148, 151-155, 157, 158,
    160-163, 165, 178, 193, 247
spiritual, 8, 15, 16, 59, 62, 91, 95, 96, 98,
    126, 128, 130, 135, 140, 142, 146,
    171, 249, 250, 256, 262, 267, 269,
    271, 273, 297
Spring and Fall, 191
storytelling, 172, 173
Strauss, 7, 32, 36
stress, 5, 73, 76, 86, 92, 93, 95, 99,
    168-170, 188, 213, 215, 217, 218,
    226, 242, 251, 252, 266, 270, 285,
    293, 294, 296-299

sudden traumatic death, 213-217, 222,
    228
survive, 3, 68, 127, 146, 173, 201, 279,
    292, 295
sutra, 105, 115
symbols, 19, 34, 130, 277, 278, 282,
    287
symptoms, 70, 73, 74, 101, 136, 167,
    217-220, 222, 227, 252

tension, 7, 168, 169, 180, 264, 298
The Day Grampa Died, 186, 193
The Dead Bird, 184, 186, 198, 209
The Little Mermaid, 206
The Magic Moth, 179, 180
The Taste of Blackberries, 190
The Tenth Good Thing About Barney,
    181, 209
The Yearling, 198
theo-centric, 106
therapeutic relationship, 8
therapy, 12, 19, 20, 40-42, 44, 46, 70, 74,
    92, 96, 118, 133-139, 143, 144, 153,
    162, 165, 170-172, 217, 225, 227,
    228, 264, 267, 269
transcendence, 91, 127
trauma, 96, 118, 119, 173, 215, 216, 218,
    220-228, 249, 252, 255, 256, 267,
    290
traumatic anxiety, 222
typology, 247

Verdi, 24
violent trauma, 224

Walter, 30, 31, 233
Where is Dead, 185, 186, 193
Williams, 29

Yang, 71-73
Yin, 71-73